D1520468

Dictatorship over Needs

Dictatorship over Needs

Ferenc Fehér, Agnes Heller
and
György Márkus

St. Martin's Press   New York

ISBN 0-312-20022-6

Library of Congress Cataloging in Publication Data

Fehér, Ference, 1933-
    Dictatorship over needs.
        1. Communist state. 2. Communist countries—
Politics and government. I. Heller, Agnes.
II. Márkus, György, 1934-   III. Title.
JC474.F43 1983   321.9'2   83-3180
ISBN 0-312-20022-6

Printed and bound in Great Britain

Contents

Foreword   vii

Acknowledgement   xiv

Part I   *Economic and Social Structure*

1   Eastern European Societies and the Western Left   1

2   Corporate Property and Command Economy   45

3   Inequality and Domination in a 'Classless' Society   106

Part II   *Political Domination and its Consequences*

4   Legitimation   137

5   The System of Domination   156

6   The Structure of Power   167

7   Ideology, Dogma, Culture   187

8   Morality and Psychology   205

Part III   *The Functioning of the System: Conflicts and Perspectives*

9   Why is Dictatorship over Needs not Socialism?   221

10   Hyperrationalist Preferences and Social Irrationality in a Planned Society   237

11   Market and Fragmented Market in Soviet Societies   264

12   The Crisis of Dictatorship over Needs   280

Index   301

Foreword

The emotional and intellectual motivation for writing this book was the exact obverse of the French maxim: *tout comprendre, c'est tout pardonner*. By contrast, and without intending to write a political pamphlet, we sought to understand the whole of 'real socialism' in order critically to expose this new and formidable system of internal and external oppression, to dissipate such illusions as exist about its genuine physiognomy. This process of 'total understanding' has necessitated, of course, an unreserved criticism of our own earlier self-deceptions. In actual fact, this book derives from the process of our own self-enlightenment on the subject of 'real socialism'. At least for some of us, the first period of sobering and adopting a critical attitude coincided with, and resulted from, the preparations for the Hungarian revolution, its outbreak and suppression, including the drastic reprisals of the subsequent years, between 1953 and 1958. If the regime watched us with constantly, nay, increasingly suspicious eyes, if it kept us (some of us always, others after a certain period of time) at arm's length from its cultural and academic positions and facilities, if it put us under direct censorship, sometimes recurring police harassment, it proved to be more clear-sighted about us than we were ourselves. For we had believed ourselves for a while to be the advocates of the regime's 'genuine interests' as opposed to the 'blockheads', 'the incorrigible sectarians', 'the bureaucrats' who had, because of some constant historical bad luck, always shaped its policies. In a later period of reformistic hopes (during which the consistently Stalinist functionaries continued to smell the adversary in us) our self-delusion became even more blatant precisely because we went *further*. We were no longer content to point up the contrast between the regime's 'ideal type' (which we alleged remained unimpaired despite historical distortions) and its 'empirical reality' (which we had already condemned by then): we demanded *actual structural changes* and these were goods the regime could not deliver.

The invasion by the Warsaw Pact countries against Czechoslovakian reform communism put an end to this ambiguity. Once again, philosophy may well have behaved like Minerva's owl and tried to fly after darkness had set in, but at least it made an effort to live up to the demands of a philosophy of praxis: it drew the theoretical consequences from what had happened, in order to act upon reality. We came to see that Stalin did not die his political death in 1953, but, and even then still to a limited extent, in 1956, in the 'Secret Session' of the 20th Congress where Khrushchev read his speech on the 'cult of personality', and also on the streets of Budapest in October that year, when a rebellious population broke Stalin's statue to pieces. Equally, Khrushchevism did not cease to exist in 1964, immediately after the coup against the First Secretary, but only in 1968, during the days of the Soviet invasion against Khrushchevist Czechoslovakia. This event, directly political in character, had important theoretical implications for us. From this time on, the world around us, in our view, no longer represented a 'perverted' or 'bureaucratized' socialism, we no longer lived under a regime whose antipathy we provoked but whose essence (of course: *reformed* substance) we somehow shared. Our surroundings appeared rather as a hostile cosmos of new oppression, and we regarded it as our socialist duty to comprehend fully its oppressive nature and contribute to its radical alteration as best we could. Since we are theorists, our contribution had to be overwhelmingly theoretical in nature. We considered all practical actions on our part (whose merit or demerit should be evaluated by others and which were anyhow modest in impact) to be simply a moral testimony to the authenticity of our philosophical position. The theoretical efforts were first shared by, and actually consisted in conversations between, a group of people usually called 'the Budapest School'. But since once uniform views have diversified, both political and theoretical responsibility for this book are exclusively borne by the three authors, while they express their gratitude to former friends for the initial stimulus. It was we who finally decided, in 1978 in Sydney and Melbourne, to write this book.

All books, except religious ones, have one common addressee: the general public, and our book is most certainly not intended to be religious. Nor does it aim at achieving 'impeccable academic standards' in any technical sense of the word. We certainly hope that it will justify itself against any professional criticism as at least one of the possible and properly founded interpretations of the Soviet systems. But we do not attempt to give it academic respectability (and, with the same gesture, intimidate the general public) by introducing either a technical apparatus or a language which sounds artificial to the politically interested but professionally untrained reader. This is why it lacks both footnotes and lengthy treatises on 'Marxology'.

Despite all the above reservations, and together with the firm intention of addressing the general public, we undeniably have one particular addressee in mind: the Western Leftist. This, again, calls for some explanation. The question that immediately springs to mind is: why should we address the Western, not the Eastern Leftist on a subject obviously much better known to the latter? The answer is simple. For a variety of reasons, the majority of which will be analysed in the course of the book, the Eastern Leftist of today is not excessively sympathetic to the type of discourse we present. Of course, in keeping with our ideas and norms we simply do not have the *right* to give up *hope* that at least some such will prove sensitive, and that the time will come when more Eastern readers are open to our arguments. But even as far as the Western Leftist is concerned, one reservation has to be indicated here in advance. In spite of being repeatedly and publicly critical of Marx, of many aspects of the Marxian legacy, we still set out from a broadly conceived Marxist framework in our understanding of the 'dictatorship over needs'. Nowadays this is an unpopular attitude among an increasing number of Western Leftists, a considerable proportion of whom are at the least indifferent, if not downright hostile, to Marx. But perhaps there is wisdom in the proverb that suggests one should make a virtue of necessity. The socialist (but anti-Leninist) brand of East European opposition that our theory represents will perhaps appeal to those Leftists whose objective is socialism as radicalized democracy, not as dictatorship of any kind.

It is necessary, further, to draw the *geographical* lines of demarcation of our analysis. What we repeatedly call here Soviet societies (in the plural), indicating by the very nomenclature that the system has extended beyond the Soviet Union as a result of Soviet military presence (irrespective of the earlier strength or weakness of communist movements), is largely, but not entirely, identical with the East European countries ruled, not governed, by communist apparatuses. We do not include in the analysis the Asian communist countries or such outposts of Soviet expansionism as Cuba or Angola. If we fail to do so, it is not because of any romantic sympathy for, or illusion concerning, either the 'advantages of the primitive' or the 'charms of the exotic'. We have no doubt that Cuba, in an ignominious corruption of the genuinely radical hopes raised by its revolution all over the world, has become a particularly nasty police state which, in addition, turns its younger generation into a kind of Foreign Legion in the service of Soviet superpower politics. Nor do we question that Vietnam is full of 're-education camps' which can be located sociologically somewhere between concentration camps and the internment camps of conservative-military dictatorships, nor that North Korea is the exact twin of the country's abominable Southern part, both as far as their respective, blatant, disregard of human rights and their nightmarishly rigid hierarchization of social life are concerned. But we are simply not acquainted (and to our knowledge very few, if any, are) with the exact historical background and the concrete sociological function of these systems. This gap in knowledge leaves different options over future developments open for the critical mind. Let us repeat: different, but not, or not necessarily, better options, and hardly ones which can legitimately be called socialist. But, for example, the near total confusion which reigns in the understanding of the character and social significance of the Chinese 'proletarian cultural revolution' demonstrates how carefully one has to tread when dealing with these societies. We venture only our hope that the conceptual framework of our analysis *could* perhaps prove useful for the self-comprehension of a leftist opposition in these countries, if there is one at all. Should there be such dissent, and should its participants be receptive towards our analysis, this would prove the existence of structural similarities with East European Soviet societies beyond our present, very cautious, expectations.

The reader may have observed a certain reservation even as far as that East European region is concerned, and the 'white spot' on the political map drawn up by us obviously covers Yugoslavia. (By comparison, despite arch-Stalinist vestiges and Maoist extravaganza, we unhesitatingly include Albania in the series of the present-day systems of dictatorship over needs.) Here, again, we are not nurturing either excessive hopes or illusions. When it comes, as it unfortunately often does, to the persecution of dissenting opinion or of spontaneous actions from below, there can be no doubt where and on whose side our sympathy lies. However, we believe that two factors countervail here against a general and unreserved degeneration into a dictatorship over needs. The first is that Yugoslavia is the *only* country in the region in which the communist regime was *self-created*, born out of a heroic war of independence. The second factor is that the Yugoslav communist apparatus granted its population such concessions as go, in all their much criticized intrinsic inconsistency, beyond the usual level of sham liberties granted to other countries' populations in times of general social crisis. The two factors result in a situation where, in our view, present-day Yugoslavia demonstrates a (not always peaceful) co-existence of contradicting social structures, institutions and trends. It is not therefore our purpose to apply our theory of the dictatorship over needs as a *consistent* social system, to this society.

One remark is appropriate here about method. Our analysis does not claim to be *historical* in character, at least not in any sense of an accurate (or even a sketchy) chronicle. We have rather tried to understand the regime in its full-fledged, 'mature' form. It nowadays presents its often barbaric oppression either in a far more covert way (it was a decade before the details of the bloody suppression of the workers' strike under Khrushchev in Novocherkass became known), or, for a variety of reasons, it has renounced 'revolutions from above', whose inevitable concomitants were recurring mass exter minations. But if the reader finds some of our formulations too harsh, if he or she objects that 'these symptoms belonged to a past which has been renounced even by the communist apparatus from the 20th Congress onwards', it is not difficult to point to Afghanistan alone where, according to gathering evidence, the Soviet military behaves in the same way as the Germans did in the Ukrainian villages. We emphasize: in more ways than one, East Europeans still live under Stalin's shadow. All his successors, even Brezhnev, a genuine admirer, have proved ungrateful to this, the true founder of the regime. They have criticized and banished him from the annals while, as far as the basic components are concerned, they have left his regime untouched, only dismantling its most brutal branches and *modus operandi*, or perhaps just moderating their brutality. Nevertheless Stalin's heirs have constantly professed their continuity with his period as an authentically socialist one despite certain 'infringements of socialist legality'. This emphasis on continuity is also a carefully administered reminder to the population, relaying to them the unspoken, but unmistakable message that Stalin's ghost (and with him: Yezhov's and Beria's) can always be regalvanized into life whenever necessary to protect the 'socialist achievements'. Therefore we have tried to understand this society (particularly in Part II which deals with the political structure) in its frightening *continuity*, even in periods when it turns a conciliatory face towards the neutral observer who lacks sufficient inside knowledge and historical experience.

It is a noteworthy fact, since it affects the tone of this book, that the bulk of it was written before the birth of Solidarity in Poland. The subsequent developments since this magnificent initiative sadly justify the originally gloomy atmosphere of the book. Nevertheless, we believe that, historically speaking, something irrevocable has happened, and that many will, or at least may, follow suit sooner or later. The 'labour commodity', up until now bereft of certain fundamental rights which it possesses in the majority of liberal capitalist countries, achieved a major breakthrough in its fight for self-emancipation by forcing a communist apparatus to *recognize officially* its semi-independent economic existence. This opens up a perspective that dissent in Soviet societies has never had up until now. It is encouraging for socialists that the breakthrough has been achieved by workers' fights in the good old fashion of nineteenth century proletarian struggles, even if with an overwhelmingly fundamentalist world view. At any rate, one should not forget that it was in Lodz, a *Polish* city, that the working class of the Russian empire organized itself against Tsarist autocracy for the first time, at the end of the last century.

Finally, a few words need to be added about the process of writing the book itself. It is a *collective undertaking* in every respect. We share basically common views regarding what we believe to be the continuation of the original (even if gradually and substantially modified) theoretical perspectives of the Budapest School. There is no major disagreement between us regarding either the evaluation or the structural description of the regime, or its perspectives. There is no divergence of views in respect of the desired world order 'thereafter' either. None of us is an advocate of a universal system of 'pax americana'. Our intention, a perspective to which we commit ourselves in a practical way, is a new, democratic and socialist world order, and the two last adjectives are to some extent tautologous for we cannot conceive of socialism without democracy. We certainly hope that, once the Soviet empire of oppression collapses, or is radically transformed, the Latin American, Asian and Afro-Arabic (capitalist or fundamentalist) tyrannies will follow suit, and the Western democracies, as *democracies*, will be radicalized in a socialist sense.

On the basis of this general agreement, it was relatively easy to work out, first, a detailed draft of the book, and then to arrange the division of labour. György Márkus wrote the first part dealing with theories analysing Soviet societies, their economy and 'class' structure. The second part, 'Political Domination and its Consequences', is the work of Agnes Heller. Ferenc Fehér wrote the third part: 'The Functioning of the System: Conflicts and Perspectives'. We have discussed each part repeatedly and made corrections as a result of these vehement but always friendly discussions. In this sense each author bears moral, political and scholarly responsibility for the parts of the two others. But this, of course, does not mean uniformity. Theoretical beliefs, individual ways of argumentation cannot be merged or concealed, neither was such uniformity our goal. The ultimate coherence and homogeneity of the book, certainly an objective we aimed at, does not even mean a total identity of views. On a number of questions (which we did not feel important enough to list here in detail) we have preserved our diverging views, as we have also retained the natural right to return to them in later writings in a way different to one or the other co-author's manner of presentation. But there is one question on which we do not have the slightest disagreement of content or emphasis. We, all three, are convinced that the world needs more, not less socialism than it has today.

Melbourne/Sydney

F. Fehér
A. Heller
G. Márkus

Acknowledgement

We wish to thank our friends, Peter Beilharz and Julian Triado, and our publisher's freelance editor, Helen Dore, for their most conscientious revisions of our text.

PART I

Economic and Social Structure

Eastern European Societies and the Western Left

The 'living spectre' of Communism

'A spectre is haunting Europe — the spectre of Communism. All the powers of old Europe have entered a holy alliance to exorcize this spectre: Pope and Czar, Metternich and Guizot, French radicals and German police-spies.' — These well-known words, so full of confidence in the future power of a nascent social force, sound almost ironic today. For the spectre of Communism has indeed been transformed into reality, the sheer power of which hardly anyone can doubt. The new societies of Eastern Europe, the societies of 'really existing' socialism, officially declare this power of existence to constitute their most essential feature. And although in countries where dialectics have taken the place of religion, it might have been wise to recall, as its old master, Hegel, put it: 'a mere being without notion, without the validity of existence . . . is an empty semblance', in this case the dialectics of notion and actuality itself is no more than a formula of exorcism, for in its very realization socialism has preserved its original 'haunting' qualities. But it does not haunt the Metternichs and Guizots of today, for they are well able to comprehend this new reality and treat it in terms of the age-old political power-game. The spectre that now haunts socialist Europe is the spectre of socialism as it has emerged in the Eastern European societies. The confrontation between the existing powers and the idea of socialism has been reversed — the idea is now challenged by that very power which proclaims itself to be its embodiment.

Living spectres are hardly worthy objects of investigation: they are no more than a source of irrational anxiety — and as such are best forgotten. This deliberately blinkered view of Eastern Europe is undoubtedly the one adopted by the Eurocommunist parties, the

largest section of the organized Left in the West; this is an attitude
which obstinately refuses to go beyond the formulas of tactical
expediency and to ask what these societies are really like. Surely
there is no need to invoke spirits from the past to find reasons for
this attitude. Any serious theoretical attempt to understand these
societies of itself would involve the acceptance of a degree of
historical co-responsibility for horrendous crimes against humanity
which were not simply irrational excesses, but the birth-pangs of a
new system of exploitation. Such a step would not only be
politically difficult for a leadership directly involved, but also a
potential cause of division of the masses within the parties themselves. Precisely because the problem of Eastern European socialism
is in this sense not an external one for the Eurocommunist parties of
the West, raising questions about its status would necessarily open
up further questions concerning their own entrenched internal
structure and their relationship with the other organizations and
forces of the Left. In a situation where such an attempt would
simultaneously force these parties to face the unmitigated hostility
of the two great world powers, the United States and the Soviet
Union, which to a large extent determine the political and economic
perspectives of Western Europe, and thereby could greatly reduce
their influence as national political forces as well, it is not hard to
understand why the Eurocommunist parties regard such a step as
tactical suicide. At one time these parties were able to invoke the
shadow of the Soviet Union to counterbalance the real possibility
of an American intervention (even if an indirect one) in the case of
a Leftist development in their own countries. Now the Communist
parties of Western Europe feel that the Soviet Union is best left in
the shadows: its reality is best forgotten.

   To understand the antinomies of a practical situation, however,
hardly justifies endorsing a political line that remains the captive of
these same antinomies. Assessing the other practical alternatives
that were or remain open is surely a matter of judgment (and
action) for those who are practically involved in the realities of this
situation. Those who find themselves outside it, like the present
writers can only indicate some of the consequences of such a policy:
doubletalk not only inevitably invokes justified suspicions about the
sincerity of the new so-called democratic political line, but itself
represents a powerful check on any true inner democratic development. The masses of the parties are again reduced to a passive role
where they are expected to give unquestioning support to a leadership that claims to know when to strike the appropriate note (for

reasons that remain unstated) in relation to the Soviet Union. As far as Marxism as theory is concerned, such a policy necessarily contributes to its deterioration into no more than an ideological façade: it is impossible to understand the modern world under the strict conditions of a self-imposed ignorance of one of its most significant socio-political constituents. If the often cited danger of social-democratization means a renunciation of the broader historical ends of the movement, based on a theoretical understanding of the contradictions within contemporary society, in favour of pragmatic exigencies, then it is important to realize that the diplomatic silence maintained by the Eurocommunist parties on the subject of the allegedly socialist societies of Eastern Europe is in itself an important influencing factor in this direction. The ethos of a movement or a party itself possesses a kind of reality. If a radical organization demonstrates a blatant disregard for its own historical aims and its own theory in its external relations (measuring the socialist character of a social system in terms of its military and economic strength as a counterweight in the international balance of power), then such an attitude cannot fail to have consequences affecting its entire internal domestic policy and inner life.

In any case a serious contribution to a radical (more narrowly: Marxist) understanding of Eastern European societies was and is attempted only by those smaller and less organized sections of the Western Left which do not bear such a heavy burden of historical and, one also ought to add, national-political responsibility. Before attempting any criticism of these theories, it is only fair that we should state the indebtedness of Eastern European dissidents to them and their representatives: indebtedness for practical solidarity and help in the form of mobilization of world opinion in cases of repression (and this definitely ought to be extended, all their vacillations notwithstanding, to the major Eurocommunist parties as well), and indebtedness in theoretical terms as well. At some point in their search for a radical-critical view of their own society, which can frequently take the form of a journey with a direct or indirect apology of the regimes concerned as its starting-point, many representatives of an Eastern Leftist opposition have often drawn to some extent on the conceptual armoury of these theories elaborated from 'outside'. As such oppositionists we would like to think that this influence and help was not just one-sided: the emergence of a Leftist opposition in Eastern Europe by its very existence and perhaps, to a lesser degree, through its writings as well, has compelled some sections of the Western Left to face the reality of all that socialism is not — and in this negative way has served to attain a better consciousness of what it may be.

But the fact that such an objective (and perhaps mutually bene-ficial) interaction between the Eastern and Western Left exists, cannot hide the problems, the uneasiness and all too often the failure which characterize their direct dialogue. Whether it is true or sheer myth, many Eastern European dissidents mention often an event that has acquired a symbolic significance for them: the meeting between Rudi Dutschke and radical Czech students at Karol Univer-sity in the early summer of 1968, which ended with the guest from the West calling the students representatives of an outdated bourgeoisie, to be charged in reply by his hosts with the epithet of 'unreconstructed Stalinist'. Though generally less dramatic, meetings between representatives of the Western and Eastern Left sometimes recall a kind of a dialogue in which the participants attempt to convince each other — with the greatest respect and attention — that it is time they shut up. Dissidents are fond of quoting the old Russian proverb: 'Only now are they coming to the fair which we are already leaving' — and in the name of their own hard-won experiences they too often simply preclude any critical discussion of their own ideas or programmes, depicting any principled criticism as an attempt to impose worn-out ideals which long ago have failed in reality. In return they may often listen to old slogans of national–cultural superiority from quite unexpected corners. If they attempt to generalize theoretically something that is not merely a personal, but a social life-experience, they are quickly reminded that this experience relates to primitive social conditions, that it is of no consequence where a working class of a much higher social and cultural development is concerned (not to mention some of the even higher developed theoretical representatives of such a working class).

It is true that this problem promises to disappear, however slowly, along with the progressive disappearance of a socialist, or at least Marxist, opposition in Eastern Europe itself. But since the difficulties of initiating a dialogue themselves constituted a factor (even if a minor one) in this process — a process which is indicative of the recent developmental tendencies of Eastern European societies — it is worth pausing to consider the causes of these difficulties that have proved so hard to overcome even under conditions of mutual respect and practical solidarity.

They are undoubtedly due in part to the fact that the participants in this dialogue have experiences of life that are not only different, but in some crucial aspects diametrically opposed. For many of the younger representatives of the Western New Left the decisive social experience which formed their views was a profound disillusion with the liberal ideology of democratic rights as a secure mechanism of rational social change. It was their realization that the institutions of a formal political democracy alone are not enough to ensure the achievement of even moderate aims of social equality and justice that set them on the path of political and theoretical radicalization. Dissidents, on the other hand, learned — often by their own example — that the lack of these rights or their effective institutionalization not only leaves the individual completely helpless against the virtually arbitrary power of the state, but at the same time makes collective control over its activity impossible, since any expression of dissent, any attempt at spontaneous public activity, can, in these conditions, be thwarted in its initial stages. Thus even in cases where there is general agreement on the principles of a democratic socialism — on the necessity to maintain and expand the institutions of political democracy together with structural changes radically transcending the limits of the merely political sphere — Eastern and Western participants in a dialogue are by their nature apt to demonstrate quite divergent sensitivities, spontaneously to attach importance to different elements in a common system of values: within a shared general framework they actually take different things for granted, tend to entertain different fears, and perhaps different illusions as well.

But these divergences reach further, beyond the question of subjective attitudes as expressions of practical life-experiences. They have to do also with the objectively different critical potential of traditional radical theories, primarily Marxism, within these different social environments, and with the corresponding theoretical and political experiences. Whatever difficulties Marxism is encountering now at the time of its crisis in the West, the primarily critical nature of this theory in face of the social realities of contemporary capitalism cannot be doubted. One may question (as many members of the Western Left now do) whether this criticism is sufficiently radical or realistic — but it remains a fact that Marxism offers a conceptual articulation and explanation (whether right or wrong) of the antinomies of society, seen from the viewpoint of its transformation into another one. Things undoubtedly stand differently in Eastern Europe and by no means only because of the well-known fact of the appropriation of Marxism by the existing power structure itself. One surely ought not to underestimate the psychological difficulties involved in remaining the 'true' representative of ideas which constitute the official ideology of the regime criticized and are therefore deeply discredited in the broad masses of the population itself. Nevertheless for a considerable time it was the revisionist intellectuals situating themselves within the Marxist tradition and arguing within its framework who generally represented the most significant oppositional element in these societies. They basically contrasted the officially professed ideology and ideals of the regime with its reality in actual terms. In the case of the history of Polish opposition Adam Michnik has shown convincingly how this ideological orientation was connected with the political expectations of a reform from above and with the strategy of influencing the 'liberal' elements within the existing power structure, first of all the party apparatus and leadership. Taking the regime at its own word was at the same time an attempt to establish a common language with the potential reformers inside the power elite. The Czech intervention of 1968 did much to put an end to these hopes and expectations, effectively demonstrating the very narrow limits within which the East European political system as a whole can tolerate reforms from above. The ensuing radicalization of the opposition (which also coincided in some cases with its more or less ephemeral political organization) also meant that many dissidents now came to the conclusion that the ideological practice of confronting the verbally accepted ideals and the reality itself may act as an 'indirect apology'. Such a critique suggests that the fulfilment of its ideological promises can meaningfully be demanded from the social system, that the non-realization of such promises is a reflection of the personal composition of the power elite, and not the result of a self-reproducing social structure of domination in stable existence. But the fact that this process of radicalization coincided with the progressive disappearance of a Marxist orientation among the dissidents (naturally this can only be seen as a broad tendency to which there are many exceptions) cannot be explained solely in those political terms to which we have schematically referred. Whatever political functions revisionist Marxism (revisionist in the sense of its opposition to the official orthodoxy) may have fulfilled in the earlier decade or decades, it remained for the majority of its representatives not just an externally imposed or accepted political device, a matter of pragmatic expediency, but the framework through which they attempted to reach a social self-understanding, a vehicle through which they stated their diagnosis of what was wrong with these societies. Now, however, as this criticism became more and more radical, directed against the whole structure of society and not just against specific features of this or that political line, many critics found that the very conceptual framework of Marxian theory did not lend itself easily to the purposes of such a critical analysis. It certainly does not require great intellectual effort or capacity to be able to demonstrate that the reality of these societies has all too little to do with the realization of those basic values and aims which socialism as a practical and theoretical movement traditionally stood for (in both its Marxist and non-Marxist variants). But those who live in these societies could hardly accept the premise that because of this these social systems are simply irrelevant to the theory and praxis of socialism. And when they attempted to articulate what these societies are in reality, rather than what they are not, they had to face the fact that precisely those features of the classical Marxian heritage which constitute its great critical force in relation to capitalist societies — its ability to go beyond the phenomena of legal—political equality to the social process of production of the relations of socio-economic inequality and their ensuing antagonisms — do seem, at least at first sight, arbitrary and confusing presuppositions in relation to social systems where politics in many important respects has a practical primacy over economics, where the notion of class, determined basically in terms of relations of property, does not seem readily applicable, and so on. The changed political orientation of the dissidents — moving away from efforts to influence the Party and sections of its apparatus to attempts to create an independent public opinion as a force of pressure against this apparatus — may have made Marxism (by now popularly discredited) a political ballast, but this was at least reinforced by a growing conviction that theoretically it cannot offer much either, in the way of a critical articulation of the deeply experienced miseries, oppressions, strains and antinomies of Eastern European societies. Leftist intellectuals from West and East equally may now face a crisis of Marxism. But the problem of being a Marxist in practical terms means different things in the East and in the West: in the latter, it is a question of whether the critical theory offered by Marxism is still actual or sufficient, while within the framework of 'really existing' socialism it is a question of whether Marxism can fulfil the functions of a critical theory at all.

It is the common conviction of the authors of this book that the Marxist tradition in its historical totality does preserve a critical potential in regard to the societies of Eastern Europe as well; that in fact, it offers both a theoretically deeper and practically more radical-critical understanding of them than what appears now to be its main alternative, the liberal theory of authoritarian political systems. (We are not speaking here of those anachronistically conservative ideas which prevail widely within the Russian opposition and which represent the other face of the Soviet system rather than an alternative to it. Judging these ideas, one ought not to forget the dictum of the young Marx: each position ought to be judged by its opposition. The great moral and artistic personality of Solzhenitzyn surely did not deserve the Soviet Union, but the Soviet Union deserved the ideologue Solzhenitzyn, as its product and its most representative dissident.) At the same time we as authors are equally convinced that a confrontation with the reality of these societies demonstrates deep conceptual ambiguities and inadequacies in the theoretical heritage of classical Marxism itself (and not just of its vulgarized or institutionalised parodies), and that these systems represent a social formation, the possibility (and the danger) of which was not only unforeseen by Marxian theory, but in a sense could not have been predicted by it. To give a critical account of these societies demands significant revisions and modifications of the very conceptual framework of Marxist theory. And for just this reason the problem of Eastern European societies has a vital importance for the theoretical fate of Marxism itself.

Those critical theories of Eastern European societies which, as from the early 1930s, were elaborated within various smaller groups of the Western Left to which we referred earlier, actually realized all the possible basic theoretical alternatives in terms of which these social systems could be interpreted within the framework of an orthodox Marxism. Consequently a survey, of where they fail in reality, of their fundamental inadequacies and inconsistencies, is integral to the claim made above. Naturally we cannot deal here with individual theories in their (often sophisticated) details — only the main types of explanation and understanding concern us with regard to their basic theoretical presuppositions. In this sense one can distinguish three basic conceptual alternatives which can be (rather conventionally) called the theories of transitional society, of state capitalism and of Asiatic formation. In fact they exhaust the answers which the Western left has produced to dispel intellectually the nightmare of Eastern societies.

The theory of transitional society

In this interpretation Eastern European societies are seen as displaying a hybrid combination of capitalist and socialist characteristics, as forming a transitional stage between capitalism and socialism, more specifically as cases of an arrested development between the two social formations. The causes of this arrest are generally located in the political sphere, in the bureaucratic distortions or degenerations of socialist development, which lead to the emergence of a privileged parasitic stratum of party-state functionaries, and keep the mass of direct producers in a subordinate, impotent position. (The causes of such a development are then often explained in terms of capitalist influence, especially in combination with Russian backwardness.) On the other hand, it is stressed with equal insistence that important elements, constituents or aspects of relations of production do in fact have a socialist character here. Liquidation of private property, absence of commodity relations in the sector producing means of production and centralized planning are the traits most often referred to in this context. The specific concrescence of capitalist and socialist features in the economic base of these societies is sometimes articulated through the contrast of the relations of property (basically socialist) with relations of distribution (basically capitalist), but it may be expressed in less schematic (and often more scholastic) ways too (see, for example, Mandel's distinction between 'mode of production' and 'specific relations of production').

It is naturally the towering personality of Trotsky that stands — acknowledged or not — behind all these theories. His is hardly an image — and for reasons that will hopefully later become clear — which is specifically popular among Eastern European dissidents, even those on the Left. The present writers as former Communist theoreticians, who, though never participating personally in the vilification of Trotsky, at any rate shared the resulting miscomprehension and mistrust of his views, should state not only that Trotsky, in his heroic struggle against Stalinism, was the grandfather of all Leftist dissidents, but also that it would be theoretically inadmissible to judge his theories in the same way as those of his successors. Trotsky's own analysis of the Soviet system under Stalin was that of a revolutionary, searching for the optimal practical perspective of an alternative social development. One certainly ought to ask whether this alternative, embedded in and guiding his analysis, was a realistic one, and even whether it was an alternative to Stalinism at all. However one answers these questions, the problem has to be related to the social–political realities of the 1930s, and not those of the present. 'The question of the character of the Soviet Union [is] not yet decided by history,' Trotsky once wrote, and these words undoubtedly contain the kernel of all theories of transitional society.

The first question about the recent variants of this viewpoint is whether it makes any sense to repeat this proposition more than forty years after it was originally written down.

Even if it is present-day Trotskyism which most typically (and in a theoretically most articulate way) represents the conception of transitional society, its influence reaches far beyond the warring groups of the Fourth International. One can encounter it in writings of radical theoreticians who have nothing to do with the political programme of Trotskyism, for example, in the 'one-dimensional man' of Marcuse. More important and rather ironical, however, is the fact that (as Claudin and others have argued) this same theory emerges each time — albeit in a diluted and deliberately confused form — when the Eurocommunist parties themselves attempt or are forced to articulate in some way their criticism of Soviet society. What is more, if one had occasion to speak tête-à-tête with the more enlightened (and more cynical) representatives of high Party bureaucracy, at least in the more liberal dependent countries of Central Eastern Europe, one could easily recognize in their own characterizations and explanations of the social situation at home the bowdlerized echo of these same theories. In a sense this silent and disturbingly ambiguous rehabilitation of Trotsky is, in our view, symptomatic. It points to the fact that the conception of transitional society acquires an increasingly apologetic function under the present conditions of Eastern European societies.

However, this statement would be not only unjust, but downright slanderous, if we did not immediately emphasize those critical elements of this theory which most assuredly deny, for the future as well as the present, not only the official rehabilitation of its originator, but even a passive tolerance of its (very rare) present-day representatives in Eastern European societies. In its consistent forms this theory undoubtedly represents an attempt to articulate the antinomies of these societies from the viewpoint of immediate producers. It is characterized by this radical momentum insofar as it succeeds in connecting organically a criticism of the undemocratic character of the political system with the existence of deep social and economic inequalities. Against a liberal critique which centres exclusively on questions of political life and which sometimes, in its vulgarly anti-socialist variants, even deduces the authoritarian character of the latter from the attempt to overcome social inequalities — to imply with complacent self-satisfaction their inevitable and natural reappearance under the ideological façade — Trotskyism in particular was at great pains to show how the very existence of a separate and even formally uncontrolled political power in the form of a privileged stratum of bureaucrats necessarily imposes inequalities, and not only in the sphere of income-distribution, but in all matters of social decision, in economics and beyond. And one can agree also with the point, most strongly emphasized in these analyses, that these relations of domination cannot be understood (even ideally— abstractly and in the very sphere of economics itself) if they are divorced from the political structure, and that correspondingly the social inequalities in Soviet-type societies are not reproduced by economic mechanisms alone.

But it is just this strongest critical aspect of the theory of the transitional society which is also the site of its inherent inadequacies and in-built apologetic potentials. The more consistent these theories are, the more paradoxical they seem to be. On the one hand, they point to the social position of the party-state bureaucracy as the funda- mental source of structural inequalities, but on the other hand, they regard the basic mechanism, through which these relations of social domination are realized and exercised, the mechanism popularly called central planning, as representing an essential counterpoint against, and restraint upon, the power of the same bureaucracy. Trotskyist writings especially (they are also the most consistent in this respect) are generally full of references to a mystical 'logic of planning' as the vehicle and embodiment of the socialist aspect of Eastern European societies. There can be little doubt that from a strictly Marxian standpoint this is a completely meaningless concept. Planning for Marx meant the rational and democratic formation of the social will of the association of immediate producers which is able to take under its control the unrestrained spontaneity and reified objective logic of economic development and to direct it effectively towards the satisfaction of those social needs which remain not only unfulfilled, but also inarticulable within the automatism of a capitalist market economy. Trotskyist writings make it clear that the actual process of planning in Eastern European societies has little to do with either rationality or democracy. Naturally, economic plans are never the expression of a mere whim of the arbitrary will of an omnipotent bureaucracy. This will is itself severely restricted not only by the material requirements of the process of reproduction in general but by a host of external and internal conditions in particular. This will ought also to be conceived (if the fundamental ideas of Marxism are deemed relevant to the analysis of these societies) as being determined, in its basic content and direction, by the very position and function this bureaucracy as a social group fulfils. But to presuppose that there is a logic of planning beyond this material and social determinants which are not counterposed, but expressed in the actual reality of power relations, is an extreme case of fetishistic thinking revealed by Marx: a transformation of Smith's 'hidden hand' into a directly mystical-divine (because devoid of any institutional correlate) force of social reason *per se*. But this is precisely the official apologetic ideology of Soviet-type societies — the objective existence of a rationality of development, independent of the conscious needs and will of the population, of a logic of the future, the requirements of which are realized through the practice of central bureaucratic planning, as the actualization of general social interests. On the one hand, Trotskyism resolutely rejects this legitimating ideology, since in Trotskyist thinking bureaucracy of a Soviet type (and it would seem, the existence of any kind of bureaucracy) represents the direct degradation and distortion of the logic of planning. On the other hand, however, by presupposing the existence of a logic of planning, Trotskyism only reconfirms the basis of this legitimation which by its very character necessarily remains an elitist one. (The antinomies of this position become particularly clear in questions of political theory, especially that of the Party itself.)

This ambiguity becomes all the more ominous, because in its most consistent form the conception of transitional society tends to identify the socialist constituents of these economies with central planning, and the capitalist ones with the market and its related economic phenomena. In this, so far as practical consequences are concerned, it coincides with the position of the most conservative (in political terms, most Stalinist) elements and groups of the bureaucracy itself, and stands in direct opposition even to the immediate material interests of the majority of the working population: a position which from the outset rejects (as measures aimed at the restitution of capitalism) all steps towards economic decentralization, towards the introduction of self-regulating economic mechanisms and market incentives is in fact resisting one of the most elemental-spontaneous liberating tendencies in these societies. Undoubtedly, the somewhat belated rediscovery of market as the universal panacea for all social ills, which sometimes appears in an extreme form among the liberal intellectuals of Eastern Europe, is not only theoretically ridiculous, but ideologically representative of the self-interest of narrow social groups (which are not themselves capitalistic, but occupy a position of dominance over the broad masses of population, while remaining subordinated to the inner core and political pinnacle of the apparatus of domination). But the fact that even these ideologies often meet with broad popular resonance and support bears witness not to the lack of a class-consciousness among a backward working class, but to the mute and correct realization that without limiting in some way the very mechanisms of a command economy, without dismantling their omnipresence and omnipotence, there can be no restraint imposed upon the power of its social vehicle, the bureaucratic apparatus itself. It should be emphasized that even in questions of income policy the central redistributive measures of the state serve not to reduce the overt inequalities of incomes in the name of social justice (as it is maintained as self-evident truth in official ideology), but rather actually to extend them, although in a covert way. And this refers not only to such distortions (actually organic constituents) of these measures as the well-known closed shop system or the widespread phenomenon of blatant favouritism in the actual distribution of the goods or services of an allegedly communal—social consumption (let us say, of resort and recreational facilities), but more so — as we shall try to demonstrate later on — to the economic content of their central elements: administrative regulation of the prices of certain basic articles of consumption, administrative allocation of certain elementary goods such as housing. Demands for the wider introduction of market principles in this sphere surely cannot be evaluated as to their actual social meaning in general abstract terms — but their popularity is indicative of an attempt to break away from the tutelage of the state in basic matters of private life, to reduce the force of the pressure which the apparatus may apply on individuals. And this also makes clearer why the apparatus as a whole usually resists these attempts (or quickly revokes, as in Hungary in the first year of economic reform, the timid measures taken in this direction). A consistent monetarization of the differences in real incomes would bring the existing inequalities into the open, which is the first precondition of their being controllable from below, and would at the same time dissolve the character of social privilege now intimately connected with them.

But the conservative character of the view, which in its struggle against the phantom of a tendency towards the re-establishment of private property, in fact defends those mechanisms through which the actual (non-capitalist) rule of the bureaucratic apparatus is exercised, reaches deeper. It militates against one of the basic experiences familiar to any citizen of an Eastern European society — the experience of impotent rage when confronted with the sheer irrationality of this acclaimed logic of planning, expressed in the production of waste (merely nominal use values) and in a staggering overdevelopment of the unproductive apparatus of organization and control. Both are organic features of an economic structure where the only connection between consumption and production is realized through the administrative decisions of a centralized and hierarchical bureaucracy. The logic of the market certainly does not embody the eternal rules of justice and equity — and this remains an uncontested fact among socialists. But when its critique is presented from the position of a mythical logic of planning, this in fact means only the effective protection of the particular interests of the central political control apparatus against those of the apparatus of direct economic management in the enterprises themselves. The traditional critique remains caught up in that false alternative, in the terms of which a ruling bureaucracy itself articulates its own internal conflict and contradictions — and within the framework of this alternative (which is completely false, because its opposed extremes in principle cannot ever be realized in pure form) only various distributions of a power of domination among various elements and groups of a ruling stratum can be formulated and imagined. One of the basic lessons which the historical experiences of Eastern European societies provide consists of the realization that the diametric opposition between planning and market (so ingrained in classical Marxism itself) is a false one which has to be transcended both in theory and in practice. The very idea of control from below demands the overcoming of this rigid alternative choice between planning or market, this fetishization of economic mechanism *per se* as part and parcel of the legitimating ideology of the very system of dominance. This necessity can be seen nowhere more clearly than in the deep inadequacies and inconsistencies which characterize the treatment received by the working class of Eastern European societies in terms of their actual position and practical perspectives, within the conception of transitional society.

The working class of Eastern European societies exists in conditions of subordination and impotence *vis-à-vis* the bureaucratic apparatus which exercises political control and manages the social organization of the process of production; the direct producers have no power whatsoever in the formulation and implementation of both economic and political decisions — this is the critical thesis of all theories of transitional society. But this thesis is immediately supplemented by the assertion that this impotent and powerless working class nevertheless exercises — not of course in a direct, but in some socio-theoretical sense — its own rule (or even dictatorship). Though the direct producers are systematically excluded from participation in the management of economy and public affairs, the state nevertheless remains in some essential-basic sense a workers' state.

This baffling notion of a dictatorship of impotence and a social rule without any effective economic and political power is at best explained within these theories in terms of the differences one can observe in the actual situation of workers in the capitalist West and the bureaucratic—socialist East respectively. Lack of unemployment, greater job security, the ensuing impossibility of enforcing an intensification of labour at the work-place comparable to the norm in modern capitalist enterprises — these are the facts perhaps most often referred to in highlighting this difference. It would be impossible to discuss in detail here the extent to which these alleged facts are real and the extent to which they remain captive of the apologetics of official propaganda, but some remarks of a general kind are surely called for.

Even if one accepts all these statements at their face-value, they prove no more than a degree of negative control from the side of the workers over the conditions of their employment and labour within the work-place or enterprise. However, this type of power is generally speaking also exercised by workers in the conditions of modern Western capitalism. Speaking about the social rule of the working class in even the most abstract theoretical sense implies, however, something decisively more, and different: elements of a collective control over the total process of social reproduction; not only an ability to influence (within rather rigid limits) the quantity of surplus appropriated and withdrawn for the producers within a given enterprise, but also a control over the direction and character of its employment, over the distribution of the aggregate surplus within the whole society. To presuppose the existence of such a control from below in the conditions of Eastern European societies would be a mockery of the facts — just as speaking about the social rule of the working class without such a control is a mockery of Marxism.

What the arguments mentioned really demonstrate is the undeniable difference in realization and exercise of the mechanisms of this negative control over the conditions of employment and labour in the West and the East respectively. Within the system of democratic capitalism its extent depends primarily upon the strength of the economic organizations of the working class; it is exercised through that collective pressure which trade unions are able to generate over the conditions of the sale and employment of labour-power. In Eastern Europe, where – up until 'Solidarity' – there have been, strictly speaking, no trade unions at all (Eastern European 'trade unions' are even formally corporatist organizations, unifying both workers and management of a given branch and allegedly representing their common interests), the extent of this control depends primarily upon the totally unorganized resistance which individual workers put up during and within the labour-process itself. That such a spontaneous and atomized resistance can be relatively effective in these societies (it would be impotent in a capitalist environment: workers withholding production, making products of defective quality, etc. would simply be sacked) definitely points to an underlying difference in the social position of producers in the two social systems. And theories of the transitional society legitimately refer here to the fact that the managers of a socialist enterprise are not capitalists (or their representatives) who privately own the means of production and can in principle dispose of them as they wish, and that their relationship with the personnel of the factory is not merely that of a temporary contract which both sides may dissolve at any time. They are the delegates of a state which claims to represent the objective and general interests of the working class (or, indeed, the whole population) itself. And the theories in question are also right when they refuse to regard this claim as mere apologetics embellishing and disguising an essentially capitalist type of relationship between the state as collective entrepreneur and the producers as mere wage-labourers. Paternalism of the state constitutes an essential characteristic of the whole process of social reproduction in these societies and it imposes definite limits over the available means of economic compulsion and therefore over the real power of management within the enterprise – limits unknown in capitalism. Where the conception of transitional society fails (and failing, turns into direct apologetics) is that it fixes on only one aspect of the changed economic-social situation of the working class. It refuses to acknowledge the organic interconnection that exists between paternalism of the state which restricts the power of management within the enterprise and the enormously enhanced (in comparison with any capitalist system) administrative power possessed by the bureaucratic apparatus as a whole (the state) in its capacity to establish directly and without any control the conditions of the sale of the labour-power, wages throughout the whole economy. And this power is naturally supplemented – at least in the form of always available exceptional measures — by the ability to exercise direct political command over significant portions of the labour force. (The economically most telling example of the latter is the virtual bondage of agricultural labourers in the Soviet Union.) The resulting 'non-market trade of labour' (to use an expression I. Szelenyi has fashioned after Polanyi) is treated in the theories discussed only insofar as it diminishes the dependence of the workers on individual managers. The extent to which it augments their dependence on the total apparatus of bureaucracy is simply not referred to. The error here lies not in the effort devoted to finding social—economic realities behind the ideological claim according to which the socialist state is the true representative of the general interest of toiling masses, but in the complete and biased inconsistency of this effort. Thus, instead of discovering a new type of social domination behind the apologetic slogans of official propaganda, the criticism ends up by endorsing the claim, though refuting all those who voice it. All the bureaucrats, both individually and collectively, have absolutely no right or ground on which to claim the representation of workers' interests, but the state in the abstract, the very institution through which they exercise their politically uncontrolled power encompassing all the basic economic decisions themselves, remains the embodiment of these interests diametrically opposed to their rule. This is indeed dialectical, but strictly in the Hegelian sense of positing the abstract universal divorced from all its empirical manifestations as the only true and at the same time hidden higher reality against all surface phenomena. Marx once called this whole procedure the secret of Hegel's 'uncritical positivism': under the disguise of an idealist hypercriticism the present is endorsed as it is. And in this case the philosophical perversion also readily turns into a directly political one: even theoreticians like Mandel can occasionally refer to the social disfranchisement of the working class in these societies, to the fact that the working class is completely deprived of any opportunity of formulating its own most elementary demands and interests as proof of its *de facto* powers and rights. It is allegedly because of the latter that the bureaucracy is unable to elaborate its own ideology and is obliged to present itself as the representative of the power of the working class. (Interestingly the same argument is not applied to capitalist societies where political power is again legitimated not in the name of those who actually rule, but through the conception of popular sovereignty.)

However, all this criticism of the conception of transitional society — a criticism which basically adheres to the framework of an orthodox Marxism — remains inadequate and insufficient in one very essential respect: it does not take into account what is perhaps the central argument offered by the theory. This argument is undoubtedly straightforward though purely negative: in contrast to all its features of bureaucratic degeneration the state in Eastern European societies remains a workers' state in one basic respect: it did and does prevent the rebirth of capitalism. And it is just this argument that brings to the fore the hidden (or not so hidden) logic of the theory of transitional society.

This whole conceptualization rests upon the presupposition that the only possible alternative to capitalism, both in theory and in practice (at least under the historical conditions of modernity) is socialism, and that the disjunction of capitalism and socialism is an exhaustive and comprehensive one. The theory then attempts to prove that Eastern European societies are not capitalist in any true sense of the word — and in our opinion it does prove its case convincingly. But they cannot be regarded as socialist either, at least not in the sense in which the whole tradition of socialist movements and thinking (Marx naturally included) counterposed this future society as a meaningful and desirable alternative to the reality of capitalism. If all three premises are granted then the conclusion is logically inevitable: these societies cannot be anything but unstable and hybrid combinations of the features of capitalism and socialism, cases of an arrested transition between the two.

In this description the whole argumentation appears to be a rather facile one: the 'first premise' is merely arbitrary. But in fact it is not: behind it stands the whole weight of orthodox Marxism and the Marxian critical theory of capitalism itself. It is not just that Marx personally could envisage no historical alternative to a socialist future (with the exception, perhaps, of the collapse of modern civilization): this view was dictated by the logic of his theory. A society in which production and consumption have an inherently social (as opposed to locally restricted) and dynamic (as opposed to socially pre-fixed) character, can ensure the necessary conditions for its own reproduction by one of only two ways. It creates them either through the mechanisms of the market which presuppose the existence of mutually independent productive units in society, institutionalized in, and through, the relations of private property, or by the effective socialization of the whole process of production which through a deliberate central plan gears production to the established needs of the social community and postulates the labour of each individual as directly social by transforming all productive organizations smaller than the whole society into merely technical units. *The exclusive and exhaustive dichotomy of market or planning already contains the similarly conceived dichotomy of capitalism or socialism as the only viable and stable historical alternatives.* This is certainly a one-sided view of the Marxian heritage, for it is equally clear that Marx did not identify planning with the existence of an uninterrupted chain of commands encompassing the whole productive organism of society and effectively determining all the economic decisions taken within it. His theory does imply (as W. Brus and others have rightly insisted) a clear distinction between *nationalization* as a legal-political act in the field of economy giving a public character to property, and *socialization* as the effective transformation of economic relations, establishing a collective-social property in the sense of the real power of immediate producers to decide and dispose collectively over the conditions and products of their labour — a distinction which theories of transitional society can accommodate, but only verbally. (What would remain of the allegedly socialist features of these hybrid economies if nationalization and planning in the sense of a system of central commands by-passing market mechanisms did not imply socialism, at least in some rudimentary sense?) And Marx in the *Grundrisse* did warn almost prophetically against the danger of the transformation of the central economic organ into 'the despotic ruler of production and trustee [*Verwälterin*] of disposition'. But this same passage also makes it abundantly clear that for him the materialization of this danger depended on a single condition: on the survival of some vestiges of market production in the new society.

Once this perspective (embedded, let us emphasize once more, in Marx's critical theory of capitalist economy) is accepted, there are only two ways one can conceptualize the empirical reality of such a society where market mechanisms are present, but subordinated to the principle and practice of central planning in the everyday, if not in the Marxian, sense. Either one insists on the non-socialist character of despotic planning and regards the case as merely a new form of realization of the unabolished logic of the market under the conditions of extreme centralization — and one then arrives at the concept of state capitalism. Or one conceives market and planning as opposed and mutually exclusive principles whose inorganic combination can subsist only as a result of accidental historical conditions — which is precisely the theory of transitional society.

Once the latter view is accepted, the societies in question appear as inherently unstable and precarious historical formations. Their supposed incapacity for systematic self-reproduction, the allegedly open possibilities they present in regard to diverse, even opposite directions of social evolution, are the conclusions dictated by the elementary logic of the theory and not the results of an investigation into their actuality. The facts allegedly supporting these generalizations have all the characteristics of hastily invoked ideological justifications for a doctrinaire position which discounts reality. For in reality the history of the Soviet Union, at least from the early 1930s, has demonstrated a degree of political and social continuity which can stand comparison even with the most stable capitalist countries. An ability to reproduce basic economic, social and political relations under severely adverse external (for example the war) and internal (for example the crisis following the death of Stalin) conditions appears to be just one of the most outstanding characteristics of this history. People living in Eastern European societies experience this ability as the immovable weight of the system reducing all attempts at individual or collective resistance to no more than an irrational and futile act of defiance. A critical theory of these societies surely does not have to endorse this attitude, but it has to give account of this basic experience. It is of course true that immobility is in a sense disproved by history — continuity does not exclude change, and it is mostly to this actual change of the system that theories of transitional society refer, thereby proving their claim to its inherent fragility. But how can the fact of historical change (even in the sense of structural adaptation) disprove the ability of an undoubtedly dynamic socio-economic formation to reproduce itself? There can be no doubt that the Soviet Union of today is not the same as the Soviet Union of 1933. But are Spain, Germany or the USA the same? No one who has lived in one of these Eastern European societies and has any sensitivity for the actual life-situation of the masses can underestimate the significance of the transformations that have taken place, especially during the transition to the post-Stalinist period. This transition has involved not only a movement away from a system of preventative mass terror to what is in practice a rather traditional form of oligarchic rule, but has also involved one from the most direct dictatorship over the needs (connected with enforced industrialization and modernization at the expense of very large numbers of the population remaining in an abject poverty) to granting a degree of autonomy to the individuals as consumers (together with the inclusion of a slow but steady rise of living-standards into the global goal-function of the system). This was undoubtedly a case of adaptation to changes that were basically brought about by the very evolution of the given type of society — no more than an adaptation, since the position of direct producers as producers remained completely unchanged. The structure and development of production (hence the overall limits of need-fulfilment) are still essentially determined by the uncontrolled decisions of a separate, united apparatus of power. But to refer to this historical example of a successful crisis-management as proof of an inherent tendency of the society in question to decompose of its own accord is just as meaningless as to see in it a guarantee that these societies will be able to overcome their next historical crisis — which all the signs indicate is not far away.

Although it is somewhat embarrassing to state such a polemical truism against allegedly orthodox Marxists, the ability to self-reproduce does not exclude the occurrence of social crises: according to Marx, so long as relations of domination and exploitation are perpetuated, the whole process is necessarily accomplished through crises of various types and degrees of intensity. Social crises in Eastern Europe certainly have their own distinct character which distinguishes them from those that occur under the conditions of neo-capitalism. In the countries of Central Eastern Europe in particular (on the most developed periphery of what in terms of its political organization comes much nearer to a vast empire than to a colonial system) they tend to take the form of political collapse. The whole vast apparatus of domination which seemed omnipotent and omnipresent the day before, disintegrates the next day (Hungary 1956 is naturally the outstanding example, but similar occurrences could also be observed, albeit on a local scale, in the cases of workers' revolt in Berlin, Poznan and Gdansk). This is surely a phenomenon which demands explanation — as does the amazing resilience of the system following what seemed to be its complete collapse. Once popular resistance is broken by external force (or even by no more than a threat of external force) the whole apparatus of domination (with a few changes at the very top) is reconstituted with remarkable ease. In an essentially unchanged form, it again attains that character of practical immovability and solidity which can even result in the memory of its collapse fading from the consciousness of its subjects — at least until the time when its next crisis approaches.

There is every reason to presuppose that a new and global crisis is again approaching in Eastern European societies — that the very consequences of the working of this system undermine the social basis on which its post-Stalinist stabilization has rested to date. But to understand this crisis, in terms of both its inherent dangers and potential, demands an understanding of how this socio-economic formation functions and reproduces itself – and not empty assurances that in the long run it does not function at all.

Theories of state capitalism

The understanding of Eastern European societies as extreme realizations of the tendency towards the concentration and centralization of capital is the second theoretical option for their conceptualization within the framework of orthodox Marxism. The historical roots of this conception again reach far back, at least to the criticism of Soviet society articulated by the council communists (for example, Pannekoek and, in a more sophisticated form, Korsch). Today the theory is dominant among various groups of the New Left and exists accordingly in a number of variants with widely different theoretical content and sometimes even opposed practical–political consequences – from the theoretical Maoism of Bettelheim to the concept of a total bureaucratic capitalism as articulated by such critics of Marx as Castoriadis and Lefort (although the views of the latter, precisely because of their critical attitude to the Marxian conception of capitalism itself, can only partially and conditionally be reckoned as variants of the theory under discussion). Here again we can make no more than some very general remarks regarding what seem to be the basic and most common presuppositions of these theories. Undoubtedly many of them are much more sophisticated than our criticism can indicate.

All these theories regard Eastern European societies as essentially antagonistic social formations within which the economic, social and political domination of one particular group, generally identified as the bureaucracy, is realized. Furthermore, these societies are themselves seen as realizations, or even consummations, of some tendencies inherent in the development of capitalism. The power of bureaucracy is expressed, at least in terms of economics, in the fact that all essential means of production have become monopolized and controlled by the single central power of the state, which in the field of production fulfils the role of a collective capitalist. When the situation of the workers in the direct production process is compared with its equivalent in both classical capitalism and neo-capitalism, it can be clearly seen as not having changed in any essential respect:

the total division between property (in its real, economic sense as power of effective control) and labour has remained intact. Eastern European societies therefore are the loci of the same basic class conflict now taking the form of conflict between managers and mere operatives.

These theories undoubtedly express a radical criticism of Eastern European societies (even if some of their isolated elements may occur in a specifically non-radical context, too, as, for example, in the so-called theories of convergence). But they seem to suffer from the defect of one curious omission. They offer no reasonable explanation for the fact that societies of the Soviet type invariably set themselves up — both in ideological and political practice — as anti-capitalist regimes, in opposition to the capitalist world-system, from which — if these theories are true — they differ only in degree. Neither the dead weight of historical traditions and origins, nor the exigencies of the political conflict between the superpowers in the world arena seem to provide sufficient reasons why these systems cling so desperately to an anti-capitalist legitimation, especially in view of the fact that this official ideology is now singularly unsuc-cessful in fulfilling its mobilizing role within the masses of the people. Further, and even more importantly, these theories seem either to operate with such a vague notion of capitalism as to make it practically meaningless (dissipating all its economic characteristics in such philosophical generalities as 'production for production's sake', 'domination of instrumental rationality', etc., or simply identifying capitalist exploitation with the appropriation of surplus in general, at least under the conditions of a dynamic economy), or they deeply distort the actual economic structure and production relations in Eastern European societies. In neither instance can they serve to promote its practical-social understanding — and in most cases they do both.

To put it in the simplest terms: in what sense can societies charac-terized by an absence of private property in the means of production, by the far-reaching reduction of market mechanisms (bordering on liquidation), by a dissolution of the institutional separation between economy and state and by a general tendency to abolish the distinc-tion between the public-political sphere and that of civil society — in what sense can such societies be called capitalist at all? (And the traits mentioned above would be granted by most of these theories; if not, so much the worse for the theories.) There seems to be only one answer to this question, which can and ought to be taken seriously: that which points to the existence of similar tendencies in the development of modern capitalism (and undoubtedly here it is the critics of Marx who can most easily and convincingly argue a case for the necessary structural character of these tendencies in contemporary Western societies). The fact that some analogous phenomena do occur in the West as well is not disputed. Nevertheless this does not seem to us sufficient to establish the conceptual identity of the two economic systems, even in the remotest theoretical sense. All these tendencies notwithstanding, in modern Western societies those basic economic mechanisms through which surplus is defined and appropriated have remained essentially unchanged. Surplus continues to be realized in the form of the differential between the market price of output and input (that is, of profit) and both the title to, and the effective power of, the appropriation of surplus remain ultimately based on property taking the legal form of ownership. As long as these characteristics of a mode of production persist, the aforementioned tendencies remain mere tendencies; it is only their complete abolition and replacement by other economic mechanisms that allows (and demands) the complete and institutionalized realization of these tendencies in Eastern European society. The difference between East and West, therefore, is not one of degree, or of the level of development of the same underlying socio-economic structure – they are different types of societies, with different modes of production.

The issue under dispute is not one of mere terminology. As long as Eastern European societies are conceived as historical variants of capitalism in however broad a sense, the way to understanding the process of their extended reproduction (that is, the direction of their economic development) remains blocked – and the limits of subjective reason appear as the lack of objective rationality of the system analysed. It is interesting to observe that while theories of state capitalism heap (deserved) derision on the concept of a transition to socialism which is so much distorted that none of its presupposed characteristics are present at all, in methodological respects these same theories simply repeat the same procedure. They operate with a basic concept of capitalism which in its application to Eastern European society makes them out to be completely irrational economies. It is something of a paradox when those who maintain that Eastern European societies represent the highest development of historical tendencies immanent and basic to capitalism, at the same time state that these economies are inherently and structurally incapable of dealing with a problem which the monetary economy of the ancient Phoenicians was able to solve (as Castoriadis so aptly once formulated): that of gearing production to meet solvent demand.

This problem of irrationality is of crucial importance for our discussion and therefore demands closer attention. Later we shall make some necessary conceptual distinctions with regard to the meaning of this highly ambiguous term. Here, however, only one point needs to be emphasized. As long as these Eastern European societies are conceived as essentially capitalist, they inevitably appear as irrational in the sense of being unable to satisfy in an efficient and coherent way the requirements of their own principle of reproduction, identified as the logic of capital. For it is indisputable that in their functioning and development they constantly and radically violate the principle of 'economic rationality' embodied in this logic. But we must immediately add: capitalism is the only known society in history which divorces (in principle) economic rationality from all underlying social-institutional limitations and considerations and transforms it into the dominating and determining principle of economic and social development. Until recently it was the privilege of some of the most conservative anthropologists to explain the obvious invalidity of this principle in the processes of reproduction of pre-capitalist societies by reference to the 'irrationality of natives'. Theories of state capitalism seem somehow to be committed to a similar position. Faced with the same situation they do not look for another principle of social reproduction (for another type of logic of development, goal-function realized through the reproduction of socio-economic relations), which naturally would be equivalent to the recognition that these societies are not capitalist at all, but rather regard this socio-economic formation as a form of capitalism which in practice functions in the most ineffective and irrational way.

The objective principle of economic rationality can be formulated broadly as that of the maximization of the output/input relation which naturally requires that the elements of both combinations be comparable through their expression in one homogeneous social medium: money. Capitalism realizes this principle in relation to and within the confines of a single enterprise by making maximization of profit institutionally an external necessity, the underlying principle of economic behaviour. It is only when monopolized means of production function in this economic context, that is, when they function as sources of profit, that they constitute capital. (Or in Marxian terms: they are capital only insofar as they are posited in the social form of value begetting more value.)

Now one can at least imagine an economic system which extends the principle of profit-maximization to the whole of the national economy, transforming the principle of profitability into that of social rentability. Already at the beginning of this century, Hilferding had theoretically indicated — under the name *Generalkartel* — such a possibility, and theories of state capitalism actually regard Eastern European societies as its realization under the tutelage of the state. If they were, they could be meaningfully characterized as essentially capitalist. But they are not. In these economies the allocation of basic productive resources is not dominated and determined by the objective of maximizing the output/input ratio in relation to either the individual productive units (enterprises) or the national economy as a whole. And this is so in a radical way, in two senses. First, these principles are not regarded simply as invalid; in fact everybody is exhorted to comply with them all the time — but the objective logic of the system (whatever this may mean) just does not seem to work in this way. Second, the fact of non-compliance cannot be regarded as a mere case of malfunctioning. Certainly it is true that the rigidity, conservativism and institutionalized irresponsibility characterizing the functioning of any vast bureaucratic apparatus cause wrong economic decisions to be taken with frightening frequency. But the irrationality we are discussing cannot be explained in these terms alone. Nor can it be accounted for by the more weighty consideration that in a system with administratively fixed prices (divorced from the relation of supply and demand) there are in many cases no criteria to distinguish between economically right and wrong decisions since in no way can real economic costs be established. (This is literally so: the great, if somewhat concealed, dispute which Hungarian practical economists have been conducting among themselves for almost two decades is concerned with the question of whether agricultural exports are really profitable on the scale of the whole national economy and actually only they keep it going, or whether in fact they are heavily subsidized and may eventually ruin the whole economy.) Because in many situations when it is absolutely clear what the right decision from the viewpoint of profitability (or social rentability) would be, the system actually prefers solutions which are irrational in regard to this particular objective. The best-known of these situations is the systematic preference given in investment policy to the first sector of industry (producing means of production) over its second sector (producing means of consumption). Nobody disputes the fact that the rate of return in the latter is as a rule significantly higher in Eastern European economic conditions than in the former. Nevertheless in

the history of these economies we can observe the following facts:
1. They regularly (recurringly) overtax even rudimentary requirements of equilibrium in favour of the first sector; 2. In situations of
scarcity of means (in relation to plan-objectives) — and they occur
constantly — the system almost invariably undercuts investments in
the second sector, but (if possible) not in the first, though this may
involve considerable political risks and costs. That is, as a matter of
basic policy of allocation these economies regularly direct the flow
of input (capital) into channels which produce fewer outputs — in
whatever way they be measured (in existing administrative prices, in
computable real prices, etc.). There are no sound economic reasons
(at least following the period of initial take-off) for this policy — and
there is no dispute about the negative effects of instability so
created, but they nevertheless constantly recur, and always in favour
of the first sector. And they cannot be explained by external causes
(military needs, etc.) either, because these phenomena manifest
themselves with a strange cyclical regularity, completely independent
of changes in the political environment and foreign policy. (The
existence of these so-called investment cycles has been empirically
demonstrated in regard to long time periods and in almost all of the
countries of Eastern Europe.)

Nor are these phenomena isolated — analogies can be found in all
sectors of the economy. Thus everybody knows that a much-needed
increase in agricultural production (and at least indirectly in state
revenue) could be achieved at quite minimal cost by investing in the
semi-private sector of agriculture (individual household-plots belonging to members of agricultural cooperatives) or even at no expense at
all, simply by changing certain regulations concerning the use of
these plots: the apparatus nevertheless consistently prefers alarmingly
risky investments in the state and state-dominated (*kolhoz*) sector
of agriculture. As a matter of fact the party–state bureaucracy
(often caught up in the investment-cycles referred to) attempts with
astonishing regularity to restrict the use of household-plots, although
these attempts are invariably doomed to failure in view of the
economic weight of their output (in contrast to their complete
insignificance in terms of the percentage of arable land held in this
way. This fact plus the precariously dependent character of their
holding makes the danger of a return to capitalism by this means a
sheer illusion.)

So it is not a mere piece of official propaganda, but a hard fact
that in the societies of Eastern Europe the principle of profitability
(and of economic rationality in general) is subordinated and even

suppressed by broader social considerations. The question is rather: considerations of what type? The official propaganda here naturally refers to the principles of socialism: social justice, preponderance of general social interests over private ones, liquidation of possibilities of exploitation, etc. It is therefore important to examine the social mechanisms really at work in such a case — and preferably one where the claims of the regime may seem immediately credible. With this in view we have chosen as an example the economy of housing.

Lack of adequate living space constitutes one of the most pressing and, one must add, most degrading shortages in Eastern European societies. There are, generally speaking, three institutional ways to reduce these shortages: the construction of new state-owned apartments by state firms; the building activity of private individuals (using both privately hired and family labour) which may or may not be subsidized by the state; and various combinations of the two, which nominally have the character of building cooperatives. Now the simple economic facts are the following. To build one unit of living space through the state housing system costs significantly more (about double in Hungary) than to do so privately, because of the enormous administrative overheads, general bureaucratic mismanagement, the application of a modern, but in these societies very costly, technology necessitated by the fact that at the official wage level there is a shortage of labour force in the building industry, etc. Rents of state-owned flats are, on the other hand, as a rule insufficient to cover their maintenance costs. This being the case, many proposals have been put forward to divert state investment into the channels of private or semi-private construction — by making the regulations upon which the availability of state loans now depends more flexible: hitherto such loans have been tied to the kind of technical conditions of construction that only the well-to-do could afford to satisfy. However, these economically rational recommendations were invariably opposed (and blocked) by the apparatus with reference to the principles of socialism: only distribution of flats by the state can allow, or rather ensure, that social considerations of real needs will override existing economic inequalities. And it is a much publicized fact that a percentage of the new state-built apartments indeed goes to the poorest, largest families. But what are the overall results of this state distribution? In the late 1960s and early 1970s representative sociological investigations were conducted independently in Czechoslovakia, Poland and Hungary into the actual allocation of the new state-owned flats. The overall results were identical. It was demonstrated that it is generally the best-paid social groups (members of the bureaucracy and professional people) who live in the highest percentage in state-owned flats, while the majority of those who live in privately owned houses are unskilled workers (the most numerous and worst-paid urban social group). These privately owned 'houses' are often no more than shacks, the building of which falls outside the necessary technical regulations, and so does not receive any subsidy from the state. The Hungarian investigation (conducted by G. Konrad and I. Szelényi) found that to obtain one unit of new living space costs on average about one-third *less* for a family in the highest income group than for a family in the lowest income group – and then such a family will probably be the first to continue to enjoy further state subsidies of maintenance, etc. through the administratively reduced rents.

And the same social lesson will emerge if we turn to other economic phenomena. Another Hungarian investigation (based on the official statistical data concerning family budgets) has demonstrated that the administrative regulation of the prices of consumer goods similarly results only in the further accentuation of already existing economic inequalities. The most heavily subsidized com modities are the ones which play the largest relative role in the consumption of higher-income families. As a result white-collar families receive on average 50 per cent more subsidy from the state in this way than do blue-collar families.

All this undoubtedly confirms the broadest and most general critical contention of the theories of state capitalism: state-ownership and planning in Eastern European societies are not economic mechanisms in some hidden way opposed to, and restricting the power of the bureaucratic apparatus – on the contrary, they are the very mechanisms through and by which this power is exercised and realized. Not only the explicit, surface political relations, but the often concealed economic relations of these societies express, in the continuity of their reproduction, a logic of domination and exploitation. But here the applicability of this theory ends. Because this logic is not that of capital. It is not as if the relentless drive for profit had been transferred in these societies, as a result of a politically accomplished extreme centralization and concentration, to the state as collective capitalist. Maximization of profit (and with it the principle of economic rationality in general) does not direct the processes of reproduction in these state-controlled economies. And this is not a defect in the functioning of these regimes, but, on the contrary, the very nature of their functioning. Their strangely regulated, well-defined and law-abiding character, we have tried to demonstrate, all clearly point to an underlying social logic which differs from that of the accumulation of capital. The task of the critical theory of these societies is to discover this specific logic of the system, and thereby the tendencies and peculiar strains and contradictions of its development — and theories of state capitalism can do no better in this respect than to declare all these phenomena signs of an 'inherent irrationality'. To revert to our earlier example: it is not sufficient to demonstrate that, behind the ideological phrases of social justice, state distribution of housing actually realizes and enhances social inequalities, that it is only one of the mechanisms through which social surplus is appropriated by the ruling strata of these societies. It is necessary also to explain why it is realized in such an economically wasteful way — since it is clear that through consistent monetarization of actual income differences and support of private house-building activities the same social result could have been achieved, only more flats would have been built. Reference to the rather obvious fact that by the former way real economic in-equalities can continue to be disguised as hidden privileges, though true, is inadequate. It is primarily an inadequate answer from the standpoint of state capitalism, since one of the great historical accomplishments of capitalism was precisely the abolition of all social privileges in the field of consumption in favour of the single privilege of having sufficient money. The point only makes clearer the non-capitalist character of Eastern European societies. But the explanation is inadequate in itself, too, because these societies are also quite successful in investing monetarized income differences with the character of hidden privilege — in extreme cases even by introducing what is actually a second type of money in circulation (chits to 'closed shops' in the Soviet Union as a normal, but concealed, form of supplementary income for bureaucrats on the higher levels of the hierarchy). So as Marx realized, critical theory cannot stop at the demonstration of the fact of appropriation of alienated labour, of surplus, in a given society — its real task is to uncover the specific social form in which surplus is appropriated from direct producers. And in Soviet-type societies surplus is not appropriated, either overtly, or covertly in the form of profit on capital.

This formulation immediately brings us to another facet of the principal difference between Eastern European and Western capitalist economies. In capitalist society the private ownership of the means of production is only the legal—institutional form through which the relative autonomy and isolation of various productive units in regard to each other is actualized. It is only through the realization (valorization) of products on the market, which establishes the social character of labour in the enterprise, that surplus acquires the form of profit. Or to use more strictly Marxian terminology: it is only through reduction to abstract labour (a process that takes place through the mediation of commodity-exchange) that the socially necessary character of concrete labour can be established at all, and it is this which constitutes — at least according to Marx — the core of all the contradictions in capitalism (and, let us add: it also remains inalterably true in cases of nationalized branches or firms within a bourgeois society). But this is most definitely not the case in the economies of Eastern European countries. Here the distinction between abstract and concrete labour does not seem to apply at all. Not only does the state appropriate the surplus from the aggregate output of a productive unit *in naturalia*, that is, as use-values, so that the majority of products never come on the market at all (means of production manufactured in nationalized enterprises are directly and administratively redistributed between the various branches of the national economy), but — at least from the viewpoint of the ideal logic of the system — concrete individual labour has an immediately social character in so far as it constitutes a part-activity determined and encompassed by the overall economic plan. In this sense these are economies that directly produce use-values, and not values at all. But here is is important to recall the Marxian idea (inconsistently realized by Marx himself): use-value always exists in some social form. The objective, institutional definition of socially necessary useful labour as 'concrete labour encompassed by the overall plan' — if taken in this abstraction — generally fails to take into account the real utility of this labour, the ability of its product to satisfy some social want. The discrepancy indicated here is, however, not a mere play on abstract discriminations: it constantly and necessarily reasserts itself in reality — necessarily so, because the overall economic plan that determines the institutional utility of labour and its products can never really encompass the consumption of individuals, since the latter (as opposed to productive consumption) is determined by the decisions of the consumers, generally those of the household. The plan can determine this consumption only negatively, by restricting the scope of available articles. The above definition of socially necessary labour acknowledges therefore as 'useful' activities without an organic relation to the consumption of real individuals through which 'a product becomes a real product' (Marx). In this sense one can accept the description of Hillel Ticktin according to which in Eastern European economies the contradiction between use-values and value is transferred to the product as use-value. Or perhaps, more correctly, one can say that one of the basic contradictions of these economies is that between the administrative use-value of the product as the form of its social recognition and its real social utility. This contradiction appears primarily in a further aspect of their so-called economic irrationality: in the production of waste – objects which cannot be used in the ways intended, being of such poor quality (a question that does not really concern the units of production, since they work to fulfil the plan and not to satisfy the socially articulated needs or effective demands), and objects which simply do not meet any consumptive requirement at all. Even in this latter sense waste may reach staggering proportions. In some Eastern European societies (and under conditions of an acute shortage of paper) about one-third of books printed has to be destroyed each year, simply because nobody wants to buy them (and one ought not to forget that those which are 'bought' are actually often administratively distributed among libraries where they stay unread on the shelves). Later we shall see in detail that it is not only 'ideological production' which is characterized by this paradoxical concrescence of shortage and sheer waste, and that waste production in Soviet-type societies possesses distinctly specific features in comparison with the superficially analogous phenomena in the capitalist economies of the West.

Now perhaps the limitations of those impossibly vague philosophical theories of state capitalism, which often attempt to articulate the ultimate identity of the two societies, can be seen. In fact they are all no more than variants of the formula: 'production for the sake of production alone'. There is undoubtedly a sense in which this formula really fits – the sense in which it is applicable to any dynamically developing economy. And this is precisely the point argued by Marx defending Ricardo against the criticism of Sismondi: 'production for the sake of production means nothing else, but . . . the development of the riches of human nature as an end in itself'. In other words, this formula is incomplete as a characterization of any modern socio-economic organism, except inasmuch as it affirms its distinction from pre-capitalist formations in general, because there is no such thing as 'production for the sake of production' at this level of abstraction and universality. The theoretically unbounded extension of production always has a historically determined direction, a definite, socially–institutionally pre-set objective. Just as capitalism, for all its technological expansionism, is unready and unable to produce, let us say, an adequate system of communal transport in the cities or nurseries for children, because it is governed by the principle of maximization of profit, so are Eastern European economies unable to produce books which people want to read, trousers that they want to wear or even razor blades with which it would be possible to shave safely — because here another principle determines the social objective (goal-function) of production (which we have yet to characterize positively). Criticism of these societies, on the basis that they acknowledge 'production for the sake of production' (and not because they acknowledge a definite type of it) is consistent from one standpoint only: from that which identifies socialism with a society that in principle checks the development of production and needs. This is naturally not an incoherent standpoint, even if contrary to the predominant tenets of modern socialist thought (Marx of course included). Since theories of state capitalism do not, however, seem to be actually committed to this perspective, there is no sense in fighting shadows. But it ought to be said that from the perspective of the hard-working majority in Eastern European countries a socialism of zero-growth would appear to be no more than the irrelevant pastime of intellectuals in rich societies, for their own society is one not of relative, but of dire, scarcity. Many elements of this scarcity are surely institutionally created, but there also exist unquestionable material limits to the satisfaction of elementary human wants (elementary at the present level of historical development). These are mostly societies that are poor (even if not in the sense of Third World societies) — and those who live in poverty see no exalted and romantic features in it.

Lastly, the principal difference between capitalist and Eastern European economies can also be argued in regard to that element of relations of production which traditional Marxist analyses have in general tended to regard as the central and determining one: that of property. In the theories discussed the real (economic) property relations (as opposed to their judicial expression in the form of state ownership) in Soviet-type societies are conceived as the concentration of capitalist private property in a sole hand: in that of the bureaucrat class. Leaving aside now the question of whether such awkward concepts as 'private collective property' and the like make any real sense at all, this interpretation seem to miss one basic point. Capitalist relations of property rest upon the complete division between the objective and subjective factors of production. Means of production are posited in relation to living labour as objects of an alien property, while, on the other hand, their proprietor has no other source of command over labour except those the conditions of which are fixed by the contract of wages. In the conditions of Eastern European societies, however, this separation of the objective and subjective conditions of production is in fact incomplete. We have actually argued this point when discussing the concept of transitional society, so here we have only to summarize the facts already referred to. In these social conditions the very apparatus which effects direct control over the disposition of means of production and the appropriation of surplus, at the same time has effective power to command by purely administrative–political means portions of the aggregate labour force (not only various forms of forced labour, now realized through conscription to the army, belong under this category, but also cases of restriction of the free movement of labourers and those of so-called social mobilization for the performance of economic tasks). At the same time — and this is much more important — the same apparatus actually determines and sets the conditions of the work contract (certainly not arbitrarily or free of objective social restraint, but autonomously within these limits), concerning both the level of nominal wages and its other clauses. The worker in these conditions is not a wage-worker in the classical sense, since in economic respect he or she is not completely free. Even legally he or she has only the right to withhold his or her labour from this or that enterprise, but not altogether, and effectively he or she can influence the conditions of labour contract only indirectly (through fluctuation of the supply of labour between various branches or enterprises, through absenteeism, spontaneous withholding of production, etc.).

The owner of labour power is under a statutory obligation to sell his labour for a price which is administratively set and which has in principle nothing to do with the surplus that labour will produce. The owner of labour is not allowed to bargain collectively or individually over the price of his labour power. He cannot decide to withhold his labour and to try to sell the products of his labour rather than his labour power. Under these circumstances we cannot speak meaningfully of a labour market.

Thus I. Szelenyi. This means that the same social stratum which effectively controls the objective factors of production, also has a degree of control over its subjective factor, over the direct producer itself. In this sense it is justified to speak of the existence of a network of impersonal relations of dependence (*Herrschaft- und Knechtschaft-verhältnisse*) in Eastern European societies, to coin an expression after the manner of Marx.

But the incomplete separation we are discussing is not a one-sided affair — it holds true in reverse as well. The actual command of the bureaucratic apparatus over the objective means of production, its effective power over their use, abuse and enjoyment is — at least in comparison with the case of capitalist ownership — restricted. In the actual process of its social reproduction and functioning, the Eastern European system as a rule does not tolerate a number of phenomena which in the West are normal concomitants and consequences of private ownership — shut-down of production in cases of non-profitable enterprises, institutionalization of overt unemployment (this, however, does not exclude the existence of various concealed types of unemployment), existence of open and explicit inequalities of income beyond a never-stated and changing, but nevertheless existing limit, etc. Undoubtedly all these restrictions are connected to the historical origin and the specific legitimation of the regimes concerned, but they are economically no less real on this account. In their total effect they impose specific social limitations upon the right of the apparatus to dispose of the resources of production — limitations that constitute the conditions of that minimal social consensus without which even the most despotic regime could not subsist, and in this (but only in this sense) they can be seen as exercised from below. One of the consequences of this situation is the fact that while the total apparatus of political—economic domination and management exercises a control over the aggregate social labour force in principle unavailable either to the class of capitalists or to the democratic capitalist state, on the other hand the means of purely economic compulsion and disciplining available to the individual manager within the enterprise are actually diminished in comparison with the West. (This holds true, of course, only of the developed, mature stage of Soviet-type societies. The mass terror of the Stalinist period fulfilled in the given respect the function of inuring and subduing the workers to the rule of the apparatus — at that time the power of the manager was directly and routinely supplemented and propped up by the power of the secret police.) And this also means that while the normal functioning of the system excludes any organized collective pressure and protest from the workers (or from any other group of people), it remains rather vulnerable to the guerilla warfare of individual employees within the enterprise; a fact that does not threaten its existence, but severely reduces its technical and economic effectiveness. To sum up: in contrast with the complete and *ex principio* divorce between objective and subjective conditions of production realized through capitalist ownership, Eastern European societies present a case where disposition and control over means of production is exercised under the conditions of a mutually incomplete separation between them and the labour force, and this creates an economic and social matrix that is systematically different to the one to be found in Western societies.

With all that said, there remains, however, one sense in which theories of state capitalism may, unfortunately, be true — a sense most clearly formulated by Cornelius Castoriadis when characterizing the Soviet regime as a part of the socio-historical universe of capitalism. This is, in our view, wrong as a means of explaining the character and the functioning of the social system concerned, but constitutes a just historiosophic evaluation of the overall results of its development. This standpoint seem paradoxical only so long as one does not take into account the frequent occurrence of parasitic societies in history — societies which subsist only in relation and in opposition to a different 'primary' social organism (which politically they may from time to time even dominate — the famous example naturally being the relation between pastoral nomads and irrigational empires). In whatever way the political—military balance and relationship between the two systems develops, in the course of their historical evolution Eastern European societies seem to become less and less able to generate significant innovations in any of the substantial, value-creating fields of social life, from technology through science to art. With the growth of a social—political conservatism there proceeds the increasingly imitative character of their development in all sectors of society — and an almost complete reconstitution of the typically bourgeois values in everyday life and in the motivation system of the members of society (together with a rather conspicuous absence of some civil and civic virtues — but this we shall discuss later on). The functioning of these societies does not proceed according to the principle of an instrumental rationality which they in fact constantly violate. But, on the other hand, they were also unable to generate a new practical principle of rationality (except as a mere ideological myth). Their own hidden logic — a logic of naked domination — can not only never be made explicit, but also seems no more than a logic of an ever-extending *status quo*, not containing sufficient criteria for the determination of the direction of economic—social change. These societies, therefore, inevitably have to fall back on instrumental rationality, a principle that they deny in ideology and cannot adequately realize in practice. In this sense competition with bourgeois societies belongs (and not only as a measure of socio-psychological mobilization) to the inherent nature of these societies — they are, so to speak, condemned to the never-ending task of overcoming capitalism (which — as one bitter Russian joke reminds us — is rushing headlong over a precipice). It is this world-historical barrenness of Eastern European societies which actually constitutes the strongest argument for regarding them as mere variants of a capitalist society — and we yet have to give an explanation for it in terms which take into account the essential structural differences between these two types of society.

The model of the Asiatic mode of production

Theories of transitional society and state capitalism are the two basic alternatives of interpretation offered and elaborated by the Western Left for the understanding of Eastern European societies. And, as we have tried to argue, this alternative is prefigured by the logic of classical Marxist theory from which it follows that under conditions of modernity (the most minimal meaning of which can perhaps be defined by the concept of dynamic social production) only capitalism or socialism can constitute viable forms of organization of socio-economic life. There is, however, a third way of their conceptualization which in principle is surely not incompatible with the legacy of Marx — an explanation which, referring to the historical backwardness of these societies (primarily imperial Russia), conceives them on the model of some pre-capitalist society. Although in these contexts analogies are sometimes drawn with feudalism, it is primarily the Marxian notion of 'Asiatic mode of production' which is most frequently referred to — rather in harmony with Marx who with predilection spoke of the 'Mongolism' or 'semi-Asiatic' character of Russian history.

True, we do not know anyone on the Left who would attempt to make this model or analogy the exclusive or even basic explanatory principle for the characterization of Eastern European societies. (The merit of consistency, dubious in this case, here belongs to Karl Wittfogel in the late, arch-conservative period of his life.) On the other hand, references to Russian backwardness and to the supposedly Asiatic character of Russian development can be found as auxiliary—secondary elements of explication in a great many theories widely divergent in other respects — their weight and importance shifting from case to case. It seems to be, however, rather symptomatic that, as well as historians who by the logic of their profession tend to emphasize elements of continuity, it is certain Leftist dissidents from Eastern Europe who tend to ascribe the greatest role to this factor of conservation of some pre-capitalist features in these allegedly socialist societies — as can be seen in *The Alternative* of R. Bahro, with its conception of a non-capitalist, because semi-Asiatic, road to industrial society. In any case it seems appropriate at least to indicate schematically our view concerning the general legitimacy of these attempts to account historically for some of the outstanding features of Eastern European societies in terms of the Asiatic or, more generally, under-developed character of their pre-Revolutionary past.

Besides the most obvious critical point made by these theories — the indication of the historical possibility of bureaucratic domination—exploitation under conditions of an absence of private property in general and the demonstration of a line of continuity in Russian development precisely from the viewpoint of this mode of domination, due to the strongly statist character of the whole social-economic organization reaching back to the Muscovite principality — they have also the indubitable merit of drawing attention to many of the dispersed features of these societies which from a historical perspective inevitably appear as pre-capitalist, as striking remnants of some traditional social organization, be it Asiatic or feudal. We have already referred in passing to a number of such phenomena: use of forced (and in the case of the inmates of the Gulag Archipelago, directly slave) labour; elements of a semi-bondage to land (or at least various forms of restriction upon the freedom of migration); the role of non-monetarized, covert privileges in the upper strata of the social hierarchy, etc. — to name only a few with directly economic relevance. In many cases these social practices are clearly linked to the traditions of the past. It does not demand great intellectual effort to perceive the connection between the Petrine Table of Ranks and the Soviet system of nomenclature. In some other cases they may be innovations or alien borrowings in terms of national history, but even so, this would only enforce the view which regards such pre-capitalistic mechanisms as organic to the very essence of the systems concerned. And in this respect it has also justly been pointed out that in the course of their historical evolution the weight of these traditionalist elements seems in some respects not to abate, but to increase in Eastern European societies. Particularly in the field of ideology the regime even seems consciously (and rather successfully) to be attempting to reconstitute such forms which in the immediate post-Revolutionary period were the main objects of its attack (nationalism has justly been indicated as the most relevant in this respect).

But even a more detailed enumeration of such phenomena would not convey what many Eastern European radicals were forced to acknowledge with a deep sense of disillusion: the stale, conservative character of life in these societies, the undisturbed survival under a socialist façade of those national stereotypes, prejudices and forms of behaviour, against which generations of the progressive tradition had struggled in the past. In the provinces especially one feels as if the phenomena of modernization have changed only the outward surface of existence. The nature of human relations with all their degrading personal dependencies and brutal inequalities, the basic types of life style and life practices have remained essentially unchanged. It is not a question of a lack of some ideal socialist form of life — whatever that might mean — which these societies surely cannot be called upon to account for, but the disturbing factor of the grotesque apeing by which the middle strata of the new apparatus of power attempt to reproduce the values and forms of behaviour of their pre-Revolutionary — mostly gentry — predecessors, and that of its social inverse: the traditional unquestioning and unhesitating popular respect of authority. Compared with all the vast human expenditure in terms of lives and suffering which the earlier abruptly radical transformations brought about, these social systems have proved to be in an important sense deeply conservative: in large population masses they have preserved in more or less intact form social habits and reflexes that are often rooted in a pre-capitalist past.

So it is emphatically not because we doubt the existence of the relevant facts or their significance in real life that we express reservations about the customary (or at least frequent) use of the qualifying adjectives 'Asiatic' or 'feudal' in many of the theories concerned. But in so far as they signify attempts to explain the specific features of these societies — specific either in respect of the existing model of capitalism or a posited model of socialism — by an exclusive reference to the backwardness of that historical ground from which they originated, they seem to us to fail principally. Of course questions of continuity and discontinuity can be discussed meaningfully only within the framework of a historical discourse and we are concerned in this book solely with the delineation of an elementary model of the functioning of Soviet social systems. Nevertheless some points can and must be made.

First, Eastern European societies cannot be described in terms of a pot-pourri of pre-capitalist, capitalist and post-capitalist characteristics. They represent an integral social system — integral in the sense of possessing a reasonable ability to reproduce themselves, with all the strains and contradictions that that implies. The specifically pre-capitalist features of these societies are inscribed in, and subordinated to, such mechanisms of social—economic reproduction which have no analogies in history and ought to be regarded as unique. To this one has to add that while the social conservatism we have indicated above seems to be an essential feature of Eastern European societies, actually becoming more and more pronounced as they evolve, many of the most conspicuously pre-capitalist institutional elements and mechanisms (which were partially enumerated earlier) seem to have a more local, temporal character: they are present in some of these societies at certain stages of their history, but not invariably and universally. It would seem to be a mistake to limit their general structural characterization to such features as the persistence of forced labour or some forms of bondage, etc. — they can do without these features as well. It is naturally characteristic that under definite historical circumstances the ruling apparatus can and does have recourse to such direct forms of oppression and exploitation, and the struggle against them is an elementary precondition of any emancipation. Their disappearance, however, only makes the system more civilized without changing its most essential, structural characteristics.

Second, this social system now exists in a great variety of national—historical environments which have very little in common even in terms of a relative backwardness or the general character of socio-historical traditions. Surely 'really existing' socialism means in many respects something different in the Soviet Union than in Hungary or in Rumania — especially if one considers the question not from the viewpoint of abstract institutional characteristics, but in terms of everyday life-practices and forms of direct social intercourse, in terms of the micro-structure of social relations which is so difficult to capture theoretically but is so important in real life. And these differences undoubtedly fit well into the pre-established, traditional patterns of national histories. Nevertheless it seems to be a reasonable and meaningful abstraction to refer to all these countries as variants of one and the same social system, social-economic formation — just as in the same way and for the same reasons it makes sense to refer to capitalism in regard to the USA, France and, let us say, Australia, although the differences between these societies, not least in the respect mentioned, are just as pronounced as in the former case.

To this the response can well be that such an analogy does not hold in one all-important respect: the present social system in the dependent countries of Central and South-Eastern Europe (and in some of the national republics of the Soviet Union itself) historically originated in external military—political pressure in a variety of forms, and is not the result of an indigenous development. Even its subsistence today depends upon constant Soviet military presence. This latter statement may be true, although to reflect upon the direction the development of these dependent countries might take, if the external limiting factor — the possibility of a Soviet intervention — were to disappear, seems at present to be a rather fruitless exercise. In any case, the relations of dependence which exist between centre and periphery in the Soviet bloc, have a decidedly different character to the relations existing between the countries of Western Europe and the USA (where even the use of concepts like centre and periphery would be rather questionable or at least much less direct). Nevertheless, even in the former case it is now only a kind of political dependence and military support, and not an external imposition of a social system. To compare the societies of Central and South-Eastern Europe with regimes of foreign occupation or with colonies is a misconception which completely disregards the question of the extent to which these regimes have become indigenous. And by this we mean not only that in these dependent countries there exist significant strata whose interests are now directly bound up with the continuous existence of the whole established institutional structure, but above all that this structure has become the framework within which the whole population articulates its plans, expectations and even its desires. The strange historical phenomenon of an immovable stability and continuity which suddenly and in a seemingly irrational way is punctuated by crises of collapse, to which we referred earlier, finds its parallel in this social perception of the system at its periphery as at once alien, externally superimposed and completely natural. Its naturalness is the result of an immobilization of social imagination which is intrinsic to the working of the system, one of the basic mechanisms through which it perpetuates itself. In this respect one can only state that once established, the whole institutional structure can be and is reproduced also under conditions which cannot be characterized as historically backward in a meaningful sense (as in Germany or Czechoslovakia), and performs under these circumstances about as well as anywhere else.

Third, it ought to be pointed out that references to Asiatic or feudal characteristics in the contexts discussed tend to have the appearance of loose analogies. That is to say, they disregard basic, determining elements of the conceptualizations they refer to, one-sidedly emphasizing determinations which in the original context had a merely derivative character. So the Marxian notion of an Asiatic mode of production (and, as a matter of fact, virtually all the relevant theories of 'Oriental society') posited the existence of a vast multitude of self-sustaining productive units, independent from each other, each itself organizing the social labour process in a traditionally fixed form, as the economic–social basis of the formation involved. The despotic (and, under given historical conditions, bureaucratic) state was seen by Marx as the appropriator of a surplus (again traditionally fixed) which was then employed (redistributed) partly in maintaining some of the general conditions of production on a social scale (the role of irrigation, establishment of reserve funds, etc.), partly – and above all – for the maintenance of an urban economy essentially divorced from the life and activity of the fundamental productive (rural) units. Naturally on the basis of this general characterization no meaningful parallel can be drawn between Asiatic and present-day Eastern European societies, because in the latter the state is not simply the redistributor of a surplus produced essentially through traditional mechanisms independent of its activity. It is the direct organizer of the production process itself, having as its aim the creation of an ever-growing amount of surplus (in a definite social–economic form) in conditions of an economy where the activity of all functional units is interrelated and inter-dependent. The question of how such a system succeeds in combining economic dynamism with social conservativism, preserving, especially in everyday life and intercourse, many features of even a pre-capitalist past (and a host of complex phenomena described by Eastern European sociologists under the headings of 'pseudo-modernization', 'semi- and sub-urbanization', etc. are relevant here), is of course a highly pertinent one. But it is not answered, only metaphorically (and misleadingly) indicated by calling these societies 'Asiatic' with some appropriate qualification.

All this naturally does not relate to the problem of the role of relatively backward conditions in the historical origin of the Soviet system (and many of the theories referred to undoubtedly address themselves first of all to this question). But the system, once evolved, is a type of modern society, even if specifically apt to conserve many features that are in the historical sense traditional, i.e. even if it has a tendency to restrict the phenomena of modernization to definite spheres, especially that of economy (both of production and consumption). And if earlier we emphasized the fact that these societies belong in a historiosophical sense to the universe of a capitalist world-epoch because they were unable to create a new system of substantive social values (either in objectified form, or as subjective motives of social behaviour), we now have to stress the fact that even this dependence on a capitalist environment necessarily takes the form of competition, in the sense of an opposition. This refers not only to the sphere of ideology (connected with the historical origin of this form of society in an attempt to overcome the antinomies of capitalism contemporary to it) or that of the politics of power blocs. The opposition is structural in the sense that Eastern European societies represent and realize an alternative way to that offered by capitalism for the social organization of a dynamic economy which reproduces even selectively borrowed values through essentially different mechanisms and therefore integrates them into a different general social context. The pseudo-socialist character of official ideology is not merely a remnant of an actually long-disappeared historical past, it expresses ideologically, that is, in a distorted way, the fact that 'really existing' socialism constitutes a society different from, and in many respects opposed to, capitalist forms of modern society – its characterization as a post-capitalist one is in this sense justified. For this reason the attempt to treat it exclusively or basically in terms of a backward national history seems to us, especially when undertaken by radicals in either East or West, to be a form of escapism – escapism from the fact that these societies, however tragic this may be, do belong to the international history of that social and intellectual movement which bears the name of socialism. Not only did they originate in a historical attempt to transcend capitalism, but they have also resulted in a social formation of a modern and non-capitalist type which represents a new form of oppression and domination. However specific the historical conjecture which gave rise to them in the first place may be, the lessons that may be learned from them integrally and necessarily belong to contemporary socialism. Just as the reality of their existence today inevitably co-determines popular attitudes everywhere to the idea of socialism, so this latter idea fails to stand up to the critique of reality if it is unable to cope self-critically with all the consequences and experiences of their existence. The intellectual attitude so prevalent in Eastern Europe, which simply dismisses the idea of any socialist future, since it believes in only one socialism — that which exists here in the present — finds both its parallel and confirmation in the intellectual attitude of many Western socialists, who actually discard the present experiences of these societies by simply relegating them to what for their own society and social practice is a backward and irrelevant past. Faced with Eastern European societies, Western socialism cannot adopt the attitude of assuring everyone that the practical social project it represents has nothing to do with the realities of these societies. However sincere and resolute the good will expressed in these assurances, it remains an act of bad faith so long as the idea of socialism does not incorporate into itself an equally clear and unequivocal criticism and negation of Eastern European social conditions and practices. And the first step towards this is undoubtedly an understanding of them which is both adequate and radical.

CHAPTER 2

Corporate Property and Command Economy

Relations of property and the apparatus of power

The working majority of the population in Eastern European societies has no control over the conditions, process or results of its own labour. Not only the technical organization of the process of production, but also all the social–economic decisions concerning what to produce and how to employ the gross product socially are actually established and made by a distinct and separate social group (the bureaucracy) whose corpus is continuously replenished through mechanisms of a selective cooptation and which is essentially self-appointed (its rule being in fact based, to use Trotsky's famous formulation, on a right of primogeniture of power). The dependence of direct producers on this dominant group is so extensive that they have no effective and direct power of bargaining, either individually or collectively, over their own share in the gross national product. This is settled by the administrative decisions of the same bureaucratic apparatus, all the more effectively because it is not only the principal employer, but also shapes (through educational policy, legislation, etc.) and to a large extent determines the macrostructure of the supply of labour-power, and simultaneously establishes the market prices for consumer goods as well. In this situation the ability of the producers to influence both the conditions of their labour and the level of real wages is indirect and rather marginal. The fact that such relations which constitute the underlying social reality behind the legal form of nationalized, public property, have nothing to do with the communal property of associated producers or the socialization of the means and conditions of production, is rather self-evident.

Up to this point most of the radically oriented critical theories of

Eastern Europeans societies are in basic agreement. Their differences — and difficulties — begin beyond this point, when they attempt to characterize positively this mode of production, and, more specifically, the economic property relations involved. To succeed in this attempt is not so much a dogmatic requirement growing out of the pre-established structure and presuppositions of a Marx-oriented theory, as a requirement of common sense. The argument that effectively demonstrates that state ownership does not involve any effective property rights for most of the members of the public, inevitably leads to the question: who then really owns the nationalized means of production in these societies? There is undoubtedly no single, straightforward answer to this question: one must first establish what 'really owning' means in these specific historical conditions. But this question cannot be side-stepped through an assumption that relations of property in this type of society do not in any case play the determining role ascribed to them by Marx (at least in the dominant interpretation of his views), since here politics dominate over economy. For it would seem to be impossible to establish the functional role and weight of property relations without characterizing them somehow first.

The difficulties involved here are partly of a conceptual nature. Though a paradox, it is nevertheless a fact that Marx — despite the indubitable importance this concept plays in his theory of social formations — never gave straightforward characterization of what should be understood by 'economic relations of property'. That is, he repeatedly emphasized (especially when cursorily treating pre-capitalist economies) the necessity of making scrupulous distinction between the legal title to ownership and the actual, 'essential' economic relations of property which the former may express quite distortedly — but in his systematic analysis of capitalism he presupposed their complete coincidence and correspondence (a not unreasonable idealization as far as classical capitalism is concerned). As a matter of fact he sometimes — as in the Preface to *Zur Kritik* — identified relations of property with the mere legal form. The problem is caused not so much by these inconsistencies (which cannot be doubted, but can be resolved), nor by the difficulty of understanding the general meaning of the distinction between legal form and economic relations as suggested by Marx. The real difficulty lies elsewhere. The legal title of ownership under the conditions of a bourgeois society unifies a cluster of dispositional rights over monopolized objects that in other societies may be sharply distinguished from each other and can belong to completely different social agents. It is clear that by 'economic relations of property' Marx meant essentially those relations of dependence between various agents of production that are stabilized and expressed through monopolized rights of disposition over the various factors of production, first of all the power of social command that the proprietor of productive resources has over both the process and products of alien labour. ('Property. . . .' Marx writes, 'in any case is a kind of power.') It is unclear, however, how these relations should be conceptualized when in connection with the differentiation between various types of dispositional rights over the same object, this actual social power of command is also in some articulated way dispersed among different social subjects.

Theories of contemporary capitalism already face difficulties at this point, since the social disjunction of the functions of management and ownership is accompanied (schematically speaking) by a tendency towards the dissociation of the right of use and that of enjoyment (with the state largely restricting the right to abuse), and correspondingly by a growing distinction between the actual power of disposition over the conditions and process of production, on the one hand, and that over the appropriation of surplus, on the other. It is a well-known fact that many disputes rage over this question – above all because the distinction is in no way clear and the two types of power undoubtedly interact. The situation, however, is much more complex in Eastern European societies, since it is very doubtful whether such a distinction can be drawn there at all. Since Marx not only fails to offer a sufficiently universal conceptualization of property relations (at least for our purposes), but there is – to our certain knowledge – a general lack of such a framework (Weber's most instructive classificatory remarks suffer at the same time from an excessive formalism), we cannot proceed otherwise than by attempting first to describe schematically the relations of economic–social power and dependence actually involved, beginning from the level of the single enterprise, and at times drawing parallels with the better-known case of modern capitalism.

Already our negative characterization of property relations clearly indicates that their subject ought somehow to be sought in 'bureaucracy' – a point on which all theories agree, characterizing it variously as the 'proprietor', 'possessor' or 'usurper' of nationalized property. The adequacy of such formulas can be decided only if one looks at its real social power in regard to both the process and the results of production.

Let us begin with the individual bureaucrat, the director of a socialist enterprise — one of the central figures in these economies. Within the given set of laws and regulations (to begin with those of the more or less detailed plan-indicators) he has the power to determine the conditions and the actual organization of the production process within the factory — more or less in the same way as his Western counterpart. In this his actual responsibilities lie only upwards, to the upper rungs of the hierarchy who decide upon his reward, promotion or removal, and not downwards to the personnel of the factory. The factory personnel is organized just as hierarchically as in the West — more so, since no workers' organization built up from below and capable of imposing some checks upon the director's power is tolerated. The restraints which operate in this respect are of a more generalized and diffused kind: the director must not provoke outbursts of spontaneous resistance from the workers, because not only the participants, but also the manager himself may well be 'punished' (though by quite different means) for the occurrence of a strike. And above all he must keep the work-force of the factory in the factory. His hold over them as an employer is economically weaker, since in most cases and for most categories, manual workers can find similar occupations elsewhere.

On the other hand, all the director's power is dependent upon one factor only — on his position in the hierarchy of the administrative—economic apparatus. There may be some vague (and changing) pre-requisites for the post — for example, political (that is, membership of the Party) or educational status — but there is no social basis or backing which would ultimately confer this power upon him beyond his being accepted by the apparatus itself. Further, the power discussed not only does not entail any entitlement to the surplus produced by the given factory, but also confers no ability to appropriate some given, determinate part of this surplus. Outwardly, the income of a socialist director takes the form of wages, just as in the case of the workers. And even if the fact of the hidden, non-monetarized privileges which accrue to this position clearly indicates that this homogenization of income-forms is misleading, it remains, on the other hand, true that the total income of the director will be largely independent from the gross profit (however calculated) of the given enterprise. The degree of their interdependence will change in practice with the various forms of economic incentives, etc. but on the whole the bulk of managerial income depends much more closely on his hierarchical position within the bureaucratic apparatus (and on his personal connections within it) than on the economic efficiency of the unit he manages. The director of a large industrial trust making constant and substantial losses will generally earn much more than the director of a small but very profitable factory.

It is clear that the actual power and social position of a member of the economic bureaucracy in Eastern Europe much more closely resembles that of a manger in the West than of a private owner—capitalist. The lack of entitlement to the surplus produced and the inability to appropriate any definite part of it, regularly changing with its sum total, makes it impossible to characterize the Eastern European bureaucrat as the individual proprietor or owner of those factors of production which he manages. His real social powers emanating from and realizing his economic function are derivative — he acts as a trustee for somebody else. But for whom?

Even in comparison with the social type of Western manager, the Eastern European bureaucrat at the enterprise level has less opportunity for economic decision-making. This is the necessary outcome of the mono-organizational structure of these economies, which naturally reduces the effective autonomy of any economic unit compared to Western capitalism. In this context we would like to underline only one point: our director is not only unable to appropriate some definite share of the surplus produced in 'his' enterprise (which for the sake of a very rough analogy one could regard as true also in relation to his Western counterpart), but he has also a very limited direct say in the distribution of this surplus as well. What in these societies is institutionally defined as the surplus of an enterprise, is for the most part directly withdrawn by the state and, generally speaking, its actual employment will be decided on by the higher rungs of the administrative hierarchy. As another aspect of this situation, basic investments determining the long-term development of the enterprise are, as a rule, covered from central budgetary (or at least centrally controlled) sources. (It should be added that M. Rakovski has rather convincingly argued that even in the ideal case of a decentralized economy within Soviet-type societies the dependence of the basic economic unit of production on the administrative hierarchy would remain of a different order than the relation between a capitalist enterprise and the state, since in the former case one and the same apparatus would preserve the control over the basic determinants of the economic environment of the enterprise as well as over all the external sources of investment.) All this does not mean, however, that the socialist manager has no influence upon the central decisions concerning 'his' enterprise (more precisely: upon the share allocated to it from the total social surplus): as we shall later try to argue, the actual process of planning is in many respects a multi-level bargaining process in which the apparatuses of the enterprise play the role of junior partners. But their bargaining position depends on their overall situation and actual importance within the administrative hierarchy: how much a director is able to obtain for his enterprise from the central organs is in practice at least as much determined by his personal contacts as by the actual economic performance of the unit he manages. For example, having a father-in-law in the Secretariat of the Central Committee would automatically give one more chance of influencing the reallocation of surplus to the enterprise than would simple ability of managing the enterprise better, in the sense of assuring a higher rate of return. In short, the ability of a socialist manager to influence the distribution of the produced surplus bears no strict relation to narrowly conceived economic performance, in the sense of profitability.

It is in this context that the basic differences in the real social situation of a Western and Eastern European manager emerge most clearly. The power of the manager of a capitalist enterprise over the distribution of the produced surplus (profit) is also a limited one. It is not only significantly greater in practice, but also limited by other means. In principle (leaving taxation and state regulation aside) it is limited by another economic agent whose power over the process of production is derived from another source than that of the manager: by the private owner-proprietors (shareholders) represented by the board who have under these conditions a socially valid title to the productive resources of the enterprise, and thereby to its profits — a title which they can always enforce at least in the form of disposing of their shares on the capital market. The actual distribution of the profits is to a large extent determined by the interaction and partial conflict of these two, differentially situated agents of economic life: one whose power primarily concerns the organization of the production process itself and is functionally based or derivative, and the other whose power primarily concerns the appropriation of some definite part of the surplus and is founded on a direct title to property. Whatever the actual relation of influence between these two groups, their interaction generally ensures the maintenance of the activity of the company in the overall direction of the maximization of surplus in the form of profit. And at the same time this also constitutes the basic criterion by which the success or failure of management is judged.

The manager in Eastern Europe is in a different social position because his actual powers are limited not by an economic agent having a different social character, but by other bureaucrats, that is, higher-standing members of the overall administrative apparatus, with more extended power than his, but essentially of the same derivative, functional type. This extension of power, however, is not merely quantitative (embracing more and more economic units), it also refers to its very content — power at the higher levels of the apparatus extends beyond the economy to other spheres of social life as well. By being in the position of dependence upon holders of such power, the economic organization of production within the enterprise as accomplished by the manager is submitted to another set of requirements than those dictated by the maximization of profit.

The managerial apparatus of the enterprises stands in variously articulated relations of dependence (of various degrees) in a number of administrative hierarchies: departmental and ministerial, municipal and territorial, etc. If one moves upward even on that hierarchy of control to which it is most immediately submitted (in most cases this will be the apparatus of the corresponding sectoral ministry), one encounters bureaucracies which are entrusted with tasks (and with corresponding powers) that in a capital environment would be solved by the interplay of market mechanisms and/or through the intervention of state organs which, however, have in general no direct right of supervision over the activities of the private enterprise and to whom the latter bear no direct responsibility. To ensure the production in definite quantities of some articles strategically important for overall economic balance; to earn a definite amount of foreign currency on definite foreign markets at definite average costs of production, while keeping productive imports within some predetermined limits; to stagger production according to some definite schedule; to keep the average wage level at some predetermined level and preserve some overall wage-structure, etc. — these may be examples of such tasks. And the higher one ascends within the hierarchy, the more economic decisions will be influenced by factors and considerations of a definitely non-economic type, whether military, internal and foreign political, social and cultural (perhaps also in that order). It is only the pinnacle that is identical for all the differently articulated functional hierarchies: the small circle of the political elite, the Party leadership, where all the basic-orientative decisions concerning the overall distribution of social surplus are made, or at least ratified. Actually this political elite acts to a large extent (taking here only the economic aspect of its power into account) as the ultimate arbiter between the competing and conflicting allocative claims made upon the available (scarce) resources by the various functional hierarchies on the basis of different considerations and priorities, of which economic efficiency is only one. It reintegrates economy in social totality, replaces political economy with an economic policy, by determining the overall conditions under which economies made within each enterprise will mean economies for the whole of the country, this being specified as the fulfilment of the targets of the economic plan which includes the satisfaction of the requirements of an input–output balance. It internalizes all the externalities: in principle it forges all the economic and extra-economic factors influencing the national income into a self-sustaining, consistent and dynamic whole.

But it does so in theory only. The decisions taken at the top and then concretized at the various subordinated rungs of the apparatuses in the form of a plan can never solve this latter task. This is not because of malfunctioning or merely (as it is often argued) because at present there exist technical (and under the given system also social) limits to the flow of the necessary information. It simply cannot realize it in principle: because, on the one hand, neither the top of the hierarchy, nor the apparatus as a whole has control over the external economic environment upon which even such a country as the Soviet Union must be dependent, and, on the other hand, because it cannot either foresee or determine by its own decisions certain important parameters of the internal economic environment: individual consumption and the supply of labour power. Concerning the first, its power – except in conditions of an all-embracing rationing system – is indirect (influencing choices through the administrative determination of prices) and negative (creating shortages in respect to solvent demand). Concerning the second– short of conditions when the whole country is transformed into one camp of forced labour – it is indirect (through the determination of wages) and incomplete (restricting the possibilities of a free movement for a smaller or larger portion of the labour-reservoir). Therefore there always will occur some accidental disturbances of equilibrium in regard to the plan-objectives, since some of the most important economic factors cannot be brought under complete control. Generally speaking, these disturbances are accidental in the same sense as the deviation of the market price from the price of production is under the conditions of a capitalist market economy. Once these disturbances occur, however, economies for one enterprise are no longer necessarily economies for the whole society, in that institutionally set meaning which is determined and specified by the plan.

Let us now look again at the situation of the enterprise and its management, from the viewpoint of its dependence upon a social power which is constituted and functioning in the manner described above. The power in question is one which reintegrates economy within the social totality — this presents itself to the management in the fact that it is confronted with a number of substantive tasks (plan targets) set from above, the fulfilment of which constitutes the main objective (and criterion) of its activity. The disputes about economic reforms in various Eastern European countries have to a large extent been over the question of the form these substantive objectives ought to take: how detailed or general, permanent or changing, etc. they should be. It was not their existence that was in question. The existence of these set objectives, however, does not completely invalidate the regulating role of some substitute for the principle of profitability. The enterprises ought to realize the targets in the most economical way possible, with a minimal expenditure of resources — therefore those concrete use-values which directly constitute the input and output of their activity ought to be made somehow comparable with each other and the differential between the (homogenized) outputs and inputs ought to be maximized. So all these economies develop, depending on their concrete means of organization and command structure, on the methods of planning applied, etc., some principle of accountancy, rentability, etc., being in fact administratively determined and institutionalized substitutes for, and variants of the principle of profitability in conditions of the absence of market relations or non-pricing markets. The actual task of management can be characterized as that of subordinating the so-defined principle of profitability to the fulfilment of the substantive tasks set by the plan, that is, organizing the process of production in such a way that the plan-targets are achieved with a minimal expenditure of costs, always in accordance with the manner in which costs are institutionally determined and accounted for.

But this is a straightforward task only so long as one does not take into account those unforeseen disturbances which in fact constantly and inevitably occur in conditions of economic activity. Given that these disturbances do occur, the objective set out above turns out to be both inadequate and contradictory. To put it in its most abstract terms: the occurrence of disturbances means that generally speaking there are inadequate resources for the simultaneous fulfilment of all the plan-targets in the whole economy. In this situation making economies for the enterprise may well involve using up resources that are needed in strategically more important

ECONOMIC AND SOCIAL STRUCTURE

economies elsewhere, etc. What is demanded of the management is
actually that in such circumstances it will act according to the
general interest of the national economy, and not that of the enterprise. The primacy of the interests of state against all individual
interests is the basic requirement which the apparatus makes of all
its members, at whatever level of the hierarchy. (What is urged upon
them in these situations is naturally the famous slogan of 'mobilizing
internal resources', that is, of utilizing resources which according to
the plan do not exist at all.) The formulation that Eastern European
managers are mere 'trustees' expresses not only the fact that their
power over the organization of the productive process depends upon
another social power which sets substantive tasks for them, but also
this requirement to subordinate their activity beyond the explicitly
specified tasks and directives (formal fulfilment of the plan) to an
unspecified 'general interest of the state'.

That this requirement is systematically violated can be learned by
reading any newspaper. But this requirement is not a mere moral
exhortation or ideal either – it is an institutionalized demand which
explains one of the basic, as yet unmentioned differences in the
power structure of the enterprises in Western and Eastern Europe:
the duplication of the hierarchy of command within the enterprise.
Beyond the managerial hierarchy and roughly corresponding to it
there exists in Eastern Europe a hierarchy of the executive organs of
the Party within the economic organizations themselves – in practice
constituted just as much from above and subordinated to a more
comprehensive apparatus than the first one. Only it is subordinated
directly to the apparatus of the central political power, and not to
one or another functional bureaucracy. The actual interrelation
between these two hierarchies in the enterprise has changed many
times throughout history but has remained chronically confused and
conflict-ridden. However, this structure with all the difficulties it
creates, remains a constitutive feature of the social–economic
organization. The management (and in general, any particular
apparatus of command at any given level) is dependent not only
upon the functional bureaucracy which is empowered to set it direct
tasks and to supervise its activity in regard to fulfilment of these
explicit tasks, but also upon organs which are to monitor its activity
with a view to checking that it keeps in line with the 'general
interests of state' beyond the fulfilment of explicit requirements,
especially in situations of conflict, and which are subordinated
directly to the political authority as such.

Interest of the state and interest of the bureaucracy

Perhaps we can now at least formulate the problem of the real economic relations of property in Soviet-type societies in a more concrete and meaningful way. Those who in these societies exercise a direct power over the organization of production (the narrowly managerial sub-stratum of the economic apparatus) act only as trustees and depend on the higher rungs of the hierarchy (culminating in one political pinnacle) which not only sets substantive tasks for their activity, but also makes the effective decisions about the distribution of the total surplus produced. At no level of this hierarchy do we, however, meet with social agents who would be entitled to the surplus or would have − at least *prima facie* − a formal and acknowledged power to appropriate it, either individually or as a definite and circumscribed social group. If the narrowly conceived relations of property − as distinguished from mere powers of disposition (*Verfügungsgewalt*) − are defined as the social–institutional power to appropriate the surplus (or a determinate part of it) produced with the help of the means owned, then it seems that in Eastern European societies there are no proprietors at all, while the bureaucracy is the possessor of the means of production − in various senses, according to its internal structuring. But this is a meaningless proposition, because the statement that the surplus is in some systematic way appropriated is no more than a tautology: the notion of 'possessor' has a specific meaning only when contrasted to the notion of 'proprietor'. Disposition over the surplus always realizes some definite form of its appropriation. If no specific social group can be located with a formally acknowledged right to the latter, then the question of property is a question of the character of these activities of distribution of surplus, and ultimately a question of the social determinants of this distribution. Or to put it another way: the question then turns out to be essentially identical with the one about the social determination and content of the general interests of the state, the enforcement of which the apparatus posits as the main requirement in regard to each of its members and which is explicated, though not reducible, in the substantive tasks specified by the economic plan.

Since it is clear that the population, the working class or in general any social group outside the bureaucratic apparatus has no institutionalized power to posit these objectives determining the actual employment of surplus and thereby its appropriation, and that they can influence these decisions at best only indirectly, by way of various kinds of informal and *ad hoc* pressure exercised upon the apparatus itself, there remain three possible answers to the question posed and thereby three various consistent conceptualizations of property relations in Eastern European societies.

According to the first view these substantive social–economic objectives are essentially determined — within the limits of material possibilities — by the arbitrary resolutions of the political pinnacle itself, that is, the narrowly understood Party leadership. It is here that the ultimate decisions about the distribution of the total national surplus are taken and though other groups may have influence, none is able to check the content of these decisions. The general interests of the state essentially express the determinations of will of the political leadership. This does not mean that the decisions in question are sociologically unmotivated: this very narrow group of persons itself shares a common social situation, therefore basically common perspectives, life-styles, values and interests. What is more, it is only a definite type of person who under existing conditions has any chance to reach the top. Ultimately, however, it is upon the personal composition of the Party leadership, and at most the relatively constant social psychology of such a group, that the actual character and direction of economic development depends.

One can regard this view as an extreme reflection of the frequently encountered phrase: the domination of politics over economy. The domination involved would then mean that under the social conditions of a Soviet system the economy does not contain and engender any principle of its own dynamism — the latter is essentially determined by the will of a politocracy. If this is so, the critical theory of these societies has to be based not on political economy but on a political science of elites that is completely absent from Marx.

On the other hand, if the above view holds true, then one is forced to accept that the dominant, etatistic form of ownership in Eastern European societies only conceals the real economic relations of a group-property. The nationalized means of production are then to all practical purposes the property of a politically constituted group, that of the top Party leadership. All the economic powers dispersed among the lower rungs of the apparatus are only emanations of this ultimate one, and the lower-level bureaucrats are actually trustees of this elite. The demand addressed to the lower echelons of the apparatus to act in the general interest of the state, even beyond the specified substantive tasks, means only that each member of the apparatus is in a sense required to act in accordance with the yet unspecified, future decisions of the political pinnacle — a rather formidable task, which actually serves to keep them, through this very uncertainty, in the position of a one-sided dependence.

Naturally, the property relations so conceived will have a number of specific structural features distinguishing them from the instance of capitalist (private or corporate) ownership. First of all the proprietor should be posited here strictly as a group which, despite a changing membership, retains its identity and perpetuity. No individual belonging to this elite would have, on his own, any effective power or right to dispose over the means so owned — and most definitely none would be able to transfer or alienate any part of them to others. Only the elite group as such exercises control over the nationalized resources (and through them over alien labour, here actually of the whole society). Second, the effective powers of disposition over the nationalized means and products in this case generally do not include that of alienation in respect of the bulk of this property, which in this regard ought to be thought of rather in analogy to estates entailed.

There is, however, no point in elaborating this conception in greater detail — though in itself quite consistent, it is hardly convincing. What perhaps militates most directly against it, is the horrendous disproportion between the power of control attributed in this way to the political elite and the actual material benefits derived from it by its members, or — to put it another way — the disproportion between the power of appropriation ascribed to the leadership as a group and as an aggregate of individuals. But we must add at once that this seems to us the less convincing point of criticism. Questions of inequality concern primarily not distribution of income, but that of (institutionalized) power. To use an analogy, capitalism remains capitalism even in cases where (as in the early periods of its history) asceticism of accumulation constitutes the dominant behavioural norm among the bourgeoisie. Actually the income/consumption pattern of the political elite would rather support a theory which takes the domination of politics over economy in the strongest and strictest sense because at the very top income wholly takes the form of non-public privileges. The very legitimation of the regimes naturally excludes the possibility of an extremely conspicuous luxury — but the real extent of this income (as far as one can judge) depends almost completely upon the changing political ethos of the ruling group itself.

Differences in this respect are, however, without any significant consequence, since the disproportionality between the economic power exercised by the ruling elite and its capability of actual private appropriation is in any case and by necessity enormous, simply because of the enormity of the first. There can be no doubt about the fact that the Party leadership concentrates in its hands a staggering and, in some respects, uncontrolled power in economic as well as political terms. The extent of it can perhaps best be gauged by its actual 'right' to misuse national resources. The history of each of the Eastern European countries (right up to the present day) abounds in cases where unbelievable amounts of labour and investment were wasted on ill-conceived or irrational projects, which were accepted by the leadership, only to be revoked or abandoned later. According to one official publication, in Hungary between 1949 and 1955 about 20 per cent of the growth of the gross national income was squandered in this direct sense.

All these facts notwithstanding, the conception under discussion nevertheless distorts, in our opinion, both the relation between politics and economy and that between the top political elite and the whole of the apparatus of power. As to the first it seems unable to explain the deep historical continuity in the development of Eastern European economies and the structural similarities between the different countries – both true independently of the very significant changes and divergences in the composition and background, and sometimes overt political aims of the concerned elite groups. What seems especially significant in this respect is the constancy (or the constant cyclical recurrence) of definite negative structural phenomena which resist entirely the will to change them. Over-investment; constant domination of a sellers' market concerning both consumption and production goods with a simultaneous irresistible increase in the volume of unutilized stocks; chronic bottle-necks in definite sectors of the economy (especially in infrastructure, agriculture and service); general overmanning within enterprises of all types, resulting in a very low rate of growth of productivity (with an actual decline of the effectiveness of resource utilization), etc. – these are some of the well-known 'irremovable' ills that plague Eastern European economies. There exists every conceivable political desire to redress them, as innumerable resolutions of the concerned Central Committees (of very different composition) bear witness. And it can hardly be argued that these are phenomena inevitable at the given material-technical level of development. These facts clearly suggest that economy plays not only the role of mere material restricting conditions whose change is simply dependent upon, and determined by, the decisions of a politocracy. The given institutional structure of economy also in the case of Eastern European societies delimits and circumscribes the possible directions of its own development, and in this sense it preserves a measure of autonomy. Or perhaps, more precisely, one has to say that since formally and abstractly speaking the political apparatus and its pinnacle hold all the power to change this institutional framework itself, the very political will of the ruling elite (this embodiment and explication of the general interests of the state) is in the last instance determined by the established economic structure of this society.

This ominous phrase, determination in the last instance, will perhaps appear less formidable, if we take into account that the decisions of the political leadership are not so arbitrary and omnipotent in a political-sociological sense, either, as the above description suggests. The relationship between the topmost political elite and the lower echelons of the bureaucratic apparatus (especially of the properly political one, that is of the Party) is not a one-way flow of power from above. Questions about the political structure of these societies will be discussed later on. Here it will suffice to say that the decision-making power of the ruling elite is in a sense restrained through the claims made by, and also through the attitudes, opinions, etc. prevalent in, the apparatus itself. Undoubtedly the appropriation of the means of communication, socialization and culture consistently realized in these societies of itself creates the most favourable conditions for the artificial fabrication of a charisma. The most was made of such an opportunity during that 'revolutionary' period when the social—economic structure of the system was first established, in the period of Stalinism. At that time a single omniscient and omnipotent leader actually also gained power over the apparatus which had created his charisma, even to the extent of being able to liquidate large portions of it physically. But with the post-Stalinian stabilization and normalization of the system, the relations between the political elite and the underlying levels of the apparatus also underwent certain changes. The political leadership proper remains the only independent decision-making body in this society. But it cannot make decisions against the prevailing attitudes of the political apparatus — even First Secretaries like Khrushchev or Ulbricht can be (peacefully) 'relieved' if they 'lose touch' with it. But these invisible checks from below ('below' strictly in the sense of the lower rungs of the apparatus of power) only take the form of external restraint and control in crisis-situations; in normal conditions they operate smoothly and internally. While the ruling political elite as sovereign determines by its decision what are the general interests of the state concerning this or that question at any given moment, this activity also enacts it as 'broker' between the various, often competing claims of the different functional, territorial and so on sections of the total apparatus of power; here it has to reassert the interests of the latter as a whole. In this sense the ruling elite also exercises its power as a fiduciary — the fiduciary of the whole apparatus.

We have actually outlined the basic arguments that can be marshalled in favour of the second (and among critically oriented Leftists most popular) consistent conceptualization of actual property relations in Eastern European societies: their interpretation as the common (collective) property of the whole bureaucracy. It is in view of this collectively exercised proprietary function that — or so many argue — members of the variously articulated and hierarchically organized apparatuses of power in Eastern European societies constitute a single ruling class.

Leaving the question about the class-character of bureaucracy aside for a moment, one has to stress that this conception of property relations maintains something more than the unquestionably true statement according to which it is the bureaucratic apparatus as a whole which actually exercises all the functions of disposition and control (*Verfügungsgewalt*) over the nationalized means of production in Eastern European societies. It also asserts that through this power to dispose over the resources and the surplus produced, this group actually realizes its common interests, that the general interest of the state, to which the activity of each members of this apparatus ought to be submitted, is actually nothing but the collective interest of this sociologically specific ruling stratum or class. The dynamics of economic development, the choices exercised by the apparatus in the actual employment and appropriation of the social surplus and determining the direction of this development ought to be explicable on the basis of this latter consideration, to make the formula about the bureaucracy as collective proprietor meaningful. And it is here that difficulties emerge: this conception either has to leave the collective interests of bureaucracy so unspecific that they become meaningless, or else it can specify them only be assuming that maximization of the total amount of the surplus appropriated by all the individual bureaucrats constitutes the determining principle of the whole process of social reproduction — and then it is simply false.

Naturally, Eastern European bureaucracies share with all ruling strata an interest in seeing their power secured and expanded. A collective interest thus stated, however, is not only historically unspecific, but also economically void — it simply leaves open the question of what kind of economic policy would secure this aim. To remain at this level of generality would mean reaffirming the arbitrary character of decisions concerning economy, only now this extreme version of the domination of politics would be maintained not in regard to the political elite proper, but to the bureaucracy as a whole. However, this would make the thesis even less convincing because, while it is true that in present circumstances the political leadership cannot act against a lasting consensus shared by the majority of the apparatus, on the other hand members of the bureaucracy (in this respect like everybody else in this society) do not have forums and channels through which to articulate and elaborate in a continuous way their own perception of their interests. They constitute the only stratum that can offer and even organize an effective internal resistance against a leadership which is drastically out of tune with them, but normally they have to trust the elite itself to act in their name as well.

On the other hand if one tries to define this common interest of the bureaucrats in a substantive way (as different from their momentary perceptions of what serves their interest), there immediately arises the question of how far members of a hierarchically organized and segmented apparatus share interests, beyond the already mentioned generality of reinforcing their common power. In a polemic against Mandel, Alec Nove once pointed out that bureaucrats both in the East and the West are perhaps primarily interested in securing promotion within the respective ladders of hierarchy — and every observation confirms the common sense and truth of his comment. This bureaucratic interest, however, is in principle non-additive, it cannot serve as a basis for the emergence of a collective interest of the whole bureaucracy: if everybody were promoted simultaneously, there would be no advance at all. Therefore, those who want to insist strictly upon the existence of a new class of collective proprietors in Eastern European societies have to take up the position that it is the maximization of the material benefits derived from their position, the drive to enhance their income and privileges (their profit) which in fact motivates members of the bureaucracy, and it is this collective interest that actually determines the basic direction of the economic policy of the state and therefore the whole character of economic development.

Now there can be little doubt that the interest so specified is both real and common among bureaucrats, in the sense that it is a powerful motive of behaviour widespread among members of the apparatus today. Nor is it questionable that some features of Eastern European economies can and ought to be explained by this material interest of the bureaucrats itself. But we have already seen, in the rather significant example of the economic policy of housing, that even in cases where this motive is certainly at work, it is in itself insufficient to explain the strangely ineffective, that is, wasteful form of realization of this objective as a deeply symptomatic feature of these economies. And many of their most specific flaws and irrationalities that seem to be intrinsically connected with their institutional structure are surely not serving the so-conceived common material interests of the bureaucracy either. In general all the arguments that can be mustered against conceiving maximization of profit as being the determining principle of the functioning of the economies would themselves testify against this conception as well, which would then carry the additional burden of the unconvincingly restrictive equation of profit with the (overt and covert) income of members of the bureaucracy. As to the latter count perhaps two remarks should be made.

First, in all probability it is true, although — due to a lack of accessible data — hardly demonstrable, that the costs of maintaining the whole bureaucratic apparatus of power (including the administrative and technical personnel directly subservient to it) are continuously increasing in Eastern European societies not only in absolute, but also in comparative terms. In this sense the bureaucracy does appropriate an increasing share of the total national income. But this is due to the irresistible, constant numerical growth of the apparatus rather than to an increased differential in real incomes in its favour. In the last fifteen to twenty years, income differences have undoubtedly become much more conspicuous in all Eastern European societies. However, this seems to be more the result of a slow general rise in living standards and a simultaneous tendency to transform some outright social privileges into monetarized benefits, than of serious changes in the comparative distribution of real incomes in favour of bureaucracy. Whether such a shift had occurred at all, is debatable (W. Brus, for example, has argued forcefully against it). In any case, if it is the profit-motive in the sense of the material benefits accruing to individual bureaucrats which, below the surface, directs the whole working of these economies, then they really are a miracle of inefficiency and irrationality. Even very high-ranking members of the apparatus regularly earn, even in real terms, significantly less than some successful small private entrepreneurs, who, on the other hand, are the social pariahs of these regimes, having an insecure, marginal existence accompanied by low status and a number of outright social disadvantages. On the other hand, while the increasing social costs of bureaucracy may well be considered as a specific form of exploitation inherent to this society, the numerical expansion of the whole managing-directing apparatus, which is its main cause, certainly is not in the material interests either of individual bureaucrats or of their collectivity – in fact it only enhances the competition between them. And this tendency actually prevails against the articulated will of the apparatus. Resolutions to reverse the constantly deteriorating ratio between those who are employed in direct production and those in administration are among those most frequently taken by the central organs, and in principle nobody opposes this aim. That all these decisions and resolutions prove to be ineffective, is again not some kind of mystical irrationality, nor does it follow merely from Parkinson's Law, which applies to any bureaucracy. In a society where all exercise of power has the character of a trustee/fiduciary relation and where systematically organized control from below is at the same time excluded in principle, a constant reduplication of the systems of supervision is an inherent and irresistible tendency. Processes of decentralization dictated by demands for greater efficiency are therefore constantly counterbalanced with attempts to impose new checks (and hence new systems of control), lest any unit (be it economic, territorial or functional) become so effective as to be able to follow its own set of objectives. It is in this vicious circle that the apparatus as a whole continues to grow, against all (sometimes drastic) attempts at its reduction. It is precisely because of the fact that the material interests of individual bureaucrats are neither severally identical with the general interest of the state, nor brought into a correspondence with the latter by any other mechanism but that of the external restraints and checks imposed by other bureaucrats, that this whole apparatus is becoming more and more cumbersome, against the will and interest of all.

Second, it ought not to be forgotten that just those characteristics of Eastern European economies which give their development a materially distinct character, the whole system of specific imbalances which is institutionally built into their process of reproduction, in particular the mechanisms artificially creating constant shortages both of production and consumption goods, serve the interests (material or other) of the bureaucracy just as little as they do those of anybody else. One should remember, among other things, that bureaucrats are also consumers. Excepting those belonging to the highest ruling elite, where the effect not only of shortages, but also of scarcity is neutralized by the privileges enjoyed, members of the power apparatus in general and collectively are detrimentally affected by the overall anti-consumerist orientation of these economies. Access to scarce goods may be — as in the USSR — one of the carefully graded privileges, but for most of the bureaucrats privileges play only a supplementary role (if any) and hardly out-balance the inconvenience of being unable to use earnings in the way one wishes because of the unavailability of the desired goods — a fact about which members of the bureaucracy tend to grumble just as much as everybody else. (Not to mention the fact that the simul-taneously occurring shortages of factors of production make the actual labour of management much more difficult and risky.) If it is the collective interests of the bureaucracy in the sense of a drive to enhance their personal profits that secretly determines the whole working of these economies, then the new ruling class is not only the most ineffective one known in history, in terms of the relative meagreness of material benefits derived from its unprecedented powers, but it is also stark raving mad since it simultaneously conserves and defends institutional arrangements which create the least comfortable conditions for the enjoyment of the profits so obtained.

It does seem that a consideration of those substantive social factors which actually determine the character of the distribution of surplus in Eastern European societies leads to a similar impasse to the one that emerged from the overview of the institutional mechanisms of this distribution. We again find only derivative powers representing and realizing an interest which cannot, however, be meaningfully characterized either as their own articulated perception of what is best for them, or as some objective common interest which they, due to their common position, actually share. The question of the kind of interest which they represent and realize in the ideological form of the general interest of the state rests, however, unanswered, and con-sequently the character of real property relations remains as obscure as it was before. Nevertheless, this failure to specify the actual socio-logical equivalent of the interests which determine the content and direction of those activities of disposition and control that are exer-cised by members of the power apparatus, is perhaps not an entirely negative result. It may be seen as an indication that the sociologically conceived notion of (objective) interest cannot play in the analysis of these societies the explicatory role in which it is used in most Marxist analyses of capitalist society.

The goal-function of the economy

In this respect it is perhaps noteworthy that Marx himself applied the concept of interest in a systematic sense only to capitalist society, that is, to a society where economic agents act free from institutional obligations, so that the institutional requirements of the system, the logic of capital (primarily the principle of profit-maximization) appear as the value-free principles of rationality in general – in the sense that their violation makes the corresponding action economically unsuccessful as a result of purely causal, seemingly natural mechanisms (and not because of intentional social sanctions), due primarily to the quasi-autonomous working of market mechanisms. When speaking about pre-capitalist societies, where the relationship between the individual and the social institutions is structured in a basically different way, Marx used another concept to discriminate the ways of their respective reproduction and functioning: he spoke of the different 'goals of production' (*Zwecke der Produktion*) inherent to these social organisms. By this he clearly meant not individual psychological motives of productive activity, but the different goal-functions of the economy determined by the structural–institutional characteristics of the society in question. With Marx, the concept, however, remained largely unexplained though it played quite a significant role in the *Grundrisse*. One can perhaps articulate it through the presupposition that each socially distinct historical type of economy (each socio-economic formation) defines in a different way – through the whole system of social relations – what constitutes costs and useful results in economic activities and thereby posits a historically specific (and not necessarily computable) principle of maximization governing the process of reproduction in the society.

It is our contention here that all those well-known so-called irrationalities of Eastern European economies which constantly and structurally characterize their process of reproduction and to which we referred earlier, are necessary consequences of the fact that in them the maximization of the volume of the material means (as use-values) under the global disposition of the apparatus of power as a whole constitutes the goal-function governing the economic activities of the state. This is the real content of that general interest which each member of the apparatus concerned with economic activities ought to represent. That is, in this society only expenditures of resources under the disposition of the apparatus count as real costs. (Neither human costs, nor strictly economic ones borne by private individuals or by communities count as *sui generis* costs in economic decisions, though they may play some role as limiting factors in respect of the political feasibility of these decisions.) And the social usefulness of the end-product is graded according to its propensity to remain during its process of utilization under the control of the same apparatus or to fall out of it. Or, to quote Konrad and Szelenyi, in these societies 'a redistributive decision only then qualifies as rational if it results in the maximal increase of the quantity of the surplus product involved in redistribution. . . . Between two productive investments with the same rate of return on capital the system of redistribution with great probability will prefer that one which extends the market of investment, and not that of consumption goods.' This specific goal-function naturally imposes another logic of functioning and development on these economies than that of profit which presupposes the homogenization of all scarce and monopolizable objectified resources and all products independently of their institutional embeddedness and the character of their possible use. From the viewpoint of such a pure economic rationality Eastern European societies are strangely and strikingly ineffective; they consistently make wasteful economic choices. This is, however, the consequence of their own objective criterion of social effectivity, of their own logic of development.

One has to insist upon the fact that such a goal-function of economic activities is a functional one given the system of social relations of domination characteristic of these societies. Let us take here one example already schematically referred to: the character of the agricultural policy. In a very detailed investigation concerning the development of collective agriculture between 1961 and 1975 in Hungary (and this is perhaps the best performing agriculture in the whole Eastern bloc), Ferenc Donath has shown that the directly state-owned agricultural enterprises have been consistently favoured as against the cooperatives (the first are supplied with more than twice as much in fixed assets per hectare as the second), though the effectivity of production in the latter form is about 40 per cent higher than in the former. Now as regards the agricultural cooperatives themselves, various subsidies, etc. from the state were consistently higher for the very big than for the smaller ones, though again their productivity (over some lower limits) demonstrates a reverse relationship. And to this we have to add the already mentioned fact of the constant recurrence of efforts to restrain administratively the use of household plots in cooperatives which actually deliver, absolutely out of proportion to the land they occupy, 40 per cent of the net value produced in this whole sector. The overall result of all these policies is the paradoxical tendency of a reduction of the land under cultivation (during the fifteen years in question by 5 per cent) in conditions of a constant demand for more agricultural products – and this tendency persists against all the direct legislative measures taken explicitly against it.

Undoubtedly such policies make no sense from a purely economic viewpoint. Viewed internally, they are absolutely consistent: the preferences of the economic policy are dictated not by considerations of profitability, but by the criterion of how far the apparatus of power retains a direct control over the means invested. In this respect, for example preferring very big cooperatives over the smaller ones, though economically counterproductive, is most logical: the possibility of the members actually participating in decision-making is generally (and institutionally) very restricted in all cooperatives, but it is reduced to pure formality in the giant ones. And this logic immediately makes sense, if one ceases to look at it from the viewpoint of a separated economy, non-existent under the given conditions, but takes into account its role in the reproduction of the actual relations of power in these societies. Attempting to maximize through its whole policy of development the means under its global and permanent control, the apparatus renders the existence of any power external to it and able to restrict its freedom of activity or the scope of its domination economically impossible. What is effectively accumulated outside the domain over which the apparatus can directly dispose, does not count as an element of national wealth, but constitutes a threat to the latter, because it can confer a degree of economic independence upon those who own it formally or practically. And this threat, unlike that of the rebirth of capitalism, is a real one. Hungarian experiences again provide a good example here. In the early 1970s, there was a long period of infighting in the higher echelons of the party apparatus to rescind the already arrested economic reforms, to recentralize the direction of the economy and, linked with all this, to syphon away from agriculture the funds necessary for a new spate of industrial investment through a sharp increase of parity. Up to 1974 it seemed that the representatives of the latter tendency had achieved victory within the top leadership. However, the first measures introduced to widen the gap beween the prices of industrial and agricultural products were answered by what virtually amounted to a strike of the peasantry. Agricultural goods, especially those produced in the households (vegetables, poultry, etc.) actually disappeared from the market and the deregulated prices began to soar. In Hungarian circumstances the householding economy of the cooperative peasantry had already become too effective, too weighty an economic factor to be dictated to by a state apparatus without resisting where its vital interests were concerned. Actually this resistance of the peasantry led to the collapse of the whole conservative political offensive. Of course, this result was not predetermined by the balance of economic forces pitted against each other. In comparison with the power of the apparatus the economic weight of any social group is inevitably marginal. The former has not only a monopoly of direct political force to be used according to its own discretion, but would also necessarily win in any waiting game. There were the easily predictable negative political consequences of both these possible courses of action which in the actual situation led to the triumph of the reformist moderates in party leadership. But this example illustrates well the social reasons that lie behind the constant economic irrationalities in Eastern European societies. Any filtering-off of resources into channels over which the apparatus has no direct control, however effective even from the viewpoint of an increase in state revenues, confers upon definite social groups some slight degree of economic autonomy *vis-à-vis* the apparatus. And this is in the last instance true of accumulation of consumption goods in private households too, since even it tends to make the pseudo-market of labour less elastic in respect of the administrative decisions taken by the central organs. What all these phenomena threaten is not the principles of a non-existing socialism, but the unrestrained domination of the apparatus, its ability to function as the sole representative of the general interest in the only real sense in which it does: by making decisions influencing the life of each and every stratum of the population without consulting it at all.

If maximization of the objective resources under the total control of the apparatus constitutes the goal-function of Eastern European economies which circumscribes the possible direction of their development, delimiting the rational options actually available to the political leadership itself, then the nationalized means of production in these societies are the corporate property of the apparatus as opposed to the group or collective property of some or all individual members of this apparatus of power. Members of the apparatus — whatever their position — have in these conditions only a power of disposition over alien labour as *Verfügungsgewalt* to which relations of property (as including the social power to appropriate products of alien labour) cannot be reduced. They act in their function as fiduciaries and trustees, as representatives of the institutional interests of the apparatus as a corporate entity. Their role is reduced (at least in principle and in norm) to this function of trusteeship primarily (though not exclusively) by the actual power relations within the hierarchically and functionally articulated and differentiated apparatus itself, through the interactions of various instances of power determined by the structure of the latter. Naturally under such conditions there constantly occur not only instances of an abuse of conferred powers in personal interests (a criminal offence though within some limits a widely tolerated one in practice, especially at the middle levels of power), but there also emerge – as we shall attempt to show – effective and powerful group interests within the various institutional sections of the bureaucracy. All these are, however, posited as anomalies.

Undoubtedly such a concept of strictly institutional property hardly fits into the Marxian schema of property forms. This is due, however, to the fact that in economic contexts Marx did not consistently draw the distinction between voluntary and non-voluntary types of organization (and therefore his conception of communal property remained a highly ambiguous one, embracing a number of sharply different economic forms). In any case corporate entities as *sui generis* proprietors are well known in economic history, the term 'corporation' being used here in a sense nearest to the Weberian concept of *Anstalt*, meaning an association that does not originate in, and is not dissolvable through, the voluntary legal act of its members. The closest historical analogy to this type of property is undoubtedly that of the Church in feudal Europe. But even this is only a far-fetched analogy: individual members of the apparatus do not have prebendary rights as members of the clergy did and, more importantly, the relationship of the institutions in question to the whole of society, and their function in it, are completely different. Through the working of the apparatus of power in Eastern European societies a definite type of economic growth is realized, and this is a task inherent to the whole system of social–economic relations. On the other hand this growth is of a non-capitalist type: while it has nothing to do with the objective of maximizing the satisfaction of needs of the members of society, it is not directed either at the maximization of returns on capital independently of their future social employment. It actually realizes a constant expansion of the volume of material means and resources (as use-values) under the direct disposal of the apparatus, that is, it constantly recreates, under conditions of an economic dynamism, the material foundations upon which the monopoly of the apparatus rests in establishing and controlling all relations of social interaction and cooperation within the whole society. The total system of social domination is not directed here at securing an expanded appropriation of surplus by one class of society, but this appropriation constitutes only the material basis for the expropriation and monopolization (in principle) of all means of socialization and social organization by a single apparatus of power.

Perhaps these considerations make it possible to give a closer characterization of the domination of politics over economy in Soviet societies. This domination first of all means that the fundamental economic relations are constituted through such an institution (the unified apparatus of power) which has an overall political character, both concerning its origin and its principles of organization. It also means that the economic goal-function specific to this type of society is inherently related to, and can be articulated only in terms of, a form of social domination that is not restricted to the sphere of economy proper, but has a universal character and embraces all forms of social interaction. On the other hand, this domination does not mean that in Eastern European societies the politically constituted pinnacle of the apparatus has an arbitrary power to determine the direction of economic development. The institutional structure of this economy once constituted again imposes its own principle of selectivity, its own logic and laws upon development: in this sense the spontaneity of economics is not overcome in this society either. This economy functions through an uninterrupted process of conscious political decision-making taking the form of central plan-commands, but the options open for decisions are delimited not merely by the material technical requirements of equilibrium, but also by the institutional requirements dictated by the existing system of social domination — and these latter may even override the former.

In this respect one more remark ought to be made about the specific goal-function of economy characterizing these societies. As we have seen this can be conceived as a historically determinate way of defining costs and returns of economic activities. It is, however, evident that maximization of material means under the direct control of the apparatus with minimal expenditure of the resources under such control does not constitute a sufficient principle of strict economic effectivity, since it does not specify the way to compare in a homogeneous manner the materially different resources and products with each other. It actually amounts to a system of preferences, in itself insensitive both to efficiency and to real social utility, since it concerns only the possible institutional employment of the material elements of wealth. If Eastern European societies have failed to create social channels through which considerations concerning social utility in the sense of satisfaction of needs may be articulated and superimposed upon the requirements of technical–economic effectivity, they did not put into effect a new criterion of the latter either. In this respect they necessarily have to fall back on mechanisms which are more or less successful imitations and replacements for the mechanisms of the market. Generally they have not engendered any criteria or mechanisms capable of giving new directions to technical development. The specific character of their economic growth only means a parasitic employment of the growth in technical effectivity generated elsewhere, according to alien, that is, capitalist criteria for a specific purpose: for the expansion of the material basis of a given system of social domination. In an economic respect this is the key to their characteristic historical barrenness.

The economic situation of the workers

So the fundamental economic relations in Eastern European societies are determined by the fact that the nationalized means of production in effect constitute the property of the unified apparatus of power as a corporate entity. However, as we have seen, under these social circumstances the division between the objective and the subjective conditions of production (between means of production and labour power) is socially incomplete. The apparatus which is effectively the sole proprietor of the nationalized means of production has at the same time a definite, though restricted, power of disposition over the aggregate labour power itself. This is partly direct: an ability to command sections of the population by administrative means or by political mobilization to achieve the accomplishment of definite economic tasks. In present-day circumstances at least this is, however, an exceptional measure, the economic presence of which becomes increasingly marginal. Much more important in this respect is the indirect power of the apparatus over labour, in the sense of its ability to establish all the conditions of the contract of labour for almost all categories of jobs. The state as (if not sole then absolutely dominant) employer actually sets administratively both the wages and the principles of remuneration. It is able to do so in conditions where (with some not unsubstantial restrictions) the employees may change their work-place and occupation, because it determines not only the demand for definite kinds of labour, but at the same time, through its uncontrolled monopoly over both general education and professional training, also the basic structure of the long-term supply of labour as well. Undoubtedly this is not an unrestricted power — fluctuations of workers between various enterprises and categories of jobs are factors which impose limits upon it and which the apparatus of management has to account for. But in conditions where employees have no right to autonomous professional or trade organizations, this indirect and spontaneous resistance can have only mild modifying effects.

On the other hand, the fact that the legitimacy of all the proprietary functions of the apparatus rests upon its claim to be the representative of the general interests imposes definite *de facto* restrictions on its command over the objective factors of production as well — restrictions which should be seen in comparison to the case of capitalist (private or corporate) ownership. These concern partly the (already discussed) limited alienability of the nationalized means, partly the character of their use. In the latter respect the apparatus cannot as a rule simply shut down units of production operating at a loss or terminate the non-remunerative manufacturing of articles unless it can provide substitutes for them in some way. Economically and socially most important, however, is the fact that overt unemployment cannot be (or at least is not) institutionalized in Soviet-type societies. As an outcome under these social conditions the unification of the objective and subjective factors of production is realized through a sale of labour-power on the 'pseudo-market of labour, where prices (wages) are basically administratively set and politically enforced, but the competition among the workers is also severely reduced. That is, this unification takes place in the social form of wage labour within a system of paternalistically operating, but essentially impersonal, relations or dependence.

To explain the latter characterization somewhat more fully, a few words should perhaps be said about the liquidation of unemployment in Eastern European societies — a topic which in any case deserves closer attention both in view of its real social impact and its importance in the discussions among the Western Left. First, the right to work coexists in these societies with the legal obligation to work enforced through punitive measures (police harassment or internment). This has to be taken in its real sense: it does not mean the obligation to earn a living through one's own labour, in any case a material necessity for the absolute majority of adult population, but the obligation to earn it in administratively recognized jobs and places of work, and in this way it is an important element of the general social–political control over the population. This excludes not only all forms of unlicensed private services or enterprises (independently of their social usefulness), but also the possibility of alternative life-styles based on irregular, casual or temporary labour, etc. In Eastern European societies marginalization (a not unattractive option for some high-school or university graduates, in view of the sheer boredom of jobs open to them in vast bureaucratic organizations) becomes strictly the privilege of well-known intellectuals, mostly of oppositional standing (needless to say, in the latter case it is a privilege which they are forced to accept). Socially much more important however, is the fact that the lack of overt unemployment means also the lack of any unemployment benefits. That is, for most of the people taking up one of the officially offered jobs (at administratively set wages and conditions of labour) is not only a legal obligation, but a direct material necessity – there is absolutely no alternative to it. It is naturally impossible to judge how many people now working would choose to be unemployed if this had been a socially recognized (that is, at some level financially compensated) possibility – but the staggering proportion (several times higher than in the West) of those in the labour force who work hundreds of miles away from their permanent home and family (often in unbelievable conditions of accommodation), the wage level for some broad categories of unskilled (mostly female) labour, well below any realistic minimum of existence for a single person, the frequency of working in jobs not corresponding to professional qualification, etc., all suggest the strong presence of a purely coercive (both legal and economic) element in the very fact of the absence of unemployment. And naturally, the more restricted the practical job-opportunities for a definite kind of work – that is, more in the case of women as a less mobile element of work-force than in the case of men, more in rural or small-town environment than in big cities, and more in white-collar or professional occupations than in manual ones – the more this impersonal dependence of labour force upon the apparatus as monopolistic employer tends to become a personal subjection of the employees to the managers of their concrete work-place. In the provinces especially job security is often accompanied by degrading and humiliating forms of personal dependence that are hardly imaginable in any modern Western social environment.

Besides all this, unemployment does of course exist in Eastern European societies, only it is hidden and socially unrecognized. As a result, its extent cannot be clearly established, though it is certainly at an incomparably lower level than in the West. It concerns first of all women, especially in definite geographical areas and age-groups. It is an absolutely established fact in these societies that in many of the industrially underdeveloped regions, a great many women want to find employment (newly opened factories have applications for jobs several times outstripping vacancies) and only stay at home due to the total absence of job opportunities in the vicinity. The only existing opportunity, labour in the agricultural cooperative, may be so unattractive in all respects that only one member in the family will undertake it to ensure the right to a household plot. Although this situation is even officially acknowledged, it does not register as unemployment. And there is naturally at any moment a quite significant number of persons who have just left employment (generally for good reasons) and are seeking more adequate jobs. In none of these cases do people receive any financial support from the state or from any other social organization.

These cases of hidden unemployment have to be sharply differentiated from what is frequently called 'unemployment within the factory' and which is not unemployment at all. It means rather the general tendency of Eastern European economies to overman all enterprises in a great many categories of jobs, resulting not only in a reduced level of overall productivity, but also in the employment of persons who are obviously engaged in completely useless pseudo-activities. While the connection of this phenomenon with the liquidation of unemployment may seem to be obvious, it is in all probability much less direct than usually supposed. It is rather a negative link: the inability to institutionalize overt unemployment only prevents the central economic management from undertaking some obvious administrative measures which could drastically counteract the above tendency. For the origin of the latter is in the specific mode of functioning of these economies, independent of employment policy. Overmanning is only a particular case of the more general tendency to create artificial scarcities which follows, as we shall presently argue, from the very organization of these economies as systems of resource constraints. Scarcities in material elements of production naturally result in constant disruptions of productive supply and therefore of the production process itself. In such a situation enterprises become directly interested not only in accumulating within their walls hidden material reserves which are not needed immediately, but also in having some reservoir of labour for the inevitable rush periods of production. (Actually, the more rigid central planning is, the more acute is this necessity.) Since this reduces the supply of labour on the market and therefore increases the uncertainty of whether workers of a given qualification can be found when they are needed, a typical case of negative feed-back develops: because of the foreseeable shortage of labour, enterprises tend to keep unneeded workers on their payroll – they hoard labour-power and thereby create and intensify the shortage.

In explaining all this it is certainly not our intention to argue that liquidation of unemployment is a socially negative feature of Eastern European economies. One of its most important social consequences is the fact that by reducing job-competition among the workers, it seriously reduces (especially in the case of manual workers at the larger factories in big cities) the economic hold which the management of any concrete enterprise has over its personnel. On the one hand, this enforces a 'paternalistic' atmosphere within the work-place. Like the population in general *vis-à-vis* the whole apparatus, the workers have no right to demand anything from the management, but are rather encouraged to ask for personal considerations and favours. On the other hand, it makes a strict enforcement of labour discipline impossible, so that the worker in the immediate process of production tends to retain some limited and purely negative control over his or her work. This results in an overall reduction of the intensity of labour, in comparison with factories on a similar techno-logical level in the West – although generalizations in this respect are especially hazardous, since intensity varies widely depending on forms of wages and available control. The broader social impact of this reduced intensity is again very complex. One ought to take into account not only the fact that a significant part of the reduced intensity of labour is due to stoppages and interruptions in the production process, which are all the more annoying and nerve-wracking because they usually reduce the size of the pay packet. Even more important, however, is the point that the reduced intensity of labour occurs at the administratively set wage-level which for many categories of workers (especially the younger ones who face the task of founding a new home) makes it a materially dire necessity to undertake mostly semi-legal work after official hours. So they actually work eleven to twelve hours a day.

In general, the liquidation of unemployment is also an integral feature of Eastern European economies in the sense that its impact cannot be simply sorted out and treated independently of the other structural characteristics of these societies. This is especially true of its other most significant social consequence: enhanced job security. This has to be seen as one of the most important components of what may be called the pervasive paternalism of the state which prevails in Soviet-type societies. Here it will suffice to point out that the totalizing social system of domination which encompasses nearly all areas of individual life and involves each individual in a complicated set of dependencies upon (and complicity with) the apparatus, has, as it were, two faces. On the one hand it means not only the lack of formal safeguards (for individuals or communities) against the actions of the apparatus, but also the actuality of an enormous pressure generated by the latter to disrupt all informal, spontaneous social connections and ties beyond the confines of the family. On the other hand, the ensuing atomization of individuals is accompanied by a system of measures which provide relative protection against chance mishaps and, more importantly, give a safe and orderly character to everyday existence. (This naturally again characterizes the developed social system and not the epoch of its historical establishment.) And most of these 'cushioning-off' measures exist not as clearly stated and enforceable rights, but as favours granted for good behaviour. Job security, a very important element in this system, also illustrates well the organic interconnection of both the aspects mentioned. For the average employee job security is very high in Eastern European societies: it is rare for anyone, whatever his job, to be sacked and most rare for an employee to lose his job for reasons of bad work or incompetence. But this operates not through regular and controllable social channels (the trade union apparatus which formally ought to safeguard it actually constitutes a subordinate element of the apparatus of management), but basically through a pseudo-personalization of the hierarchical relations at the work-place. Therefore it immediately ceases when individuals 'misbehave'. If conflict with the management of a particular enterprise regularly involves demotion or loss of job, conflict with the apparatus as such, that is, 'political misbehaviour', generally results in a stigmatization of the person concerned for the whole of his or her professional career. In the context of a generally prevailing job security this attaches such a high risk to any such act (even leaving other possible consequences aside) as to make it appear irrational. In this way state paternalism in both its aspects constitutes an important element in the legitimation, and therefore in the reproduction, of the social system.

Bureaucratic planning as a social process

As far as economy proper is concerned, however, the basic mechanism through which the extended reproduction of the whole system of social domination, primarily the actual appropriation of social surplus by the apparatus as a single corporate entity is realized, is nothing but central bureaucratic planning. We have already argued that planning as practised in Eastern European societies bears almost no relation to the Marxian idea of it, except for the common negative element present in both: negation of the regulative role of market mechanisms. We should add that it has equally little to do with the common, everyday meaning of planning. It does not mean a forecast of basic future alternatives and an elaboration of guiding schemas of strategic decisions for these cases in view of present-day exigencies and needs, but an integrated system of binding orders which aims to determine the essential characteristics of the economic behaviour of all subordinate units for a longer period of time. This kind of planning remained unchanged in all the attempted reforms in Soviet bloc countries – they involved only changes in what indices of economic activities ought to be regarded as essential and therefore represented only variations in that margin of freedom which every central plan necessarily leaves to the underlying units. Whether to call such a practice planning at all is, of course, a semantic question. In response to that question one should decide whether to apply the expression 'planning an itinerary of travel' to the case of a very elaborated directive of how to reach Novosibirsk from Moscow whose observance lands one – due to unforeseen circumstances – in Vorkuta. Along with many others, in this situation we personally prefer to speak not of planned, but command economy.

Joking apart, one of the most elementary and important facts to take into account about planning is that no plan has ever been fulfilled in any of the countries involved. To speak on these occasions about 'good approximate' fulfilment (95 per cent or the like) is rather meaningless and quite misleading at the same time. As to the first, any comprehensive economic plan has to represent a system of material balances. Even two per cent under- or over-production already signifies either a neglect of the most elementary requirements of equilibrium in the original plan, or enormous dislocations in national economy. (As a matter of fact the first historically applied plans tended to disregard even the basic demands of equilibrium, but planning has seriously improved over the years in this respect — which also demonstrates that the problem lies not with the competence of the planners, but with the working of the system.) As to misrepresentation, this involves not only distortion of the actual state of affairs, although that also occurs constantly (in the Stalin era through blatant doctoring of data, today more as a result of the in-built — and tendentious — inadequacies of information-gathering and statistical methods applied). Much more important, however, is the fact that reports concerning the fulfilment of one-year or five-year plans do not and cannot reflect either what happens in reality at the level of productive enterprises, or what concerns the long-range, strategic tendencies of economic development. Total figures by their very nature tend to equalize the discrepancies occurring in the real units of production and at the same time are already the results of sudden, drastic modifications demanded by the central organs against the original plan of the enterprise. It is naturally impossible to give a quantified characterization of the average extent of these 'corrections' — but one has only to speak to practising economists and managers to learn about their frequency and the problems they cause. (The fact that non-fulfilment is, as a rule, significantly higher in regard to one-year plans than the five-year ones, gives some indication of the global importance of this phenomenon.) The practice of command economy actually amounts, at this level, to a system where enterprises do not adapt themselves continuously, on the basis of information they themselves gather, to their economic environment (including demands or needs to be met). Rather, they have to wait for unpredictable and intermittent directives from above which generally demand prompt and considerable reorganization of their activities. On the other hand, in regard to the determination of long-term objectives of national economic development, the Eastern European practice of 'planning' proved a complete fiasco. The failure of Khrushchev's famous prediction that the Soviet Union would overtake the United States in per capita output by 1970 perhaps remained somewhat more clearly in popular consciousness, but it was only the most spectacular case. One has only to read the preambles to the various five-year plans to realize the ludicrous discrepancy between the long-term goals set, and what turned out to be the economic reality. So both on the micro-level of the actual day-to-day activity of elementary economic units and at the macro-level of the basic, strategic decisions concerning the overall strategy of total economic growth, command economy turns out to be the exact opposite of a planned economy in the meaning of a system which through the harmonious and unbroken integration of all units of production succeeds in realizing collectively and consciously established, distant social objectives.

We have already discussed the principal causes of this constant discrepancy between plans and reality in Eastern European circumstances and we shall return to this question. But to understand the basic consequences which necessarily follow from the very structure of such a command economy, we shall first look more closely at the very activity of planning as a social process. In reality planning – the formulation of an integrated system of lasting economic commands (we shall take here only the case of five-year plans) – represents a very complicated process of semi-institutionalized competition and bargaining between the various horizontally and vertically articulated bureaucracies.

Naturally we can characterize this process only in the most schematic and idealized way. Within these limits we can refer to three basic phases or components involved:

1. The making of claims for recognized objectives in the plan from the corresponding main functional, territorial, etc. bureaucracies: very roughly speaking, a process of competition between the horizontally coordinated organizations for scarce material and budgetary funds available in the future.

2. The overall strategic decision about the basic objectives accepted and the corresponding distribution of resources made by the political leadership with the collaboration of the central planning organ in the role of experts: the general bargain struck by the main parties in competition.

3. The transformation of this decision into a balanced system of plan-directives in a process of reiterated bargaining, now between the levels of corresponding bureaucracies hierarchically subordinated to each other under the overall control of the central planning bureau. Each phase in this process has its own characteristics which all contribute to the structural determination of the emerging plan.

As to the first stage, the claims made upon the plan, their most important feature is that they are overstated in some and understated in other respects. They are overstated as to the objectives themselves. The state does not have unlimited budgetary funds to dispose of. To try to increase their own share in the available national resources is not only a necessity dictated by the competitive power struggle between various bureaucracies, but also a requirement of the task they are entrusted with. Each section of bureaucracy is directly responsible in principle for the optimal, in practice for the smooth functioning of a definite domain or region of social life. Understandably, the greater the resources over which it disposes, the better and more easily it can fulfil this job. So it will systematically overvalue the beneficial effects of proposed projects (or the negative consequences of their non-implementation), in particular the expected economic effectivity of requested productive investments. No outright cheating is necessarily involved in all this. We are dealing here with cases of probable estimates: the apparatus concerned will (and has to) represent the optimal one. In general, it will always ask for more than it itself considers necessary, since it knows well that it will in any case receive less than requested and that its competitors all do the same. But if the objectives themselves are overstated, their costs will invariably be understated — and by the same logic. Everybody knows that the most important single task is to get some programme or project in the plan: to get the apparatus officially committed to it. Then not only considerations of prestige, but also those of effectivity, will usually ensure its continuation, even if the original cost-estimates are severely exceeded — it would be uneconomic to abandon a large project in which enormous funds had already been invested. So one can always count on the central organs to help out in some way. From the standpoint of the apparatus itself all these are surely symptoms of an inadequate consciousness on the part of individual bureaucrats, and they are continually exhorted to give priority to the interests of the state. And this is undoubtedly their duty (as a result, some may from time to time be punished for exceedingly flagrant cases of transgression), but it is not the task for which they are directly responsible. As a matter of fact, even if they wished to act in this disinterested spirit, they would not know how to do so. They have no systematic information about the real situation, needs, etc. in all those fields of social life which are not under their direct control. In reality they can contribute to the emergence of the general interest in only one way: by simultaneously over- and understating their claims on the plan in the manner described, thereby ensuring that in the competition for funds between the various bureaucracies each behaves in a similar way and none can create by ruse a specifically favourable starting-position for itself. But since it is an inherently irrational process, having no clear-cut limits, how far they dare to go in this cheating as a necessary constituent of normality depends basically on their perception of what they can get away with: on the power position of the concerned bureaucracy. So already the initial claims move in favour of organizational strength as opposed to 'real needs' in any sense of the term.

It is the task of the central planning organ to prepare suggestions for the political leadership, outlining how far and in what way these competing claims can be partially incorporated in a balanced set of economic objectives taking into account the actual situation of national economy and the predictable trends in consumption at home and in foreign trade. In this respect the planning bureau itself is in a paradoxical situation. It has a direct interest in ensuring equilibrium, in providing for cases of emergencies and in concentrating funds on a limited number of larger projects, since it will be responsible for the translation of the five-year plan into a balanced set of yearly objectives which cannot be done if the above conditions are not met. But, on the other hand, its direct responsibility consists in ensuring the optimal dynamics of growth under the existing conditions and only such a policy can also provide the maximum of resources under its own disposition in the next round, enabling it to act more flexibly. Therefore, even in cases when numerical growth, for political reasons, is temporarily regarded as a secondary goal, it will give systematic preferences to productive investments over unproductive ones, to investments in the first sector over those in the second, etc.

But the last decision between the competing claims will be taken by the political leadership itself: it is the ultimate broker, and without appeal. But it is hardly an impartial one. Most of the members of the Politburo (or of the Central Committee) are either heads of the largest functional and territorial bureaucracies or else are responsible within the Party for the control over their functioning. The actual ability to influence the hierarchy of institutionalized objectives is very unequally distributed and directly dependent upon the (relatively stable) power relations between the organizations concerned. The latter constitutes one of the most important determinants structuring the priorities actually conferred upon various objectives – naturally within the changing context of overall political considerations pressing at the moment. In such a way – to take the most glaring example – the consecutive plans will always give preference in respect of the geographical distribution of funds to the capital city and to the few great industrial centres (whose Party bosses are, as a rule, themselves members of the decision-making body) as against the claims made by underdeveloped, provincial regions (whose heads are less important members of the apparatus). This is so even if an unhealthy geographical concentration of the economic, administrative and cultural life is an openly acknowledged problem which the leadership itself wants to redress.

Under this system social needs and demands can appear in the form of articulated claims only insofar as they are translatable into bureaucratic objectives whose legitimacy is recognized by the apparatus, and — as has been already effectively argued by Bahro — the terms of the reconciliation between the various claims, of the bargain struck, will be determined by the logic of the apparatus and by its fundamental power-structure.

The strategic decision taken by the political elite is ultimate: it cannot be directly challenged. Formally no more than a mere elaboration and breakdown of the plan remains, down to the level of the basic economic and administrative units. Actually this is a new, reiterated process of bargaining, this time between the vertically subordinated units, and not about the objectives themselves, but about their predictable costs (through which, in fact, even the original hierarchy of objectives may be significantly modified). In this process merely budgetary sectors and units (related to non-productive aspects of social life) are in a fairly ineffective position: the most they can do is complain. This is not so, however, of the various administrations representing the productive sectors and units of economy. Of course, formally they are also in the situation of one-way dependence and subordination in relation to those superior organs which now present them with a set of determined objectives in the form of definite plan-indicators. But the actual relationship is much more complex — not only because the superior organs are actually responsible for the functioning of the subordinated ones and so cannot be completely insensitive towards their complaints (which is true in all domains), but also because they need — as we shall see — the goodwill of these lower levels of economic management to help them out informally in cases of constantly occurring emergencies. And these inferior rungs of the management still possess a quite significant economic weight: due to the very character of command economy there is an irresistible tendency towards administrative centralization, especially at the very base, at the level of enterprises. (In Hungary, for example, the number of enterprises in nationalized industry has been reduced by one-half over twenty-five years.) So even the most inferior participants in these processes are actually monopolists in respect of some products needed for the national economy as a whole, and hence the argument 'under such conditions we cannot deliver according to the plan' carries a lot of weight: all the more so since this is often true and the subordinate organ, as far as information is concerned, is always in a better position to make this claim than are its superiors to disprove it. It is also obliged to make some such claim, since it ought to attempt to provide the possible optimal conditions for the fulfilment of those tasks which the plan specifies: this is precisely its responsibility. And since the most important among these conditions are under the disposal of the superior state organs, now that the objectives are settled, haggling at all levels begins over the resources needed for their fulfilment. This may take the most various forms: bargaining about forms of subsidies, the amount and terms of credit, relaxation of import-limits and so on. But just as earlier the objectives themselves were systematically overstated, now their costs of achievement will be overstated. The greater and more powerful the administration concerned (and the better the informal ties its chief bureaucrats have with higher organs), the more chance it has of succeeding in this bargaining. In this way even the centrally posited balance will always be tilted further towards the largest and politically most powerful productive organizations, whatever the actual economic demand.

This very rough sketch of the process of planning perhaps gives some indication of how in Eastern European societies the planned distribution and appropriation of the surplus actually accomplishes — independently of the will of decision makers — a maximization of the means under the direct control of the apparatus itself within the limits of perceived political feasibility. At the same time this analysis sheds light upon further structural characteristics of these economies. As we have seen in the process of elaboration of the command system, directing these economies over a period, both objectives and costs become (though at different stages) systematically and necessarily overstated. Actual economic (and social) demand enters this process — in the form of bureaucratic estimates — only at its beginning; then it is systematically and uncontrollably inflated in an institutionally defined, well-determined direction. The only effective checks concerning both goals and costs are the ones posited by the physical availability of inputs which the apparatus can mobilize. The actual restraints upon the process of growth are set not by the structure of demand (under a given system of prices), but by the extent and technical composition of available resources. In this respect Soviet-type economies are — as Kricman had already recognized in the 1920s and as Kalecki and Kornai have argued in detail — economies of resource-constraints as opposed to classical capitalism as a system of demand-constraints.

Shortage economy

This means, therefore, that they are shortage economies in the sense that they systematically produce and reproduce artificial shortages both of production and of consumption goods. Since it is only resources that effectively delimit the demand for factors of productive input, every plan turns out in practice to be an overstrained one. At each level the central organ will naturally try to ensure reserves for such overstrained situations, and this may be a major objective in the original draft of the plan. But these reserves will leak away from it, partly in the process of bargaining with subordinate units over their inflated cost-claims of plan fulfilment, partly due to the necessity to help out those units under its management which are in trouble since their investment-plans were accepted only as a result of an original underestimation of costs. So there is never enough input left over to balance out those disruptions which inevitably occur because of unexpected technical problems on the one hand and unpredictable changes in consumption behaviour at home and in markets abroad, on the other. And since in this situation of un-expected insufficiencies no manager can be sure even about the actualization of planned deliveries, while it is certain that he will be unable to procure vital elements of production quickly in the case of various unforeseen emergencies, each will now further inflate his demands concerning conditions of plan fulfilment, even beyond the level of an operational optimum. It is always safer to have things hidden away in reserve somewhere. This makes the pressure upon central reserves — and thereby the shortages themselves — even more acute: we have already seen this mechanism of negative feedback at work in the particular case of the employment of labour-power (overmanning) and there is no need to repeat the argument here merely in a generalized form.

However, an economy which constrains growth only through the actual shortage of resources, does not achieve a means for their effective utilization — it is actually an economy of resource-waste in the direct sense, that is, independently of the socially meaningful or meaningless character of the very objectives of growth, because shortage and waste necessarily presuppose and mutually condition each other. At any given level of technological and economic development delimiting the possibility of effective substitutions, shortage of some definite factor of production means that other available factors of production, which ought to have been combined with the first, remain unemployed. Bottlenecks involving one type of resource result in the enforced underutilization of other resources. If there is, for example, a lack of certain raw materials, they either have to be substituted with economically or technologically less effective ones or, if this is impossible, machines and workers will stand idle. Both are cases of waste.

Furthermore, shortage in the economic sense cannot be identified with physical lack as such — it means that some type of resource is unavailable when needed at a certain place and time. Since enterprises can insure themselves against the endemic occurrence of shortages only through the policy of semi-legal hoarding already described, it may very well be, and actually most frequently is, the case that the factor vitally necessary for one enterprise will be kept as non-utilized reserve at some other productive unit. But since these reserves by their very nature have to be concealed from the higher administrative organs of management (trusts, ministries, etc.) and there is no systematic vertical connection between the productive economic units themselves, the given input will remain as a rule non-mobilizable. In other words, within the framework of the national economy the factor will be both wasted (underutilized) and in short supply, the latter causing further waste and therefore interruptions in the production process and output which will necessarily affect other enterprises. It is just this vicious dialectics of shortage and waste which specifically characterizes East European economies as one of the basic components of their irrationality. These economies produce shortages even of what they have in sufficient supply, and nothing proves this better than the fact that unforeseeable shortages remain chronic though in its gross value the fund of unutilized reserves constantly grows in the national economy and (as everybody realizes) is well beyond the limits of technical and economic necessity. *In abstracto* there are reserves, only not of what is needed at the right time and place. There is only one way (apart from hoarding) to counteract this tendency. It consists of developing a network of personal relations through which each manager, at whatever level of the hierarchy, may be assured of help from others in case of emergencies. So behind the economy of scientific planning there burgeon primitive give-and-take transactions (the so-called 'third economy' to which we shall return) which extend beyond all the formal bureaucratic boundaries. It eliminates the worst dysfunctioning in the actual working of the unbelievably cumbersome administrative system, just as it helps to create it, since by divorcing the official from the actual economic reality, it introduces a further factor of uncontrollable accidentality which makes the real effect of central decisions even less predictable.

This circumstance gives rise to a very specific case of the complementary nature of shortage and waste in Eastern Europe economies, which deserves to be mentioned here. Since the strategies open to an enterprise to counteract the disturbing effects of material shortages created by its outside environment (both hoarding and the system of informal personal relations of assistance) tend to create new dysfunctioning within the framework of the national economy as a whole, the higher levels of economic bureaucracy now have to attempt from their side to counteract them. Since these strategies, however, are hidden and informal, the only way to gain control over them is to increase the extent of information that the higher organs demand from the lower ones. But because these are informal mechanisms they constantly readapt themselves to these means of control, creating only a renewed need for further information. The result is a situation which has been well described by Bahro or Parkin: a simultaneous surfeit and dearth of information at all levels, which not only contributes to the constant growth of the unproductive apparatus of administration, but also makes it practically impossible to distinguish between 'noise' and 'message'.

Production and consumption

In these last paragraphs we have already had to refer to the systematic distinction which exists in Eastern European societies between the official and the actual reality of economic life. Up to this point, however, we have been able to describe at best only a few of the symptoms of this distinction, insofar as we have examined how the official economy actually works. But we did accept the fictitious abstraction that it is the administrative apparatus of the state which constitutes the sole economic subject in these societies. It is now time to remove this abstraction, and thereby gain a better insight into the segmented character of these economies.

The problem about the inherent restrictions imposed upon the economic activities of the state by other economic subjects arises even within the framework of the official ideology of the regimes concerned — and is used for apologetic purposes. According to this view it is the existence of two forms of property — nationalized and therefore fully socialist, on the one hand, and merely cooperative (notably in agriculture), on the other, which explains their transitory character and many of their inadequacies in relation to the Communist ideals, since cooperative property as such imposes limits upon the rational planning activity of the state and hence on the realization of general interests as against the particular ones of the members of cooperatives. There is hopefully little need to examine this so-called theory in detail. The especially brutal ways in which the cooperative peasantry has been exploited during most of the history of these societies, the constant disparity between industry and agriculture always to the detriment of the latter in respect of the policy of prices, investments, etc., all give it a resounding lie. These facts demonstrate how little in practice the cooperative form of property in agriculture and in some of the services restricts the power of disposition and control by the central administration over the means and products so owned. And many (see for example the related works of A. Hegedüs) have argued convincingly and in detail that in conditions of Eastern European societies the difference between nationalized and cooperative property concerns only the legal form of ownership and not the real economic relations involved. The latter (in our terms, the corporate property of the apparatus over both nationalized and cooperative means of production) differ only in the form of their realization and exercise (direct—administrative versus more indirect—economic), at best in their extent, but not in their character. Admittedly the existence of a private economic sector, to some degree present in all these societies, constitutes a problem of a different order, and we shall later argue that its functional role may be more significant than its small economic weight in terms of total national output would indicate. Its very existence, however, is the result of deeper structural causes and it is the latter that must be looked at first.

Our analyses have already clearly suggested that the basic restrictions upon the economic power of the apparatus emerge not in the sphere of production proper, but in that of individual consumption, on the one hand, and supply of labour power, on the other. It is here that we had earlier to locate the basic internal causes of those resistances and frictions which introduce an element of permanent uncertainty into the mechanisms of command economy. These uncertainties emerge because of the unpredictable character of the global outcome of the innumerable consumption choices and of the decisions taken on the pseudo-market of labour — actions which the apparatus can only severely restrict, but cannot control. If, from the viewpoint of the organization of production it is a meaningful idealizing abstraction to regard Eastern European economies as those which admit the action of a single economic subject only, from the viewpoint of consumption they present us with the activity of millions and millions of economic subjects — in principle — independent of each other. These are the individual households which attempt to maximize their incomes (from wages) and minimize (in relation to the needs to be satisfied) their expenditures to achieve a balance between income and expenditure, thereby providing a strictly economic activity. The scope of the latter is severely limited by the fact that the state apparatus as dominant employer and supplier of goods essentially by its own authority, administratively sets the conditions under which households can both derive and spend income. But as long as the whole country is not transformed into a labour camp with a strict system of rationing, as long as individuals have some choice between the administratively offered jobs (at set wages) and available consumption goods (at set prices) the economies in question necessarily represent a dual picture of administratively centralized production and atomized consumption, both having their own subjects following different principles of economic activity. The two dualistically counterposed spheres can naturally coexist only because there is an institutional interconnection between them. And with this we have of course arrived at the most disputed feature of Eastern European economies: at the existence of the market, or more exactly, of the different kinds of (non-unified) markets in these societies. Because of the practical and theoretical importance of this problem, it ought to be set — even if very sketchily — in a broader context.

Any modern industrial society faces the *prima facie* antinomistic requirement of connecting an inherently social production with a highly differentiated and individualized consumption and choice of labouring activities. Capitalism solves this task by subordinating social production to particular, privatizable ends, organizing and developing it according to the principle of profit-maximization, subordinating it to the logic of the accumulation of capital. As a result this system satisfies social needs only insofar as they are transformable (under the given conditions of market sale of labour power) into effective private demand on the commodities market. It subordinates the production of social use-values to the logic of market exchange and channels needs into forms adequate to the accumulation of the capital. Eastern European societies solve the above tasks in a basically different way. They organize social production in principle from one administrative centre, developing it according to the corporate power interest of this unified apparatus and subordinating it to the principle of the maximal extension of the material basis of the domination of the apparatus over society. In this sense they subject the satisfaction of needs to an alien logic just as much as capitalism does. Yet not only is this logic different to that of capital, but also the means of its superimposition differs. It primarily takes the form not of channelling needs into socio-economically pre-figured forms of demand, but rather that of the restriction of the supply itself (and thereby of satiable demand too) partly in a direct material sense, through endemic shortages of desired consumption goods, partly indirectly, through the suspension of demand—supply mechanisms by the administrative fixation of prices. In its pure form, therefore, this system tends to act as a brutal dictatorship over needs. But none of these two systems actually operates, at least in developed form, in such purity. To ensure the general social—political preconditions of the reproduction of profit-dominated market relations, the capitalist state has not only to intervene in their functioning (to counterbalance their socially most destructive dysfunctioning), but also (as is underlined by Habermas, Offe, O'Connor and others), in some areas of the public sector, it has to replace the working of market mechanisms in favour of the satisfaction from public funds of politically articulated social needs. (Against all the facts of temporary successes of a monetarist counter-offensive in the West, we would endeavour to maintain that these elements of welfare state economy are structurally necessary to advanced capitalism and constitute the conditions of its social stabilization.) Similarly, the post-Stalinist stabilization in Eastern Europe could take place only through a relaxation of the strictness and directness of control over needs, through the extension of the scope of possible consumption choices on the administratively regulated market of goods accompanied by the (officially tolerated) appearance of various segmented markets of price-fixing type. Essentially similar processes have taken place simultaneously on the pseudo-market of labour as well. That is, the social stabilization of the relations of command economy itself required an extension of the relative role of supply—demand mechanisms, although the general principle of a dictatorship over needs, that is, the determina-tion of social production through the uncontrolled decision of a unified apparatus of power (and through its underlying logic) still remained in force. In this sense there exists a broadly conceived analogy between the functioning of both social systems in their relatively advanced form. Both can ensure the overall social condi-tions of the reproduction of their respectively dominant relations of production only by injecting into the very functioning of economy alien elements potentially disruptive to them. And just as capitalism can contain and pacify the tendencies thus generated as long as it succeeds by means of depoliticization in confining the social articulation of needs to the sphere of distribution proper, Eastern European societies, with their lack of an institutional division between economy and politics, can achieve the same result as long as they succeed by means of a strict atomization in confining tendencies of autonomization *vis-à-vis* the decisions of the apparatus to the privatized sphere of household consumption only.

As against both these existing types of social organization of economy the Marxian idea of a free association of direct producers undoubtedly involved the project of an immediate connection between the social character of production organized on a communal and self-managerial basis, on the one hand, and the unrestricted development of many-sided individuals, including naturally the free choice of activities and the satisfaction of differentiated, personal systems of needs, on the other. In conditions when the objectives of production are determined in a direct democratic way by the members of the association themselves, there is no longer a need for reified social mechanisms to mediate between production and consumption, although the task of minimizing social expenditures in the realization of these pre-established objectives remains actual. It becomes, however, a merely technical task of pure computation, of establishing the optimal balance between existing resources and pre-set productive goals. As such, as a mere function of social book-keeping it can safely be delegated to a central organ.

It is this complete institutional divorce between the social task of establishing the very objectives of production and the merely technical calculative problem of their optimal implementation as a question concerning only the management of things which provides the key to the Marxian project of socialism as marketless economy (as articulated in *Capital*). But it is not difficult to see (and this was argued in a rather detailed way in an earlier work written by G. Bence, J. Kis and G. Márkus) that this divorce is possible only under very specific conditions. In actual fact it can only take place in a society where expenditure of technically and socially homogeneous labour constitutes the only scarce resource which needs to be economized, that is, in a society of abundance which knows only a technical division between essentially similar and socially equivalent productive tasks. In *Capital* Marx actually spelt out (though in an implicit and disconnected way) a number of these preconditions in detail: the reduction of all directly productive functions to simple labour due to technical development; the existence of a fixed natural upper limit in the case of all material needs; the very slow change — in practice, constancy within the life-span of one generation — of the consumption need-structure even within these limits; the essentially costless character of the satisfaction of all cultural needs, etc. The mere enumeration of these preconditions perhaps also demonstrates that in the circumstances of the second half of the nineteenth century it was not unreasonable to presuppose them or their realizability. But from the viewpoint of our own experiences they are misplaced historical expectations. If socialism is not to be thought of as an attractive utopia of such a distant future that it is even unclear how we could contribute towards its advance, but rather as a practical social project for today, then its economy ought to be reconceived as one able to function under conditions of a relative scarcity (beyond that of labour which, as Marx underlined, always remains a scarce resource since labour-time is part of the very finite time of life) and of a not merely technical, but social division of labour. In such circumstances, however, the radical separation between the social and technical aspects and phases of communal decision-making envisaged by Marx is unrealizable. In a situation where not all needs can be satisfied (which is the meaning of relative scarcity), decisions have to be taken as to what needs to satisfy and to what extent, and these necessarily depend on technical considerations concerning their costs, but the social costs of production of any given use-value remain indeterminate as long as the extent of its production is undefined. In this situation any decision taken by a central planning organ is not merely a calculative–technical, but a social one, giving preference to some needs over others, and with the existence of a social division of labour, when the structure of needs is determined not merely by the chance element of irreducible personal differences, but by structural determinants, as a rule this means giving preference to the needs of some groups and communities over those of others.

Planning and the market

Behind this well-known formal–economic difficulty (the so-called 'paradox of planning'), which can be overcome by some institutionalization of a process of democratic planning understood as interplay between variously articulated associations with each other and with

their representative delegative organs (not envisaged in the dichotomic schema of Marx), lies, however, a deeper one. In the situation
outlined the presupposed direct–immediate unity between the
social–communal organization of production and the free development of individuality, including freedom of choice of productive and
non-productive (leisure) activities (consequently of consumption,
too), no longer holds. There is a necessity for social mechanisms
mediating the individually differentiated patterns of activities and
consumption, on the one hand, and the requisite system of division
of social labour, on the other, to which democratic planning itself
does not provide any kind of solution. Planning can establish only
the general proportions and extent of production of various goods.
When these, however, do not cover the full range of communal and
individual needs, there must be some mechanisms through which the
particular preference patterns can systematically be transformed into
rationally motivated choices between the available, but scarce, types
of products and activities – and in such a way that reacts back
(correctively) on the system of production itself (a necessity, since
the outcome of individual choices is never completely predictable).
Neither history, nor – and this has to be emphasized – theory
provides us with an example or project of institutionalizing these
mechanisms except that of the market. In Marx's own schema the
necessity for such mechanisms of mediation never arose. And those
of his followers in the West who seem to give some account of this
problem under modern conditions, at the same time tend to replace
it by moralizing perorations about the 'ideological revolutionalization
of the workers' (Bettelheim) or their 'identification with the society
as a whole' (Ticktin) as both precondition and outcome of a truly
democratic practice of planning. 'Cultural revolution', understood
here as a process of transformation in the very system of needs which
any institutional transformation can and should only initiate, is
certainly a basic element in the very project of socialism. Moreover,
utopias concerning its possible distant consequences are not meaningless as ways of exercising and stimulating social imagination or
transcending the confines of the present. But they are pointless as far
as socialism as a real and realistic alternative to the presently existing
systems of social domination is concerned, that is, as far as we have
to think of it as a practical society functioning under conditions of
relative scarcity and social division of labour. The existence of these
conditions means that the interests of producers and consumers,
furthermore those of the various groups of producers and consumers,
are not directly and objectively identical with each other, and no

raised level of consciousness can find an immediate identity where there is none, where on the contrary it has to be created by a process of incessant mediation between competing and equally justified claims. In these circumstances references to cultural revolution and socialist consciousness not only replace Marx with Rousseau (because the former certainly did not think of socialism as a society of virtuosi of morality), but are altogether beside the point. To put it crudely: if there are more individuals (or collectives) who wish to obtain some definite good than there is available, then even the highest level of a communal ascetism will not help to solve the question of who among them should or should not receive it. This either has to be left to the decision of the consumers themselves who allocate their means among the available use-values in a systematic and homogeneous way, that is, in the form of money on the commodities market, or the goods have to be distributed independently of these choices, according to some objective criteria; that is, differentiated consumption has to be transformed strictly into a matter of privilege enforced and superimposed by some organ standing above society. And the same applies naturally to the question of the choice between various socially required and acknowledged types of activity of labour as well.

Under these circumstances it is no more legitimate to explain (apologetically or critically) the subordinated existence of some elements of market regulation in Eastern European economies as remnants of capitalism, than it is justified to identify the subordinated presence of market-replacing actions (and strictly limited planning) of the state in advanced capitalism with ready-made elements of socialism. In both cases the interpretations involve a resignation from the basic intentions constituting the Marxian idea of a free association of producers in the name of a strict orthoxody. Our historical experiences demonstrate (against the Marxian predictions) that the correspondence of the requirements of a social organization of production with those of free individual development cannot take place directly and automatically, because relative scarcities tend to characterize economic development even after the satisfaction of the most elementary human needs became at least a possibility. If we designate exactly this structural situation by the name of 'modernity', we can see that the alternative of planning *or* market is meaningless for any 'modern' society. Eastern European social systems prove that no such society can completely repress demands of individual autonomy through a rigid and strict system of social privileges, while the facts of Western development demonstrate the impossibility of ensuring the broad social preconditions of a production which is inherently social in its character merely through the blind play of uncontrolled market-mechanisms. The project of socialism as opposed to both of these social realities means again not replacing the market by planning, but giving to both these economic mechanisms a changed character and creating a changed interrelation between the two.

Under conditions of modernity the question about the possibility of socialism is economically to a large extent equivalent to the question of whether it is possible to establish real social–communal control over the indispensable market relations from above and below simultaneously (which, of course, involves not only their restriction, but also their definite replacement through directly allocative and egalitarian distributive mechanisms in certain economic spheres). There is nothing in our historical experiences which would make the Marxian criticism of market relations obsolete. The market is not a neutral instrument of equilibrating production and consumption in circumstances of a relative fragmentation of social interests and economic units (both objectively determined facts under conditions of modernity) – it does not merely express, but through a reified mediation enormously enhances this very fragmentation. Only if it is possible to counteract the spontaneous tendencies of the market, by opening up new ways of determination and articulation of both demand and supply, can socialism be a real alternative at all. This requires, on the one hand, the subordination of the overall, long-term direction of economic development to the explicit, conscious articulation of social needs through a process of real strategic planning as rational choice affected by the whole population between plan programmes expressing existing economic alternatives under conditions of free discussion and the widest political democracy. On the other hand, it demands the generation of new types of pressure and new criteria upon the very character of technical development (beyond the mere effectivity of employment of social capital) through the articulation of the needs of producers as producers via processes of self-management under conditions of a wide decentralization of economy. It has to be emphasized that while both of these processes represent effective restriction upon the role of market mechanisms, they can be coupled with each other only through the mediating and equilibrating function of the market itself.

This brief discussion perhaps makes it clear that radical critics of Eastern European societies cannot adopt a once and for all, predetermined 'for or against' attitude concerning those economic reforms which — as elements of a crisis-management — are undertaken in these societies and strive to give a greater function to mechanisms of demand and supply in the economy. They cannot be judged at all in the abstract, but only in their concrete economic and social consequences — most importantly in their interconnection with, or ability to stimulate, the processes of political democratization, and those of self-management of various collectives (primarily, but not exclusively, at the work-place).

The market certainly does not constitute a universal panacea against all social ills in the circumstances of Eastern Europe either. Insistence upon this fact, trivial for any socialist, cannot, however, overshadow the other aspect of the problem: without a simultaneous extension of the function of market regulation, both the processes of political and economic democratization necessarily run against narrow and structurally—economically determined limits. In this sense (and in this sense only) Eastern European dissidents of a socialist conviction ought to be — and mostly are — themselves 'pro-reform' (in the above meaning).

The specific Eastern European solution to the problem of modernity consists, as we have argued, in a dualistic combination of an administratively centralized production whose sole subject is (in principle) the unified apparatus of power and of an atomized consumption undertaken (in conjunction with the sale of labour power) as an economic activity by millions of independent households. These two spheres and their corresponding subjects, following distinctly different principles of activity, are submitted to discrepant logic. The economy can function as a whole, of course, only because these two spheres are interconnected. They are interconnected primarily, though not exclusively, by the administratively regulated psuedo-markets of consumption goods and labour power respectively which at the same time subordinate the economic activities of the households to the reified logic of production through a direct restriction of the extent and conditions of supply of commodities, on the one hand, and that of the demand for definite kinds of labour, on the other. The fact that both of these markets have essentially a non-pricing character is in principle synonymous with the statement that they are closed in relation to, and separated from, each other. Changes in demand for articles of consumption do not lead through the feed-back mechanism of prices to a readjustment in the structure of production, and therefore to corresponding changes on the market of labour power, and vice-versa. It is this relative fragmentation which ensures that the role of market relations is restricted to distribution proper, that they exercise no directly equilibrating function between production and consumption and so allow the former to follow that logic of social domination which we have described earlier.

There are two interconnected consequences of this state of affairs. Firstly, under such conditions the unification of production and consumption remains incomplete. The unified apparatus of power and economic management can only restrict by its commands the activities of the households (both as consumers and suppliers of labour power), but cannot determine the limited choices exercised by them in both respects. As we have argued, this is at least one of the basic causes of those disequilibria which are inherent in the functioning of a command economy and which lead to a constant production of both shortage and waste. But if these phenomena necessarily follow from the subordination of production (and the whole society) to one unified and separate apparatus of power, their occurrence at the same time makes the existence and functioning of this apparatus an economic necessity. Because − and this is the second point − under such conditions, when the market plays no equilibrating role, it is only the corrective actions of the central apparatus which can re-establish again and again the relative correspondence between the previously disjointed spheres of economy. Yearly plans and the intermittently undertaken modifications of the plan (that is, the bulk of the activity of central apparatuses of economic management) to a large extent fulfil just this function. In this sense, by the apparent defects of its own functioning, the apparatus constantly reproduces the conditions which make its existence necessary. In general bureaucracy is no more an abnormal carbuncle, a mere parasite on the social body of Eastern European societies, than capitalists under the Western conditions: both are organic elements of their respective processes of reproduction. Just as the impossibility of any spontaneous formation and expression of collective group interests from below makes the administrative establishment of a compromise between the bureaucratically articulated competing claims by the very top of the apparatus a functional social necessity, so the lack of any systematic connection between the directly productive and consumptive units of the economy (the respective multiplicities of enterprises and households) renders the system of administratively superimposed corrections from above an economic necessity. In this way the liquidation of the equilibrating function of the market creates a unique economic basis for the social domination of the apparatus, and the latter cannot be success-fully challenged in other spheres and in other aspects as long as a restricted reinstatement of supply and demand mechanisms does not make this economic function of it superfluous as well. Western Leftist critics of Eastern European economies often seem to forget that any programme of decentralization (as a preconditon of a system of self-management in some meaningful sense) is possible only if the enterprises can rely in their activity on some objective indicators (that is, on market prices) reflecting the overall changes in the external economic environment. Otherwise their concerted function-ing can be ascertained only through signals, instructions and commands received from above. The broadly understood demand for a wider role for market mechanisms and incentives is therefore in this sense part and parcel of the attempt to emancipate both individuals and collectives from the universally present and all-encompassing tutelage of the state — although in isolation from other emancipatory tendencies such attempts may merely intensify those processes of social atomization which actually stabilize the domina-tion of the apparatus over society

In addition, it is not difficult to comprehend that an economy which can ensure the relative balance between production and consumption only through the administrative intervention of central organs after disequilibria have reached overall and glaring proportions, necessarily functions in a very cumbersome and wasteful way. The difficulties of its working, however, diminish precisely to the degree that demand is less differentiated and more centralized. This is one of the important reasons for the fact that this type of economy functions much more effectively in the initial period of take-off, when there are a few clearly marked priorities of development that have to be satisfied at all costs, than in the later period of intensive growth. At the same time this makes the armaments industry the only kind of production for which this economic system is really adequate, for here at least the split between production and consumption disappears. One has to realize that the manufacture of armaments is organized in these countries in a way which differs in principle from all other branches of production. The representatives of the army (that is, of the consumer) are in most cases directly present in the factories involved, exercising a controlling function over the whole labour process, and it is invariably they who fulfil the task of quality control. In a sense production here is directly subordinated to consumption — a solution made possible not only by the specific irrelevance of cost-restraints in this sphere, but also by the fact that in this case there is only a single institutional consumer. This difference in the very principle of organization also explains the paradoxical fact that in Eastern European economies the armaments industry does not fulfil its usual historically driving function in technical development. The transfer of modern technology into branches of civil production does not proceed in smooth, obstacle-free way; the differences in organizational structure lead to a technical insulation of the military industry and to a growing disparity of the levels of technical development between these two sections of the economy. While the priority given to armament production in the Soviet Union is clearly politically dictated and in other respects constitutes an enormous burden on the economy, it is, however, significant that the whole system functions at its best in this sphere: by virtue of its structure, it is most effective in production for war.

In all other spheres and branches of the economy the possibilities of a dislocation between production and consumption — with all its disequilibria, shortage and waste — are present and are all the more pronounced, the more pluralistic, differentiated and decentralized is the demand in question. The inherent contradictions of a command economy in the given respect therefore emerge most clearly in the sphere of production of consumption goods. Here the system in its undiluted form can function only so long as it imposes a drastic dictatorship over the needs of the absolute majority of the population, an enforced homogenization of demand (through chronic shortages) at the level of bare necessities. The post-Stalinist stabilization of these societies, however, could take place only on the basis that the regimes concerned have incorporated the tendency towards a very slow, but constant raising of living standards into the system-objectives of the economy. The attendant emergence of an increasingly differentiated and volatile demand concerning consumption goods could not be met in principle by pure mechanisms of command economy. This not only constituted one of the important stimuli towards economic reforms, giving a greater functional role to market mechanisms within the official system, but at the same time enforced a further segmentation of economic life, or more exactly made much more pronounced and widespread those phenomena of fragmentation which were never completely absent in these societies.

The three economies

At the present we can see in these societies a very uneasy, but functionally necessary, interaction and interpenetration of three economies which are governed by quite diverse and opposed mechanisms. (In the characterization of these three economies we depart from the analysis given in the works of A. Hegedüs and M. Márkus.) The official system of command economy (in which supply and demand mechanisms on the state-controlled pseudo-markets of commodities and labour-power may play a larger or smaller, but always subordinate, role) has of course an absolutely predominant and determining position, especially where the direction and dynamics of economic development are concerned. This is due both to its preponderant economic weight and to the fact that the apparatus managing it at the same time concentrates in its hand the political power through which it can always at least restrict the possibilities of, and set the overall conditions for, the working of the other economies. But since this official economy, with its rigid and immobile organization essentially depending on central signals and commands from above, is in principle unable to provide goods for highly differentiated and variable types of demand, with the rise of the latter it had to suffer a supplementation through a second economy working according to more or less strict market and profit principles. This is the second economy of private enterprises and activities which in some countries may even achieve a preponderance in some branches (especially in services, in the production and/or trading of semi-luxury goods — including house-building and seasonal commodities). This second economy is constituted not only by small private enterprises proper (including workshops of independent artisans and private stores), but also by the activity of cooperative peasants on their household plots, and the enormously widespread practice of moonlighting among workers together with many other 'grey areas' of economic life, although the latter types of activity are much more directly determined by the needs of the households concerned than by the profit motive. All are regulated, however, by actually uncontrolled, though very segmented, market forces.

This second economy fulfils the indispensable function of filling in those gaps between production and consumption which, as we have argued, are inevitably posited by the structure of official command economy. In this sense it is definitely supplementary to the first, and its development during the post-Stalinist period was and is an important factor of stabilization, since it contributed substantially to a better satisfaction of consumption needs. And it plays such a role not only in the economic respect. By relaxing the control over legal and semi-legal private earning activities, the apparatus has opened up channels through which a very significant part of the population can improve its own lot through its own initiative. Since at the same time all forms of public—collective activity remained as much suppressed as earlier, this development stimulated enormously the processes of social atomization, which is the precondition of the uncontested social domination of the apparatus itself. This effect of the second economy is made even more pronounced by the fact that its very existence creates significant differences and conflicts between strata and groups who otherwise seem to occupy the same social position, since access to it is very much differentiated according to specific profession and job. (A television mechanic certainly finds it much easier to earn in some way or other in the second economy than a miner does.) So the second economy acts as a factor of social fragmentation as well.

While in all these respects the existence of a second economy seems to be both necessary and functional in the societies of Eastern Europe, it exercises a highly disturbing effect in other ways on the dominant system of economic relations: it both supplements the working of the first, official economy and introduces new obstacles into its functioning. To begin with, its very presence means that there now exists a double system of wages in the economy: the official wages, and those the worker can earn through free bargaining for private activities or for those performed within the framework of private enterprises (in both cases the bulk of labour is provided after official working hours by worker-employees of state enterprises). The latter wage is, as a rule, several times higher than the former. The understandable result is a lowering of the intensity of labour in the sphere of official economy. Those workers who have a regular opportunity to make earnings in the second sector, become positively interested in doing bad work in their official work-place, the state enterprise, since disorganization allows them to reserve their energy for after-hours labour, or even making things on the side during official working time. Naturally, the two-tier system of prices relates not only to labour, but also to a very wide range of commodites and services of consumption. The second economy fulfils an integrative function because it produces goods which are in short supply on the state-controlled market (in relation to the demand generated at the official price level) and which are therefore available to the consumer only through connections or by chance. The second economy makes these commodities available, only at a much higher price, and thereby it reduces the labour of purchasing for households, which otherwise would be simply unmanageable. (Similarly, the goods and services obtained through the second economy are in general of much more reliable quality than those offered by the official economy of the state.) But since many of these articles and services of consumption are semi-luxuries only in the perverse sense that most of the population cannot obtain them through the normal channels of state economy — and this above all else refers to the acquisition of an independent flat for young couples — people have to buy them through the second economy which they can afford only if they also earn through it, since the official wages are complately inadequate in relation to prices in force on the 'free' market. So the second economy constitutes an expanding circle which increasingly undermines the productivity and effectivity of the first. According to an estimate recently published in the central organ of the Hungarian Communist Party, about half of the whole population and more than 70 per cent of all the wage earners draw some income (in the absolute majority of cases supplementary to official wages) from the second economy. And the distinction between the two can become so pronounced that in some Eastern European countries there is actually a double system of currency· some consumer goods and services are available in the GDR almost exclusively for West German marks only, while in Poland the accepted currency for such goods is American dollars.

This enormous expansion of the second economy is made possible, paradoxically enough, by the fact that it is not really integrated with the first. The official economy needs this supplementation just as much as it is unable to provide normal conditions for its functioning (and even the most draconic measures of the Stalinist period could not succeed in the eradication of the second economy; they simply forced it underground, reducing it to a black market level and thereby increasing the risks and prices involved to such an extent that its services were available only to the lucky few). The real task of the second economy is to fill in the gaps between demand and supply in the sphere of consumption created by the first, but the logic of the command economy makes supplying the second (with raw materials, tools, etc.) the last in the order of its own priorities. In cases when some relevant shortages occur, it is the provisioning of the private enterprises which will of course suffer first. In these conditions the second economy could not function at all, were its activity really determined through these legal—official channels of contact with the first. But it is not. The workers who do private jobs for individual households after hours, work with tools and materials (as a rule unavailable in the stores) stolen from the factory, private entrepeneurs flourish because they have their chains of contacts, beginning from the respective Ministry and ending with salesgirls in the shops. It is this host of semi-legal and outright illegal activities which makes the majority of the adult population able to participate actively in the second economy. The result, however, is an increasing 'criminalization' of economic life which in most cases is now considered normal by the population itself (even in countries where earlier a strong work-ethic and a norm of honest business has predominated). On the whole, if the second economy helps to integrate production with consumption, it does so at the price of disintegrating production itself, at least in its subjective aspect, from the point of view of work-motivation.

This criminalization of the economy could never have proceeded so far were the transgression of official rules and the by-passing of official channels not already a practice embedded in the actual working of the first, official economy itself. And here we come up against the phenomena of the third economy. If the second fills in the gaps left open by the command economy primarily in the sphere of consumption, the third fills in the gaps concerning the very organization of production within the first economy. If the second is regulated essentially by pure market mechanisms, it is the mechanisms of an exchange of generalized equivalences and reciprocal services, better known from economic anthropology than from descriptions of modern societies, that dominate transactions in this third sphere. The third economy is that of personal, informal relations of assistance in case of shortages and other disequilibrating emergencies, mostly between the various members of the bureaucratic apparatus of management which extend beyond all the administrative boundaries and which we have already described when analysing the actual functioning of planned economy. The actual role of these relations in the normal working of economy can hardly be overestimated. The administrative reorganizations of the last years of the Khrushchev period had a disastrous effect in the Soviet Union (and contributed greatly to his downfall) primarily not because they confused the official lines of command, but because they completely destroyed all those informal ties which managers at the various levels of the hierarchy had built up and carefully cultivated throughout their entire careers and on which they invariably relied in their work. All these connections and transactions are, strictly speaking, illegal (at any rate they violate existing regulations of some kind), although they are often entirely unconnected with the motive of direct personal gain and are dictated merely by the desire or need to ensure a greater efficiency of the entrusted economic unit. Nevertheless, the fact that all these activities are formally illegal, makes it impossible to differentiate them from cases of outright corruption. It is therefore not surprising that the second economy usually links up (in cases of larger private enterprises) to the first through the mechanisms of the third.

In their post-Stalinist period of development Eastern European societies have shown a marked tendency towards enhanced segmentation in the above sense and at the same time towards the informal, uncontrollable integration of the diverse segments of the economy. In consequence, they have created an ever-growing cleavage between the official and the actual reality of economic life. The second and third economies actually achieve a secondary redistribution of incomes and – to a lesser extent – of factors of production which goes on in secret. Under these circumstances, not only planning in a substantial sense, but also meaningful command becomes more and more difficult, because the long-term consequences of economic measures turn out to be completely unexpected for the planners themselves, since they take place in an environment which does not exist for them and is radically different from their reality, that is, from the officially acknowledged situation. A typical example of this kind of problem occurred in Hungary in the late 1960s, when everybody in charge was so convinced of the inevitable emergence of widespread unemployment in the wake of economic reforms that some precautionary welfare measures were even taken with a view to ameliorating its social impact. As it turned out, the reforms resulted in a near catastrophic shortage of skilled labour in the larger industrial state enterprises which could be redressed only by introducing stop-gap measures administratively restricting the movement of labour power, an effect contrary to the whole aim and spirit of the reform.

This growing divorce of the two realities is only one of the signs of the deepening contradictions of these economies that seem to point to an approaching new crisis of Eastern European societies which in its intensity may well surpass the one following Stalin's death. There are some indications that the other type of segmentation, between civil and military industry in respect of levels of technological development, also becomes the source of growing structural tensions. Without underestimating the success of the Soviet armaments drive, it should nevertheless be pointed out that even in this most preferred field Soviet industry seems to be having trouble in keeping pace with the newest technological advances, especially in respect of computerization and miniaturization. It is at any rate unclear how far the technical insulation of the armament industry from the rest of the economy may go and where the disparity between the two imposes limits upon technological progress in the first sphere as well – in any case the costs of this insulation have to be increasingly high and burdensome for the national economy.

But the most important indicator of a coming social crisis is the serious fall in the overall growth rate which is now occurring simultaneously in all the countries concerned and which is beginning to threaten the very basis of the post-Stalinist (relative) stabilization itself. Even if the case of Poland – a country with a negative growth rate and which has been on the brink of economic bankruptcy for years – is an exception, and the state of affairs there is the result of particularly foolish economic policies, the general drop in the growth rate, together with that in the rate of increase in productivity of labour and yield on investment, has now reached a level in almost all the countries concerned which makes it very doubtful whether the economy can any longer provide both for the armament drive and for the perceptible and sustained rise in the living standards of the population, however slow this may be. In these conditions the logic of the system – even independently of all other political considerations – leaves no doubt whatsoever over which of the two requirements would be dropped and some of the newly adopted five-year plans in the countries of Central Eastern Europe clearly demonstrate that even on the basis of officially set aims the population of this region can at the very best expect a stagnation in the level of real incomes. However, this means a repudiation of the terms of the post-Stalinist social compromise. Since the Soviet Union seems definitely set on importing its own economic difficulties into the dependent countries (by applying more and more political pressure for their direct participation in the most capital-intensive Soviet investment projects), the situation on this 'periphery of the empire' may become extemely insecure. In the face of an inevitable political crisis of succession within the 'gerontocratic' leadership in the Soviet Union (these countries have so far been unable to find an institutional solution for the problem of succession) the social consequences of growing economic difficulties may be especially grave – and unpredictable.

Naturally one ought not to underestimate the economic reserves of these societies either, nor the enormous resilience of their systems of social domination, the economic aspects of which we have attempted to analyse here. Soviet-type societies represent a specific social—economic formation, well able to reproduce itself in all its contradictions and demonstrating a rare power of resurrection even after apparent collapse. Since the corporate property of the apparatus constituting the material basis of its domination at the same time represents only the economic facet of a monopolization of all the means of social organization and intercourse, the question of whether, under these conditions, sufficient (and sufficiently organized) social forces can be generated from below which might be able to use the situation of a crisis for the imposition of new directions on social development, is not one which would encourage facile optimism. Especially not if one takes into account the fact that this question ought to be posed above all in relation to the power centre and lynchpin of the whole system — to the Soviet Union itself.

CHAPTER 3

Inequality and Domination in a 'Classless' Society

We have characterized the basic economic relations of Soviet-type societies as being constituted by the corporate property of the apparatus of power over the objective means of social production incompletely divorced from its subjective factor (labour power itself); we similarly expressed the fundamental developmental tendency of these economies in terms of a reference to this apparatus as a corporate entity. It is now time to look more closely both at the relationship of the apparatus as an institution to its members, the individual bureaucrats, and at that of these latter as a social group (of whatever type) to the rest of the society. It is the question of the character of the social structure in these societies – a question which we, dealing with their abstract model only, can answer at best as far as the principles of social stratification are concerned, since characterization of social structure is a task that cannot be undertaken in abstraction from the widely divergent historical realities of the countries in question.

The organization of the bureaucratic apparatus

When we refer to the apparatus, we mean the integration and unification of all the hierarchically organized bodies of social decision-making, execution and control into one all-encompassing and centrally administered hierarchy. Two aspects seem to be of primary importance here. The first is the well-known observation, constituting the starting point for all critical theories of these societies, that in them no social organization has an institutional autonomy, that all the corresponding partial bureaucracies relating to the various sectors of social life and covering all the significant economic, political, social and cultural spheres are effectively unified in, and subordinated to, one centre: these countries are in this sense — to use T.H. Rigby's expression — mono-organizational societies. On the other hand, however, this single unitary hierarchy of power is not realized directly through one formally homogeneous administrative structure, but through the unification and subordination to one centre of all the partial bureaucracies which have their distinct chains of command and which at various levels interact with each other and by necessity develop and represent at least partially divergent interests. But this interaction is not the result of explicit transactions and compromises between the concerned bureaucratic organizations and their members. It is ensured by the existence and activity of a separate organization, that of the Party, which, on the one hand, penetrates all these structures of administration and control, and at the same time has its own hierarchy, the top of which exercises command over each of them. In this sense this unification is inscribed into the very logic of the organization of power itself.

The unity of the apparatus is expressed and secured by a number of characteristics which will be discussed in detail in the following chapters which deal with the analysis of the political structure proper. Therefore we shall only enumeratively indicate them here in a succinct way. First, though the partial bureaucratic hierarchies are formally constituted in different ways (appointment from above, election from below, etc.), actually both access to these organizations and their functioning is subordinated to the same rules and principles which are identical in all spheres. This is ensured through the purely formal character of election at all levels and through the invariably enforced domination of the executive organs over the formally elected ones. In these conditions access to membership in any of its functional segments actually follows the principle of self-recruitment and self-formation of personnel by the apparatus itself.

Second, this disappearance of the distinction between appointed and elected bodies already indicates that the apparatus cannot be conceived as bureaucracy in the proper, narrowly Weberian sense of the word. Weber's strong emphasis on the executive—expert character of bureaucratic power connected with the formal rationality of the choice of means for pre-set goals cannot be applied to the organization of power in a society whose most prominent characteristic is precisely the tendency to submit all spheres of existence to the same logic of domination through a unified and all-encompassing system of commands originating from a single self-appointed centre. In these conditions the functions of goal-setting, task-achieving and rule-implementing become intricately interwoven in the activity of the apparatus of power and though one of these roles may take preponderance in that of its particular members, they cannot be completely divorced in the work of individual officials either. They are bureaucrats therefore only in the sense that their power depends solely upon their holding an office, but not necessarily in the stricter meaning relating to the nature of their activity.

Third, the structural imperative of this system to transform all specific bureaucracies into functional organs contributing to the implementation of a single set of centrally posited goals finds its subjective—normative expression in the demand made of each official: to submit his activity not only to the explicit rules and directives of office, but simultaneously to the general interests of the state, that is, to a set of changing and at best vaguely specified substantive universal objectives. This norm of the supremacy of state interests results in an increased dependence of each individual bureaucrat upon the apparatus as a whole. Since each official should have to satisfy in his activity two sets of non-coinciding and often opposed requirements (formal rules versus universal goals), he can always be in the wrong. It is the acceptance of this fact which each office-holder in this system must internalize, and this creates the specific ethos of this bureaucracy in which loyalty to the apparatus as such ('the Party is always right') takes precedence over both values of formal correctness and purposive effectiveness.

Fourth, this unification is accomplished through the fact that while various bureaucratic structures are formally independent of each other, there is actually a very high degree of circulation of personnel between them, especially and notably in the leading positions. This circulation not only counteracts (at least to a degree) the tendency of individual bureaucrats to identify themselves with the office held instead of the apparatus as such, but it also renders the various functional hierarchies homogeneous in the sense that it practically establishes an equivalance of rank among the most diverse and seemingly incomparable administrative positions — a fact to which the Soviet system of nomenclature gives only a rigidly formalized expression.

However, as we have already emphasized, the decisive element in bringing about this integrated power structure is the Party itself. The leading role of the Party is actually the supreme principle of unification of all potential centres of power into one. This principle has two fundamental aspects. It means, firstly, that the decisions taken by the top of the separate Party hierarchy, by the actual Party leadership, are incontestably obligatory for all organs of power and for all social organizations. All broad, far-ranging social decisions are the actual monopoly of the central apparatus of the Party which at the same time determines all questions of personal appointment to leading positions in each and every functional bureaucracy. This sovereignty of the Party is, secondly, supplemented by the control which ubiquitous Party organizations with their independent functionaries — members of the separate Party-hierarchy — exercise over the activity of the corresponding state, economic, etc. organizations and their bureaucratic heads. It is in this way that potential tendencies toward autonomization on the part of partial bureaucratic systems are kept in check. Especially at the lowest, basic level the party organizations are posited as the watch-dogs of the higher rungs of the Party apparatus over the work of professional bureaucrats. If the top of the Party hierarchy coordinates the activity of formally separated power and organizational structures by determining the substantive, universal objectives they ought to follow, the bottom of this hierarchy attempts (at least ideally) to enforce the priority of these objectives against any of the particularistic tendencies that may grow out of the segmentation of power and the indubitable plurality of social interests. In this way the party welds together all the differentiated and diversely articulated organs of social management, regulation and command into one immense structure of power.

But just this necessity of welding together demonstrates that the whole apparatus, though integrated and unified, is not monolithic in the proper sense of the word. The separation of the various functional bureaucracies related to the various sectors of social life is not pure formality or mere appearance. Though none of them can ever attain autonomy, they are not just cogs in the machinery of power, harmoniously complementing each other. The specific bureaucracies do develop — and by necessity — their own, more or less particular interests. Their interrelation is (as opposed to the norm of functional complementarity) actually in some respects competitive and they act out this competition in specific forms of bargaining. This latter moment, one should emphasize, though an anomaly from the viewpoint of the pure ideal of the system, is not only inevitable within it, but also actually forms an organic part of its functioning.

The fact that each partial bureaucratic structure develops its own immanent particular interest, follows partly from the general logic of hierarchical organizations in which the possibilities of an individual's advancement on the ladder of power become intricately interwoven with the relative growth of the weight and province of activity of the specific bureaucracy he belongs to. In this way an interest of office is consolidated which clashes with that of equals in other administrative and organizational structures. But it would be a gross oversimplification to reduce the constant tendencies towards a particularistic segmentation within the apparatus to no more than these well-known phenomena of inter-office rivalries. In Eastern European conditions the latter themselves become expressions of deeper-lying conflicts of interests.

In Soviet-type societies each individual member of the apparatus ought to be no more than the representative of the whole. In a sense this is his direct–formal responsibility too. He has first of all to ensure that the goals and directives transmitted from above will actually be realized within the domain of his authority. But in a system where any unexpected occurrence is a social disruption and, more specifically, where any sign of opposition and resistance, even that of spontaneous organization from below, is perceived (correctly) as a major threat to social stability, officials are in fact just as much responsible for the smooth and peaceful functioning of the managed domain as for substantive task-fulfilment. These two sets of responsibilities do not, however, coincide. To minimize the possibility of such disturbances, to keep the field under their own authority pacified, each section of functional, territorial, etc. bureaucracy must try to influence the set of universal goals in a direction which expresses at least some of the objective particular interests of those who, in one way or another, are involved in or directly affected by the activities of the given sector of social life. In this way interests of office become to some extent expressions of various broader social claims. It is only in the form of inter-office rivalries that the latter can be at all articulated within this system. The most important element of this structurally determined clash between the various bureaucratic organizations is the competition among them for central budgetary funds. We have already seen the way this works in the process of planning as bargaining (see pp. 77–83).

The development of specific, particular interests by various functional bureaucracies appears in this system as a regrettable anomaly, expressing the lack of consciousness of individual officials. And this is a correct perception in so far as the unchecked evolution of such a process, the identification of individual bureaucrats with their office (instead of that with the apparatus as a whole) or – much worse! – with those managed or represented by this office, would directly endanger the very principle of domination of the unified apparatus as a corporate entity over the society. The Party therefore keeps these separatist tendencies under a constant and tight control. Its ruling pinnacle establishes itself as the sole, all-powerful broker in the competition of various bureaucratic interests, while the lower rungs of its own apparatus check the working of each and every organizational structure against the resurfacing of autonomistic tendencies. But within certain limits the latter are not only inescapable, but also highly functional for ensuring the normal reproduction of this whole system of domination. In view of the complete lack of a public political arena within these societies, the different and partially opposed social interests of various groups of the population can find no other regular channel of expression but the voice of those bureaucracies which are responsible for keeping the specific groups in question pacified. Since no political system can in the long run impose completely arbitrary decisions on the population, absolutely neglecting the subjectively perceived needs of the largest social groups, since there are limits of suffering which any power must take into account, a degree of selective identification of the partial bureaucracies with the interests of the sector they manage is constitutive to that process of political tatonnement in which the interests of the apparatus become superimposed on all particular social claims within the bounds of tolerance. In this sense the functionally differentiated bureaucratic organs fulfil — as A. Arato has emphasized — an important screening function. They do this not so much by impartially signalling the objective and subjective needs of the sector managed upwards, as by transforming those underlying social interests which are compatible with the given system of social domination into specific bureau-interests that they represent. A specific, institutional selectivity is the key element in this process. In any of these countries one can always be morally certain that the President of the Academy of Sciences (a middle-level member of the apparatus) will fight tooth and nail to get central funds committed to the founding of some new research institute, that he will constantly lament the insufficiency of finances for the upkeep of resort houses, nurseries, etc. for the workers of the Academy — and that he will never raise a single question about the principle of censorship of scientific publications. The fact that the person in question may well be an elder scientist himself, one who in all probability personally considers the further proliferation of academic institutes to be a mere folly, while deeply detesting the power which formal or informal censorship gives to the young and semi-educated headhunters in the cultural apparatus of the party over their scientific elders, will not change his behaviour one iota. He could never become President of the Academy if he were not ready to represent the particular interests of his domain in so selected and filtered a way. It is in a constant process of integration of the particular bureaucratic interests constituted in this way that the unity of apparatus as a sole corporate entity comes into being.

To what type of social group do the members of an apparatus of power which is structured and functions in the way just described belong? Do they constitute a new class — the ruling class of Soviet-type societies? This is undoubtedly the most important — and most widely disputed — question concerning the social structure of these societies.

Perhaps we should begin by asking whether members of this apparatus do in fact constitute any one social group. To answer this question in any detail would involve dealing with such problems as the degree of homogeneity of a group so defined (in view of its relative functional differentiation and hierarchical articulation, the closed or open character of its social reproduction, the presence or absence of any consciousness of common interests, etc.) all concrete empirical questions that can be treated only within the framework of historical and sociological analyses. In the present context we have to restrict ourselves to the elementary and, it seems to us, incontrovertible observation that during the history of these societies the personnel of the apparatus has undergone definite processes of homogenization and consolidation into a distinct, unique social group. Originally, just after the anti-capitalist transformation, the apparatus of power was, as a rule, manned by people originating from two distinctly different social environments and having clearly differentiated functions: by political functionaries, often though not exclusively of working-class origin performing the task of goal-setting and control, and also by bourgeois specialists from the traditional strata of intellectuals and professionals providing the technical expertise. In the course of the evolution of the regimes, however, the sharp distinction between the two social types of the agents of power and functions they have fulfilled respectively has been diminishing to a great extent, though it has not disappeared completely. Undoubtedly there remains a vague difference between technocrats and political bureaucrats and there are often strong feelings of resentment between these two. These are, however, phenomena well known under Western conditions as well. As a matter of fact, the disparity between these two sub-groups is in principle of less significance than in the West because in Soviet-type

INEQUALITY AND DOMINATION IN A 'CLASSLESS' SOCIETY

societies access to positions in both instances rests on fundamentally identical principles, and the originally very pronounced differences in cultural level, life-style, etc. are rapidly disappearing. Their over-accentuation has more to do with the tactics of bureaucratic in-fighting and with psychological mechanisms of over-compensation than with social reality.

Further, if in the early phases of development the apparatus of power was built up through processes of very rapid and widespread social advancement and the turn-over of its personnel was very high (if one can use such a euphemism for the bloody purges of the Stalinist period encompassing the officials of the regime themselves among their victims), Eastern European societies have since created an almost unprecedented security of office (under the fundamental condition of a proved loyalty). This downward immobility (as Alec Nove has aptly named it) at the same time characterizes not only the career of the actual members of the apparatus, but in a broader sense the social (generational) reproduction of its personnel as well. Of course offices are not inherited in these societies. In general, there are no social mechanisms which would automatically ensure the placement of the offspring of an official, however high his standing, within the hierarchy of power. Access to, and advancement in it always ultimately depends on one principle: acceptance of the given individual by the apparatus itself. In these conditions members of the apparatus do not (and in our opinion cannot) constitute in regard to their social reproduction a completely closed group. Then again, their children have great advantages, because of the partly formalized (for persons in higher positions), partly practical privileges their parents enjoy in securing for them access to higher education, which has become the most important formal precondition for advance-ment, and also because of those personal connections through which the parents can assist their career. This whole subject is naturally under the strictest taboo and therefore no reliable statistics are available, but both the sparse data as well as everyday experiences confirm that there is a definitely growing tendency towards the social closure of this group as an important aspect of its consolidation.

Lastly, one cannot deny the existence of a consciousness of separation from those who are ruled among the members of the apparatus. The character of legitimation this system of social domination requires and provides, excludes the emergence of even a rudimentary class-consciousness among the bureaucrats in the sense of an awareness of an opposition of interests between them and other social groups. Not only the historical origins, but also the social character and the structure of rule exclude the open admission and defence of existing inequalities: all officials of these regimes are in principle posited and aware of themselves only as the representatives of general interests. On the other hand this very factor gives rise to a strong and unifying consciousness, like that of a traditional conservative officialdom: 'they' — those who are directed, managed and controlled — are a lazy, egotistical, irrational mass who never understand the superior reasons of the state and do not appreciate 'our' hard and difficult labour. Naturally this ideology is most widespread and explicit where this system of power has the longest-standing tradition and has become most ossified: in the Soviet Union.

So it seems to us absolutely legitimate to regard the members of the apparatus — against all phenomena of functional and hierarchical differentiation — as a single, reasonably homogeneous social group, even if its boundaries — as we shall see — are blurred. There is also no doubt that the members of this group occupy all the positions of social power and command in Soviet-type societies and that they use these positions to reproduce and extend the material and social conditions of their own corporate dominance. Does this group then constitute a new ruling class? The answer to this question clearly depends on the adopted definition of the concept of class; nevertheless it has more than a mere hagiographic or emotive significance within the Marxist tradition. Its formulation is necessary to articulate both similarities and differences in the basic mechanisms determining social structure in West and East respectively.

The Marxian concept of 'class' and the bureaucracy

The very meaning of the Marxian concept of class is the subject of a long-standing dispute and no scrutiny of the classical texts would, in our opinion, help to solve it in an unequivocal way. The relevant textual fragments of Marx themselves seem to be ambiguous or at least open to divergent interpretations. It is easy to pick up even from within the same period of Marx's *oeuvre* formulations which would suggest a very broad application of this notion to all examples of antagonistic group interests based on a general distinction between producers and non-producers (as, for example, the famous enumeration of typical cases of class-conflict throughout history in the *Communist Manifesto*) and contrary statements which restrict the existence of classes (at least in their pure form) to capitalist society (in the *German Ideology* for example). In view of this predicament it seems to be more fruitful to look at the actual *use* of the concept in the theoretical practice of class analysis. Three (rather elementary) considerations seem to arise out of such an approach as to the basic constituents of the meaning of the term in Marx. First, class is a correlative concept, since it is introduced primarily for the explanation of the structural determinants of social conflicts, that is, individuals constitute a class in so far as they stand in a fundamental opposition of interests to some other class. This focussing on the problem of conflict determines, in the second place, the understanding of class composition and membership. Classes are conceived as large-scale social groupings to which individuals belong as a result of their positions in the network of production relations which objectively confer upon them an unequal access to, and command over, its conditions and results, thus serving as an ultimate basis for a structurally determined opposition of interests. Property relations are undoubtedly conceived by Marx as constituting the fundamental determinant of class composition although – as his remarks about the ideological strata of the ruling class demonstrate – class membership cannot be treated exclusively in these terms. Third, the whole enterprise of class analysis centres around the questions, what is the relation between the structural groupings so conceived, which are rooted in a shared objective position in the social process of reproduction, and the conscious (political, ideological, etc.) activity of those social groups which attempt to realize their interests in a clash with others, that is, who are the directly, empirically given subjects of apparent instances of conflict in society. In other words: whether, under what conditions and in what form 'class-in-itself' can be transformed into 'class-for-itself' is the central problem for this type of analysis.

Those who argue that such a concept of class is inapplicable to Eastern European societies as a rule make the point that under these conditions, due to the domination of politics over economy, a definition of classes on the basis of property relations (and more generally in economic terms) is inadequate, since it is unable to explain either the origin of the power, or the actual composition of the ruling social group in question. From this argument they usually conclude that it is necessary to modify the Marxian concept of class, mostly in the direction of a greater generality by subsuming economic power under some broader concept of social domination. These (divergent) attempts at redefinition naturally have to be evaluated on their own merits. But as far as their often professed explicit aim is concerned, that is, to make the notion applicable to both instances of modern society, they seem to fail, because they do not take into account some more abstract, but theoretically also more fundamental, reasons rendering the original conception of class inadequate to the case of Soviet-type societies, at least as far as the characterization of their ruling group is concerned.

As can be seen from the above, the Marxian concept of class primarily refers to an aggregate of individuals (a point made clearly by A. Giddens, for example) whose unity consists in the fact that they share a definite objective position and function in the material process of reproduction and who are therefore constrained to act in this process in an essentially similar way. But this constraint (and this ought to be emphasized) is not due either to social sanctions in cases of deviance or to a community of values and aims. It is the result of a mere adaptation to the quasi-causally working automatisms of economy. The reality of class is primarily woven through this logic that is conferred by economic (or, in a broader sense, social) relations upon the formally free social action of individuals as character masks. Hence the question: how far and in what forms can a grouping so constituted act as a real social group (in the sense of community based on the conscious interaction between its members) in instances and spheres where no automatisms secure the concerted character of its action. (As can be seen, our views at this point coincide with those of Max Weber: the strict concept of class is applicable only to societies where market plays a regulative role.)

Now this concept could be applied to the case of Soviet bureaucracy through its rather simple generalization if it were a fact, that in Eastern European societies not merely economic, but some broader social mechanisms conferred such an objective unity upon the behaviour of the members of this ruling group in some relevant sphere of social action. But the dominance of politics over economy means something much more radical here: due to it the ruling group is constituted in a way that is in principle different from a class. The members of the apparatus are not constrained to act in a definite way by the position they occupy in the structure of social reproduction; they have to follow consciously the rules and objectives pre-set by the apparatus — otherwise they would be sanctioned, that is to say they would lose the office to which their whole position of authority is tied. The difference here from the class of capitalists cannot be reduced to the observation that the power of bureaucracy is not — even in the primary sense — a mere economic one. The most essential contrast emerges through the fact that in this latter case membership in an organization is the pre-condition of, and therefore logically prior to, any structural position of power the individual may occupy. It is the process of being recruited, coopted and accepted by the apparatus that makes someone a bureaucrat. It is in virtue of this principle that the apparatus is a corporate entity. To put it crudely: a person is a capitalist whatever his relations to other members of his class — though he will lose his class-position (by losing his capital) if consistently and in the long term he exhibits an economic behaviour contrary to the logic of capital. On the other hand, a person can be a member of the apparatus of power in Eastern Europe only if he is able to interact with the other members of bureaucracy according to the prescribed rules and objectives of his office, otherwise he will be stripped of it as a result of the concious action of his superiors. This type of social grouping (quite contrary to the case of class) is based on the primacy of a definitely organized group ('corporation') over the individual and it is this which makes the central objective of class analysis — the question of how individuals in a similar objective position reach a common conscious-ness and organization — objectless as far as the ruling stratum of these societies is concerned. The application of the Marxian concept of class is theretore apt to result in this case in pseudo-problems and in completely meaningless assertions. So when, for example, M. Rakovski maintains that in Soviet-type societies not even the ruling class is in a position to organize itself, one is at a loss to grasp the meaning of such a statement. What is the apparatus of power in these societies, if not the organization of this ruling group? Should its members perhaps create another party beyond the Party to get themselves organized?

Therefore, as far as the principles and social mechanisms of its composition are concerned, the ruling group of Eastern European societies (the bureaucracy) cannot be considered a class in the strict sense which the practice of class-analysis would confer upon this term. As a matter of fact this type of social group demonstrates more analogies with groupings to be found in some traditional societies (for example, with estates) than with classes proper. Not only the fusion of economy and politics, but also the authoritative allocation of positions in a hierarchical order of ranks with corres-ponding spheres of explicit duties articulated through rules and norms (and with ensuing privileges) constitute elements of this analogy. But all such historical cases of comparison will again break down in equally crucial respects: bureaucratic membership is based (contrary to the general case of estates) not on ascriptive criteria, but on the principle of individual achievement. The rules and norms in question are not tradition-sanctioned, but consciously established and dynamic. The hierarchical relations of authority have here a definitely impersonal character and so on. Members of the apparatus in Soviet-type societies form a unique social group which has no convincing parallels in history and we lack a suitable term even to designate it. Since questions of terminology do not preoccupy us much, we shall call it a corporate ruling group, the pinnacle of which constitutes the ruling elite proper.

But the concept of class in Marx refers not only to definite principles and mechanisms of large-scale group composition, but primarily to a definite relationship between the groups so composed. As a relationally correlative concept, class designates a group whose members stand in opposition to the objectively defined interests of another, similarly constituted group. And one can well argue that the stricter concept of class referring to the determinants of its composition (which we discussed above) is nothing but an application of this broader (and manifestly more vague) notion to the actual structure of capitalist society. In any case it is clear that the question of the class or classless character of Eastern European societies cannot be answered merely upon the basis of considerations concerning the internal structure of its corporate ruling group — the relation of this latter to the majority of population controlled and dominated by it is of decisive importance here.

As has often been emphasized, the Marxian concept of class in this broader sense involves the idea of an essentially dichotomous relation of conflict between classes. What is in question here is not the simplistic view according to which Marx proposed an ultimate reduction of social stratification in any concrete society to just two fundamental classes. The correlative, broad concept of class presupposes a reciprocal relation of mutual opposition of interests centring around the disposition and appropriation of surplus product, and so its applicability to any concrete case depends upon whether those relations between large-scale social groupings that are the basic sources of potential conflict in the given society can be treated in terms of a number of such dichotomies (certainly interacting with, and perhaps subordinated to, each other).

To decide the question of whether such a concept is of use for the critical understanding of Eastern European societies, we have first to characterize somewhat more closely the social boundaries and extension of that group which in them all occupies the positions of power — as far as this is possible within the framework of such a general discussion. We have earlier identified this corporate ruling group as the members of the apparatus of power. This characterization must now be amplified and concretized.

First, we have to reiterate that the members of the apparatus in regimes of Soviet-type societies cannot be simply identified with bureaucracy or officialdom in the strict sense of the word. The integration of all bodies of social authority into a single hierarchy in practice blurs to a large extent the differences between the functions of goal-setting, task-achieving the rule-implementing in the activity of their individual members. Therefore not only those who preponderantly make or implement administrative decisions, but also those who predominantly provide the necessary technical expertise or information for such decisions belong to this apparatus. It is so partly in the direct sense that they are, in the majority of cases, embraced by the same organization, and partly because in these conditions there is no way to draw a clear-cut distinction between the two types of activity. Further, we have to agree with those who argue that members of the officially recognized cultural elite providing the ideology of the system do actually belong (and not only through their function, but also through their actual social situation and influence) to the same social group, even if they do not occupy any administrative position. Correspondingly, 'members of the apparatus' should be understood in the broad sense as embracing all those who perform the activity of social command and control in the various organizational structures of social authority as well as those who provide the necessary information or supporting ideology for this whole process of social command within these same structures (or in rarer cases around them).

Similar considerations together with the fact that tertiary education has undoubtedly become the main avenue of access to positions within the apparatus have motivated some critics of Soviet societies (Konrad-Szelenyi, Gouldner, etc.) to identify their corporate ruling group (usually conceived as a class) with the intelligentsia as such. At this point we wish to make only two critical remarks of a sociological character to indicate why we find this view untenable. While it is true that higher education has become the most important channel for entering positions of power (and the privileged access children from the corporate ruling elite have to it is one of the important sources of the tendency toward a cross-generational continuity and stabilization of the ruling group), it is certainly not the only avenue, especially for positions related to the political apparatus proper. It is important to note that the degrees which the regime officially regard as equivalent to those which can be achieved through higher institutions of learning are often actually conferred upon political bureau-crats already in (mostly middle level) positions through short-term courses in specifically created institutions (such as higher Party schools, etc.). This fact itself demonstrates that admission to the apparatus (at least to some actual key positions) does not depend upon the possession of definite intellectual skills which can be acquired only through formal learning. Conferring degrees upon middle and senior officials is actually a practice through which the system attempts to homogenize the social prestige, etc. of the higher strata of its ruling group in spite of the remaining educational and cultural differences. Further, and this is the more important point, if higher education is today the most important and regular avenue of access to bureaucratic power, acquiring it certainly does not constitute a sufficient condition for entering the ruling group. Indeed the most numerous professional group among the intelligentsia, that is, teachers, comprises people who are not only among the worst paid in these societies, but who for the most part live in situations of an oppressing personal dependence upon low-level officials (in small towns and villages) and are without any social influence. It would be merely perverse to regard them as members of a ruling group in any sense. So if one is to take the argument for the identification of the members of the apparatus with the intelli-gentsia in an empirical sociological sense (and not as a matter of an arbitrary and somewhat confused terminology), it is patently false. Not only are a great many members of the apparatus not intellectuals in any meaningful sense of this word, but the majority of those who constitute the intelligentsia do not belong to the apparatus of power. Because although many positions presuppose specific kinds of expertise (and therefore prior knowledge attainable through formal education), the ability to function as a member of the apparatus is in general not based on the monopoly of some mystical new kind of knowledge, but just on simple, old-fashioned political and admini-strative skills which can be learnt only in practice. It is simply that access to this practice is safeguarded and restricted by the apparatus to those whose loyalty it accepts as being beyond doubt. This does not mean that the theories in question have not offered some important critical insights, not least of all as an antidote against that substitutionist ideology by which Eastern European intellectuals tend to regard themselves, following a long historical tradition, as the divinely appointed conscience of the nation. Without the slightest self-critical hesitation they identify their own, sometimes very grave, sometimes petty, troubles with the most onerous social ills of the population. But theories of the intelligentsia as the actual or latent ruling class are rather to be seen as ideological reactions to the above ideology, not as effective critical theories of Soviet-type societies. They are the Eastern European variants of that frustrated masochism of radical intellectuals which is certainly not unfamiliar in the West either.

If we have encountered difficulties when trying to draw the social boundaries of the corporate ruling group in the horizontal dimension, these are only compounded when we attempt to answer the question of where membership of the apparatus of power actually ends in these societies. First, the actual bureaucratic structures naturally encompass a very great number of persons whose position and activity have nothing to do with social decision-making and command: office workers of various types who perform elementary, semi-manual (white-collar) functions of administration, accounting, etc. within the apparatus. No doubt the work of these people is purely subordinate and their situation is often characterized by a much higher degree of defencelessness and personal dependency upon petty bearers of power than that of the productive workers proper. Nevertheless in some sociologically relevant sense these persons do belong to the apparatus, and their social situation and status is not the same as of those who are merely managed by it. They usually have a more direct access to the real bearers of some power and therefore may participate if not in their privileges then in some of their favours, and since it is frequently they whom clients of the given institution first and most regularly encounter on the everyday, face-to-face level, they may partake in a spurious way in its authority too. Actually on the level of empirical consciousness the conflict between those who perform commanded (white-collar, unproductive) labour within the apparatus and the direct producers outside it is usually very strong and clearly formulated.

Further, and more importantly, since the whole apparatus of power is unified into one enormous hierarchy, the activity of all its members, with the exception of the political elite proper at the very top, is commanded and commanding *simultaneously*, with a continuous narrowing of the sphere of authority as we descend its rungs. So inevitably there is a numerically very significant group situated between the agents and subjects of this type of domination: these are the actual mediators between the various institutions of power and those who are managed and controlled by them. These mediators are social agents who merely implement decisions taken elsewhere and transmitted to them from above, but it is they who translate them into directives and dispositions addressed to a small group of concrete persons, or directly supervise their realization, like checkers, foremen, or even the lowest-grade engineers in the industrial organization proper. This is not only a very broad, but also a heterogeneous group and the social situation of many of its members does not differ substantially from that of the workers. On the other hand, as such positions are very often conferred as the result of political or personal favouritism, they bring with them a degree of personal power and may serve as stepping stones for a further career.

Naturally, groups with similar or even identical functions do occur in capitalist societies as well. However, under conditions where all power has one and the same source and access to it is regulated by identical social mechanisms, the presence of intermediary strata has different significance and consequences from in a capitalist environment, where it is really the plurality of kinds and sources of power which constitutes one of the most important legitimating principles of the social system. In Eastern Europe where all positions of social authority and control are fulfilled on the basis of the principle of trusteeship, where all power of persons is actually the emanated power of the apparatus itself, the uninterrupted and imperceptible gradations through which one can descend from positions of seemingly unlimited and all-encompassing authority to those of complete dependence and subordination not only create empirical difficulties in defining the exact limits where membership of the apparatus as participation in the corporate ruling group ends, but in a sense also make such a demarcation conceptually arbitrary. That is, in some respects the all-important lower boundaries of the ruling group are objectively blurred and this fact expresses one of the important tendencies that co-determine the social structure of these societies.

This point may become clearer if we turn for a moment to that official self-image of these societies which may not correspond to their professed doctrine, but which in the most diverse ways is constantly disseminated and reinforced for popular consumption. In this view the whole of society constitutes one vast and all-encompassing pyramid in which each individual has his own place and function in the variously articulated apparatuses of the state, according to his ability. Nearly everybody is a state employee, therefore everyone is a representative of the state, whether he is the First Secretary of the Party or the Prime Minister, or an unskilled factory worker. Doing their own job, fulfilling their specific duties (which are inevitably also accompanied by specific rights) each of them contributes in his own way to the common good embodied in the sacred image of the state. This is in truth already a classless society, because, on the one hand, it replaces the accidental nature of the relation of the individual to his social station by true principles of meritocracy, and, on the other hand, because everybody is in fact a member of the apparatus of power, only occupying different functional positions within it. If one wished to give a theoretical expression to this simplistic imagery, then it could be said that this view conceives the social structure of the societies in question as one based solely on the principle of an all-comprehensive technical division of labour — where 'technical' in a perverted sense relates not only to the choice of means for the realization of ends, but also to the selection of ends.

This last point is naturally the most important, and the one which is deliberately obscured by this apologetic ideology. It is falsified not just by everyday experiences (this is proved by sociological investigations of the most elementary kind) which demonstrate behind the flimsiest veil of a meritocratic façade the working of social mechanisms constantly reproducing the privileged position of certain groups. (In Hungary, it was found that children from an academic or professional family environment have an eighteen times better chance than young people of peasant background to enter the institutes of higher education.) Even more significant, however, is the fact that this ideology hides behind the formally universal characteristic of 'state employee' the crucial social difference between those who define the ends (or contribute to and influence their determination) and those who merely handle the means of their realization: the point where the technical division of functions becomes the social divide between power and dependence.

So it is not difficult to see through the apologetic function of this ideology which actually is nothing but the positive inverse of the critical idea of totalitarian classlessness in terms of which many liberal theories conceptualize Soviet-type societies. But the evident falsity of this ideology should not blind us to the fact that it is more than just a distorted representation. In fact it expresses one of the important tendencies of the system which is embodied in a number of actual social practices. By this we mean not only that the apparatus of power would naturally like to see everybody behaving as a responsible agent of the state, correctly performing his duties and all the time controlling others to see that they also fulfil their tasks, but that it directs a barrage of exhortations at each person, from early childhood on, to foster such attitudes. Beyond this verbal propaganda the system constantly creates and tolerates objective situations in which people with no actual power at all may behave against other individuals (in their roles of private persons) as all-important representatives of the state. Bureaucratism in its popular sense, a favourite target of Eastern European satirical journals, is one of the most pervasive and ingrained features of everyday life. It is an important compensatory mechanism which allows the lowest-grade officials or employees to identify themselves with that power upon which – for their own position and situation – they wholly, and in the most painful manner, depend. Those who have lived in any of the Eastern European societies know only too well that this phenomenon, in a broad sense, is not restricted to the walls of offices, but is encountered in all walks of life. If you ask for a less stale loaf of bread from a shop assistant (an occupational group at the lowest wages and status level in these societies), you may suddenly find yourself in the situation of an applicant currying some specific favour from an official of the state and you may receive instead of bread a rambling lecture about responsible consumer behaviour and decent demeanour, or even about your clothing. And it is hard to tell what is more degrading as an experience: to be the object of this incessant, enervating petty domineering, or to see it crumble instantly if the 'official' facing you suddenly perceives by some sign that you are the bearer of some real power. For if a worker, incensed by mindless bureaucratism, expresses his opinion in a few blunt words in an office, he may easily find himself in the nearest police station. But should a dissident intellectual – hardly a favourite of the system – in a moment of irritation invoke some of the sacred slogans of the regime against a petty official, all the latter's haughtiness may give way in a moment to abject servility. It is precisely by self-assurance and the knowledge of these meaningless phrases that he has created the impression of being one of those who have the right not to request, but to command – and then he may be (most subtly) reproached for not having said so from the very beginning.

It is through this etatization of all forms of (non-private) intercourse, through the attempt to fashion all non-personal relations according to the model of interaction between a client and an official of the state, that Eastern European social systems attempt to create situations in which each and every person may enjoy at least moments of identification with the apparatus of power. But if this is undoubtedly one of the objective tendencies in these societies, it is also by necessity an ultimately unsuccessful one. The identification of the whole society with one vast pyramid of power in which every person participates, since each individual at least in some situations assumes the role of authority and control over others, is for those who are at the bottom of the pyramid and constitute its foundation merely a way of vicariously compensating for the inability to determine their own work and life. It is a phenomenon of a socially induced distortion of personality, and not of the social structure proper. And more importantly, even this mechanism of psychological substitution breaks down in the case of the largest group at the bottom: the industrial and agricultural manual workers, who cannot even for a moment dominate anything but the material of their labour, who do not command anybody else, but are only commanded. If a hierarchically articulated, etatistic homogenization is an objective tendency in Eastern European societies, then it never really counteracts the effects of the much deeper-lying social division: the dichotomy between those who can and do decide upon the lives of others and those who merely implement such social decisions.

Class dichotomy and division of labour

Whatever the difficulties (empirical and conceptual) in drawing the exact boundaries of the corporate ruling group, whatever the mechanisms which allow a vicarious identification with power to those who are in reality outside its range, nothing can eliminate or even disguise the opposition of interests that exists between those who monopolize all form of public authority and enjoy all the ensuing economic, social and cultural privileges, who realize in their activity the domination of the apparatus over the whole society, and those who not only have no say in the everyday matters of social life, but are dependent even in their private activities upon uncontrolled decisions taken by others. If the concentration and fusion of all kinds of power into a single type sets into motion some secondary mechanisms of an apparent social homogenization, in other respects it makes the antagonism between 'them' and 'us' especially apparent. In the 'core' cases there is never any difficulty in drawing this distinction. Naturally, even the narrowly conceived group of productive workers cannot be designated under Eastern European conditions via the concept of 'working class' in the sense this term has in classical Marxist theories of capitalism. Not only — as we have argued earlier — is the economic position of direct producers different under these conditions, but their social situation *vis-à-vis* the members of the apparatus cannot be conceived on the model of the relationship between the proletariat and the bourgeoisie. Both the great antagonistic classes of capitalist society consist of individuals who are free to pursue their own (individual or collective) interests against each other — naturally within the framework set and the chances established by the economic–social institutions of this society. In Eastern Europe, on the other hand, the direct producers constitute the social grouping of those who not only have no real chance, but also no formal possibility and no right to articulate their own interests (individual or collective) themselves. The members of the apparatus face them as the self-appointed representatives of their best and real interests, and any questioning of this institutionalized right of representation amounts to an outright rebellion. The two fundamental classes of capitalism equally have the right to organize themselves, although their access to the material, political and cultural means of organization is structurally unequal. Under conditions of 'really existing' socialism the corporate ruling group is *eo ipso* organized, it constitutes a group simply because its members belong to a definitely articulated social organization (the apparatus), while the direct producers in principle cannot organize themselves, even in elementary forms and at local levels, autonomously, at least as long as the basic mechanisms of social domination remain un-challenged and intact in these societies.

Therefore it seems to us evident that the actual social relations between the two fundamental groups are essentially different in these two basic cases. However, this is not meant to deny that the relation between the corporate ruling group and that of the direct producers in Eastern European societies is in fact a specific historical type of social antagonism. The appropriation of social surplus by the apparatus as a corporate entity which constitutes the material basis of its overall social domination (and which is effected through the control its members exercise over the whole process of social produc-tion and the distribution of its results) stands in sharp conflict both with the immediate material concerns and the long-term social interests of the productive workers themselves, and more generally of the whole ruled majority of population. Nor does this opposition of basic interests remain unconscious. Certainly, as long as the system functions normally there is no possibility of giving it any articulated, organized expression. But the experience of the conflict between 'them' and 'us' informs the behaviour of the majority of producers at their own work-place. Quite deliberate slow-downs of production, absenteeism, maltreatment of machinery, constant infringement of technical regulations and rules of labour discipline, widespread theft of material and tools, etc. — all these are the everyday forms of resistance by which workers deprived of all possibility of self-organization individually wage their guerilla struggle against the apparatus, attempting in an atomized way to express, and in a degree to enforce, their own interests. So if one uses the concept of class in its broad (and rather vague) relational-correlative sense, there are good reasons for regarding Soviet-type societies as a new historical form of class societies. Or — as we shall see more exactly — there are deep structural tendencies in these societies due to which a dichotomous opposition of interests is constantly reproduced between the corporate ruling group and the unorganized and amorphous grouping of direct producers, which is the source not only of incessant skirmishes between the two, but also of a possible open conflict. Because, it can be argued, in the moment of truth, at the time of recurring overall social crises (on the periphery), this great division between the two classes suddenly becomes crystal-clear. There is no modern society where rebellious masses could so certainly count on such overwhelming support or at least sympathy from the whole population — with the exception of the members of the apparatus itself — as in those of Eastern Europe. When the normal reproduction of the system falters and its repressive apparatus is paralyzed, it is truly a question of the struggle between 'them', the rulers, and 'us', the ruled — and therefore the crisis can be overcome only with the assistance of foreign troops (or at least by the threat of such an intervention).

But if these moments of sudden political collapse are seen as revealing the truth, the deep hidden structure of these societies, then the ease with which the whole apparatus of dominance is reconstituted after what seemed to be its complete disintegration, perhaps no less belongs to their essence. The generalized and local collapses which — especially on the periphery of the Soviet 'empire' — un-expectedly interrupt and punctuate their overwhelming social—political immobilism, are for these societies not only their moments of truth, but equally those of a *citoyen* enthusiasm. For it is only in these short periods of political exaltation or elementary existential despair that the whole of the ruled population or even the vast stratum of direct producers can discover itself to be a unified social group having — in an antagonistic relation to the apparatus — the same predominating interests. In the day-to-day functioning of these societies even the 'class' of productive workers turns out to be heterogenous, not merely ephemerally, but structurally articulated and divided (in various, non-coinciding dimensions) into groups with different, to some extent even conflicting, interests.

If someone were to succeed in writing the real social history of these countries over the last twenty-five years, it would undoubtedly demonstrate the persistence and the importance of such subterranean and unarticulated conflicts of interests which definitely cannot be reduced to the antagonistic dichotomy discussed above. The most evident case of the latter is the incessant tug of war between urban and rural strata of population (in respect of which both dwellers of small provincial towns and commuting industrial workers represent a specific and intermediary group) which pervades a whole range of social problems, from questions of parity of pricing between industrial and agricultural products to aspects of cultural policy, and which is distortedly and selectively reflected and at the same time exploited by various sections of the bureaucracy in their infighting. And in periods of 'thaw', of that very restricted 'liberalization' which from time to time these regimes are forced by various economic–political reasons to allow, one can often observe the articulation of quite unsuspected group interests. So during the discussions of various projects of economic reform in Central Eastern Europe and especially in the social reactions to the half-hearted attempts at their implementation, differences emerged not only between manual workers and intellectuals in the broad sense (for example in their typical attitudes to, or at least preferred interpretation of, the principle of a sharper income-differentiation), but – rather as a matter of general surprise – also between the workers of small and middle-sized industrial enterprises, and the employees of big concerns. And these differences, though usually completely un-formulated, often find expression not only in rather conspicuous ways in styles of life and leisure, but also in the survival of some traditional (and quite divisive) prejudices and in a psychology of suspicion concerning other groups. So large numbers of industrial workers are inclined to believe that even now 'all peasants have money under their skin', while the older generation of cooperative peasantry still thinks in stereotype of a homogeneously sinful big city whose inhabitants are all 'big spenders' with no idea of what hard work really means. At the same time the actual bearers of power always find it relatively easy to evoke, when needed, sharply anti-intellectualist reactions from both groups.

Therefore we do agree in principle with those (Ossowski, Hegedüs, etc.) who emphasize not only the extreme abstractness of a reduction of Eastern European social structure to a case of class dichotomy (in the sense of the existence of various intermediary and secondary strata), but also its fundamental inadequacy due to the role the social division of labour plays in the determination of the real social position of individuals and in the formation of social groups which on the basis of structurally defined similarity of positions and interests may potentially become subjects of common social action. It constitutes the third, and – as we shall argue – the most important objective principle tendentially articulating and structuring these societies. Only social division of labour should not be simplistically identified with the subsumption of individuals under occupational categories (and therefore the emphasis on its role in our understanding is not equivalent to the proposal to replace class analysis with stratification theory which – being both scientistic and apologetic – has become in the meantime the favourite conceptual tool of the officially promoted sociology in Eastern Europe). We cannot attempt here a clarification of this notoriously problematical notion and therefore merely state that we understand by it those mechanisms that subsume individuals under such broad social categories of activity that in the given society involve differing life-conditions and social opportunities (due to differences both in the social character of activity and in the mechanisms of participation in the total social product). So explaining social structure in terms of the positions which individuals occupy in the system of social division of labour definitely does not mean explaining away social inequalities by reference to the technical differences in the labour functions performed by these individuals. Just the opposite, it represents an attempt to articulate, behind the evident, but seemingly gradually distributed inequalities in income, prestige, etc., those basic differences in the material conditions of activity and ways of life, on the foundation of which there can emerge concrete social groups with various interests which are partially, or in some cases totally, opposed to each other.

However, in contrast to theories of class division (in whatever sense) this approach emphasizes that the social structure of these societies cannot be reduced, even in abstract and bare fundamentals, to a case of dichotomic antagonism or, more generally, to a number of such dichotomies superimposed upon each other (in this way allowing for intermediary positions) but all being constituted in a single dimension, determined by a single principal source (be it monopolization of social power, appropriation of social surplus or whatever).

Taking the social division of labour as the most important social mechanism and principle objectively structuring these societies means laying the emphasis on the irreducibly multi-dimensional (and therefore inherently dynamic) character of social group formation in their everyday reproduction and functioning. The extreme poles of rural/urban, manual/intellectual, male/female, large-scale collective/ privatized individual labour designate some of the most important dimensions in which the actual social positions of individuals and their potential social groupings are determined. But these, as we have already stated, cannot be discussed in such an abstract generality. Their actual composition and importance differs in the various countries of the Eastern European bloc, depending on their historical past, their level of economic development, etc. But there is no doubt that in all of these countries the socially most important dimension of the division of labour is the one marked out by the extremes of commanded labour and the labour of commanding. In it also, as in all the other dimensions, there occurs (as we have seen) a number of intermediary positions between the two extremes — but here there prevails an objective tendency towards the antagonistic intensification of the conflicting polar interests which at specific historical moments may and do overshadow all other social differences, positing those who command the labour of others — the members of the apparatus as corporate ruling group — in overt antagonism to the whole working population as such. So the emphasis on the role that the division of labour plays in Eastern European societies does not have to, and should not mean, the denial of the indubitable truth contained in attempts at their class analysis: the existence of a strong, structurally determined tendency which at moments of outright social crisis objectively reduces all the differences of group interests to this single and implacable dichotomy.

But it would be extremely formalistic to understand the fundamental character of the social division of labour as the principle of social structuration merely in the sense that on its basis one may well also give account for, or theoretically encompass, the dichotomizing tendencies present in Soviet-type societies. We tried to argue that their actual social structure is determined by the co-presence and interpenetration of three objective processes and tendencies (etatistic homogenization, antagonistic dichotomy and interaction between multi-dimensional group interests determined along the lines of the social division of labour). The tendency towards an etatistic homogenization of the whole society, though certainly neither ineffective nor inconsequential, is in the final analysis that of a manipulative surface only. So the problem finally boils down to the question: what is the relation between the tendency towards the extreme intensification of the antagonism between the corporate ruling group and the direct producers (indeed, the whole ruled population) which erupts at times of sudden outbursts, socio-political crises, on the one hand, and that of subterranean conflictual interaction between variegated and multi-dimensional group interests which divide the working population itself and which are constantly at play in, and reproduced through, the normal functioning of these societies, to a large extent determining the everyday life, behaviour and consciousness of individuals, on the other? Further, this question relates to the way the two tendencies objectively interact with, and mutually condition each other.

At this point we have to return to the idea with which we ended the analysis of the economic system of Eastern European societies: in these countries disposition over, and appropriation of, the social surplus exercised and realized by the apparatus as a coporate entity constitutes only the material foundation and economic component of a monopolistic expropriation by it of all means of social organization and intercourse. Its social domination over the whole society rests upon the fact that no social group outside it has either the opportunity or the right to articulate and to attempt to realize its own particular interests either *vis-à-vis* the apparatus itself or in relation to other social groups. It is this fact which puts members of the apparatus in a position of fundamental opposition to the whole ruled and dominated society. At the same time it is precisely this which makes the existence and functioning of such a separated organization of power, uncontrolled by the population, within the given conditions, a social necessity as well. It is not only in the sphere of economy that — as we have already argued — the corporate ruling group fulfils an organic function: it does so in a broader social sense too. As long as the various and partially clashing group interests, structurally determined by the existing system of division of labour, are suppressed and unarticulated, there is no other way to achieve the necessary balancing and reconciliation between them except through the self-imposed representative and mediative function of the apparatus itself. The suppression of all group interest and of civil society both creates, gives substance to, and perpetuates the antagonism between the corporate ruling group and the rest of society. In so far as the various particularistic groups of society are completely deprived of any possibility of organizing themselves, they have no other channel to assert their own specific interests to some degree, except through exercising some amorphous, atomized and spontaneous pressure upon the apparatus as a whole, and at the same time accepting the representative role of that part of it which is directly responsible for their sphere of activity. We have already encountered a number of factors due to which this whole system of etatistic mediation as a specific screening process, in which the institutional interests of the apparatus become actually superimposed over those of each and every social group, regularly tends to break down. In these moments all the various and divergent social pressures and resistances tend to coalesce into one enormous social explosion against the apparatus as a whole. But if it is merely a case of breakdown, if the various groups, which at this moment of political enthusiasm find themselves suddenly united, do not succeed in developing simultaneously, at least in rudimentary forms, their own organization, then re-establishing the domination of the apparatus in an unchanged form is a relatively easy task, since such a form of organization of unified power is in a sense needed by such a society. This is, in our opinion, the key to both the specific vulnerability and the enormous resilience of that type of social domination which Eastern European societies exemplify.

So, to conclude, our opposition to those critical theories which ultimately conceive this social structure as a new historical variant of class societies, rests not merely on theoretical considerations concerning their extreme abstraction or inadequacy, it is also, and primarily, an opposition of a practical character. But one should remember that the very notion of social conflict, constituting the living core of Marxian class analysis, has itself a connotation which cannot be exhausted solely in descriptive–theoretical terms. Conflict in this sense means not only an antagonistic opposition of interests, but also social struggle which in the future can radically change not only the relative power positions of the groups concerned, but also the very basis of their antagonism. It is just in this practical respect of a possible emancipation that class theories of Eastern European societies seem to us to be most drastically inadequate. To the apologetic idea of a homogeneous society disseminated by the official ideology they counterpose its inverse: the critical idea of a society whose members are homogeneously united (as to their basic interests) against a relatively small ruling class. This view forgets that this unity of all those ruled (of the working population, of the direct producers, etc.) is merely a negative one. It certainly exists, but only in so far as all individuals in this society − except members of the apparatus itself − are systematically and equally excluded from any exercise of social power, from any participation in, and control over, real social decisions. This fact, however, does not obliterate the existing essential differences in the actual life-conditions of these equally powerless individuals, differences which originate in their different positions in the system of social division of labour (the level of which cannot be momentarily transcended and changed at will) and which give rise to particular interests that in many respects collide with each other. With all due respect for the radical intentions of, and many true critical insights contained in, the class theories of Eastern European societies, they seem to bring with them the danger of a new substitutionism. The practical orientation they strongly suggest towards an imminent, all-decisive clash between the two fundamental 'classes', seems to lose sight of what is for us the most important practical principle in regard to the emancipatory possibilities of Eastern European societies: a grass-roots, autonomous and pluralistic self-organization of the various social groups constitutes under the given circumstances the basic precondition for initiating historical processes capable of challenging and changing not only the personnel of, or perhaps the principles of selection for, the apparatus, but the very social basis of its domination.

PART II

Political Domination and its Consequences

CHAPTER 4

Legitimation

The legitimation crisis

If a social order survives for sixty years, it is appropriate to raise the question of its legitimacy. We can regard it as highly unlikely that a system of domination which conceived of itself and is conceived of by others as a unified continuum of the same coherent whole, would not have collapsed during over half a century had it been upheld only by various types of interest, including the imposition of fear. According to one formulation of Max Weber, a social order is legitimated if at least one part of the population acknowledges it as exemplary and binding and the other part does not confront the existing social order with the image of an alternative one as equally exemplary. Thus the relative number of those legitimating a system may be irrelevant if the non-legitimating masses are merely dissatisfied. This is even more markedly true in various kinds of non-democratic systems, for in them dissatisfaction cannot be expressed, at least not continuously, and the lack of legitimation does not manifest itself except in sporadic outbursts that the ruling elite can easily cope with. Consequently, the Soviet social order can also be conceived of as a legitimate one, even though only the Party or perhaps only the leading bodies of the Party acknowledge the order as exemplary and binding. Further, there are no masses of any kind which would be able to confront the existing social order with an alternative concept they could present as exemplary. Accordingly we cannot speak of any legitimation crisis in Eastern European societies unless one of these two conditions of legitimation disappears or fades away. In the Soviet Union both prerequisites of legitimation seem to be met and that is why the social order has to be regarded as a legitimate one. In other Eastern European societies, primarily in Czechoslovakia, Poland and Hungary, the two former conditions are, however, not met, as they may be said to in the Soviet Union. Not only is the relative number of subjects who legitimate the system very small (being basically restricted to the ruling elite itself) but the over-whelming majority of the population does have an image of an alternative political order — that of the Western European or North American liberal-legal state — which is acknowledged by them as exemplary. Thus Eastern European societies, and in particular the three mentioned above, continue to exist in a permanent legitimation crisis. That is as true of Hungary as it is of Poland or Czechoslovakia despite the popular support lent to the present government in Hungary. Legitimation means not so much the legitimation of government as of a form of domination, and relative popular support is given to the Hungarian government precisely because it practises the otherwise rejected form of domination in a more tolerable fashion than is the case in other countries.

However, a protracted legitimation crisis does not inescapably lead to the collapse of a social order. Even setting aside for the time being the dependent status of these societies and the presence of the Soviet army on their territories, it is conceivable, though not probable, that their structure might survive, even though this will probably not be the case. The legitimation crisis only leads inevitably to collapse if both pillars of legitimation are shaken, that is to say, if the members of the Party or of the ruling bodies of the Party also lose their belief in the exemplary character of the order and no longer find it binding. This happened in Hungary in 1956. Those who admired the open dissent within the Chinese ruling elite, and contrasted this with its absence in Eastern European countries, missed the important point that the Chinese leaders were never threatened by the second aspect of legitimation crisis, except perhaps in the case of Shanghai. Most Eastern European countries, however, have been legal-democratic states for a longer or shorter period of time and their inhabitants are ready to consider democracy as itself a part of their own tradition. The subjects of these countries (the term 'subject' is appropriate here instead of 'citizen', for without a relatively independent civil society, there is no citizenry) generally have access to books and information about the 'other world', and personal contacts and experiences as well. If open dissent occurs in the Party or within the Party leadership, the alternative images held by the majority of the population and the aspirations of one or other Party faction may coincide in that they may actually or apparently share the desire for, and the prospect of, a change. That is why the slogan announcing the purity of the Party and calling for the expurgation of all open dissent from it is more than mere ideology or neurosis; in fact it is highly rational from the standpoint of the social order. Communists, often including the most sincere ones, who plead for inner-Party democracy do not understand the logic of their own social system.

In Eastern European single-Party systems the Party is a poly-functional organization. One of its functions is precisely the legitimation of social order. Only those who meet this criterion may be admitted to the Party. No achievement in production, culture or administration is in itself sufficient to guarantee admission; only the readiness of emphatic legitimation will do, but this will suffice even without any kind of achievement. The Party member should not only accept the ruling order but, at least in principle, also believe in its absolute validity. That is to say, as far as he is concerned no other social order should have any kind of validity. Of course, this is not how things have always worked out in practice, but Party members should behave as if this is what happened.

From the aforementioned, the conclusion may have already become clear: in the Soviet Union the social order has to be considered legitimate, whereas this is not so in the most important Eastern European states. However, the type of legitimation has not yet been analysed.

We have seen that the Soviet social order may be described as a system of domination that conceives of itself as a unified continuum and is understood by others, too, as such. However, the same system of domination has been and still is legitimated in three totally different ways: the 'classical' types of legitimation have been in the past and still are in the present always combined with auxiliary ones, which are applied not only to the Soviet Union, but also to almost all despotic single-Party systems of our times.

Earlier phases of legitimation

The first phase in the development of the Soviet Union can be described in political terms as a form of Jacobin dictatorship. Its main characteristic was that it did not lay claim to any kind of legitimation proper (and not only during the Revolution). For the sake of clarity, we must look first at the mode of self-justification of the dominating party, which cannot be identified with self-legitimation; second, the growing indifference of the ruling elite regarding the attitude of the majority of the population, and third, the role of negative legitimation, particularly before the stabilization of the regime.

The Bolshevik Party conceived of itself as a revolutionary power, as the embodiment of a complete break with Russian tradition — for it, traditional legitimation was out of the question. However, it made certain attempts to construct a new tradition. It was a matter of great urgency for the new regime to erect the statues of Marx and Engels and to propose the establishment of a Pantheon for the heroes of the socialist movement. This was, however, devised as a tradition for the movement and for the successful Revolution, not for a social order. Legal legitimation was attempted but had to be abandoned. In all the elections after the Bolshevik seizure of power (in the election for the Constituent Assembly, in those of Georgia and the Ukraine) the ruling party suffered a devastating defeat. It became entirely clear that the system of domination ran counter to the will of the vast majority of the people: the authority failed to establish itself as legal. The possibility of a charismatic legitimation was, again, out of the question. Lenin was anything but a charismatic leader — his charisma was a posthumous and ideologically motivated product of his followers. He had never been acknowledged as 'the leader' by the peasant masses (otherwise they would not have voted for the Social Revolution (SR) Party). All Lenin possessed was a very high degree of authority, within his own party. Bukharin seriously considered his temporary arrest and the final consent of Lenin's opponents to his proposal regarding the Brest–Litovsk peace-treaty was not the consequence of his personal charisma but of a rational calculation. Lenin's threat to found a new party unless his proposal was accepted was an act of blackmail based on his enormous authority, and as such, it was contradictory to the image of a charismatic leader. His lack of charisma had little to do with his personality; it was mainly due to the absence of the *Führer-Prinzip* in socialist movements, even in their Bolshevik version. The theory of Plekhanov that 'great personalities only execute historical necessity', which meant that one could always be replaced by another, was deeply rooted in the self-understanding of all socialist parties in the first two decades of this century.

The self-justification of the ruling elite — roughly speaking, of the old guard of the Party and of those who joined the victor, for they considered victory as justification in itself — had been constituted by different, though related, elements. The Party's self-image was that of the executor of a world-historical necessity, of the vanguard of world-revolution, of the repository of the future, of the embodiment of the real interests of the proletariat inside and outside Russia. This self-justification was binding to a very large extent but it did not at the same time imply the recognition of a social order as exemplary. This was principally because the new system of domination was not understood as a permanent social order at all but as the bulwark of coming revolutions, as a prelude to a future world social order. Lenin's remark that after the victory of the European revolution Russia would once again become an underdeveloped country, is very telling in this respect. Except for the expropriation of the previous ruling classes all measures taken were rationalized by the references to the 'emergency state'; the system was understood as temporary. The revolution was not yet completed — it had only just been set in motion.

As we have seen, the reference to the objective interest of the proletariat was a constituent of the self-justification of the regime. Needless to say, that interest in itself is no principle of legitimation even if real interests are used for that purpose. However, during this particular period only the interest of the self-justifying party was real; the interest which it supposedly represented was imaginary to an increasing extent. The language of Lenin was clear: in 1919 he stated: 'We recognize neither freedom, nor equality, nor labour democracy if they are opposed to the cause of the emancipation of labour from the oppression of capital'. In 1921, Radek put it even more bluntly. The workers do not support us, he said, 'but we must not yield, we must impose our will on them'. This language betrays indifference towards legitimation. Despite this indifference, the Bolsheviks at least appealed to the proletariat for its support but they did not ask for the support of the majority of the population, except during the civil war. The bulk of the peasants — the so-called 'middle peasants' — had to be neutralized; that is to say, no legitimation was sought with regard to them, but they were required to withdraw their recognition from the adversary social force.

The civil war had been won not as the result of the generally recognized legitimation of the new regime but as the outcome of the legitimation crisis of the preceding one. The slogan of peace proved to be a good catchword, for the soldiers were tired of war; however, it was not so much this promise as the land reform and repartition of the huge estates that really mattered. The White armies imperilled this achievement in that they represented the old regime. The Mensheviks and the SRs supported the Red side as well: the future under the Bolsheviks was as yet unclear but the Tsarist past was very well-known. Non-Bolshevik socialists could not be certain whether they were going to be crushed by the new power but they could and did know for sure that such a fate had been awaiting them under the old regime. Although the main elements of the new system of domination had been present from October 1917 onwards, the system itself had not been established completely until 1921. At the 10th Party Conference Lenin's motion for the abolition of factions was accepted, as was Radek's proposal to outlaw and crush the Menshevik and the SR parties completely.

The need for the legitimation of the social order became at least partially necessary with the programme of 'socialism in one country'. It is well-known that until then the dictatorship of the proletariat meant terror. The principle of rule by terror, however, is no principle of legitimation. Proclaimed (openly practised) terror is the execution of sheer power and not of domination; in it popular consent is simply bracketed. 'Construction of socialism' was, however, understood as a revolutionary measure which needed the cooperation of the majority. Hence the power had to interpret itself as domination and increasing terrorization could no longer be practised openly. Instead of entering into historical details it will suffice here to point out that Soviet political domination underwent its first legitimation crisis in the twenties. True, the inner-Party debate expressed this crisis in a fairly distorted manner and triggered off basic economic changes at the same time. The outcome of the crisis was the establishment of the totalitarian state. The first milestone in the transformation of the Jacobin dictatorship into a totalitarian despotism was reached, as we have seen, in 1921, and the last in 1929–32 by collectivization. The legitimation crisis finally concluded in a new form of legitimation: the charismatic version.

It is easy to grasp why the inner-Party debates of the twenties were a distorted expression of the legitimation crisis and not simply a struggle for power, although there was a power struggle as well. Trotsky's rejection of the formula of 'socialism in one country' was linked with his endeavour to continue the course of self-justification without any kind of legitimation. He further insisted on open terror on the one hand (more emphatically than Lenin ever did) and on an inner-Party democracy, the spirit of the corps of the ruling elite, on the other. The perpetuation of this warrior attitude only made sense, however, from the perspective of the permanent revolution – inside and out. It is interesting to follow Kamenev's argument against Trotsky's plea for inner-Party democracy. He said: 'For if they say today, let us have democracy in the Party, tomorrow they will say, let us have democracy in the trade unions, the day after tomorrow, workers who do not belong to the Party may well say: give us democracy too . . . and surely then the myriads of peasants could not be prevented from asking for democracy.' Kamenev was but a mere spokesman of Zinoviev's negative attitude towards democracy which was related to the remilitarization of the Party and the programme of forced industrialization in economic policy. From the beginning Bukharin recommended a different kind of legitimation through the raising of living standards and the support lent to the peasantry which may have been devised together with concessions to the masses and consequently with a certain kind of liberalization. Stalin's desire for power was − again from the beginning − related to the desire for charismatic legitimation. That is why the various options of economic policy were of secondary importance for him. Immediately after Lenin's death, he deliberately fabricated a charismatic image of the deceased leader.

However, in the twentieth century charismatic legitimation is inextricably linked to the idea of the totalitarian state: Stalin's charismatic leadership presupposed the totalitarian state and he implemented his project in the most brutal way.

Both Bukharin's and Zinoviev's programmes regarding the need for legitimation were patently of primarily economic character. Here we are confronted with a new attempt at legitimation, namely legitimation through substantive rationality. In recent years, certain experts Eastern European societies (Konrád−Szelenyi, Rigby) have made the theoretical proposal to interpret these societies as being completely or at least chiefly legitimated by the principle of substantive rationality. Let us now briefly analyse this principle.

The categories of goal-rationality, value rationality and substantive rationality are related to action (behaviour). In Weber's view value rationality means that values are acknowledged as valid and accepted as regulative ideas in behaviour and in the assessment of the behaviour of others irrespective of the success of the action in question. Goal-rationality is a proper choice of means to realize a particular goal. In it, rationality is proven by success, in other words by the realization of the goal. Although neo-Weberians modified the meaning of these categories, their basic interpretation remained unchanged. The notion of substantive rationality, mentioned only occasionally by Weber, is less clear. It can be distinguished from value-rationality only if goals themselves are not values, but are set in keeping with the interests of a group (or a class). It can be distinguished from instrumental rationality only if the same goals are 'substantive' in so far as they encompass a well-defined change in the

social structure as a whole, based on a preliminary (mostly scientific) knowledge of all the means employed in order to realize it. The Party did make unjustified claims for substantive rationality by stating on the one hand, that the goal presented by it embodies the interest of the proletariat – the 'masses' – and on the other, that the same (substantive) goal is set according to 'scientific' knowledge about the socialist transformation of society. If one takes substantive rationality seriously, both the failure to represent the clear-cut and manifest interest of the group (class) and the failure to realize the goal (or the 'sub-goals' of the all-encompassing one) reveal the irrationality of the action involved. This is precisely what happened in the case of Bolshevism. As soon as the party started to realize its substantive goal, the very class whose interest it was supposed to represent, turned against it. This class did not recognize its own interest in the interpretation of the Party. The only interest the Party in fact represented was its own, namely the interest of maintaining its own power. For obvious reasons this could not be publicly admitted, and consequently substantive rationality became a mere myth. On the other hand, to claim scientific knowledge in respect of the substantive goal is in principle an ideological overdetermination of scientific prediction. If prediction is taken seriously as prediction, not as an ideological creed, and if one has to admit the unrealizability of the sub-goals – if the inadequacy of means has to be considered – this concern triggers off a kind of rational discussion, at least among the experts. Under such circumstances formal rationality and the pluralism of opinions have to serve at least as corrective principles. In this case, however, the dogma of infallibility cannot persist and the way back to some kind of formal rationality is only a matter of time. As soon as substantive rationality serves only as an ideology for the centralization of economic decisions it becomes a sheer myth – and myth needs mythmakers, as well as the belief in the infallibility of either charismatic or traditional legitimation. Legitimation through tradition was not practicable in the late twenties: the new regime lacked any kind of meaningful tradition in the generally accepted sense. Only two courses remained open: the real acceptance of substantive rationality which sooner or later leads to lawful legitimation (through elections) or the use of substantive rationality exclusively as myth, as an auxiliary form of legitimation complementing the charismatic one. Totalitarian state plus charismatic legitimation together bring about a political order of particular provenance which we are going to call terroristic totalitarianism.
    Jacobin dictatorships can only have a short-term life. In all

probability they may conclude either in terroristic totalitarianism or in the so-called 'Thermidor'. During the Terror of French Jacobinism, one of the leaders, Robert Lindet, had predicted the possibility of a new 'Tamburlaine' and one only has to remember Bukharin's description of Stalin as Genghis Khan to see that the prediction was highly realistic. Trotsky and all the others who explained Stalin's seizure of power as a result of the underdevelopment of Russia missed the important point: in the late twenties only a certain type of terroristic totalitarianism could preserve Lenin's work, and in this respect this was a necessary conclusion of this work. Lenin would not have appreciated this form of preservation, but he would not have appreciated the disappearance of the system created by him either. He had no options.

The idea of substantive rationality was inherited from Marx, which, however, does not account for why this thesis was widely received while others remained neglected. It is obvious though, without going into historical details, that the belief in formal rationality, more precisely in its beneficiary results, had for different reasons been shaken to its foundations in the first three decades of this century. The experience of the disenchantment of the world on the one hand, the vast irrational by-products of formal rationality (world war, economic crises) on the other, prompted a readiness to accept different types of substantive rationality as alternative solutions. In the first place, it motivated the replacement of society by community, formal–legal regulation by direct action, pluralism by homogeneity. Needless to say, these two types of constituents were characteristics – in different ways, with different kinds of ideology – of all totalitarian states, and this despite the considerable difference between the economic and social structure of the respective regimes. Like Stalin, Mussolini and Hitler legitimated their own systems by the confrontation between them and the Western types of capitalist democracy. And like Stalin, Hitler and Mussolini also boasted that they had put an end to unemployment – and all three 'mobilized' the population for 'great industrial achievements' (for example, the Autobahn-network in Germany). Ever since, the ideologies of 'modernization' and 'revolution' as auxiliary forms of legitimation of modern despotic states with single-party systems became fairly widespread, particularly after the Second World War in the former colonies.

In spite of all parallel phenomena, it was the Soviet experiment that fully realized this model, primarily because the ideology of the Bolshevik Party was devised and conceived of as science proper, as the only true science of society, the arcanum of knowledge regarding the necessary advent of the socialist future. Even if it had been applied as myth, it had never been interpreted as such. The leaders of the Party really believed that they were equipped with the only true knowledge and that it was their historical mission to shape the raw material of society in the direction of the historical goal, even when the 'material', that is to say the people, would not yield. This was intended to be a revolutionary transformation of society from above. However, when Party leaders came face to face with the task of economic and social transformation, they became helpless and this was true first of all of Lenin. 'Science' turned out to be impotent when it came to application. In order to totalize a social system the principle of substantive rationality had been applied, but it only proved to be rational politically, not economically or socially. Universal rationality was nothing but an obligatory creed. The terrible waste of human energy and life exceeded the worst fiascos of any misconceived instrumental rationality and the achievement itself had substantially nothing to do with the posited goal. Even the real achievement, the vast though badly organized industry, was officially not allowed to be identified with the goal proper. Stalin in his *The Economic Problems of Socialism in the Soviet Union* rebuked Yaroshenko severely for positing industrial growth as a telos.

However, substantive rationality as ideology did become an auxiliary principle of legitimation. It could not be otherwise, for the irrationality of its application was experienced and observed by anyone with the smallest amount of common sense. Common sense itself had to be eliminated, the senses had to be ideologized, perception had to be distorted in order for mythical substantive rationality to be accepted as rationality. This had been achieved by charismatic legitimation.

We have called the totalitarian state with charismatic legitimation 'terroristic totalitarianism'. However, these two constituents do not necessarily coincide. According to A. Davidson, Italy did not become a totalitarian state until 1926. In the Soviet Union the state was already totalitarian when charismatic legitimation had gradually been established. And after Stalin's death the Soviet Union ceased to be a terroristic totalitarian state but never a totalitarian one.

The distinction between 'totalitarianism' and 'terroristic totalitarianism' is thus an exigency of our times. When the notion was first applied to theoretical and political discourse, totalitarianism was identified with the political terror regimes of Stalin and Hitler. This identification became obsolete after Stalin's death.

It is advisable to accept the definition of totalitarianism formulated by the founding father of totalitarian Fascism. Mussolini wrote: 'The Fascist concept of the state is all-embracing; outside of it no human or spiritual values may exist. Thus understood, Fascism is totalitarian, and the Fascist state, as a synthesis and unit which includes all values, interprets, develops and lends additional power to the whole life of the people.' Thus totalitarianism is identical with political society (submission and liquidation of civil society), with the elimination of any kind of recognized pluralism. Pluralism of values may, of course, exist but it is outlawed and persecuted. The degree of punishment may vary in different countries and at different historical times but the principle remains the same.

The notion of totalitarianism denotes a system of political domination and this is why it defines the socio-economic structure from only one aspect. Quite different socio-economic structures can be totalitarian in the same way. Likewise, the term 'Asiatic despotism' does not give an account of the particular socio-economic structure of a country, only of its system of domination. Moreover, although we obviously prefer all types of liberal—legal state to totalitarian ones, we do not use this notion with a necessarily unambiguously evaluative content. There are, even in our present times, non-totalitarian societies (military dictatorships, for example) which are in many respects far worse than Mussolini's totalitarian state.

Charisma legitimates totalitarian systems in all cases when they cannot be legitimated by tradition. Hitler was a charismatic personality, Stalin was not, although he created his charismatic image no less successfully. Charisma means a quasi-religious creed whose basic tenet is belief in the omnipotence of a personality, not just his superiority. Omnipotence has to be proven on a daily basis by the mobilization of the masses for ever-new victories. The image of permanent dangers which can only be overcome by the wisdom and will-power of the Führer is an integral part of charisma's creed. If there are no real dangers, substitutes have to be created. Moreover, the creed has to be the creed of the masses — and this presupposes the distortion of rationality, of common sense, of everyday perception. Finally, *there is no creed without generating universal fear.*

In saying that terroristic totalitarianism was the necessary outcome of Jacobin terror if Lenin's work was to be preserved, we did not mean to imply that the unbelievable dimensions of Stalin's mass terror were necessary as well. The more than 20 millions exterminated (according to Conquest) by the leader, were victims of this particular leader; their fate cannot be explained by the social system alone.

However, the terroristic totalitarian system in the Soviet Union could not have been established without a great number of victims, principally because the perpetuated war had to be an 'inner-directed' one. The Soviet Union of that time was too weak to start a war against its 'outward' enemies and it was wise of Stalin not to risk power in any such venture. On the other hand, he established a terroristic totalitarian system, as is always the case, with a single party. But this single party was not totally ready for its task.

Despite military discipline, overcentralization and readiness to wipe out whole groups of the population which were labelled as 'class enemy', the Party Stalin inherited was far from appropriate for the implementation of terroristic totalitarianism. A leadership appropriate for such a task has to consist of unscrupulous murderers, and the Bolshevik leaders, although prone to exercise mass terror, did have certain scruples. For example, they opted for decreased terrorization in the aftermath of collectivisation, even though this contradicted the terrorist totalitarian type of rule. There was no Führer-Prinzip in the Party. A famous joke which circulated in the higher ranks of the Party after the Kirov assassination testifies to this.

One day Stalin summoned Radek, who was well-known as a cynic and given to spelling out things which others did not even dare to think of. Stalin said to him, 'I was informed, comrade Radek, that you are speaking of me in an ironical manner. Have you forgotten that I am the leader of the world proletariat?'

'Sorry, comrade Stalin,' Radek replied, 'this particular joke was not my invention.'

Moreover, the system of domination that parties of terroristic totalitarianism had in mind before seizing power was practically identical with what they subsequently realized, but this was not so in the case of the Bolsheviks. From the socialist movements they had inherited traditional humanistic ideas which they did not observe in practice but whose validity they did not question. The first Bolshevik leaders were not brought up to be hostile to democracy but rather to hate Tsarist autocracy. The direct democracy of the early Soviets did not vanish completely either: minds once trained to rational discussion could not be re-educated by a simple declaration of creed.

Of course, unrestrained ruthlessness against both the actual and the potential enemy, and readiness to silence all dissent both inside and outside the Party by coercion predetermined the Bolshevik Party so that it was easily transformed into a terroristic totalitarian one. None the less it had to be transformed. Conquest's notion that by 1934 Stalin planned to transform the Party into an obedient tool by means of exterminating the majority of its leaders and a huge percentage of its membership, and that he took the idea from Hitler's way of treating Röhm and his comrades, may well be true. However, mass support for such a procedure could be achieved only by mass terrorization, by regular, consecutive periods of hysteria and relief and by Stalin's own skill in making people believe that whereas others were responsible for the phases of rise in terror, he himself bore exclusive responsibility for its phases of decline. As he succeeded in making almost the entire country co-responsible for all the crimes committed, his charismatic legitimation was thus also based on the natural instinct for self-defence. Not only the beneficiaries of terror hailed his name: so did the victims. Starving and humiliated in the concentration camps before their execution, they blessed their executioner. And even those who hated him ascribed everything to his personality, to the superhuman wickedness of his nature. Charismatic legitimation had completed its course.

In the charismatic type of legitimation the legitimation of the system and of the leader is one and the same; the leader is the symbolic incorporation of the system. The so-called 'personality cult' is only an expression of this identity. Hence only terroristic totalitarianism, not totalitarianism as such, makes it impossible to differentiate the regime from the ruler.

Charismatic legitimation in the Soviet Union became historically obsolete after the victory in the Second World War. From that moment on the same system of domination could have been legitimated in a different way as well; government and system could have been differentiated, and so the elite could have governed without resorting to the terroristic totalitarian type of rule. Moreover, in a sense it could only survive by having transformed a terroristic totalitarianism into a non-terroristic one.

However, this transformation did not take place at once. Terroristic totalitarian regimes disappear either with the death of their leaders or by defeat in war. Whether or not Stalin was insane in the last years of his rule remains undisclosed. What we do know is that he continued to act according to a terroristic totalitarian logic, at least after a historical moment of hesitation. He kept artifically creating crises, producing scapegoats both inside and outside the country in a new wave of extermination. He was co-responsible with the Western powers for the Cold War and with China for the 'hot' war in Korea, he set up regimes after his own image in the occupied territories, once again sent millions into camps and recommenced the assassination of his own loyal guard. The latter event is telling from our point of view. After the 'Yeshovshchina', he never endangered his close collaborators — they were his creatures. The unexpected change in his behaviour may have been due to a hidden crisis of legitimation after the war. One may be right in assuming that Stalin's entourage felt the change and tried to put an end to the complete identity of the system with its leader. The convocation of the 19th Party Congress with Malenkov as the new speaker could be seen as the corroboration of this thesis. However, what was the second legitimation crisis in Soviet history became overt only after Stalin's death. In this respect it would be particularly interesting to know whether he was murdered or died a natural death.

Terroristic totalitarianism died with Stalin, not because no one else qualified for charismatic leadership but because it became superfluous during Stalin's own lifetime. Even during its period of mourning, the country felt a deep sense of relief.

Khrushchev drew the obvious consequences from the situation by terminating wars both inside and outside the Soviet Union. Prisoners were released from the camps, the politics of détente were launched. In order to effect an open break with terroristic totalitarianism the image of the charismatic leader had to be annihilated. Only those who have never lived in a terroristic totalitarian state can underestimate the symbolism of renaming Stalingrad and removing the embalmed 'father of the nation' from the Mausoleum in Red Square.

The charismatic type of legitimation had now been discarded. Negative legitimation, with which we are familiar from the times of Lenin's Jacobinism, was again out of the question. It would not only have meant a break with Stalin but also a break with the whole system of domination legitimated by his charisma. It would rather have been a prelude to a new system of domination which contradicted the interests of the ruling group, including Khrushchev. (It is true that some of the Communist leaders, above all Imre Nagy, acted counter to Krushchev's intention by accepting a different system of domination based on the sovereignty of the people.)

Khrushchev was an experimenting spirit, a man who was constantly effecting change. If one looks at his different experiments and projects it becomes clear that even his most impracticable ideas were somehow related to the realization of substantive rationality. His greatest ambition was to surpass the most developed capitalist countries in *per capita* production and thus attain the promised land of Communism. He even forecast the exact date when this would supposedly happen. Krushchev promised more production of consumer goods and better living standards; he initiated new, even if ill-conceived, plans for the rapid increase of agricultural production; when he was in the United States, he boasted of the superiority of the planning mind. For the second time in Soviet history substantive rationality had been proposed as the main type of legitimation. Once again it failed, and for the same reasons.

Almost all ruling strata are capable of overcoming their legitimation crises if these can be overcome at all. But in the case of the Soviet Union in the 1960s no mastermind was needed to accomplish this task. The Party leaders were simply never shaken in their firm conviction of their right to rule by virtue of tradition. The Party had ruled the country for half a century: it had already created a socio-economic structure that was completely adequate to the system of domination. As a result of the subsequent waves of extermination no alternative political forces were left in the country. The Russian Empire won its greatest victory since the Napoleonic wars. The Soviet Union gradually became a superpower, an equal partner of the United States, making co-decisions on the fate of the world, and increasing its own sphere of influence, and once again this happened under *their rule*. It is no wonder that self-legitimation by tradition appeared to them as natural. Reliance on tradition was self-evident for the ruling elite and not a shrewd scheme devised in order to obtain mass support. Legitimation by tradition was more than self-legitimation, it became legitimation proper.

Legitimation by tradition

The new traditional legitimation is a combination of two traditions: that of the Russian (national) one and that of the Soviet rule since 1917. Stalin had begun to experiment with reintroducing the idea of a nationalist Great Russia as an auxiliary form of legitimation. In his view of history, however, the figures of great dictators and 'modernizers' served as paradigms, as the archaic Russian forerunners of his charismatic leadership — Ivan the Terrible, Peter the Great and other military leaders, the conquerors with whom he once again identified himself. In the recent type of traditional legitimation Nation and Empire are more emphatic and the responsible part of the ancient ruling elite gets its share of recognition. But the part of traditional legitimation directly compared to the Soviet tradition is the overwhelming one. An exclusively nationalist tradition runs the risk of challenging non-Russian nations, the danger of which in a multi-national country did not escape the leaders' vigilance.

In order to legitimate the system of domination by Soviet tradition, the latter has to be conceived of as a continuity. The immense resistance to Khrushchev's de-Stalinization by the Party leadership was not the result of any Stalinist creed or inclination on the part of the ruling stratum. As we have said, terroristic totalitarianism died with Stalin. In fact it was already obsolete before his death and no one could or would reintroduce it. Quite fundamental interests have been involved in this common decision to bury Stalin's system of government: after all, every one prefers to die a natural death instead of being tortured, hanged or shot. However, the vehemence of de-Stalinization, the persistent investigation of past crimes, endangered traditional legitimation, for it could bring into question the leaders' right to rule. That is why they had to get rid of the legacy of the 20th Congress, even though the revelations of past crimes during the 20th and 22nd Congresses fell far short of exposing what really happened. But even this small degree of exposure was more than sufficient for the traditional legitimation. For the purposes of self-legitimation and legitimation proper the rulers had to turn the page dealing with Stalin in the book of history and erase him from popular memory as well. They did so with success. In a meeting with young people seven years ago, Yevtushenko made an improvised survey regarding their estimation of the number of Stalin's victims: he was told that there had probably been as many as thousands.

Legitimation by tradition implies conservatism and the present Soviet Union can well be characterized by this denomination. It is ruled by a 'gerontocracy'. All social and economic experiments, typical of all preceding periods, are now banned. The slightest change is rejected, even promised reforms are not realized. Culture is completely fossilized, family life and education are conservative to a degree. The state has not, of course, lost its totalitarian character, pluralism is not less outlawed, but this tradition had to be formalized too. Formalization became necessary because reference to the emergency state is no longer feasible in traditional legitimation.

What is the secret of the Soviet leaders' success with their traditionalism? The answer is that the present system of domination in the Soviet Union is in fact traditional and is accepted as such.

It is common knowledge that there had never been a democratic system in Russia. There were, however, movements towards direct and representative democracy. Needless to say, under Stalin all those forces were successively exterminated. No father remained to convey a different image of rule to his children. In addition, the relative number of those who had participated in the Russian people's first attempts at self-emancipation, in the revolutions of 1905 and February 1917, in the soviets and in the government agencies between February and October 1917 was small, and consequently there had been constant signals predicting that the Revolution would be 'betrayed'. The silent acceptance of whimsical decisions on the part of the authorities, the myth of the sacred ruler, the attitude of meeting calamities with passive endurance, the belief in fate that cannot be changed, in other words the behavioural patterns of serfdom, were deeply rooted in a population moulded by centuries of autocratic rule. These habitual modes of behaviour had to be reinforced in order to cast the relatively new democratic pattern into complete oblivion. Today even those who are aware that democracy may be an alternative system of domination no longer have the social imagination to grasp what this really means. All habits, attitudes and abilities, even language itself were created by totalitarianism, which has become part of everyday life and second nature to the human beings living under it. Their dissatisfaction with it does not contradict the lamentable fact that the system became natural for its oppressed subjects. Nothing illustrates this more clearly than the attitude of a substantial number of dissenters. Of course, every dissenting opinion has a progressive function in a totalitarian state, and every open act of dissent even more so. Having said this, one should immediately add that a considerable number of the dissenters are characterized by a belief in the superiority of the old Russian way of life over the so-called decadence of the West, a contempt for democratic procedures, the rules of civility and formal rationality, and by their predilection for obscurantist world-views, quasi-religious beliefs in catastrophe and redemption, and the paternalistic way of handling issues. One can see from the way the most determined of the dissidents look at the world how difficult (if not wholly impossible) it is to recover from certain social ills.

Differences between the Soviet Union and Eastern Europe

The types of legitimation in Eastern European countries can be conceived as miniaturized imitations of those in the Soviet Union, though in different sequences and variations. However, there is a main divergence which cannot be neglected. In certain Eastern European countries — initially in Poland and Hungary, and later on even in Czechoslovakia — the mass basis of legitimation has never been so broad as in the Soviet Union. It was roughly identical with Party membership at least until the death of Stalin. From then on, however, an important change can be observed. We have already mentioned that one of the main functions of Party membership is to legitimate the system. The Party membership is selected in such a way that it has blindly to accept the system of domination as exemplary and binding. But in Eastern European countries this function has been lost. The private conviction of the Party members differs in no way from the opinion of those who never joined the Party. The leaders are perfectly well aware of this and that is why they are increasingly interested only in the public performances of the Party members. Moreover, that is why they no longer use the Party as a body of legitimation in its entirety. Thus self-legitimation has become identical with the self-legitimation of leading function-aries, bureaucrats and members of the top technocracy.

The second feature of the way the Eastern European pattern differs from the Soviet paradigm is that in Eastern European countries nationalism, national power and dignity could never have been used successfully as forms of auxiliary legitimation. Such attempts have been made and have been rejected with contempt by the population of the occupied countries: these attempts could become a – relative – success only in Rumania, the only Eastern European country that plays at sham-independence and that has never ceased to retain certain 'Mussolinist' features of totalitarianism.

Almost all the Eastern European countries established a pluralistic-legal state after the Second World War, though limited by the presence of the Soviet Army and its direct interventions in the balance of power. In keeping with Stalin's plan these regimes were transformed into terroristic totalitarian states. Mini-Stalins were created, whose artificial charisma was but the emanation of the charisma of the 'Father of the Peoples'. They could be dismissed, imprisoned and murdered by him, and even their show-trials were fabricated by a foreign secret police. Not even their fellow-murderers believed in them, they knew that they were nonentities, they played a role in a drama whose origins were unknown to the population and even to the Party members. Here too terroristic totalitarianism died with Stalin – abruptly in Hungary and slowly in the other countries. The legitimation crisis, however, could not be solved here.

For a while, after the crushing of the 1956 revolution, Hungary repeated the Leninist model of self-justification. The Kádár govern-ment in its early period made use of a negative legitimation. It constantly referred to the legitimation crisis of the preceding government (to the crimes of the 'Rákosi clique' and the 'counter-revolution'), and combined these references with open terrorization. The transformation of the then prevailing type of legitimation into a traditional one had to face unresolvable difficulties in all Eastern European countries. The only tradition the rulers could conjure up was not their own but that of the Soviet Union. That is why the 'leading role' of the Soviet party and the 'national way to socialism' had to be accepted and professed simultaneously. The gap could be bridged only by extensive pure pragmatism. The ruling stratum insists, of course, on its right to rule, but the question of what gives it the right to rule is not raised sincerely, if at all. Allusions to the 'division of the world' as a fact, to the necessity of the Soviet presence, to 'order' as such (identified, of course, with the existing order), in other words, rationalization through interests, are part and parcel of increased pragmatism. Defensive and shaky self-legitimation makes the rulers susceptible to auxiliary forms. In Hungary pragmatism is supplemented by the well-known remedy of legitimation through substantive rationality. The government established by Khrushchev could never completely rid itself of the marks of its heritage.

But — as has already been argued — legitimation through substantive rationality fails of necessity. If it aims at transcending the limits of self-legitimation, that is to say, to be professed as a sheer myth, it has to reintroduce a certain amount of formal rationality, a kind of pluralism, and finally it has to tolerate the transformation into a different system of domination. If this is not the case (and it would mean the abandonment of domination on the part of the ruling strata, which would be an impossibility) substantive rationality has no legitimizing power. It eventually rationalizes the pragmatism of the government, a rationalization which occasionally has to be combined with the bare and brutal display and use of non-legitimate power, once again in a pragmatic way. That is why the permanence of the legitimation crisis in Eastern Europe is not only due to the presence of the image of an alternative and at the same time exemplary system of domination in the social fantasy of the population, but also to the incapability of the ruling strata to elaborate a meaningful and binding formula of self-legitimation and to the lack of a party to internalize and represent it publicly. These three constituents are interconnected and shape the pattern of the whole.

CHAPTER 5

The System of Domination

Sovereignty

The Soviet state was originally defined by its rulers as the state of 'workers and peasants', and later on as the state of 'the people'. The principle of the people's sovereignty has, however, never been accepted, not even formally, within the Soviet state. Although the question of sovereignty and of the system of domination are not identical with one another, the second cannot be answered without the first. Hence in order to define above all the structure of domination, the following dilemma must be resolved: what (or who) is the source of all powers in the Soviet Union?

Let us start with a commonly known fact: the Soviet Union is a one-party political system. A 'one-party system' does not necessarily mean that there is only one party in the country. A one-party system can be identified by the following characteristics:
(1) All powers (executive, legislative, judiciary) are centralized.
(2) All public issues (economic, social, cultural and political) are decided by that central authority.
(3) The central authority is identical with the supreme organs of the party.
(4) The supreme organs are only elected by the members of the party.
(5) All other organizations (elected or appointed) are controlled by the party on every level (local, national, all-Union) and should represent and execute the supreme will. Thus a one-party system excludes by definition all organizations with essentially alternative programmes in the field of politics, culture, economy, etc. and with it also the possibility to propose such alternatives. It excludes at the same time contractual relations among individuals and collectives independently of the state. A one-party system oppresses civil society. Its ideal type, its overt (or hidden) goal is totalization, the complete submission of society to the state.

Obviously, the totalization of society does not take the same course in different totalitarian societies. In Fascist Italy or in Nazi Germany the state had to subjugate an already existing civil society, whereas in the Soviet Union civil society was only *in statu nascendi* at the time of the Bolshevik take-over. The elimination of private property was not aimed at by Fascist Italy and Nazi Germany, only by the Soviet Union. One can, however, observe a feature common to all types of totalization, namely, that the ideological aims of the totalizing party have to be modified by some economic exigencies. The Nazis could not realize their original anti-plutocratic creed, and the Strasser group, which had taken the original ideology seriously, had to be exterminated. The Bolshevik Party was compelled by the same necessity to reintroduce some quasi-market-relationships — once again, counter to the original ideological creed.

Critics of the Soviet regime often wonder why the duplication of all central institutions in 'Party' and 'state' organs is necessary. They argue that the submission of civil society by the state can be accomplished by the state alone. This is, however, an unacceptable assumption. A cursory glance at the duplex power will suffice to convince any reasonable spectator that its parts do not have equal authority and influence. The basic principle of the Soviet type of domination and at the same time the only one which has been realized in practice consequently in all periods of Soviet history is *the leading role of the party*. All basic decisions are within the exclusive reach of Party institutions and all state organs are subordinated to them. This being the case, duplication of power seems then to be superfluous, for there is no need for state institutions. This again is a wrong assumption. Although everything is decided by the Party, the Party cannot rule without the state institutions. What, then, is the particular function of the Party? Simply this: in the one-party system the party is the sovereign, it is the source of all powers.

Formally, the sovereign is identical with the Party as a whole, that is to say, with the sum total of its card-carrying members. They elect their representatives, in an indirect way, for the Party Congress, (which is the parliament of the Party), and they elect the ruling bodies (the government of the Party). Many important posts of the leading organs are occupied by appointment.

Already from the 'ideal type' of party sovereignty it follows first, that the people's sovereignty is excluded in it, and second, that the majority of the population has no say whatsoever — not even formally — in the most decisive question of the system of domination, namely, regarding who will rule them. No census before the institutionalization of universal suffrage could have restricted the right of voting and of being elected to a larger extent than the one prevailing in 'the people's state'.

There is, however, an immense gap between the ideal of the Party sovereignty and its reality. (Of course, there is a gap between the ideal of the people's sovereignty and its realization in Western countries as well, but of a different kind.) In this respect, it is important to note that the Bolshevik Party and the parties created in its image have never been democratic. The principle of the so-called 'democratic centralism' already criticized by Rosa Luxemburg, was a principle of overcentralization from the start. Overcentralization implies the exclusion of the most important element of democracy: in it there is no room for the rights of the minority. Even the majority rule was observed — in the periods when it was observed at all — only at the top: the lower echelons were militarized and the rank and file in the party had no choice but to obey.

The organization of factions was forbidden as from 1921 and alternative political programmes could not be circulated, not even among Party members. The minority of the Political Bureau or the Secretariat could never appeal directly to the sovereign proper (the Party membership). More precisely it was attempted only once by Trotsky, which in itself was a sign of being new to the Bolshevik power apparatus. When a Party Congress is being convoked, the upshot has already been decided by the leading organs. In other words, the totalitarian type of rule was practised within the Party before it was realized in the country. Further, there is a basic difference in the functioning of the people's sovereignty and the Party sovereignty. No leader can 'choose' a population for himself; the Party membership, however, is chosen by the Party leadership itself. The constitution, the programme and the organizational principles of a party are formulated by those who establish and who run it. Hence the sovereignty of the Soviet system of dominance was the actual derivative of the leader's will, and the party is a sovereign without power: it is the source of all powers in name only, not in reality. This in itself is not an unusual phenomenon. Kings in modern democracies are nominally sovereigns of the nation, though they have no power of their own and are not sources of all powers either. In the case of modern monarchy, the people's sovereignty prevails in reality, though not in name. In the case of the Soviet Union, there is a nominal Party sovereignty, but in practice it is the leading bodies of the Party (the apparatus) that function as the real sovereigns.

The sovereign and the state

With Louis XIV, the Party leadership can rightly say: 'L'état, c'est moi.' It is quite significant in this respect that criticism of Party leaders — not only of their policies, but also of their responsibilities — gossiping about disputes or internecine strife in higher circles, or telling irreverent jokes about them, is labelled as '*crime against the state*'. It is always more dangerous to criticize the First Secretary than the Prime Minister or the President of the state. There is no doubt about who is the real master.

The identity of the sovereign (the Party leadership) and the state can best be demonstrated by a short analysis of the four Soviet Constitutions. Three of the Constitutions (that of Soviet Russia in 1918, and those of the Soviet Union of 1923—4, and of 1977) analyse in their preambles the world situation, the goals of the state and its leading principles in exactly the same way as the Party Conferences and Congresses of the periods in question. Chapter V/9 of the First Constitution speaks for itself: 'During the actual phase of transition the fundamental task of the Constitution of the USSR consists in establishing the dictatorship of the proletariat of the cities and the countryside, in the form of an all-Russian Soviet power . . . and in *establishing socialism in which there will be no division of classes, nor state power*.' Chapter 11 of the Fundamental Law of the state prescribed as the task to ensure the victory of socialism in all countries. The Second Constitution states: '. . . the unstable character of the international situation and the danger of a new aggression make the creation of the military front of the Soviet Republics inevitable in the face of capitalist encirclement.' The last Constitution of the Soviet Union (1977) states among other things: 'The fundamental tasks of the state are the following: to create the material and technological basis of Communism, to perfect the social relations of socialist type and transform them into Communist ones and to form the man of Communist society'. The same article declares that '. . . the Soviet people is guided by the ideas of scientific Communism and remains loyal to its revolutionary tradition.'

Of course, all constitutions have substantive elements; civil rights themselves are formal and substantive at the same time. However, if concrete guidelines for a future economic, political, social and, more-over, world-historical development are set down as the function of a state in its fundamental law, this excludes all further discussions, because the guidelines themselves are binding for the subjects; thus all different goals, values, programmes with regard to the development of the society are by the same token considered as anti-constitutional. The programme of the Party (irrespective of whether real or imaginary) is a law for the state. Even the freedom of organization — guaranteed in the 1918 Constitution — could be granted, in principle, only for those who were organized to carry out the substantive goals set down in the constitution, in other words the programme of the Party. It may be astonishing at first glance, that the only Soviet Constitution which resembles a real one is that of 1936 worded by Bukharin and authorized by Stalin during the great purges. It has much too often been contended that the 1936 'Stalin'-Constitution was merely a trick, a rather skilful piece of camouflage for tourists or fellow-travellers abroad. But this ingenious contraption deceived only those who sought for self-deception. The Constitution of 1936 is the only one in a long series of similar documents that localizes the sovereign precisely. Article 126 says that the Communist Party 'presents the leading nucleus of all workers' and state organizations'. This is very clear language. The right of organization guaranteed by the same Constitution can be read only in the following way: everyone has the right to join all social or state organizations which are directed by the party (they are even listed in the constitution).

The identity of sovereign and state is, however, called absolutism, hence the Soviet Union can be described as an absolutist state without using an excessively journalistic phrase. This particular kind of absolutism is characterized by a constitutional legalization of the absolutist rule. Hence its correct description is a *contradictio in adjecto*: constitutional absolutism in which it is not absolutism but 'constitutionalization' that calls for explanation.

In absolutist states the sovereign is the acme of social life; its orders have to be carried out in all state and social institutions. But the administration of a huge body of state cannot be handled by the sovereign alone. In old-time absolutist states the low-level agencies of administration were inherited and simply transformed by a new bureaucracy in order to execute the will of the sovereign. Soviet absolutism, however, is an outcome of a revolution which has destroyed all forms of traditional organization so that an entirely new one has had to be created. The easiest thing to do was to transform the institutions which emerged in the wake of the revolution, namely the Soviets, into the bodies of administration. They were tamed by, and submitted to, the sovereign in order to execute the latter's will. In no way could the nominal sovereign as administrative body be used, for different reasons. In the beginning this was practically impossible: taming the Soviets in itself aroused resistance and rebellions (for instance, in Kronstadt); disbanding them would have led to a complete withdrawal of support from the state on the part of all workers and poor peasants. In addition the administration of the state by the nominal sovereign would have led to an increase in the number of the Party membership, endangering all other functions of the Party listed under the heading of its 'leading role'.

In short, the new system of administration had, perforce, to render itself legal and this is precisely what has been accomplished by the Constitutions. It is worth mentioning that in the first two Constitutions of Soviet Russia and the Soviet Union there was a latent (and again nominal) contradiction between the absolutist character of the state and the structure of state administration formally based on the Soviets. The absolutist state is always emanative, but the indirect elections to the supreme bodies of the state (Soviets) legalized an administrative system with a different logic, with that of the shabby remnants of direct democracy (from the bottom to the top). The 1936 Constitution resolved this contradiction again by introducing direct elections at the top, and thus the emanative logic of the system became coherent. All members of the Supreme Soviet are nominated by the sovereign before the poll takes place and the poll itself becomes nothing but a comedy. The concrete outcome of the poll had been fixed too by the Party leadership prior to the actual event which is in this sense a purely symbolic act. The joke that the elections in Eastern European states allow the population to choose between two white elephants is a correct assessment of the gist of the matter. But all this confirms that the 1936 Constitution cannot be regarded as a simple device of deception. The duplication of institutions in 'Party' and 'state' organizations and the total subordination of the latter to the former belongs to the basic structural features of constitutional absolutism. It cannot function in any other way.

In the foregoing the Soviet state has been defined as 'constitutional' absolutism with Party sovereignty. All absolutist states make attempts to totalize society, in other words, to homogenize a system of values, patterns of behaviour and institutional procedures according to the will of the state, society's sovereign ruler. Absolutist kings always crushed religious dissent ruthlessly, for the state religions were the state ideologies of their times. They either tamed or liquidated all social forces and institutions which attempted to remain relatively independent of the state — the self-organizations of the estates no less than the first germs of civil society. They, too, 'modernized' society according to economic plans and conceptions, pushed through industrialization at the point of the sword. De Tocqueville hinted at the similarities between Jacobin terror and *ancien régime* French absolutism. Pipes and Szamuely, on the other hand, pointed out the resemblance of Tsarist absolutism of the old Russia to the Soviet state. It is no accident that Soviet historiography and literature promoted and fostered the idea of progressive absolutism and that Stalin recognized his own forerunner and kindred spirit in Ivan the Terrible.

The dimension and degree of totalization is, however, not always the same. It has to be more complete in societies which have already been familiar with political pluralism, either in its actual or, at least, in its ideological forms. In a sense, modern absolutist states have had to become totalitarian in order to survive.

The widespread concept of the totalitarian state can be accepted for purposes of systematization although it does not describe the phenomenon correctly. The absolutist state does totalize but it is not the state that is totalitarian, rather it is the society which is being totalized by the state. Totalitarian societies are political societies, even though not all political societies are totalitarian ones. Political society means the identity of the private and public sectors, the identity of man and *citoyen* (or subject), a society where there are no life manifestations outside the state. The political society is totalitarian only in the extent to which this identity has not developed in an organic way, but has arbitrarily been superimposed on a society which already distinguished between state and society. This reunification has to be effected by a central power which represents only one political alternative among the many that exist and thus excludes all others by force. Thus in a totalitarian society the identification of public and private goes hand-in-hand with the definition of the obligatory creed and politics of the subject by the state. In short, society is totalitarian if pluralism is outlawed in it.

But pluralism can only be outlawed if it has existed previously. No totalitarianism has ever existed without prior pluralism. In the main, this fact remains hidden in terroristic totalitarian states for there fear is too great and dissent withdraws into the most intimate recesses of private life, into the very minds of individuals. The suppressed existence of pluralism becomes, however, explicit in post-terroristic totalitarianism. Pluralism of values, even political pluralism make their public appearance, as it were — to different degrees and at different times, in different states, of course, but practically universally. The totalitarian state can evolve a kind of pluralism-tolerance whose barriers vary according to the will and calculation of the leading organs of the party. Pluralism-tolerance is a concession to the civil society which can legally be withdrawn at any moment, pluralism being outlawed, even in times of concessions. Soviet peasants can take an aeroplane every day if they wish and carry their baskets of flowers or fruit and vegetables to Moscow, for the second market is virtually tolerated. But they cannot know which day the police may knock at their door to arrest them for having done something which was tolerated yesterday but no longer is today. Intellectuals can distribute their oppositional writings if this is tolerated; but there is no telling whether the state will strike back, and if so, when and how. All present Eastern European societies are totalitarian, independently of the degree of their pluralism-tolerance. In them, pluralism has been outlawed to just as great an extent as before and this is precisely what totalitarianism by definition means.

This situation is correctly reflected in the Soviet Constitution of 1977 (and in other Eastern European Constitutions too, such as the Hungarian). According to the wording of the Constitution (articles 50, 51):

Freedom of expression, of the press, of coalition, of meetings and street demonstrations are guaranteed to the citizens of the USSR in conformity with the interests of the toiling masses and in order to consolidate the socialist regime. The citizens of the USSR have the right to associate in the social organizations, in conformity with the objectives of the construction of Communism.

It has been mentioned already that contrary to the 1936 Constitution and following the patterns of those of 1918 and 1923—4, the 1977 Constitution includes a description of the substantive goals of the state. On the other hand, the 1977 Constitution is characterized by a greater degree of formalization than the seemingly real Constitution of 1936. This is apparently a contradiction, but only apparently. The Constitution of 1936, through its famous article 126, nullified the validity of all other articles concerning human rights. The formal character of the Constitution was spurious, for it gave a list of all the organizations that could be joined, together with the leading role of the Party. The articles in the 1977 Constitution quoted above restrict human rights, but the constitution does not give the list of the organizations which a citizen can join and in which — exclusively — one is allowed to profess one's opinion. In other words, the specific degree and content of freedom of speech and self-organization is not defined, whereas the demand that it has to conform to the substantive goals of the state is. Hence it is a matter of definition, whether or not a particular act or idea conforms to these substantive goals. The definition is, again, in the hand of the sovereign, of the Party leadership. Hence pluralism is wholly outlawed, but the sovereign can rule in all given cases, what particular action should be defined as dissent. The same act can be defined as being in accordance or at variance with the construction of Communism according to the will, decision and pragmatic calculation of the Party leadership.

The outlawing of pluralism is fundamental to all totalitarian societies. As a result everything that does not conform to the values, goals and will of the sovereign is outlawed in these societies. By implication, the measure and content of what is considered illegal depends on the goals, values and will of the sovereign as well. Thus in different totalitarian societies varying types of actions, organizations and values are outlawed, and to a varying extent. To support a Jew in Fascist Italy was not considered illegal as it was in Fascist Germany for the simple reason that anti-semitism did not belong to the accepted ideology (value-system) of the Italian Fascist Party, whereas it was fundamental to its German counterpart. Moreover, if a number of societies are totalized, this does not imply their socio-economic identity. The ideology of the Bolshevik Party included the nationalization of industry and the liquidation of all forms of private enterprise. In order to totalize society and to fulfil the original social mission of Bolshevism, private enterprise (individual as well as collective or communal property) had to be eliminated and a new mode of administering production had to be established. The ideology of the Fascist Parties did not include this programme; that is why in their case totalization could be politically all-embracing without touching the basic structure of capitalist economy. But it is worth mentioning that Fascist Parties started to control production to an ever-increasing extent as well. Mussolini ended his career with a large-scale nationalization of Italian industry, and war emergency, an organic ingredient in Fascism, also took complete control over economic life in Germany.

Bearing in mind, however, the basic values of the Bolshevik Party, it makes sense to argue that in the times of the NEP Soviet society was not a totalitarian one. A restricted degree of economic pluralism was recognized by law which, of course, contradicted the basic principles of the sovereign and can in retrospect be considered only as a temporary tactical move inspired by pragmatic considerations. Since that was the political and ideological, but not the economic, will of the sovereign, totalization was not totalization proper. The Bukharin group had no objection whatsoever to complete totalization. Its basic argument was of a pragmatic nature: it considered the Soviet economy was not yet ripe for economic totalization. That is why it has been argued in the previous chapter, that the totalization of Soviet society went on over an extended period. Before 1921 this society was not totalized at all. It was during that year that the totalization of the Party and the political-ideological totalization of the whole country was launched, but society as a whole became totalitarian only in the process of forced collectivization, in the real abolition of free enterprise both individual and collective. Real abolition is mentioned here because the land had been nationalized in 1918 and was used only by those who cultivated it; we speak also of the abolition of individual and communal free enterprise, because not only the peasants' own land was appropriated, but also the land of the free communes which had been established during or immediately after the Revolution too. This totalization meant two million human beings lost their lives — some were killed and some perished in the subsequent famine. However, the will of the sovereign was executed.

The will of the sovereign is not generally very elastic, but a certain degree of elasticity is not excluded. In the terroristic-totalitarian period of Soviet history it was altogether rigid, indeed it acted on whim. Worst of all, it was so elusive that no one knew precisely what the sovereign's will really consisted of, at least within a given framework. Then the same will became less capricious and somewhat more elastic, both within the Soviet Union and, more markedly, in several Eastern European countries. This was mostly the case as far as non-political cultural creation was concerned. As to increased elasticity in economic life, it is worth mentioning that the small peasant's private ownership is no longer illegal in Eastern European countries, that Hungarian cooperatives are far from being identical with the *kolkhoz* model of Soviet collective farms, etc. Private enterprise in social services is once more legally recognized. Forced industrialization with the obligatory primacy of Department I (heavy industry) has been terminated, plans are more or less adapted to the limits of exploitability of natural resources. Economic reforms with the objective of decreasing the irrationality of over-centralization were launched, even though they were never realized. It is not completely out of the question that in the economic sphere the ruling elite at least tries to replace totalization by the hegemony of the state in society. This in itself is a sign of weakening self-legitimation and runs counter to the logic of the system of domination itself.

CHAPTER 6

The Structure of Power

The Party leadership is the source of all power. This is identical with the assertion that all power emanates from the Party leadership, but not with the other assertion that different organizations would have no power at all. The sovereign is the only independent power in the sense that all other powers are dependent on it. No power can be exercised against the Party, but all emanated power can be exercised against the population. The relation between the centre that emanates power and between the organs that receive such power cannot change in the Soviet system of domination, for such a fundamental power balance constitutes its very essence. What can, however, be changed are:
(1) The balance of powers inside the party leadership, hence the type of rule.
(2) The balance between the emanated powers.
(3) The modes of the execution of powers.
(4) The mechanism of feedback to the emanating power.

Types of rule

Three different types of rule can be easily distinguished in Soviet history: *aristocratic, autocratic* and *oligarchic*.

The application of such terminology needs some explanation. It is perhaps bizarre to describe types of rule in an industrial society in terms of antediluvian categories, yet they seem to be entirely adequate in the case of the Soviet system of domination. The Soviet Union has to be conceived of as a political society, a social structure that, since the differentiation of state and civil society, has completely disappeared from the Western European scene. It was Aristotle who properly described the alternative types of rule in all kinds of political societies as: monarchy, tyranny (autocracy), aristo-cracy, oligarchy, democracy. Political society as democracy is practicable only in very small integrations (city-states); in a huge country like the Soviet Union there are only three possibilities left: aristocracy, oligarchy and autocracy. Hence the application of the above terminology is justified by the very fact that the Soviet Union is a political society and as far as the type of rule is concerned, it is indeed antediluvian despite its modern forces of production.

The notion of 'Party aristocracy' is not a new invention. The leading functionaries who played an important role in the Party before the seizure of power, were unofficially called 'Party aristo-crats' in the Party itself. In the case of a revolutionary organization such a denomination is adequate, however strange it may appear. All Bolshevik-type parties had their own aristocracy, and whoever belonged to it stood in high esteem before autocratic rule took over. Trotsky in his time justified the predominance of the Party leader-ship with its 'primogeniture' in the Revolution. The reference to the feudal right of heredity meant just what it was supposed to mean: the noblest have the right, even the prerogative, to rule. Party 'aristocrats', mostly — even though not exclusively — of intellectual middle-class origin, declared themselves to be the cream of the working class and thus the repository of its historical mission. They were the crusaders of the liberation of the world, the New Jerusalem was their promised land and their patrimony. They extolled a way of life based on a constant danger of death, on borderline situations, on self-sacrifice and also on the conviction that they had the right to sacrifice others mercilessly. They were heroes and thugs at the same time. Their attitude was warrior-like: their sufferings were their decorations. The number of years spent in prison or in deportation, or who had joined the Party earlier than others, became matters of the highest importance. Those who had joined the Party later or had been less persecuted than others generally occupied a lower rank in the hierarchy of nobility. The early Bolsheviks fostered *esprit de corps* on the one hand; on the other they nurtured obscure grudges against each other which went back as far as 'prehistorical' eras but never faded with the passing of time. Even small offences were taken as *points d'honneur* — of the Party, of course. But a point of honour can by the same token be a matter of revenge: personal enemies were denounced as traitors or agents of the police. The 'aristocrats' were at once over-confident and over-suspicious. They could never get rid of their past, because this would be tantamount to becoming a 'commoner'.

Rosa Luxemburg wrote: 'But here is the "ego" of the Russian revolutionary again! Pirouetting on its head, it once more proclaims itself to be the all-powerful director of History – this time with the title of *His Excellency the Central Committee*.' Indeed, 'His Excellency the Central Committee' became the first sovereign of Soviet Russia.

Let us once again make clear that the notion of aristocracy here is no mere figure of speech. Aristocracy in this context means 'meritocracy', and the content of 'merit' is strictly defined as the virtue of a warrior or a particular organization which directs history. Aristocrats stood on an equal footing with each other, but one among them became 'more equal' or *primus inter pares*: this was the First Secretary. The First Secretary was increasingly surrounded by a quasi-mythical aura. In times of aristocratic rule he presumably had no more real power of his own than all the members of the leading bodies. It was this mythical aura rather than his real power that made him 'more equal', in that he was the symbol of the Party. It is true that Stalin very skilfully pushed himself to the acme of autocratic rule. However, no manipulation and intrigue could have been that successful, without being reinforced by respect for, and the religious connotations attached to, his position by his fellow-rulers. Even Lenin's 'Testament' was not sufficiently powerful to force the General Secretary to resign. Nothing is more telling in this respect than the behaviour of the exiled Trotsky, who as late as 1932 warned his followers not to accept the slogan 'down with Stalin', because 'this would almost certainly benefit the forces of counter-Revolution'. In order to establish autocratic rule, the Party aristocracy had to be decimated and liquidated as a stratum; moreover, as Conquest correctly points out, it had to be morally annihilated as well. Only a minority of the second- and third-rate ancient aristocrats could survive, and these were the flexible ones who were always ready to relinquish their independence and to accept without misgivings a merely emanated power. The First Secretary alone became the actual sovereign.

The slogan of 'collective leadership' after Stalin's death meant a break with autocratic rule. As a result, the new structure of power inside the sovereign of the state can be described as 'oligarchic'.

Obviously the problem of heredity has to be raised here. There can be no question about the fact that political power is not hereditary in the Soviet system of domination. In spite of the common principle of selection of the leaders, there is a difference, here too, between aristocratic and oligarchic types of rule. It was characteristic of the Party—aristocracy, and not only in the Soviet Union, but in other Eastern European countries as well, that the so-called aristocratic families had predominance. The wives of Party leaders were usually politically active themselves and occupied real political positions, though mostly minor ones. A great deal of 'inbreeding' went on in leading Party circles. Brother and sisters, whole family clans occupied vital positions. This was more than a simple comedy of protectionism as it is today in Rumania and Bulgaria, for the members of the families were real comrades in arms. Also the children of the leaders stood in high esteem, even if they were quite insignificant. The political lifetime of this generation was, however, too short to allow even speculation about the possible future position of these children, although a 'conditionally hereditary' rule was not excluded. Stalin's fervour in liquidating whole families even after the death of their heads may serve as an indirect proof of such a possibility.

Stalin managed to crush the families of the new aristocracy and ensure a completely bureaucratic selection based on long and obedient service. In this respect nothing changed after his death. Today Soviet oligarchy is a product of this type of selection. The rulers themselves climbed slowly upwards on the ladder of power. However, getting to the top no longer means exclusively prestige and power. It also means wealth and privilege. Privilege in itself is wealth, though a particular kind of wealth: it cannot be monetarized, it is exclusive, it goes with the top position only. That is why it is appropriate to describe the present sovereign of the Soviet Union as oligarchy.

The expression 'oligarchic rule' denotes a structure rather than any individual psychology. Just as some of the Soviet aristocrats were greedy, so presumably some of the oligarchs are not greedy at all. Greed was, however, an atypical personal character trait in times of aristocratic rule; asceticism was preferred to greed which had to be, as it were, morally 'accounted for' or excused in some way. To be wealthy, and to make use of privileges is, however, the norm in the case of the oligarchy. Even if someone feels uneasy about accepting what is due to him, none the less, he has to do it or face excommunication.

In one respect, however, oligarchic rule repeats the *status quo ante* of aristocratic rule. Oligarchs are equal, but the Party Secretary is 'more equal'. The will of the First Secretary is more significant than the will of his fellow-rulers. The removal of Krushchev however — an act the like of which never occurred in the era of aristocratic rule — shows that the mythical aura surrounding the First Secretary is gone. His priority is more a matter of tradition, power concentration and pragmatic calculation than of quasi-religious belief.

The unification of the three powers

There was an emphasis when defining the one-party system in the previous chapter on the concentration of the legislative, judiciary and executive powers in one and the same hand. It is obvious that if all powers emanate from the Party leadership, be it aristocratic, autocratic or oligarchic, the three branches of power cannot be divided at all. Constitutions have to be approved by the Party leadership before they are passed in the Supreme Soviet or in the Parliaments (the latter is only a formality). The same is the case with all laws. In important cases — not only in cases of political, but also of economic 'crimes' — the sentence is decided directly by the sovereign and the judge acts only as an executor. In practice the unification of the three powers means that there is only one power· namely, the executive. First of all the sovereign makes up his mind (in autocratic rule this really is a one-man decision), the laws are subsequently created and the courts, as executing bodies, are instructed how to act. Hence it is no wonder that in the hierarchy of the organizations of emanated power those that have the task of execution are always at the top, and those at the bottom serve simply as means of execution: legislative and judiciary powers. Thus the emanated power of parliaments is practically nil. The judiciary power of the bodies of jurisdiction is, again, virtually nil; their emanated power is that of execution. However, as far as political cases are concerned, even the executive power accumulated in the field of a so-called jurisdiction is very small. The real power is in the hands of the political police, which executes the will of the sovereign without much formality (and at one time without any formality). Formalities adopted in order to limit the power of the political police after Stalin's death, expressed again exclusively the will of the new sovereign: above all they protect Party officials against a possible attempt to reintroduce autocracy. Apart from the political police the greatest emanated power is concentrated in the ministries which, again, is an executive power.

The ministries are responsible for the control of society; they are huge sub-systems of power, but their power is far from being equal. The balance of power between these sub-systems has changed several times historically and is by no means the same in different countries. As a result, our description will take the form of a generalized outline rather than an accurate account of any particular case. The most powerful of the ministries is invariably the Ministry of the Interior. A simple comparison of its actual say in decisions with that of the Ministry of Justice will suffice to demonstrate, again, the subordinated position of judiciary power. The Ministry of Justice depends not only on the Party, but, to a different extent at different times, on the Ministry of the Interior as well.

Next in the power hierarchy come the different ministries of industry, and eventually the Ministry of Agriculture too. The power balance between the ministries of industry is, again, shifting. Their power depends — at least partially — on the national importance of the branch they control and that is why they are deeply interested in expanding it. Expansion is not identical with efficiency, rather with increasing their relative share in the budget. Moreover, efficiency of an industrial branch does not necessarily increase the power of the ministries. Hence there is a conflict of interest among them; they are huge pressure groups intriguing against each other in order to acquire the bigger share. At present, in the post-Stalinian period, the sovereign has to take into consideration the interest conflicts between its own emanated powers and maintain their balance within a given framework. The limit has already been described: pressure groups cannot exercise their power against the Party. To exercise pressure means to influence the Party in order to acquire a bigger share of the national budget, political influence, promotion and the like. In certain Eastern European societies pressure can even be put on the Party by various ministries in order to attain greater efficiency, but this pressure can only be limited.

Republican ministries in so-called 'federal' states are emanations of the central ones. Their power never extends beyond local matters; moreover, they are directed by the national leadership — an emanation of the sovereign as well. They have, however, a sufficient amount of power to remain masters of their own territory. Republican ministries are, again, interested in expanding their own republican industry which triggers off an interest conflict among them and has to be outbalanced by the centre. Moreover, federal republican govern-ments compete with each other as well: the more they get the more they can control and the more power they possess. In the balance of national powers, however, the greatest emanated power lies in the given case *always* with Russia; under all Soviet governments all other nations and federal republics are underprivileged. Moreover, the power balance among all other nations does not mostly or even primarily depend upon the pressures of the republics, but upon a central political decision. Federal republican governments (and thereby whole nations) can be punished by the withdrawal of a considerable amount of their share in the all-Union budget, a portion of their investment funds and even of their food supply. This occurred, as is well-known, in the Ukraine after the War. In short, all powers emanate from the sovereign, but the balance of power can change, although only on the same level of emanation and not between different levels.

Even if it is true that normally the greatest emanated power is in the hands of the political police, this does not mean that this power is their own. Rather the reverse. There can be no comparison between the power of the political police in Western democracies and that of their Soviet counterpart, and this is no less true now than it was in Stalin's time: the whole Soviet population is at the mercy of the political police. At the same time no political police in Western countries has so little independent power as the Soviet because democracy is unable to control them, whereas the sovereign in the Soviet Union controls its own totally. It often happened in Soviet history that the party leadership (even Stalin) pretended to have no part in the actions of its secret police. Party bosses still allow rumours to circulate about the 'bad guys' who take measures without their knowledge. This is nothing but a deliberate pattern of deception, a scenario with set roles, with the Party Secretary as an eternal personification of the 'good guy'. But, of course, this cannot be taken seriously. The Party has a very firm hold on the political police and the reasons for this are easily understood. Any independent power of the police, could endanger the execution of the will of the sovereign; moreover, it could endanger the sovereign itself, and sound precautionary measures are taken to prevent this from happening. Eastern European countries are, in this respect, in a different position. The Soviet Union does not have any great confidence in the Party leaders of the dependent countries. That is why the political police organs of those countries are directly controlled by the Soviet secret police. Of course, Soviet control over the national services does not mean that *all* detentions, arrests, imprisonments and even executions have to be effected in consultation with the sovereign. In Stalin's time, there was a quantitative limit to it: the very dimensions of the purges. Stalin, however, was a competent manipulator of his own secret police; he let them loose on their enemies and then, their work done, he sent them to the same execution cells. Today the Soviet leaders exert a similarly firm, if less dramatic, hold over their police.

The power of the army is also of an executive character, but its importance and strength have frequently changed in the course of Soviet history. Without going into historical details one can assume that the power of the army depends entirely on the decision of the Party, and more precisely on whether internal terrorization or external warfare is on the agenda. During the Great Purges the power of the army was very limited, not only because its leaders had been executed by Stalin (he subsequently eliminated the leaders of the secret police as well), but also because the war had been turned inwards. The growth of the army's power was natural during the Second World War, but it had immediately been withdrawn when the war ended. This situation did not dramatically change in Khrushchev's time, but it has since Brezhnev came to power. For in the last fifteen years, in harmony with the transition to traditional legitimation, the Soviet Union has launched a type of foreign politics practically unknown in its preceding history, that of political imperialism. (Political imperialism, not imperialism as such, because economic exploitation is far from being the major target of this politics, if indeed it is one of the targets at all. The goal is to increase political influence and gain dominance in new spheres all over the world in competition with the United States.) Armaments are now a first priority in Soviet industry and the perfection of the army is the main target: only a strong army can back imperialist politics. That is why the power of the army increased considerably, perhaps equal to that of the political police. The army is one of the greatest (if not the greatest) pressure groups in today's Soviet state. We must reiterate, however, that no pressure group, whatever the scope of its power, can have any power against the Party. Thus the Party has a complete hold over the army as well. Were it otherwise, the whole system of domination would be basically endangered. This is unlikely to happen, but, of course, it cannot be completely excluded as a possibility.

The modes of execution of power

In order to comprehend the mode of the execution of power in the Soviet system of domination, one has to analyse *bureaucracy, police activity, the penal code* and, last but not least, *paternalism*.

It is a view generally held that the Soviet system is basically characterized by the rule of bureaucracy. This is, however, an inaccurate description. All Soviet leaders, from Lenin on, regularly blamed the inefficiency of the system on bureaucracy; they launched campaigns against it, against the dimensions of paper-production, against the lack of initiative and the narrow-mindedness. But these charges cannot be taken seriously, not because they were not true, but because they localized the source of the decay in the wrong spot. The Soviet sovereign has never been bureaucratic, nor is it bureaucratic at present either, although the leaders are mostly selected from the ranks of *ci-devant* bureaucrats. Bureaucracy had and still has only emanated power, more precisely, emanated-executive power. The bureaucratic mode of the execution of power is a consequence of the system of domination and not identical with it, even less its cause.

All centralization increases bureaucracy: over-centralization increases it further. The totalization of the whole society (economy included) cannot function without a hierarchic administration of immense dimensions. Over-centralization and totalization have been accomplished by the sovereign: in order to realize its set aims, it needs bureaucracy. The Party leadership may blame the bureaucracy for its inefficiency, but this has been caused by the sovereign itself; it may blame the bureaucracy for its lack of initiative, but in a totalitarian system no one can take initiative except the sovereign, thus the accusations do not make sense.

What are the main characteristic features of Soviet bureaucracy (some of them identical with or similar to those of its Western counterparts, some completely different)?

In the Soviet Union there are no bureaucracies in the plural, but just one huge apparatus of power with different branches, which are interconnected with each other and at the same time carefully hierarchized. In a political society the whole apparatus is of a political character, its economic branches no less than the Party or state administration branches.

The members of the Soviet apparatus are not civil servants, not even in a theoretical sense. They are not responsible to the citizenry, but exclusively to their superiors, and in the last analysis — through mediations — to the sovereign. Those who have any contact with the citizenry exercise their power against them, and this is expressed in the very rude and domineering attitude they adopt towards them. By implication the population is afraid of the apparatus, its characteristic attitude towards it is one of humility. The population has no rights vis-à-vis the apparatus, it can only ask for favours. If an *apparatchik* settles a matter, he is doing a favour, not fulfilling a duty. The good guys do more favours than the bad guys — that is the only difference between them. To put it more precisely, subjects of the Soviet-type state have just two rights: *ius supplicationis* (the ancient feudal right of asking for favours) and the right of denunciation. It seems shocking that these rights should be referred to as matters of fact, but they are in fact mentioned as granted in the Soviet Constitution itself. Article 49 of the 1977 Constitution says: 'Every citizen of the USSR has the right to make suggestions to the state organs and social organizations regarding the improvement of their activity, and the right to criticize the insufficient aspects of their activity. The responsible persons are bound . . . to examine the suggestions and requests of the citizens.' However, these 'rights' exist only nominally; it can prove exceedingly dangerous to try to enforce them. One has to be very cautious about the favour one is seeking; the requests themselves are approved or disapproved regardless of whether favours will be granted or not. Disapproved requests find their way into the subjects' files and can be turned against them in due course in the form of accusations. A good subject is one who asks for favours, for this is a sign of trust in the state, but it is important to know what the proper requests are. For improper ones exceed the constitutional right of requesting and thus become illegal; the applicant can be legally persecuted as a result of it. This becomes obvious from the wording of the article of the Constitution quoted above: the requests of the subjects have to aim at the improvement of the activity of the apparatus. Which suggestion or request serves this purpose and which does not is only a question of definition.

Soviet bureaucracy, like all other bureaucracies, has its inner hierarchical tensions, but it becomes a phalanx of unanimous solidarity when defending its own logic against the subjects of the state. In the case of grassroots criticism the bureaucrat's spontaneous reaction is to protect all his fellow-bureaucrats. However, should the criticism come from the top, solidarity is replaced by a complete atomization of bureaucratic organizations — in such situations, withdrawal of solidarity and mutual accusation is a matter of survival, or at least, of staying in office. It is worth mentioning that all accusations published in the press express exclusively the dissatisfaction of the sovereign. This double face of the Soviet apparatus (a closed phalanx toward the subjects, atomized towards the summit of power) is, again, a consequence of the system of domination. On the one hand civil rights and the pressure of public opinion are lacking; on the other, the power of the sovereign is total. The inefficiency of this bureaucracy which sometimes assumes truly catastrophic dimensions is, at least partially, due to this contradiction, which, however, no one can eliminate from the Soviet system of domination.

According to Max Weber, bureaucracy applies rules and it is thus that it realizes the very principles of formal rationality. Personal common sense and understanding do not enter into the matter, the individual character of a particular problem is not taken into consideration, the particular case is subordinated to the general rule, the individual can hold no responsibility. Hence bureaucracy is an administrative machine of instrumental rationality and is pragmatically extremely efficient. However, the lack of formal rationality in Soviet society has already been pointed out, as has, at the same time, the bureaucratic mode of power execution. This is seemingly a contradiction to be solved.

The Soviet apparatus applies rules as every bureaucracy does: in this respect all the Weberian characteristics fit into the picture of Soviet bureaucracy. The Soviet bureaucracy, however, does not only follow rules; it executes *ad hoc* directives as well. A phone call from the superiors immediately invalidates all the rules. Counterposed to an order, no rule has any relevance at all. The word of the Party is always command. Hence the rules of the Soviet bureaucracy are binding only in the interim between two commands. If, however, the command comes from a superior of relatively lower rank, the bureaucrat does not know what to do, his loyalties are divided. He has to decide for himself what to do, which is never the case when only rules are applied. He has to decide, but he is afraid of so doing; as a result, he passes the decision to another bureaucrat, who again passes it on, and so on and so forth. The bureaucrat's position and, in hard times, even his life is at stake: someone has to make the decision but no one wants to take the responsibility. It would be better to do nothing, but this may prove dangerous as well. That is one of the reasons why Soviet bureaucracy is not characterized by formal rationality.

Moreover the rules themselves are formulated in such a way that their application cannot be rational from a pure pragmatic viewpoint. The leaders occasionally want to break rules they themselves have set. It is primarily the leading economic managers who are aware of the fact that observing the minimum requirements of formal rationality demands bending the rules prescribed by central authorities. In this case, however, why are these rules set at all?

All this raises, once again, the question of the inefficiency of Soviet bureaucracy. In a strange way, it is not a question of the failure of those bureaucratic organizations. The Soviet bureaucracy *has* to be inefficient in order to accomplish its true aim: to stem the tide, to defer the satisfaction of the population's needs. In the case of a food shortage, the bureaucracy has to be inefficient in distribution; in the case of an accommodation shortage, the bureaucracy has to adopt a tactic of deliberately disheartening the applicants; in the case of a machinery shortage, the bureaucracy must constantly delay in issuing machinery to factories that cannot function without it. Hence, paradoxical as it may sound, Soviet bureaucracy executes at least one of its sovereign's wishes by being inefficient. Its function is primarily to practise dictatorship over needs, and this is being done thoroughly. The system of directives (orders) is a corrective one (or at least is meant as such): it clears the way for the break-through of ideological, doctrinal priorities. We only have to add that in some Eastern European societies a system of directives may clear the way to the (partial) realization of instrumental rationality as well, even though in a restricted manner, and that in the Soviet Union the armaments industry is exempt from the power of bureaucracy precisely because it has to be efficient.

The second mode of execution of power in the Soviet system occurs through police activity and judicial procedures. We have already mentioned that the latter have nothing or very little to do with jurisdiction proper, they simply execute the will of the sovereign. The impact of different organizations of the political police in the history of the Soviet state is too well-known to dwell on here; it is only necessary to point to the change of its function after Stalin's death. In earlier periods of Soviet development crime detection was definitely not the task of the political police or, at any rate, was not an important one. The sovereign indicated the target groups to be destroyed (*ci-devants*, members of outlawed political parties, members of the Party opposition, *kulaks*, experts, writers, old Party members, members of foreign parties, etc.) and the police struck at them indiscriminately. During the great purges practically the whole Soviet population served as a target group. After the 20th Congress the system of indiscriminate extermination had been abolished and that is why prevention and crime detection on a mass scale has become the primary task of the political police.

Because of the emphasis on socialist legality, it is important to look briefly at the Soviet criminal code. According to Montesquieu, the constitution of a state does not wholly define the subjects' actual situation. Their freedom or slavery alike depends on the penal code. (In certain societies, this is the crucial factor.) Which actions are considered unlawful and what are the penalties to be inflicted, is the decisive issue in that respect. It has often been asked why Stalin needed a penal code at all, what difference it made anyhow, if innocent people were shot after a cursory trial or without any trial at all? The need for the show trials was obvious, they were aimed at the moral destruction of the Party opposition, but where did the need for secret trials come from? Hundreds of thousands had been liquidated without trial, but the system of extermination usually functioned by way of trials. Yet this apparently superfluous procedure had one function, namely, an ideological one. In times of overt (Jacobin) terror formalities could be negelcted, the principle of the regime being that even innocents can be crushed. Lenin openly formulated that, during a brawl, one cannot select who is and who is not responsible, one has to hit out indiscriminately. However, Stalin wanted to create the impression of general guilt. Lacking the ideological armour of a Hitler (the doctrine of superior and inferior races) he chose a very plausible means of psychological pressure which he exerted on the population. This was the politics of general involvement: no one could possibly state that whoever was executed was non-guilty. If anyone did make such a statement, this was proof of his own guilt. This ideology provided Stalin with the same vicious circle that was a basic tenet of Hitler's ideology: anyone who casts a doubt about the inferiority of other races proves that he himself does not belong to the superior one.

Even the shortest and legally most absurd trial is, however, impossible without the application of some articles of some sort of penal code. That is why such articles had to be formulated. Here is a random sample of them: the punishment of the family for the 'crimes' of its head was incorporated into the penal code; capital punishment could be passed and executed on fourteen-year-old children; the different sub-paragraphs of article 58 of the penal code declared that all propaganda which might weaken the Soviet state was unlawful, as was keeping such literature in one's home; deliberate non-fulfilment or careless execution of duties were equally crimes, etc. One can detect a sufficiently wide compass to render all human activities criminal according to the whim of a tyrant.

After Stalin's death the Soviet penal code underwent some kind of formalization; offences were defined in a less nebulous way. It was precisely this formalization that exposed the draconic character of Soviet law. The death penalty was extended in May 1961 to large-scale economic offences, including forgery; in July 1961 to serious infringements of currency regulations; in February 1962 to attempts on the life, health and dignity of the police and members of volunteer guards, and to certain forms of bribery. All this happened at a time when the death penalty had been either abolished or considerably restricted (as compared with formerly) in nearly all Western European countries.

Parallel with, and complementary to, the above-mentioned formalization, a new form of eliminating politically unsavoury elements was invented: they were forcibly hospitalized in the mental asylums of the secret police. Nor did internment and forced labour camps disappear either. Although the dimension of the present-day Gulag cannot be compared with the all-embracing system of concentration and forced labour camps in Stalin's time, and may not necessarily be lethal as they were then, the police has not lost the prerogative to consign subjects to camps without any kind of judicial procedure. All totalitarian − Fascist or non-Fascist − states are police states, of necessity.

The self-image of the state in the Soviet system is that of the father. This is the source of its all-embracing *paternalism*. The state, not the subjects, makes all the decisions, but the implication is that all is being done for the subjects' benefit. The paternal authority metes out punishments to its naughty, disobedient and rebellious offspring; it approves or disapproves of its children's behaviour: those who behave well will be rewarded, even decorated. To no smaller extent does the sophisticated system of state orders and medals express the father image of the Soviet state. It is up to the subject-children to feel remorse when offending their father; even the idea of an offence is conceived as a challenge to authority, which then has to be 'repented'. The 'dialectics' of criticism and self-criticism is an 'objective law of social development' in the Soviet system.

The Soviet Union is one big family. Everything that a subject may get (consumer goods, a flat, heating, clothes, theatre tickets, etc.) is 'due to the state'; it is not granted as a right or given in exchange for something else, but provided as an amenity that can be revoked. It goes without saying that it is the citizen's duty (legally as well as morally) to experience and demonstrate his gratitude for such magnanimity. And since the state is but an emanation of the Party, the good Soviet subject has to have the same obedient and grateful attitude to the state as a good Christian has to God and the Church.

As has been mentioned, Soviet subjects ask for favours, their right proper is *ius supplicationis*. If the favour is granted they have to give thanks for it, to the state and the Party; if it is refused, they have to accept this decision as the expression of the justice and wisdom of the state and the Party because these paternal authorities always know better what is right and what is wrong, what is due to the subjects and what is not. In a broader sense, one can say that the subjects are wholly dependent on the state and the Party. In this capacity they get from the state everything that ensures their reproduction as dependent on the state. This means (a) the necessary minimum material to ensure their survival; (b) services which grant the control of the person by the state. The amount of goods defined as 'necessary to ensure survival' is not less historically determined than the value of labour as described by Marx. There were times when even the minimum for survival was not granted: two waves of mass famine have been recorded in Soviet history, and the Soviet leadership was at fault in at least one of them. There were, again, times like the present, when the minimum on which one can exist is granted for everyone. In Eastern European societies the necessary minimum has always meant more disposable goods for the subjects, even during classical Stalinism, and particularly at the present time. But in any case, the necessary minimum is always prescribed by the state, although in different ways at different periods and in different countries. The types of service which ensure control by the state do not, however, change, although in some Eastern European societies several minor deviations from this pattern have taken place in the last decades.

The above-mentioned paternalistic services are described in the Soviet Constitution of 1977 as so many different 'rights' of the citizens. They are: right to work, right to rest, right to protection of health, right to pension, right to housing (shelter), right to education, right to the benefits of culture.

According to the formulation of the constitution, 'right to work' means guaranteed employment. It entails, however, something else too, namely compulsory employment, at least for all adult male and single adult female subjects of the state. The Eastern European proverbial joke according to which 'everything that is allowed is compulsory' can be applied to this right as well. Thus being employed is in itself no favour for the very reason that the state can have a hold over its subjects only if they are working. To be employed 'according to one's capacities' which is presented as a basic right of citizens in article 40 of the Constitution is, in fact, a 'favour'. Promotion necessitates gratitude to the state, to the Party, who decide who should be given promotion, what his rank should be, etc. In the formulation of the article regarding the 'right to rest', the state grants the citizens so-called mass sport facilities and provides them with the conditions for so-called entertainment. The 'right to education' ensures compulsory secondary education. The state even grants free tertiary education, but the question that is so relevant here is not raised in the Soviet Union itself – namely, by whom the costs are paid. There is not only no real progressive taxation in the Soviet Union, but the higher one stands (in terms of income and non-monetarized amenities) the more privileges one gets. So it is not unjustified to speak of a regressive system of taxation. It is obvious, therefore, that the costs of tertiary education are paid by those who (together with their children) never benefit from it – the more so since upward mobility, especially in the huge rural regions of the state, is far smaller in the Soviet Union than in the United States. The 'right to culture' means the right to, and the obligation of, being culturally indoctrinated, for the simple reason that no alternative culture is available.

Paternalism is, then, state control and as such, another aspect of the dictatorship over needs. Regardless of its real function it is often used as one aspect of auxiliary legitimation by substantive rationality. This aspect belongs to the category of negative legitimation in that it points to the alleged superiority of substantive rationality through the 'legitimation deficit' in capitalism. Since the emergence of the welfare state, however, the impact of negative legitimation has decreased and with the exception of the 'right to work' a vast amount of deception and self-deception is needed to take it seriously. The fact of the growing unemployment in the West serves without any doubt as a main argument for the negative legitimation by substantive rationality at the present time as well.

Forms of feed-back

The character and the forms of feed-back are of great importance in every power structure. In the Soviet system of domination there are three possible types: the feed-back of the population, the feed-back of the apparatus and the feed-back of the experts (technical and economic professionals).

Popular feed-back can take only one form in a totalitarian society: revolt. By revolt we do not exclusiveiy mean revolution, but all types of violence directed against the state, the Party, the symbols or representatives of the sovereign. It can be revolution, armed revolt, rioting, destruction of symbols, lynching of functionaries or even of shopkeepers (if there is a food shortage), strikes. There have been uprisings in all Eastern European states, and not only once. The answer of the state to the challenges is, of course, bloody reprisal in all these cases (and it should be added that the cruelty of retaliation always exceeds, in terms of victims, that of the uprising). Yet the direct cause of the uprising is usually eliminated even if only partially and intermittently. The repeated strikes and riots in Poland serve here as a good and well-known example. Due to the lack of a contractual system, of channels for expressing the popular will, of the organs of negotiation and compromise, revolt is the only way in which people can change anything, even though in a very restricted manner.

The feed-back of the Party and state apparatus belongs to the very essence of the power structure. All organizations on all levels were and are obliged to send regular reports to the higher authorities about the general atmosphere among the people, whether workers, peasants or intellectuals. It was part and parcel of the duties of bureaucratic institutions to report reactions to measures taken, overt and covert mass opinion regarding the most recent decisions of the authorities, prevailing moods in various strata. However, in times of terroristic totalitarianism the feed-back was only nominal, never real The apparatus reported precisely what the sovereign wanted to be fed back. (The only exception could be at certain times the feed-back through the channels of the secret police). Whoever misunderstood the will of the sovereign and failed to make the right report was imprisoned or executed. The reports at this stage had to fulfil two (only apparently contradictory) requirements. Firstly, they had to stress that the whole country stood as 'one man' behind the most recent decision of the Party; secondly, they had to emphasize that there were enemies everywhere, like saboteurs, *kulaks*, counter-Revolutionaries, 'bandits'. During the purges it was by no means easy to accomplish this double task, for both the glorious results and the dangerous enemies had to be invented. Further, one had to find out the exact proportions and localize the protagonists of the murderous fairy-tales precisely. But of course, real feed-back is not functional in terroristic totalitarianism where the decimated population is much too terrified even to dare think of any resistance and where the will of the autocrat is carried out without any regard to the price the country has to pay.

Under oligarchic rule, however, there is an opening for a real or at least partially real feed-back of this type. First of all, because oligarchic rule is characterized by a constant struggle for greater power and some members of the sovereign body want to increase their power at the cost of the power of other members. Real feed-back concerning the consequences of a decision of a certain member of the Political Bureau may be very useful for other members who want to get rid of him or at least push him downwards on the rungs of the power hierarchy. Brezhnev and his allies, when competing against Khrushchev, collected a vast amount of correct data about the outcome of the latter's adventurous experiments. In Hungary the so-called 'workers' opposition', a group of hardliners from among the upper echelons of the power elite, succeeded in discrediting the partisans of economic reform and in ousting them from the leadership; once again, the data collected were conclusive. A further need for a feed-back system consists in the wish of the oligarchic leadership to avoid, if possible, spectacular social clashes. High-ranking party functionaries have to be aware of tensions in order to reduce them, although this is usually done in such a way that they create a new tension which has to be reduced again in due course. Thus oligarchic leadership in a non-terroristic totalitarian country has to develop an ability of manoeuvring which can only be accomplished with an amount of confidential information provided by the reports of the *apparatchiks*. One should not overestimate, however, the sense of reality that becomes manifest in these reports. Even if *apparatchiks* intend to report what is really going on (and this is practically never entirely the case), they understand their world in terms of their own authoritarian doctrine which by its very structure prevents them from using their common sense: they see only what they are supposed to see. Nevertheless even from such a distorting viewpoint some scraps of reality may be grasped and reported according to the requirement of the new form of rule.

The third type of feed-back in the Soviet system of domination is that of the experts. Here one has to differentiate between feed-back proper and advising.

By experts we do not simply mean people with a university degree. In the higher ranks of the elite one can find numerous experts, but their political power has nothing to do with their academic background. They are mostly engineers or economists trained in highly specialised branches who have never practised their profession, or only for a short time, and whose training would no longer qualify them. Nor do they need their learning, for it is quite different skills that make a good *apparatchik*. The same is true of the leading politicians. In this respect the Soviet Union does not differ from other countries. Kennedy's skill as President of the United States had nothing to do with his Harvard training.

In the Soviet Union experts are highly qualified professionals, who do nothing but exercise their expert skills. Academics or engineers may be employed by the apparatus, but they do not belong to it. Even less can they belong to the corps of the sovereign. Experts represent, as they do all over the world, the spirit of goal rationality. And this is exactly why they cannot have any political power in the Soviet system of domination, not even emanated power. It is a mistake to speak of 'technocracy' in the Soviet Union, and even more of a mistake to conceive of the power structure as a domination of intellectuals. Of course the majority of intellectuals everywhere support the establishment which ensures their privileged position (in salary and/or in prestige) and offers them the possibility of exercising their skills. However, Soviet intellectuals are not less controlled by the sovereign than the members of any other social strata. Of course, the sovereign concedes a higher level of need satisfaction to intellectuals than to workers and peasants. It must be said that their position within this general framework has changed several times in the course of Soviet history and that in certain 'people's democracies', especially in times of 'economic reforms', their prestige and influence can be considerable. Later on the role of the ideological intelligentsia will be mentioned, now it is only the experts who are being analysed: for the two types of intellectual have completely different functions in the Soviet system of domination.

As we have already seen, experts have no political power whatsoever in the Soviet Union. Their power is of an economic or technical nature and lies in their disposable knowledge which is indispensable in an industrial society. Their work is badly needed, but at the same time objectively they are alien elements in the system of domination. The reason for this is that the system of domination is totalitarian, hence all power has to be political. The power of the experts cannot be political – they embody the limits of totalization by their very existence. Their support of the establishment mentioned above does not solve this contradiction.

In arguing the thesis of the intelligentsia as a ruling class, to which we referred critically at an earlier stage, Konrád and Szelényi revitalized the experts' dream, namely the total engineering of a society and the hostility of this social stratum to any kind of popular democracy (we are, of course, describing their diagnosis, not their position). The existence of such a dream cannot be denied, nor can the experts' hostility to the behaviour of the layman. Whatever the ideology of the experts may be, they can only function properly in pluralistic states. They may not like them, but they need them.

Formal rationality runs counter to the logic of political society: the absolutist sovereign acts totally in the spirit of its own principles if it refuses to share power (the right to rule and decide in political matters) with experts. With the exception of concrete industrial and economic matters, experts can only give the worst advice to the ruling oligarchy as far as the proper functioning of a totalitarian system is concerned. (Military experts may possibly represent a special case here.) Moreover, formal rationality is unable to avoid conflicts — it creates them. Were the sovereign to follow the logic of formal rationality, this would put an end to the Soviet system of domination. But all ruling elites are clever enough to know where their own interest lies. Hence it is quite impossible for the experts to obtain political power in the Soviet Union, but it is not completely impossible for them (although at present only in certain Eastern European states) to obtain a big share of extra-political power and thus to become a vast pressure group — which may contribute to the detotalization of the system.

The real function of the experts in the present Soviet state is that of the feed-back of formal rationality, either in the real sense of the word or in the form of advising. In the case of real feed-back experts assess plans and instructions from the standpoint of formal rationality and report back. If a project cannot be realized or seems to be irrational for other reasons they work out their alternative solutions. The feed-back is itself a form of advising. If, however, experts are ordered, despite their protest, to realize the unrealizable, they no longer have any say, and consequently no final decision can lie with them. The result in the case of direct advising is similar. This happens if experts are asked for their opinion before or during the process of decision-making. The sovereign may or may not pay attention to professional advice — decision-making remains its privilege. In a legal state the expert whose opinion has been rejected can turn to public opinion or to other powers or can pursue his idea independently (if he can obtain the resources to do so). If, however, the Soviet state closes the discussion, the expert has not even a hypothetical right of appeal. The religion of formal rationality visibly cannot be exercised freely in totalitarian states. Clearly, this is a tension, a conflict of interests between experts and the sovereign. Nevertheless, the feed-back of experts is acquiring growing importance in Eastern European states. As long as professionals are treated as learned servants, they can be of great use for the process of manoeuvring in the higher regions of the state.

CHAPTER 7

Ideology, Dogma, Culture

It is common knowledge that ideology plays a decisive role in Soviet social systems. Here we must deal with:

(1) The special character of this ideology.
(2) Its functions in the socio-political system.
(3) Its main tenets.
(4) Its effects on culture as a whole.

Contrary to the preceding chapters in which the categories of Max Weber have been applied, here the Marxian notion of ideology will be used as a frame of reference.

Ideology is a meaningful world-view which expresses and formulates coherently the interests of one social class among many in a covert manner, that is to say, with the pretension of expressing the cause of humankind based on a knowledge of human nature. Hence ideology pretends to be universal although it only universalizes particular interests and life-experiences. Universalization of particularity aims at the persuasion of the whole society in order to influence the motivational system of different social classes. Thus the liberal utopia of the self-regulating market was a typical ideology with all its implications.

It is not too bold to say that what is nowadays called 'Soviet ideology' is in fact no ideology at all. Although some characteristics of ideology can be discerned in the so-called Soviet ideology, others are completely missing. This is not entirely true in the case of Lenin's Marxism, but has become increasingly relevant since the acceptance of 'Marxism—Leninism' as the official creed of the Soviet Party and state.

Firstly, while ideologies express class-interests although they pretend to be universal world-views, Soviet ideology pretends to express class-interests (those of the proletariat) which in fact have been replaced by Party sovereignty as a goal in itself. Ideology becomes the expression of the will of the sovereign. Stalin put it correctly: dialectical materialism is the world-view of the Marxist–Leninist party. Secondly, ideologies proper are in competition, they go out into the market, they are always in the plural. Soviet Marxism–Leninism, however, does not compete, it excludes all other ideologies from the state and thus itself ceases to be an ideology in the proper sense of the term. Soviet Marxism–Leninism does not try to persuade either: whoever wants a chance in society must accept it. Last but not least, the coherence of the world-view also becomes superfluous. Once it is no longer exposed to criticism, it may consist of different articles of faith that are very loosely interconnected, or even contradict each other. To be meaningful is not a prerequisite of this world-view either, and for the same reason: the meaning has nothing to do with the text, but with its *interpretation* by the sovereign. It is coercively stipulated that this interpretation is always true and, moreover, that it is the only true one. Hence the equal right to interpretation of the text is banned. In so far as the sovereign does not offer the correct and only true interpretation, one can only guess at the message of the script: one cannot *know* it. Should the higher authority decide that the message has to be read in such a way as to show that democracy and dictatorship are identical or that the state has to be strengthened in order to abolish it, no one can argue. The meaning given by the one and only correct interpretation is the meaning of the text. One cannot reflect upon it, one is obliged to believe it.

Hence Soviet 'ideology' is not an ideology but a dogma, a doctrine, although a very special kind of doctrine. This doctrine is called science and it is based on the work of the founding fathers, Marx and Engels. To grasp the essence of the Soviet doctrine it is important to comprehend the function of its self-identification with science. By claiming to be science, the doctrine obviously pretends to be rationally proven. Science, however, can be falsified; moreover, social science is dependent on the time at which it was formulated and this was spelled out by Marx. This double character of science proved to be very useful in the Soviet system of dogma. On the one hand the slightest lay criticism of the official world-view was rejected out of hand as non-scientific, obscurantist, as the expression of hostile and alien classes which could not, for reasons of principle, have access to truth. On the other hand it is carefully stated that the founding fathers could not possibly foresee the events of the twentieth century, they could not invent solutions for the problems of the present, hence the interpreters were free to replace almost all

Marx's statements by totally different ones. If it came to the credibility of these substitutions all those who referred back to the corpus of Marx only proved that they had not understood what science is, namely, that it was to change with time, that it can be falsified. Hence the interpreters not only succeeded in fossilizing a scientific work as a system of dogma, they also changed the original corpus completely. Both could be accomplished with a reference to 'science'. Thus one can understand why 'dogmatism' was disapproved by the interpreters of the doctrine. Turning back to the originals, the texts of Marx or Engels were and still are described as dogmatism, because the only non-dogmatic, that is to say, 'scientific' interpretation of the script was (and still is) always identical with the last resolution of the Political Bureau or — as in Stalin's time — with the last obscure statement of the autocrat. To develop Marxism—Leninism further is always the prerogative of the sovereign. The identification of doctrine and science is thus polyfunctional: it opens the gate to all kinds of tampering with an ideological heritage.

All further developments of the doctrine are simply manifestations of the will of the sovereign. What is being manifested can be the interest of those dominating society but not necessarily so. No interest can account for Lysenko's becoming a 'scientific' agrobiologist or for Stalin's decision that language does not belong to super-structure. The prerogative of the only true interpretation of dogma often became an obsession, and not only with Stalin. Despite the growing pragmatism of oligarchic leadership, despite the reluctance of certain leaders to practice that prerogative, it has nevertheless to be affirmed. Party Secretary Brezhnev too was awarded the Marx Prize by the Soviet Academy of Sciences for his merits in developing further the science of Marxism—Leninism.

'Free discussion'

The assertion that the interpretation of Marxism—Leninism is a prerogative of the sovereign is not identical with the other: that there is always only one possible interpretation of the theoretical heritage as a whole. First of all, it is for the sovereign to decide whether it uses its prerogative completely or only partially. The sovereign can arbitrate on the only true Marxist—Leninist standpoint concerning cybernetics or fine arts if it so pleases but it can also abstain from this, simply fixing the limits of interpretation and leaving the rest to the experts. This is what is called 'free discussion' in Soviet terms.

The so-called free discussions (so-called, because the limits fixed by the sovereign cannot be transcended) are, again, polyfunctional. Sometimes relatively free discussions are triggered by the leading organs of the party themselves when they realize that the arbitrary nature of their own decisions endangers their own rule or some of their own vital interests. This is what happened in the case of cybernetics. 'Free discussions' fulfil the function of reducing tension as well. The Soviet system of domination is characterized by the recurrence of periods of temporary tension-reductions following periods of great tensions. Although the tensions of Stalin's time and those of the present cannot be compared, the dialectics of tension and tension-reduction are no less applied now than in the earlier periods. After being forcibly reduced to silence for years, the intellectuals are 'encouraged' to pursue debates; moreover, the party blames them for their 'servility' and lack of ideological initiative. Matters then usually take the following course. Some of the intellectuals obey by starting sham discussions, thus creating a seemingly freer atmosphere whereafter the less cautious also appear on the scene and discussions start in earnest. The Party stands by for a while as a simple observer. After a certain time has elapsed, the Party organs intervene, 'using administrative measures', as they put it. This means an official resolution containing a positive assessment of the fact of the discussion (which is, after all, a decision of the sovereign), and a condemnation of the 'deviations' in it. 'Left'- and 'right'-wing deviationists face police harassment; in the very liberal countries they are simply sacked and a new period of tension begins. In all 'free discussions' the last word invariably lies with the sovereign: the decision which of the arguing partners were right or wrong, is the sovereign's. Indeed, it cannot happen otherwise, as the sovereign is the repository of true Marxism—Leninism, and nothing but true Marxism—Leninism is accepted as true opinion in any kind of discussion.

In harmony with the sovereign's prerogative of developing Marxism—Leninism further, even the most loyal and officially accepted philosopher is limited to explaining the doctrine; the interpretation of it is a manifestation of the sovereign's will. The question of what the subject matter of 'free discussion' can be, where its limits lie, what its allowed duration may be, is no less an expression of the Supreme Will. 'Free discussions' are never launched for the sovereign to draw some lessons from them in an open-minded way. The Party knows the answers before the discussion begins and knows them better than the arguing parties can ever do, it is just that for one reason or other it has not yet disclosed the correct answer. That is why in the course of 'discussions' the loyal and (professionally overcautious) official theorists of the regime try only to find out what is on the sovereign's mind, what position the Party wants them to adopt. Thus 'free discussion' is a sort of quiz-show in which all who guess the thought of the sovereign correctly win, and the others lose.

The interest of the sovereign is not necessarily expressed in the content of the accepted article of faith, but rather in the fact that its acceptance depends on its own will. Thus the article of faith in question can be changed, but it can never cease to have been the expression of the sovereign's will. Not infrequently the interpretation of the Party has been identical with an earlier theoretical standpoint at that time deemed a 'deviation' by the same authority. But a later shift in the sovereign's mind does not mean that the erring theorist will be rehabilitated: the Party is always right, even retroactively, even when its present standpoint contradicts its former statements. The ways of the Party are enigmatic, indeed it is Kierkegaard's God that is embodied in it: no one can ever be in the right against it. The Party is all-wise – its utterances are expressions of a wisdom which the average human mind cannot grasp, but can only believe in. The term for this absolute belief, however, is 'acceptance of a scientific truth'.

The infallibility of the Party does not necessarily exclude the admission of some past mistaken judgements and policies. But once again, it is the privilege of the Party (that is to say, of the leading bodies) to criticize and rectify its own mistakes. Of course, the mistakes admitted by the Party are never substantial ones, only minor blunders that not even a god can avoid; the victorious construction of Communism has never been seriously endangered. There are no mistakes in the present, they were all and could only be committed in the past, they became mistakes only as from the moment the Party came to consider them as such, and only those confessed by the Party were mistakes, nothing else. Experienced Party members know, however, that even in the case of admitted past blunders, it is preferable not to speak of them. Subjects who are narrow-minded, forgetful and obedient are deemed the most loyal.

Teleology of dissent

The statement that Soviet ideology is not ideology proper but rather a system of dogma does not imply that there have never been

ideologies in Soviet societies. First of all, as we have seen, the transformation of Marxist ideology into a state doctrine was itself a slow
process. In the years of the aristocratic rule non-Marxist theories
were banned from the whole ideological life (at least from 1922
onwards), but all members of the aristocratic ruling body had an
equal right to explain and interpret the common theoretical legacy
and they did it, too, in different ways. That is why the sovereign
body could not define a single true standpoint concerning the interpretation of Marxist philosophy, economy, psychology or art theory.
Lenin's disapproval of the philosophy of Bukharin did not prevent
the latter from reformulating and publishing his ideas. Disaccord in
the sovereign body makes disaccord regarding the interpretations
generally possible. The early 1920s are justly famous for some real
discussions and achievements within the theoretical framework of
Marxism. Every school or tendency in economy or philosophy could
refer to someone in the Political Bureau or Secretariat who shared
the views in question. Pluralism reigned supreme within Marxism
and the different conceptions freely clashed with each other. They
universalized different kinds of interests, they used rational arguments
and wanted to persuade the partisans of the other conception. They
really functioned as ideologies proper, although in a limited sense of
the word, because even at this time an official framework existed
which could not be transcended and within which all discussions
took place: the viewpoint of the 'enemy' was never refuted by
arguments, only denounced.

The situation changed totally in the second half of the decade;
Marxism–Leninism became simply a doctrine from the late 1920s
and early 1930s. Ideological Marxism, however, did not cease to
exist as an undercurrent even after this period.

In the Soviet system of domination all ideological types of
Marxism are outlawed for the simple reason that they embody
pluralism by their very ideological nature. They were, however,
always present in all Soviet states even during the period of terroristic
totalitarianism. We are entitled to call them ideological types of
Marxism, because they interpreted the theory of Marx, Engels and
Lenin in an individual way and contrasted this interpretation with
others, mainly with the official doctrine. The interests they
expressed in a universalized way were often those of the ruling Party
itself, but they gave voice to it in the form of a rational argumentation, in order to persuade others. They often contrasted the ideal of
the Soviet state with its reality. They paid lip service to the doctrine,
otherwise they would not have had the slightest chance of survival.

Despite that, they were harassed and treated with the utmost suspicion. The representatives of ideological Marxism ascribed their harassment mostly to the stupidity of certain official theorists or to a kind of irrationality in their behaviour. This was false consciousness, indeed. Doctrine cannot tolerate ideology of any kind, and Marxist ideology least of all. The sheer existence of a Marxist ideology challenges the indisputable right of the sovereign as the sole inter-preter of the doctrine. The acceptance of the slightest degree of pluralism within Marxism would have made the prerogative question-able. Even at the present time and in those Eastern European countries where there is a greater amount of pluralism-tolerance in practice, plurality of Marxism cannot be openly professed, but at best practised in secret.

The contradiction between doctrine and ideology cannot be solved in the Soviet system of domination. This explains a number of facts which in themselves may astonish the observers of Soviet history. For instance, once the situation on doctrine and ideology is under-stood, the 'Lukács mystery' is no longer a mystery. When he accused Lukács of Stalinism, even Deutscher did not grasp the basic issue. Lukács might accept as many theories of Stalin as he was prepared to, but he could not become a Stalinist for the simple reason that he practised Marxism as ideology. His Marxism was 'illegal', it represen-ted pluralism regardless of the content of his writings. He simply did not give up his right to the independent interpretation of the theory, which was not granted. When it was announced from the pulpit of the 22nd Congress of the Soviet Communist Party that no single serious book has been published on Marxist economy, philosophy or theory since 1929 there was no reason for surprise. The logic of the system did not, and will not, tolerate independent and original social theory, at least not without consequences euphemistically labelled as 'administrative' by the regime.

Totalization and control

In discussing the functions of the doctrine one has to reassess the notion of substantive rationality described in the first chapter as an auxiliary form of legitimation. The prerogative of the sovereign in the interpretation of the 'only true science' is identical with self-legitimation through substantive rationality. This prerogative, however, transformed ideology into a system of dogma and that is why the substantive rationality itself became unreal, a myth.

The auxiliary form of legitimation is, however, not the main function of the system of dogma disguised as substantive rationality. The main function is to totalize and control the society. One should bear in mind once again Mussolini's definition of totalitarianism according to which in a totalitarian society all values are homogenized by the state. The doctrine interpreted by the Party is an obligatory creed for all members of the society: all other values and interpretations are precluded, that is to say, they cannot be openly expressed, or at least they have to be related, sometimes in a most awkward way, to the last utterance of the sovereign. Herein lies the necessity for the Party to have a 'scientific' opinion regarding everything, not only political matters. If there were no Party resolutions in the fields of fine arts, music or linguistics, loose threads would be left for interpretation based on heterogenous value preferences contradicting totalization. The extent of totalization has to be controlled again and again and thus reinforced. In this way the caprice of the Party constantly to pass new, often even contradictory resolutions on the same subject, has its function as well. It is a test of control. Not only the totalization but also the readiness of the population for immediate and unconditional belief has to be tested. The population is well-controlled only if it is ready to follow the Party in changing its mind from one minute to the next regarding all issues. In addition obedience has to be all-embracing. The successive acts of reinterpretation of the doctrine in fact regulated the degree of obedience and made it all-embracing by physically liquidating, imprisoning and dismissing from their jobs all those who were reluctant to obey at once, who were not malleable enough to accept all the new interpretations instantaneously. Those who hesitated could not expect a come-back, or perhaps only occasionally. 'Self-criticism' – in real terms, self-abasement and self-degradation – was the price to be paid for the come-back. It involved not only the denouncement of one's former point of view and the acceptance of the Party line, but the self-denigration of one's own character and motivation as well. The doctrine controls the society in that it repeatedly crushes assertive individuality. Only where no individuality is left, only when the subjects no longer know their own opinion, is the battle of totalization won.

De-enlightenment

The two main functions of the doctrine (totalization and its control) conclude in a process that may be called the process of de-enlightenment. If, according to Kant, enlightenment is humankind's release from its self-incurred tutelage, de-enlightenment means the relapse into that same tutelage. If enlightenment requires the use of one's own reason, de-enlightenment requires that one should never use it but should rely upon the collective intellect of the Party which does the thinking, instead of the person's own intellect. If enlightenment requires that one should reflect before acting and find out whether one's option is good, de-enlightenment requires that one should never reflect, but unhesitatingly obey the Party. Enlightenment emphasizes personal responsibility, de-enlightenment substitutes sheer obedience for personal responsibility. De-enlightenment 'liberates' humankind from moral, intellectual and political freedom. Nothing is more characteristic of the norm of de-enlightenment than the slogan of the Komsomol, the Communist youth organization and 'primary' school for future Party members: 'The Party is our reason, honour and conscience'. This slogan holds the secret of de-enlightenment: self-alienation becomes a publicly professed creed.

Self-alienation in the de-enlightenment process has particularly devastating psychological consequences. People not only lose their capacity for thinking for themselves, but have to pretend that they still are. The final interpretation of the dogma, with all its practical implications, has to be accepted not passively, but actively. One is obliged to analyse it, to expound it in public, to argue for it, to internalize it. If, however, the interpretation changes, one has again to expound, analyse and internalize it to the same extent. All Party members are supposed to be 'agitators'; they have to persuade those outside the Party, at least seemingly. Even though such persuasion is never real, personal involvement in it has to be emphatic. In this process there are only two possibilities left. Either one preserves a total incognito and thus participates in actions without any personal commitment, or even acting against one's own commitment, or one induces oneself really to accept everything actively and passively. Both positions lead to serious personality disturbances: either to an excessive degree of cynicism crippling normal behaviour, or to an excessive degree of self-deception, with similar symptoms. The stress exceeds the ego's capability of endurance and the personality falls apart. It is relevant here to refer to some typical reactions of Soviet intellectuals. In the main they meet the requirements of the sovereign, demonstrating their readiness to accept and (at least, seemingly) internalize the Party's latest interpretation of the dogma. Thus they become completely incompetent in their own *métier*, they cannot follow its logic, their products are mere waste-products despite receiving all possible and impossible awards and medals from their master. Most of them are aware of their incompetence: they know they could have done better and that is why they become the regime's most faithful watchdogs. Their guilt-feeling is transformed into hatred against all those who have preserved their personality; the annihilation of such a 'living reproach' becomes an obsession with them. The leading Party organs merely have to give the signal, the watchdogs do the rest. The smallest amount of real freedom would mean that their own lives were a failure, and they defend their own lives in destroying the lives of others.

Another group of intellectuals pays all the lip-service required, but seeks for a piece of firm ground untouched and unsoiled by the doctrine and thus preserves the dignity of the intellectual and the possibility of creativity. This is, in truth, a kind of heroism, for, so they are told, their production has no connection whatsoever with practice and indeed it has none. The ivory tower, of course, does not offer protection against the sovereign, only against the loss of personality.

A third group, a mere handful of men and women, the so-called dissidents, are the product of only the last twenty years. They bring into question not only the prerogative of interpretation of the doctrine, but the doctrine itself. The deeper the roots of the system, the more enraged the dissidents have to be. Their attitude is mostly prophet-like, which may seem strange, sometimes even ridiculous to Western eyes, but not at all to their own. They are indeed prophets, telling obvious truths to an audience which forgot about the obvious decades ago.

The language of domination

The language of the doctrine is constructed from different clichés, like those of television advertising. At the same time it has a menacing tone for it is the language of domination and power. In the Soviet Union the totalization of society was successful enough to generalize the language of domination. No one can use any other language while speaking in public; it has even entered the private sphere, and subjugated cultural production, at least in all kinds of social theory. When language ceased to be the vehicle of self-expression it precipitated the destruction of personality. Opposition, too, is compelled to speak the language of domination unless it is ready to invent an artificial language which is not spoken by ordinary people. This is, however, not the case in other Eastern European societies. Here the language of domination is spoken exclusively in public or in official documents. The leading articles and the Party resolutions are written in a quite different language from, say, that of art critiques in the press. Consequently no one any longer reads the language of domination simply for reading's sake. People read for a different purpose, namely in order to find out where the wind is blowing. Whoever is familiar with the patterns of the language of domination is able to guess the practical–political meaning of the presence of one cliché and the omission of others. A particular cliché may forecast the gathering storm in a general social sense; another may express a threat in one or another aspect; yet another may promise concessions towards the population.

The vocabulary of the official language is partly that of warfare and partly that of paternalism. In it, everyone is on the 'front'. There is a 'cultural front', a 'work front', 'economy front' – and on all fronts one has to 'fight'. There is a 'peace front' too, obviously a symbiosis of incompatibles. The country is a 'fortification' in the 'peace front'. One has to 'fight' for the realization of the five-year plans; the production of coal is a 'battle for coal'. According to this vocabulary all fights are won, never lost. The 'offensive of the enemy' for example on the 'culture front' is always flung back and the offensive of socialism on the same front is always victorious. Lenin's Party is the 'victorious Party'; socialism is the 'victorious socialism'; the plan is the 'victorious plan'. At the same time the socialist 'camp' (a betraying term in itself) is 'one big family' – among whose members relations are always 'brotherly ones'. The Party scolds the subjects if they behave improperly and praises them if they behave properly. The Party leads the population, it grants privileges, imposes limits and above all teaches. 'The Party teaches this or that'; the 'Party knows it'; 'the Party helps'. Hence the Party is – according to its own language and the self-image mirrored in it – a military leader and an authoritarian father.

In a strange way, it is always the text that is important, never the spoken voice; it is the text and not the voice that threatens. Bolshevik leaders are not orators, they usually read their speeches in a dull, lifeless tone. Hence the voice, the gesture, even the situation is completely meaningless. If a particular leader has personality, his tone when answering questions may be more colourful than the text, but everyone knows that it is only the text that matters.

A strange feature of the language of Bolshevism could perhaps be best described as perverted *Lebensphilosophie*. The Party raises a claim not only to the exclusive interpretation of the theoretical heritage, but also to the expression of 'life' as well. The Party embodies life in its real, profound sense. Social theorists are always chided because they 'have not kept pace with life'. Life is always with the Party, the Party is the heart, the soul of life. Life is happiness and devotion, it is a good one, it is optimism, confidence, *élan vital*, it is magnificent. The standpoint of life is the standpoint of the Party. Sadness is 'decadence'; it is bourgeois, sceptical, fossilized, dead. The dissatisfied and the sad do not know what life really is, hence they do not belong to it. Life is the deep reality contrasted with the 'superficial' one, which is reality without life.

Dialectical materialism

The substance and the status of the basic doctrines shows the same sordid picture. Dialectical materialism is the world-view of the Party. Hence dialectical materialism, Marxism–Leninism, is, as Castoriadis formulated it, the language of domination. Djilas is unquestionably right in stating that at the present time there are almost no Party leaders left who would pay heed to what Karl Marx said on any topic. The text of Marx is hardly read and has no bearing at all on Marxism–Leninism which is a ritualized formula, and precisely therein lies its function. The Party has to have a philosophy of its own in order to totalize and control society, in order to exclude all world-views and philosophies proper, all kind of reflections from it. Dialectical materialism is being lectured on in every university, every Party school or union school; there are legions of philosophers in all Soviet systems. Dialectical materialism is, as was often emphasized, a state religion — following thereby the usual pattern of all absolutist states. The specificity of the Soviet state-religion which calls itself philosophy is, however, that it bans the standpoint of the 'double truth' — truth is one and undivided. The content of dialectical materialism can change, but not its exclusivity.

Besides the interdiction on all philosophies proper, both components of dialectical materialism have a particular function of their own. The acceptance of the religion of materialism plays a very important role in the totalization of society. So-called 'militant materialism' represses all religious world-views. Religious world-view is outlawed or forcibly relegated to the background (with the exception of Poland) even if religious practice is tolerated (whereas it has not been tolerated in the Soviet Union for many decades). No god can accept a competitor. If no one can be in right against the Party, there should be no God, but one — the traditional has to be interdicted. At the same time the materialist creed is useful for the control of natural sciences, or rather, the natural scientists. The disobedient (or only hesitatingly obedient) are stigmatized as 'idealists'. In times when the Party has a definite opinion regarding natural sciences everyone who does not accept it immediately or raises the slightest doubts with regard to it is deemed idealist. The particular function of dialectics is different. Dialectic, so we are told, teaches that everything is in a state of change, that everything is interconnected with everything else and that opposites are identical with each other. Hence those who do not follow the changes in the interpretation of the doctrine by the sovereign are anti-dialectical: everything changes, thus the truth of today has to be different from the truth of yesterday. At any rate, the thesis that everything is interconnected with everything else is itself a direct expression of the goal of totalitarianism. Those who do not perceive that dictatorship and democracy are identical; that in order to wither away the state power has to be strengthened; that there are no classes (or only friendly ones) in the Soviet Union, yet the class struggle is intensified; that socialism overpowered capitalism, yet there is still a capitalist encirclement of socialist states, are anti-dialectical, because they do not understand the identity of opposites. Although both aspects of dialectical materialism have particular functions of their own, the materialistic aspect has been emphasized more often than the dialectical one. It is easy to grasp the reason for this. The materialist creed could only be applied as a state religion; dialectics, however, could be used in a subversive way too (for example, not everything that is real is rational, the existing deserves always to be transcended) and indeed occasionally have been applied this way. That is why even in the case of Lenin's philosophy *Materialism and Empiriocriticism* became more official than the *Philosophical Notebooks*.

Dialectical materialism has to be applied to the period of socialist construction. Contrary to the dogmatic homogeneity of philosophy, however, here one is confronted with statements which are very loosely interconnected with each other, if at all. The political economy of socialism has always been a mess: the best the student could do was to enumerate the data of economic successes, taken from the most recent address of the First Secretary of the Party, memorizing thereby all the meaningless numbers about the gross

200   POLITICAL DOMINATION AND ITS CONSEQUENCES

production of steel, coal, etc. The same holds true in the field of politics. One can always score high if one states the following: Socialism is in every respect superior to capitalism. The history of the Soviet Union and that of all socialist states is a history of successes. The socialist economy is a planned economy, all plans have been fulfilled and over-fulfilled. Collectivized agriculture produces *x*-times more than individual production in agriculture. In industry, Department I has to grow faster than Department II; Soviet industry produces to meet the needs of the population. The needs of the population are ever-increasingly satisfied. The economy is sound; economic crisis is unknown. Exploitation of men by men has been abolished; there is no surplus-value in socialism. The Party is stronger than it ever has been. The whole population stand as one man behind the Party. The Soviet state is the dictatorship of the proletariat, and later: the Soviet state is the state of the 'people'. The Soviet state — and its leading force, the Party — expresses the interests and needs of the proletariat, the peasantry and the intellectuals; everything is done on behalf of the population. The socialist state is the highest form of democracy. The national states of the Soviet Union are brothers — the national question is solved according to the norms of the Leninist national policy. There are no classes (or there are only friendly classes) in the socialist states. There are 'remnants of capitalism' in the heads of some people, reinforced by capitalist encirclement and propaganda. The enemy has to be crushed or cut out from the same body of the Soviet society which is a community. Vigilance is needed in order to defend socialism against the enemy which is always ready to strike. The construction of socialism has been terminated and the construction of Communism begun (not in *all* countries, but primarily in the Soviet Union). The world-power of socialism is increasing day by day, capitalism is losing ground. 'Under the victorious banner of Marx, Engels, Lenin' (and, in his time, Stalin) socialism is always 'marching forward'. Some mistakes are still being made, but the Party corrects them all in due course. It is the wisdom of the Party that leads us, the Party never lets us down. It led us to the freedom of real socialism, liberated us from the oppression and slavery of capitalism, it will lead us to Communism in our country and on the whole earth as well.

If a student is familiar with these basic tenets, he knows everything there is to know about the application of Marxism–Leninism. Only the data of the latest successes have to be attached, the newest target-groups of the political police identified and denounced, the most recent Party-resolution memorized. It is a simple formula.

Soviet doctrine and culture

The pernicious consequences of the doctrine for cultural life as a whole are, first and foremost, palpable in the Soviet Union. Although the same doctrine has done a lot of harm in other Eastern European societies as well it could not succeed in fulfilling its task there. The reasons for this are well-known, nor is there any need to tell the story of Soviet culture either. The immense contribution of Russian art and social sciences to world culture at the beginning of this century is generally known, as is the fact that it was a radical art and social science regardless of the political commitment of the artists and scientists. Part of this radical culture even continued to develop during the first decade of Soviet rule, for at least the radicals of the Left were able to pursue creative activity further and they were granted every facility to distribute their products and cultural ideas. The totalization of society, however, brutally put an end to these achievements and endeavours. From the late 1920s and early 1930s Soviet culture was successively transformed into a desert. Everything that can be called culture in the Soviet Union at the present time is oppositional in the sense that it embodies pluralism by its very existence.

Western artists and social scientists are often astonished (maybe even envious) when they observe the popular interest in a poem, a novel, a painting, a book on sociology or philosophy, even if they are far from first-class. There can be no doubt that creative culture of quality exerts a tremendous influence in Eastern European society, for the simple reason that it respresents dissent by the very fact of its existence. The enthusiasm of the reception is only partially due to artistic and scientific qualities, it is primarily due to the challenge of thinking, writing or painting in a different way. But there is no reason to envy the popular Eastern European intellectuals. An enthusiastic reception triggers punitive sanctions on the part of the sovereign, and as the sense of the inherently artistic or scientific value of the production is of secondary importance for the recipient, the creator cannot know whether the product is of real value or not. The influence is a political one, but in a mutilated form, for cultural products cannot trigger political actions, at least not more frequently than in the Western world. The function of culture becomes rather like the function of pornography in a Victorian environment; it hints at something we think of and desire, but do not do – or only in a clandestine way, never publicly.

All Bolshevik-type parties have agitprop sections and pursue a cultural policy. Cultural policy is the application of the interpretation of the doctrine by the sovereign to culture as a whole. The Party secretaries responsible for cultural policy have to apply the doctrines concretely to all cultural fields. It is not enough to prescribe, for example, that art should be 'socialist–realist', philosophy 'Marxist–Leninist', etc.: the requirements have to be detailed as well. Among other things, novels, for example, have to be optimistic, have to be focussed on so-called 'positive heroes' (the most positive among them have to be Party members), have to depict socialist construction, above all work activity. 'The content and character of a book should in every respect respond to the demands of socialist construction; it should be militant and deal with political themes of the present day,' says a Central Committee resolution of 1931. Philosophy, to take another example, not only has to be Marxist–Leninist, it is prescribed as well how many 'points' dialectics should have (five or twelve), how Kant, Hegel or Socrates have to be interpreted (whether they ought to be analysed as reactionaries or part of the progressive tradition), how materialism has to be described, how epistemology has to be discussed, etc. Moreover, all individual works get a good or bad mark, they are approved or blamed and censured. The authors themselves cannot foretell with certainty whether their work will meet with approbation or criticism. And if later the detailed and all-embracing character of prescriptions is eased, the limits remain set.

It is not surprising that the members of the leading organs of the Party (at least in the Soviet Union and some Eastern European societies) treat 'cultural workers' as common servants who are useful only if they obey. For the most part, they do become real servants, though not without occasional grumbles and complaints. The Party is firmly convinced that by virtue of being the source of all political powers it is the source of all cultural powers too, hence its decisions have the magic capacity of actually making cultural products not only accepted, but good as well. Even an intelligent cultural functionary, once himself an intellectual, the Hungarian József Révai, told Lukács that the value of a philosophical work is defined and ascertained by the Party, and no work can have any value at all if rejected by it. Renown gained despite the Party's censure causes no confusion among the ranks of functionaries either: success is due to the conspiracy (or the politically biased propaganda) of the enemy. Strange as it may seem, they apply their own standards to a different world.

In a political society, even more so in a totalitarian society, every-thing *is* politics, both for those who govern and who are being governed. That is why the differentiation between political and non-political culture is out of the question. Every cultural product expresses either apology or opposition (and the latter is culture proper). No wonder that the (hesitant) acceptance of a realm of political neutrality is one of the greatest concessions to civil society. This concession has been granted in the last decade by the very pragmatic Hungarian leadership. Here all cultural works are divided by the sovereign into three groups: supported, tolerated and prohibited. The tolerated group is supposed to be politically neutral. Although the works belonging to the tolerated group can be prohibited and lose all support, and so their position is temporary and uncertain, their transient acceptance is regarded as a basic step forward in the process of liberalization.

This dichotomy of culture under Soviet rule (apology or opposi-tion), in other words, the politicization of intellectual production in general, is, however, only one expression of the politicization of society, although a highly important one. Some further aspects of this politicization will be discussed in the next chapter. One of them, however, is particularly related to the control exercised by the doctrine and its consequences on culture. This is the problem of forced consent.

Forced consent

Hume was wholly right when he ridiculed Locke's category of 'tacit consent', the assumption that everyone who does not revolt against a social order, who does not initiate overt political opposition to it, by the fact of his abstention gives tacit consent to the same social order and thus accepts obligation towards it. It is totally legitimate for a socialist when analysing Western societies to criticize the concept of tacit consent as an expression of mere liberalism (a solution by definition insufficient for socialists) and a theoretical obstacle in the face of the tasks of radical democracy. The present book, however, is an analysis of a society which is the product of a de-enlightenment process, in contrast to which even mere liberalism appears as an embodiment of human freedom. Apparently, Hungary is (or was until the Polish August) the only Eastern European country in which the sovereign occasionally accepted a certain kind of tacit consent. Kádár's statement according to which 'whoever is not against us is with us' is indeed an expression of liberalism. The dilemma does not consist in whether tacit consent is a real consent or not, but whether it is accepted as such by the sovereign. As a rule, it is not accepted in the Soviet system of domination. Contrary to Kádár's statement it is the explicit creed of the sovereign that 'whoever is not with us is against us' which, in other words, means the eviction of tacit consent. The subject has no right to be politically indifferent or neutral while obeying. At the same time obligation is not understood as the consequence of a certain kind of promise and it cannot be: the ideological conception of contract is evicted from this society. All subjects of the state are under binding conditions by very reason of the fact that they are subjects of the state — they must give their overt consent to everything decided by the sovereign. The obligation entails the expression of positive consent at every given minute and in all matters. The question is not whether the consent is genuine or simulated — it is mostly simulated. What really matters is that it is enforced through, and guaranteed by, punitive measures against everyone who has not given his consent in an overt manner. Hence it is forced consent. Hume in his time argued, that if he asked the man on the street whether he gave his consent to the government he would not understand the question. The Soviet subject would, however, understand it very well and answer in the affirmative — according to a long-lasting education in forced consent.

The concept of forced consent seems to be a self-contradictory one, yet it is a precise description of the gist of the matter. Soviet society cannot be properly controlled (although it can be legitimated, of course) without the unceasing and public appreciation and enthusiastic consent of the subjects. That is why appreciation and consent become the subjects' obligation towards the sovereign. At the same time, the sovereign needs not only appreciation and consent but also the appearance that these were granted by the subjects of their free will: they could have refused the decision of the sovereign, but they accepted it for they considered it to be good and true. The lamb of the parable was devoured by the wolf in spite of his rational arguments. His Soviet counterpart has to do more than that: he has to recognize the action of the wolf as justice.

CHAPTER 8

Morality and Psychology

Any examination of the morality of a society has to begin with the validity of its accepted norms of ethical behaviour. It is a reasonable assumption that the norms are generally observed or seemingly observed and that their open violation provokes not only punishment, but also disapprobation.

Needless to say, in totalitarian societies there is only one system of norms which is recognized as valid. In one-party systems it is the moral code of the sovereign that is being generalized. All other norms have to be suppressed or subjugated to the valid ones and in case of a conflict the former have to be neglected, the latter obeyed. That is why it seems to be relevant to discuss Bolshevik morality in order to understand the ethical system of the Soviet societies.

Lenin and morality

Because of the frequent references to Leninist norms we should begin the discussion with a brief analysis of Lenin's own understanding of morality. We will see that in this respect there was very little to refer to: Lenin's party could not observe the moral prescription of its founder.

Although Lenin did not touch very often upon moral questions in a theoretical way, his random remarks are consistent enough to offer an insight into his basic conception. All his formulations manifest a fairly coherent version of utilitarianism. All moral norms are based on interests: either on class interests or on the general interest of social co-existence. The class norms are changing, for different classes have different interests; the norms of social co-existence, which were called elementary norms by Lenin are, however, stagnant. The observance of both is guaranteed by the state in all class-societies.

This is a most simplistic ethic, but one that is far from being a product of de-enlightenment. It is nothing but the application of liberal–bourgeois theories of 'rational egoism' to social classes. Even the notion of natural law is preserved in the concept of elementary norms.

The application of the theory is, again, a simple procedure. Everything is morally correct that is being done in the interest of the proletariat, moral good is identical with the behaviour that realizes these interests. The interest of the proletariat, however, cannot infringe the elementary norms, for the goal of the dictatorship of the proletariat is the withering away of the state which could only happen if the elementary rules were observed by everyone without state enforcement.

Although Lenin did create the very organization (the Party) which became the instigator and the guiding force of the de-enlightenment process and of a morality adequate to it, his arguments for doing so were utilitarian ones. He had a personal inclination to Jacobin virtue (for example, in matters of sexuality), but he was not sufficiently Jacobin to describe terror as a moral issue. He instigated and defended it as a necessity – once again in utilitarian terms.

All utilitarian ethics are self-contradictory. For the purpose of this analysis, however, it is sufficient to glance at the self-contradiction in Lenin's version of the theory. The structure is as follows. Thesis one: moral notions and norms express class interests. Thesis two: everything which is done for the interest of the proletariat is good. If the thesis that moral notions express class interest holds true, one could act in the interest of the proletariat only by accepting its moral notions and judgements. If, however, the second thesis holds true, that everything that is being done in the interest of the proletariat is good, the moral notions and norms of the proletariat are either superfluous or they do not express the interests of the proletariat: in both cases they can be neglected. And they were, in fact, neglected.

It is obviously irrelevant to command: 'Act according to your interest'; but it is very relevant to command: 'Act according to the interest of others.' Lenin's statement was a hidden commandment of the second type. The thesis according to which everything done in the interest of the proletariat is good has to be read in the following way: act in the interest of the proletariat! Hence it had no relevance for the proletariat which would anyhow follow its own interests. It was a commandment directed at the Party (and the Komsomol), that is, at organizations (and members of organizations) which supposedly were nothing but the expressions of the interest of the proletariat.

However, the very fact that actions serving the interests of the proletariat had to be commanded for them as good was an expression of the fact that they did not represent the interests of the proletariat in practice, although they should in theory.

As mentioned, the Russian proletariat very soon expressed its interests as contrary to those of the ruling Party. Thus Lenin reformulated his utilitarian thesis as follows: 'We recognize neither freedom, nor equality, nor labour democracy if they are opposed to the interest of the emancipation of labour from the oppression of the capital.' By 'We' was meant the Party, which did not recognize labour democracy. From this it would logically follow that the Party does not represent the interests of the proletariat, but — through the identification of the 'emancipation of labour' with the programme and actions of the Party — only its own interests. The interest of the Party was openly substituted for the interests of the proletariat which was only an open recognition of a more or less ever-present situation. We have seen, however, that 'following our interest' cannot be morally required, that it is a matter of calculation rather than observing norms. Utilitarian ethics made sense (in spite of being innerly contradictory) up until the seizure of power, for the imperative, 'Act according to the interest of the proletariat' was a commandment which could trigger moral motivations. After 1921–2 utilitarian ethics made no sense at all unless a cynical (Mandevillian) version was used predicting that the vices of the Party serve in the long run the benefit of the proletariat. Undoubtedly there were certain representative politicians who drew precisely this conclusion (Radek is well-known among them). However, even if they were numerous, they were still exceptional cases. No society can survive without some kind of moral motivation. It is beyond the plasticity of human nature to base its activities exclusively on calculation and accept vice as an indifferent factor for the sake of success. (There is also of course the fact that calculation cannot cement an organization, for everyone may calculate in different ways.) Thus Bolshevism very soon worked out its own morality. The Party, the substitute of the proletariat, itself became the highest value. 'The interest of the Party' no longer had a utilitarian meaning, it had nothing to do with the interests of its members, of its leaders, it became a symbol. If Communists were told, 'this is the interest of the Party,' they could not answer, 'We are the Party,' they could not ask 'Why?' or 'How do you know it?' 'How did you find it out?'. They had to accept it, and — usually — they *did* accept it as the exclusive norm of action, as the embodiment of 'good'. Reflection itself would have meant a kind of doubt, and the slightest doubt would have been a sign of not being a good Communist, hence a sign of moral evil.

The supreme Soviet virtues and shame-culture

Bolshevik morality is based on the two supreme virtues related to the Party: loyalty and obedience. Everyone is considered to be good, who obeys the will of the sovereign and is loyal to it; failing to do so is considered a moral transgression, a crime; whoever does so repeatedly is positively wicked. Every action is a good one, if the actor obeyed the sovereign; every action has to be blamed which stems from disobedience or disloyalty. The Party is not only the source of all powers, but also of all virtues. If a concrete value formulated in the code of the sovereign clashes with the main virtues — loyalty and obedience — the former has to be subordinated to the latter two, according to the hierarchy of values. For instance, the increase of industrial production is a value in the moral code of the sovereign, but if loyalty to the Party requires the political denunciation of the most able engineer in a factory, local Communists responsible for increased production have to do it immediately. The family is a value according to the Soviet moral code, but if loyalty to the Party requires that you leave wife, husband or parents, you ought to do so without hesitation. Hence the 'burdens' of moral freedom, choice or deliberation do not belong to the ethics of good Communists. Not only the duty, but its observance and application to any concrete situation, are always known. The Party clearly prescribes how a task is to be performed, in which situation, towards whom, when, etc. Hence the question of whether actions required by the Party were good cannot be raised: they are good for the simple reason that they were commanded by the Party. There are no other values left as the measures of good or evil.

The same self-alienation faces us, then, as the one formulated fairly comprehensively in the already quoted slogan of the Komsomol: 'The party is our reason, honour and conscience.' There is no individual conscience left, conscience becomes completely estranged, embodied in an organization outside the individual, or rather, in the mythical will of his organization.

The development of conscience, or morality proper, was the only progress human ethical behaviour achieved in the course of history. The obedience to concrete behavioural patterns was replaced by the internalization of norms and by the reflected application of the same norms by the individual, and all this was called moral autonomy. Of course, conscience never superseded shame completely, not only because the latter is an innate human feeling, but also because shame has always been reinforced by the system of habits prevalent in all kinds of society. The feeling of remorse when we have done something wrong in terms of our moral standards and the feeling of shame when deviating from the average pattern of behaviour were always simultaneously present. These two feelings, however, could clash with one another and individuals even became able to accept shame for the sake of a good conscience.

In Bolshevik morality something extraordinary came about. If persons do not internalize moral norms and become unable to apply them individually any longer, one would be entitled to speak of the reintroduction of shame-culture. Bolshevik ethics produced a shame-culture for the simple reason that norms were not applied individually, and they had to be accepted without any reflection. The shame functioned (though only with faithful Communists) as if it were conscience, since the norms supposedly embodied a rational interest. A good Communist was not ashamed of denouncing his friends and relatives, of betraying his lovers, maybe even of denouncing himself, nor did he feel any qualms of conscience either. A good Communist was not only afraid of being caught red-handed if he gave a piece of bread to an enemy of the people, but he really felt qualms of conscience because of the disobedience and disloyalty against the Party inherent in such an act. If someone felt that he had been done an injustice (which might occasionally happen), he did not refer to his own sense of justice. In one of his famous poems even the individualist Majakowskij appealed to a future Central Committee to do him justice and acknowledge his right, as allegedly did Bukharin in his — perhaps apocryphal — letter 'on the right to the last word' before execution.

Shame functioned, then, as a quasi-conscience only in the case of the good Communists, but all ethics have to be judged on the example of those who observe their norms. That is why one is justified in speaking of internalized shame even if shame was not at all internalized by many, most certainly not by the majority. It is most telling that in the trials of the leading Communists there were only few who displayed symptoms of refusing such an internalization. Pleading not guilty does not in itself mean the resumption of one's individual conscience. It may also mean: I have always been loyal and obedient, what happens to me has to be a fatal mistake. Ter Vaganjan, an Armenian Communist, is a clear example of the very few who resumed their own conscience when saying: 'If my Party, for which I lived, and for which I was ready to die any minute, forced me to sign this, then I don't want to be in the Party.' Even though Stalin's times are over, the internalization of shame has not yet been terminated. It became less spectacular and less murderous in its consequences, but it is still present, at least in the leading circles.

To give an example of internalized shame, one can refer to curricula. Every subject of a Soviet state has repeatedly to write curricula extending sometimes to the most intimate details of his private life. One of the leading norms of loyalty to the Party is that whereas one can (perhaps even must) lie to one's fellow-creatures, one must never lie to the Party. To lie to the Party does not mean only to give false items of information: even an omission from one's curriculum is considered to be a lie. After submitting his curriculum to the proper authorities, a Soviet citizen suffers constant inner tensions while asking himself whether he has left something out that may be of a certain consequence (and no one knows what may be of consequence). The majority, of course, have worries of only a practical nature and the possible consequences are no longer fatal. But there are always some who feel a pang of conscience not only because they may be exposed (perhaps they forgot to describe their feelings as opposed to their deeds), but also because they have 'lied' to the Party.

Needless to say, the ethics of Bolshevism are in themselves a manifestation and a main constituent of the de-enlightenment process. Loyalty and obedience to the sovereign as supreme values belong to a world prior to enlightenment. However, as far as Western Europe was concerned, even the ethics of feudalism were more pluralistic than those of Communism. Obedience to God and to the Church, and observance of religious values could have been contrasted with loyalty and obedience to the monarch. Christian conscience has never been totally identical with the conscience of the faithful subject. Moreover, not only did the subject have moral obligations towards the sovereign, but the reverse was also true: the sovereign had moral obligations towards the subjects as well. Bolshevik ethics, however, inherited the Pravoslav tradition void of pluralistic institutions in matters of moral behaviour. The de-enlightenment process went back to this tradition, to the ethics of Russian autocracy. It was transplanted into the Communist movements with different historical and religious backgrounds, though rarely with the same success.

In a totalitarian society loyalty and obedience have to be all-embracing. The new sovereign abruptly and brutally overpowered not only the party members but the whole population. One should not forget, that though loyalty and obedience were traditional values in autocratic-Pravoslav Russia, the concrete values and behavioural patterns prescribed by the new sovereign were far from being traditional. The Russian population was religious in its majority and the Communists themselves inherited from the ancient social-democratic Marxist movements a quite different set of values. Even utilitarian ethics, as demonstrated, were not identical with a moral roster whose acme was loyalty and obedience: it included reflection and at least a certain amount of responsibility for the population, above all for the real interests of the working class. The process of de-enlightenment had to be repressive in a very high degree, suppressing all values previously accepted and followed, and pushing them into the sphere of the unconscious. It is, however, inconceivable that self-repression could continue without inner conflicts. Presumably there has been a continuous inner tension between the oppressed previous values and the confessed ethics. It is not too bold to assume at the same time that it caused neurosis in a very high degree, a sense of guilt that no one could get rid of.

It is very difficult to prove the prevalence of the guilt-feeling directly, but there is some indirect evidence.

There is documentation of the fact that certain of the Bolshevik Communists, among them the most dedicated terrorists, turned to religion while in prison or before being executed. Jagoda's form of reasoning is particularly interesting from our point of view. God has to exist, he said, because he deserved only gratitude from Stalin, but punishment from God for his deeds. It is characteristic, again, that those early Communists who left Communism, dedicated their whole life to the cause of anti-Communism with a kind of cold hatred that could only be matched by their previous loyalty. The more obedient and loyal they had been, the greater their hatred became, radically transcending the state of mind necessary for an objective critical attitude towards Bolshevism. Clearly, this became an obsession with them. The charge of renegade in modern politics is typical of Bolshevism. There have never been Nazi renegades. If former Nazis recognized that they were wrong and what Nazism really meant, they fought against their previous creed passionately, but never with the same obsession and fury as former Bolsheviks. Nazism was an openly reactionary and racist doctrine; nothing had to be repressed when following its practice and accepting its message. Bolshevism, however, accepted at least some humanistic values while practising just the contrary: repression and a feeling of unconscious guilt was an inevitable consequence of this. It was precisely this unconscious guilt that came to the surface in the obsession of hatred.

The third indirect proof of the sense of guilt is the phenomenon of excessive zeal. Every crime the Party required to be committed was 'overdone' by loyal Party members and even by many outside the Party. The NKVD officer who shot Kamenev and spat on the collapsing body is a perfect symbol of this neurotic and exaggerated zeal. Or, if one analyses the mass denunciations during the purges in the thirties, one can see that in them self-interest was one possible motivation (for example, to get the flat of the denounced, among other things), but this alone does not account for the immense number of disinterested denunciations. Nor can personal grudge and hatred be an explanation for this phenomenon where men and women were denounced en masse by accusers to whom they were personally unknown, nor for the sadism involved (they could not become voyeurs of their victims' sufferings). It is hard to find any explanation for this established fact, other than a sense of guilt which people wanted to rid themselves of by becoming really guilty, but unconsciously again, which led to new crimes *ad infinitum*.

The fourth indirect proof for the prevalence of the sense of guilt is that almost everyone felt themselves guilty with regard to the Party, even when they had always been loyal and obedient. People who believed in the Party and participated in its action generally felt that they had done something wrong, but they localized the source of the rot in accordance with their accepted morality (obedience and loyalty): they felt guilty towards the Party, not towards the people they inwardly knew they were wronging. Several Communists confessed that they felt a sense of relief when they were arrested. 'It is all over,' sums up their feeling at the time. What was all over? Partially the fear of being arrested. But why was the arrest (which might lead to execution) a relief in comparison with the fear of being arrested? The external tension was, obviously, not over, it was going to be tremendously increased. Inner tension had, however, been terminated. Punished for crimes they had never committed, they might unconsciously feel that they were punished for crimes they *did* commit, by a moral law, *not* by the Party. It is better for the conscience to feel a victim rather than a murderer. (Communists persecuted by the Nazis never said that they felt relief when being arrested.) Only a haunting and repressed sense of guilt can account for such a strange kind of relief. The greater the qualms of conscience, the more intense the estrangement of conscience and the fear of the unknown. Whoever witnessed the events of 1956 in Hungary, whoever watched Communists until so recently truly loyal, but now panicking not only from the fear of being punished, but also from the fear of being exposed as common criminals, will understand this very well. More than a million Party members melted away into limbo within five days, and this cannot simply be ascribed to sheer cowardice — the more so since at least a handful of them lived up to the suppressed conscience later, in the wave of persecution of 1957—8.

Admittedly, all this can be regarded simply as a direct result of fear, and it was, undoubtedly, a real fear that persisted along with the unchanging face of despotism. One should not forget, however, that in the Soviet social system *the source of all powers and the source of all virtues are identical*. Loyal Communists are afraid both of the physical consequences of their behaviour, and equally of the disapprobation of the Party. Even uncommitted Communists are not only afraid of being arrested or losing their jobs, but also of the shame that stems from such a disapprobation. The Party plays the role of a gigantic, authoritarian father. Thus it is a double fear amplified through more or less unconscious anxiety, the offspring of the suppressed individual morality and conscience. Fear and the sense of guilt belong together, they increase each other's intensity. There is, again, an indirect proof for that too: Communists, who lived in a state of permanent anxiety and fear, were liberated from the same fear in the war. They had to face no less mortal dangers but the sense of guilt was gone. And this holds true not only in the case of Communists.

The purges and Party ethics

In this respect, the concept and practice of the Party purges are most characteristic. Purges have repeatedly been practised by the Bolshevik Party and other Communist Parties as well, based on the doctrine that the Party is fortified by purifying itself from 'opportunist' or 'careerist' elements within it. The words 'purge' and 'purifying' are telling, referring as they do to 'cleanliness'. Everyone is clean who qualifies for the double fear, who acknowledges the Party not only as the source of all powers, but also as the source of all good. As a result, a mass murderer can be clean, but a person whose only guilt is a failure to be completely convinced of the Party's constant infallibility is unclean. Those who were re-accepted during the purges proved their cleanliness; the more alienated their conscience was, the cleaner they were. The unclean ones became immediately objects of suspicion, second-class citizens, pilloried not only by the Party, but by everyone as morally inferior. In times of generalized purges, not only good Communists, but others as well believed that whoever was hit by the terror had really done something wrong, even if it was not exactly what he was accused of (if indeed it was known what he was accused of). Friends who had known each other for decades made frantic efforts to find out what crime the other might have committed – and they usually found something. And those who are still adherents of Communist morality in our time believe exactly the same: the attitude has not changed for those who still share it.

   It is virtually a sociological or moral law of the Communist mentality that members of the ruling elite are ready to do practically anything in order to remain in the centre and not be compelled to move to the periphery. It is too simplistic to explain this phenomenon exclusively in terms of a desire for power. It is well-known, for instance, that in Stalin's time those who did disappear from the view of the tyrant had a greater chance of survival than those who remained at the centre, although far too many who were aware of this still remained there. Is the desire for power stronger than that for self-preservation? It is well-known that Trotsky's attitude was different in this respect. Was his thirst for power less than that of his fellow rulers? By way of explanation one may point out that he was not educated as a Bolshevik and thus did not share the Bolshevik morality completely. To be in the centre did not only mean being in power, but belonging to the elite, according to Bolshevik morality. Whoever had to move to the periphery lost not only power, but honour as well – it meant proscription. The schizophrenia in the attitude of some loyal Communists is clearly perceivable. Even if they disapproved of certain measures taken by the Party, even if they realized that something horrible was going on, they felt dishonoured when left out of the ranks of those who committed the crimes they themselves condemned. To be left out meant political exile, a wound which never healed. Even insincere self-criticisms were often sincere in one respect: self-humiliation was a price paid willingly for belonging to the elite. To be in 'good grace' was experienced as elevation, as self-confirmation, even if the person from whom the grace stemmed was despised.

   Lenin's conception was the point of departure for this analysis. It is now appropriate to refer back to his idea of the primacy of certain elementary norms of human co-existence. Even the most superficial survey will show that precisely these elementary norms were destroyed by the supreme virtues of loyalty and obedience. The most simple norms of solidarity, mutual help and goodwill, the most simple moral feelings of sympathy and empathy, the unobtrusive moral gestures of confidence, of support to our fellow-creatures in borderline situations disappeared, moreover were regarded as crimes. Fidelity and charity to those in need were all gone, either suppressed or practised exclusively against the tide. Anyone who gave shelter to a harassed person, a piece of bread to a deported person's child, anyone who maintained allegiance to their own husband, child, parent or friend now in disgrace, or was reluctant to give false testimony against their own neighbour was a hero. The normal became extreme and the extreme normal. The ten commandments were outlawed as well.

Social atomization and mass-neurosis

Phenomena of mass-neurosis are — at least partially — the consequences of a total atomization of society. There has never been a society more atomized than the Soviet societies. In them not only have all organic ties been cut, not only have elementary norms lost their validity, but the formation of any kind of new communities and movements have been blocked as well. Atomization was accomplished in Stalin's time and no Eastern European society could completely recover from it, least of all the Soviet Union. A situation was created in which no one could expect anything from anyone. Everyone was afraid of everyone, suspicious of everyone. To confide in an old friend was a risk most persons did not even try to take. Love could be brought as a testimony against you, more so those thoughts which had to be hidden deeply in the soul, even from oneself. A neighbour was a possible source of danger, so was a colleague, so was a lover. If you applauded in a crowd you watched the person standing next to you to see whether he was watching you. Have you cheered loudly enough? Have you clapped visibly enough? Everyone could be a spy. There were real spies in sufficient number but those who were considered as potential spies far outnumbered the real ones. If someone visited you, you asked yourself, why? If someone told you that he agreed with your opinion, you asked yourself again, why did he say so? When someone told you that he was in love with you, you asked yourself, why did he want to gain your confidence? If there was ever a completely lonely crowd, it was this crowd in real socialism. Everyone was left alone with his own guilt-feelings and very few could cope with them.

It is necessary to distinguish between mass-neurosis and mass-hysteria. Mass-hysteria is a very rare phenomenon in Soviet-type states and if it occasionally occurs it is directed against the regime. In this respect the psychology of Soviet societies radically differs from that of the Fascist societies. Italian and German Fascism regularly instigated and triggered mass-hysteria. Riots were daily occurrences; SA and SS-men attacked Jews, socialists, Communists, they destroyed and killed in a bloodthirsty frenzy. Bolshevism has always had its Gestapo, but never its SS. 'Arbitrary' action and conduct was energetically discouraged. Mass-hysteria is an open aggression, an outburst of hatred directed against an out-group. In this case it is appropriate to argue against Freud: xenophobia expressed in mass-hysteria, at least as far as the majority is concerned, is usually not the upshot of a repressed sense of guilt, but of repressed inferiority feelings. Moreover, in mass-hysteria rage, not fear, becomes manifest. The SA men who murdered Jews and socialists were not afraid of them and they were not afraid of their own party either. Killing was their great revenge against life and their own frustrations. (And incidentally, while all the Nazi leaders had been previously frustrated for one reason or another, most of the representative Bolshevik leaders were not.) Those Germans who felt the sense of guilt were not rioting: they did the same as their Soviet counterparts — denounced with fear.

It is difficult to account for the lack of mass-hysteria in Soviet states by reference to historical tradition. Russia, no less than Germany, had a tradition of rioting, maybe even more from Stenka Razin to the pogroms, above all in the Ukraine. However, the Bolshevik Party had always feared mass-hysteria: perhaps because it got far smaller popular support than the Nazi Party did and wanted to keep the genie in the bottle; perhaps because its target groups were not identical with traditional ones and that is why xenophobia could not have been used as means for the chosen ends. The reasons are, however, of secondary importance. The consequence was that the crimes of Soviet citizens were more subtle ones. Most of the dirty work had been done by the security organs: the blood was not on their hands, the average citizen acted through others. Fear of committing a crime and, at the same time, not committing it, fear of the retaliation of the Party or of the reproaching eyes of the victims, fear of everything, above all fear of oneself — this is mass-neurosis.

As long as Bolshevik ethics remain binding in wide social groups, mass-neurosis will re-emerge again and again. In recent decades it became less binding: less in quantitative terms of those still under its spell, less in the Soviet Union, but even less in Eastern European societies. The de-enlightenment process is over, at least for those who no longer believe in the values of obedience and loyalty. What usually happens is that the Communist quasi-religion is replaced by a more traditional kind of religion or the former is replaced by open cynicism: the values of Communism proved to be false, as a result all values are false; the Communist morality proved to be irrelevant, as a result all morality is irrelevant, or so many argue. Rational argumentation, civil courage, tolerance, objectivity, respect for a different way of life, civility, practices based on the universal values of freedom, personality and community, combined with the elementary values of decency, are advocated and represented by all too few.

PART III

The Functioning of the System: Conflicts and Perspectives

CHAPTER 9

Why is Dictatorship over Needs not Socialism?

The general findings of our analysis so far can be summarized as follows. The new society, the 'dictatorship over needs', is neither a novel, modified form of (state) capitalism, nor is it socialism — it is 'something else'. It is a social formation completely different from any that has existed in European or world history to date and it is equally different from any relevant conception in terms of which socialism, either 'scientifically' or in a utopian manner, has ever been conceived. Nor is this social formation a kind of transition between two states of social affairs, one existing (capitalism) and one not yet existing. It is a self-reproducing social order in which many elements declared to be 'transitory' (for reasons of camouflage) are constitutive of, and indispensable for, the functioning of the system. But even if there is an enormous practical, as well as theoretical, importance in understanding and admitting that the new social order is not socialism, it must none the less be recognized as a type of response to capitalism and its contradictions. As such, it is not totally independent of socialist ideas and movements either. We also believe that this new system cannot be deduced totally from the economic and social backwardness of certain countries which would confine the new social entity to underdeveloped areas, even though it undeniably has a certain affinity to backwardness. This is, then, a universal system, or at least a system that has universalistic aspirations, it is not a regional solution. Our attitude to the new formation is unambiguous. As a *dictatorship* over needs we consider it a value degradation, a demolition of the potentially free individual whose voluntary association would form an emancipated society, in the imagination of Marx and every socialist. For us the dictatorship over needs is a historical dead-end despite its self-reproductive capacity.

The attentive reader will immediately see that this summary of the foregoing analysis actually contains *two* methodological steps. The first was the statement that all movements and ideologies which have implemented the new system originally had a socialist intention. Any attempt to deny this would transform the analysis into a farce; nevertheless, this fact has repeatedly been denied and for perfectly simple reasons. If representative socialists (such as Rosa Luxemburg for instance) considered committing suicide at the outbreak of the First World War, as they regarded this event to be a terrible defeat of the socialist cause, one can easily imagine what later generations of socialists may have felt when confronted with the 'real socialism' of Stalin and his successors. This is why they resorted to a number of defence mechanisms in order not to be compelled to realize the upshot of their own, often heroic, struggles. One of these mechanisms, but not the only one, was to conceptualize the movements and their results as mere ideological façades for the 'bourgeois industriali-zation' of backward, overwhelmingly agrarian, Tsarist Russia which needed a pseudo-socialist ideology for the enormous thrust whose end result has, however, no bearing whatsoever on the real status of socialism in modern world. The sometimes noble motives of such a mental operation are fully understandable but we are not prepared to accept its easy excuses and comfortable outlets. Socialism as a whole, if it is ever to transcend its present miserable state, needs radical self-criticism of what has happened in the last sixty years. No socialist movement has ever existed which would even experiment with the idea of such a nightmare as the Soviet Union under Stalin. In this respect, all comparisons between Stalin and, for instance, Nechaev are exaggerated and biased. It is equally true that there have been many socialist movements which warned against the various social ills inherent in certain Marxist or non-Marxist socialist aspira-tions. But no such socialist movements (once again, neither Marxist, nor of any other kind) would have been completely exempt from any of the latently dangerous tendencies or policy objectives. Nor were there any which would have given a forecast of the horror, or even a vague prediction of the totality of social cataclysms socialists can elicit, under the disguise of reforming social ills, if unaware of the dangerous potentialities of their doctrines and practice. And since socialism does not exist except as the sum of its historically existing varieties, nineteenth- and early twentieth-century socialist doctrines are at least co-responsible for the 'real socialism' of today. even if we reassert our statement that the upshot is not socialism in any meaningful and acceptable sense of the term.

And this last statement leads us to the second methodological step. We have argued to a considerable extent in Part I, in the section which criticized rival interpretations of the new societies, against any theory that identified dictatorship over needs with capitalism. But in a way we have taken for granted that it is not socialism either, and therefore have presented no counter-arguments. We shall now deal with this point. Our argument is twofold. Firstly, we cannot accept any value-free definition of socialism. Without the valid existence of certain fundamental socialist values, socialism, however it is interpreted, is inconceivable as a social state of affairs. These values are freedom (in its 'formal' and 'substantive' version); equality (in all its forms and, in certain theoretical versions, in conflict with the former); and, (this latter only in the Marxian conception of socialism), the acquisition of the wealth of species by every individual, or at least a dynamic pointing in this direction. Excepting the official propagandists of 'real socialism', there is now a consensus between the enemies and the supporters of socialism that none of these values is observed (or even respected) in the societies which nowadays call themselves socialist. Instead, only a shabby structuralism would list a few features, such as the 'leading role of the Party', 'the state property of the forces of production', the 'expropriation of capitalists' and the like, as allegedly criteria of the existence of socialism. Such a list would neither be traditionally socialist, although it contains at least certain elements common in many (or all) socialist ideas, nor expressive of the genuine will to socialism.

Secondly, even though we do not conceive of socialism in a 'chiliastic' way, as a mystic *'promesse de bonheur'*, as the 'resolved riddle of all history', but rather, and more modestly, as a response, an ideology and a movement confronting the painful dilemmas of the modern age, we shall be able to draw up a catalogue of problems as a response to which it was in fact invented. These problems are roughly the following: social oppression within a particular type of society (in the form of class-, group-, or elite-oppression); national oppression between various states and nations; poverty; liquidation of individual and collective civil liberties already gained (or their formalization to a degree where they become meaningless); the socially eliminable pains and burdens of modern industrialization; the catastrophic and non-rational character of modern social development following the above mentioned (and other) factors; local wars; the burdens and threats of the armament race; and the danger of a universal nuclear war. Once again, with the exception of official propagandists the consensus is that the societies labelled socialist do not diminish but in fact add to the gravity of this catalogue, or at the very least they leave the original problems unresolved. It is in this double sense that we deny that Eastern European societies (or any of their extensions elsewhere) can justly claim to be socialist.

But all this provides us with a new 'cunning of reason' rather than with any solution. The 'why' has not been answered, or it can only be answered seemingly in a Hegelian way: the new universal class, the proletariat, created a 'realm of bourgeoisie' out of the projected 'realm of reason' just as, according to Engels, the former universal class, the bourgeoisie did. But Hegelian *aperçus* very rarely solve social enigmas. They are particularly worthless here where, according to our firm conviction, it was not the proletariat that created the new social order (which was created only in the name of the proletariat) and it was not the realm of any bourgeoisie that came about but rather the elitist dictatorship over needs. The social protagonists remain unidentified, the result of their efforts mysterious. The real upshot of struggles of movements with various socialist projects (which is at the same time Lenin's genuine and irrevocable historical contribution) is something negative: the closure of the world-historical period in which capitalism seemed to be naturally given. Capitalism can, in principle, be restored (even if this is at any rate a highly unlikely option), but its 'naturalness' is irretrievably lost.

There are two easy answers to the problem, to the historically unexpected result of contrary aspirations, both of them logical, but neither acceptable for us. The first is the well-known 'Thermidor' explanation which has many versions. Its inventor (as so often in the history of twentieth-century Marxism) was Trotsky. His is a consistent reply in that it argues that because of backwardness, weakness of the proletariat or a combination of the former and many other factors, power, the class character of which had been socialist up to a certain point, was torn out of the hands of socialist forces and taken over by an anti-socialist one. This is a straightforward sociological solution but one which could only find justification if the ensuing social state had become capitalistic in any interpretable sense of the word. We believe we have proved that this is not the case. The second answer is neo-Burkean, and it is anthropological rather than sociological in nature. According to this interpretation, for reasons which are somehow rooted in human nature all attempts at reforming social ills must lead to even graver maladies. We are convinced that the external elegance of this argument is fraudulent. It is nothing but an inadmissible hypostasis gained from a certain amount of undeniable pragmatic experience of how Jacobin attempts at moral dictatorships have always to date degenerated into utterly immoral tyrannical states, and at the same time a claim to 'true knowledge' about the future of all anthropological-radical reforms which is nonsensical and misleading. But we know full well that we have thus far at best only refuted certain popular explanations, not explained anything. The problem remains to be solved.

The first step in the analysis of this spectacular world-historical fiasco is the necessary self-criticism of socialism as a theory and a movement (in its various guises). Any 'this-worldly' conception of socialism demands that several fundamental aspects and elements which are contained in nearly all socialist doctrines and have contributed to the undermining of the enlightenment lineage of socialism, be isolated, because it is precisely these that can be mainly held responsible for the monumental 'cunning of unreason', for this negative fulfilment of a Hegelian dialectic. Especially in the movements which resolutely set out to realize their allegedly socialist programme, though not only in them, socialism has lost its powerful enlightenment character. It turned into a doctrine which many call a 'religion' but which perhaps can be more properly called a 'cult of unreason' and an undoing of that release from 'man's self-incurred tutelage', to use the phrase coined by Kant, which was the main achievement of the Enlightenment, the culmination of which socialists have traditionally considered to be Marx's *oeuvre*. As a culmination of de-enlightenment it ceased to be socialism.

The first negative complex within the socialist tradition was the Jacobin legacy so sharply and wittily criticized by the young Trotsky (who later became one of its main representatives) and by Rosa Luxemburg (who remained its enemy until the moment of her death). Since our analysis is not a historical study, it will suffice to mention the main constituents of the Jacobin streak in socialism. First and foremost a 'double anthropology', so characteristic of Robespierre himself, has constantly been inherent in several shades of radical socialism, with a very wide gap between an uncritically maintained idea of human perfectibility, even a deification of man as the public doctrine, and that of virtue in minority, a desperately pessimistic view of human substance, as the secret doctrine. The latter, in itself, and in blatant contrast to the optimism of the public doctrine, provoked the use of terror as an inevitable means of 'moral improvement' and as an organic part of government. It is an unacceptable excuse used by so many, so often, that the early and unrestrained administration of mass terrorism by the Bolsheviks can primarily or even exclusively be explained by an emergency situation. The famous debate between Trotsky and Kautsky about the obligation of work and 'state slavery', and particularly the arguments used by Trotsky regarding man's innate laziness and the necessity and legitimacy of coercion to discipline it, testify to the fact that Bolshevik—Jacobin terrorism has always had a moralistic and pessimistic ingredient which renders necessary the punishing cane of the educator. The second, similarly fatal, constituent of the Jacobin legacy was the allocation of moral perfectibility in an omnipotent political state, master and tutor of an egoistic and imperfect society, a universal remedy for all malaises of human nature. Despite the fact that, for instance, Marxist socialism simply wanted to abolish the state as such, coexistent with the uncritical acceptance of that highly unrealistic perspective there was a tendency to adopt in fact the Jacobin position and practice of a dictatorship which had an educational function (with constant apologetic references to its merely transitory character, of course). The greatest representative of this trend is Lenin, and the main responsibility for it lies with him.

To set the goal of the abolition of the state, on the one hand, and tacitly to accept on the other the idea of a dictatorship, in other words, an unusually strong state as the transition to that end, has for decades been called a superior dialectic. In more humble, and perhaps more reasonable, terms, it is a flagrant contradiction at the very heart of the theory and, as such, one of the roots of evil in it. But it had a further, specific, and very dangerous consequence. Marxist socialism declared the work of political emancipation to be completed when it was only just begun, and its fruits to be irrelevant in comparison with human emancipation. It did not only want to relativize the absolute rupture between bourgeois and citizen, to mediate between these totally separated spheres, but to produce a complete homogenization, a merger of these two aspects of human social life. This meant a practical liquidation of the political sphere as a whole, ignoring all theoretical and practical problems of a democratic and socialist political establishment. Socialist parties with a Marxist education, particularly the German socialist party, used vague phrases about a 'people's state' but yet were unprepared with regard to the whole problem-complex of state, law, power and their separation, principles of a socialist constitution, and the like, even *before* socialist radicals were cynically manipulating democracy as the 'suitable battlefield' for their struggle for a dictatorship. The unrealistic programme of the 'withering away of the state' was not only insincere, but also contributed only negatively to the development of a Marxist theory of politics.

A further important, and equally negative, component of the legacy was the technocratic-statist spirit, the most influential apostle of which was Saint-Simon. The impact of 'socialist technocratism' was negative in a twofold sense. Firstly it involved the absorption (or even the annihilation) of all other fundamental socialist values in the name of an exclusive growth of social material wealth. This arose from that 'productionism', so vehemently and rightly criticized by Castoriadis, the forebears of which are the socialist technocrats rather than Marx. Secondly, the specific argument of this standpoint did not lie in any moral consideration but in the alleged incompetence of civil society as against a technologically trained elite (the latter judgement delivered from the perspective of a general goal-rationality). Its partisans were just as contemptuous towards the 'dilettantish' character of civil society as the zealots of 'virtuous minority' despised 'immoral majority'. The practical results of the two different standpoints were not so far from one another.

As a further component of a problematical legacy, we should mention here the Babuvian violent homogenization of human needs which had a strange and unique fate in socialist doctrines and movements. Its well-known basic principle is that 'actual equality' (*égalité de fait*) can only be realized by a total (and if necessary, violent) uniformization of all individual needs, and their general reduction by the elimination of all 'artificial' ones. The Babuvian Communist has no inhibitions about paying the inevitable price for this operation: the proscription of free individuality. Babeuf's tenets had a quite unique fate precisely from the viewpoint of our theory. His radical spirit was the first to go far enough to grasp the (anticapitalist) social problem at the really fundamental level of needs and need regulation and after a short but vehement conflict with Jacobinism he gave his *a posteriori* consent and blessing to the 'permanence of guillotine'. But irrespective of the fact that he is generally called the 'first Communist', his doctrine has always been, except perhaps for a short period of the Chinese cultural revolution, only partially accepted by later implementers of originally socialist tenets by the founding fathers of a dictatorship over needs. As is well-known, Stalin and all his successors were vehement enemies of the petty bourgeois idea of egalitarianism. The element of Babeuf's writing and political personality which they put to use was the very invention of the dictatorship over needs, that is to say, the idea that the subjection of the 'rebellious' and 'individualistic' private person to a 'superior wisdom' has to be started at the level of his needs system. The inherent paternalistic streak of socialist theories had added its share to all this. Dostoevsky's famous and malicious *aperçu* that one of the greatest forces of attraction to socialism is the fear of having an opinion of one's own was totally calumnious at the beginning of the nineteenth century. In an age when the state was either the general master of society (and in this capacity, it condemned all self-protecting activities of the workers) or an open agency of the well-off safeguarding an electorate which never went beyond the wealthy upper strata of the middle classes, socialist paternalism had been aimed at guarantees then deemed to be dangerously radical innovations, but which are now normal routine functions of the welfare state. However, parallel to the increase of the statist element in socialist doctrine, paternalism had gradually been transformed, and assumed a strongly anti-enlightenment character long before the attempts at realization of the doctrine. In this respect, the whole emphasis on the importance of the Party within socialist theory and practical activity (even long before Bolshevik pseudo-religious mystification) was the herald of an epoch in which Dostoevsky's malevolent comment turned out to be a tragically accurate description of the state of social affairs.

Finally, the eulogy of backwardness as something superior, because potentially more revolutionary than the 'bourgeoisified' developed countries, become increasingly preponderant in radical social theories which were originally almost exclusively centred on developed Western Europe. As we now know, Russian Marxism, a joint undertaking of the two rivals, Trotsky and Lenin, played a specifically fatal role in this process. They shifted the epicentre of Marxist (and, generally, socialist) ideas to the East and this 'geo-political' turn resulted naturally in a growing contempt for the democracy and liberties of a Western civil society, in themselves indicators of 'embourgeoisement' in the eyes of the radical. In a deeper sense still, it was tragic for socialism to have accepted the alliance (more so, the merger) with the representatives of the tradition which saw socialism as the mere negation of the rule of bourgeois private property. Marx had a much too obscure and sociologically vague premonition of this danger when he wrote about the 'mere negative transcendence of private property'. He described this social possibility as 'crude Communism', and also tried to separate the 'authentic' types of socialism from the 'inauthentic' ones, but these warnings remained fragments of an intellectual experiment. Marxism (and socialist theories in general) were much too self-indulgently 'value-free', in the positivistic sense typical of nineteenth-century theories, to make unambiguously clear the conditions, the fulfilment of which would constitute socialism: (and conversely, the conditions, the want of which constitutes an anti-capitalist formation, which however cannot and should not be identified with socialism).

But theories, good or bad, humanist or anti-humanist, do not engender social formations. For dictatorship over needs to come about, the confluence and combination of two factors were necessary, one of them purely ideological, the other directly social. To start with the second: whereas in vast areas of what is nowadays called the second and third world there was a social will to modernization carried and made manifest by the most variegated social classes, strata and human groups, all these efforts had practically, with the sole exception of Japan, either petered out or become paralysed. For hundreds of millions in these areas this forced standstill appeared as the crime of Western liberal capitalism. Even if we now have a more complex view of the intrinsic difficulties for large non-European cultures of establishing an autochthonous capitalist-industrializing transformation, this historical verdict must now be accepted as essentially justified. This general feeling made huge masses sensitive to the reception of a version of Eastern Marxism. They were drawn to the doctrine (created by Trotsky and by Lenin separately), which expressed a sometimes uncritical and inconsiderate contempt of Western parliamentary and civil liberties together with their insightful criticism, a theory that preached the primacy of a (rhetorical or Machiavellian) activism, one which increasingly replaced the original Marxian bourgeois-proletarian dichotomy by the conflict between pauper and rich nations, states and regions.

By introducing this second element in the interpretation of the genesis of the dictatorship over needs, we are not returning to the theory of backwardness (of mostly Trotskyist provenance) as an explanatory principle. Firstly, the result of the confluence of Eastern backwardness and Eastern Marxism was a Jacobin political revolution, a typically Western invention. It was not a figure of speech but a statement of a sociological fact when we described Lenin's regime as Jacobin. Secondly, at a later stage of this analysis we shall try to indicate the limits of generalizability of the regime but we will not deny its universalistic tendencies. Moreover, it is precisely through this intrinsic universalistic dynamic that we explain what is otherwise called 'Soviet imperialism'. And it goes without saying that a social system which has universalistic claims cannot satisfactorily be accounted for, not even as far as its genesis is concerned, by any theory of backwardness. What actually happened, was a three-stage occurrence. Initially, the impossibility of modernization had widely been experienced as general social suffering, and this generated an ideology adequate to the expression of universal frustration. The combination of social frustration and a transformed theory enhanced the problematical aspects of the doctrine originally inherent in it. Further, this confluence gave the theory, which even in its transformed shape could have remained an academic matter, a social function. Finally, the merger of the two (complemented by factors which we shall shortly analyse) produced a new social formation. But there is no hidden historical necessity lurking behind this meeting of disparate factors, as a Hegelian explanation of history would conceive this unexpected turn. It happened thus, but it could have happened otherwise. But since it happened in the way it did, and since the result is a society with universalistic claims, we have to approach it as a new stage of modern history with global consequences.

The third component of our account will make even clearer why we cannot accept any theory of backwardness as a general conceptual framework of explanation. In our view, there is a solid material basis of the new society in the 'negative utopias' of modern industrialization. In other words, there have always been trends inherent in industrialization irrespective of whether or not industrialization develops in a capitalist or non-capitalist social organization, which have at least promoted such a development. It is a stunning critique of the allegedly socialist character of dictatorship over needs that tendencies latent in capitalist industrialization which could, however, become only partially manifest in liberal capitalism (precisely because of the alliance between capitalist industrialization and democracy, or at least liberalism) could emerge in an unrestrained form in the new society.

The first of these tendencies is the growing centralization of the management of all social affairs in the hands of an increasingly powerful state, master and tutor of society. After a very short period of unadulterated *laissez-faire* non-interference which, in Polányi's view, was more the utopia of liberal capitalism than its completed reality, the state increasingly interfered with production, distribution and the preconditions of both, and generally with all social affairs pertaining to them, as it did under capitalism. But for a variety of reasons (the most important of which is the absolute necessity of competition as a pre-condition of capitalism) there are limits to centralization under capitalism which disappear in the new society; the most important limiting factor is, naturally, the market itself. Of course, this transcendence of liberal—capitalist limits (in themselves actual safeguards of personal liberties whose removal concluded in a new and abominable system of dependency) should not be conceived in terms of a 'diabolical conspiracy'. Even if later we face again the problem of the crisis of rationality and its false transcendence in dictatorship over needs, the original need for going beyond liberal—capitalist limits appeared as a mass protest against the insufficient centralization of the allocation of natural and socially produced wealth, as a protest against the irrationality of liberal capitalism. The strongest proof is the very historical moment in which Jacobinism *sui generis* was born: the historical year of 1793 in which the Paris *sans-culottes* forced a politics of maximization and centralization on a most hesitant Montagnard political elite as a protest against Girondist *laissez-faire* policies which they felt were egoistic, irrational and criminal with regard to the interest of the poor. But when this measure, conceived as protective against reckless exploitation, had been coupled with dynamic industrialization and when the 'checks and balances' of an even moderate liberalism had been removed from the social context, it became a new system of tyranny, the burdens of which proved most unbearable precisely for those masses who had historically initiated its emergence.

A further 'negative utopia' of capitalist industrialization, constantly latent in it, albeit never wholly realizable, is the total subjection of the work-force to the power centres of capital. This remained a dream and a utopia, partly because even though capital used the alien work-force as outright slave labour, it still had to retain remarkable vestiges of the once free condition of its own workers, sometimes even corrupting them (as in Fascist Germany), and partly also because capital in all such social experiments had simply to divide the working class into two separate entities, one totally dependent, in its legal and practical situation perilously close to resembling ancient slave workers, and another organized in keeping with modern liberal principles. This division is clearly visible in the example of South Africa or earlier, that of colonial regions in which white and coloured work-forces coexisted. There were even historically brief periods and limited areas (such as the southern states of the United States before the Civil War) in which a whole economy described by Engels as capitalist (but one which was hardly industrial) used slave labour in legalized forms. But in all such cases the alliance of industrialization with capitalism, the adequate state of affairs of which is limited liberalism, puts restrictions on these latent negative utopias.

The system of dictatorship over needs relies on these inherent tendencies of industrialization and extends them to an unheard-of extent. It actually realizes the total subjection of the work-force to the commanding centres of industrial development. But here again the objectivity of analysis is necessary. First of all, and despite the fact that millions of the prisoners of the Gulag Archipelago had been exploited to the greater glory of 'real socialism' as actual slave workers, the only parallel to which was Hitler's use of Slavs, Jews and other inferior races, it would not be accurate to describe the entirety of Soviet labour conditions as a system of slavery. The Soviet work-force is subjected to the state but the wage-earners are not state property, either formally or actually, not even during the worst and most nightmarish periods of Stalinism. Despite all the severe limitations (which would be totally unacceptable for the working class of any liberal capitalist country), there remained certain minimum levels of personal freedom (the choice of family relations, personal consumption and the like) incompatible with actual slavery. But the necessary objectivity of analysis cannot and should not conceal the monumental 'cunning of unreason' in this respect as well. Originally, the total subjection of the work-force to the state had been advertised as a 'higher principle of industrial organization eliminating capitalist irrationalities'. But it became, economically, one of the main limiting factors of economic growth, and politically, one of the sorest points of the social structure of the dictatorship.

Thirdly, the central political—economic category of our whole analysis, command economy itself, is inherent in every type of industrialization, and for a variety of reasons. Industrial development very soon becomes world economy, and there is a constant tension between the emergence of world economy and the very existence of the nation states which realize it. The latter are 'disturbing factors' obviously limiting and upsetting its general calculability and pre-dictability (a wish, to be sure, rather than a scientific reality) whereas the command economy (and its vehicle, the omnipotent political state) with its universalistic claims, promises, but only promises, global planning and planetary harmony. Further, it is only global industrialization that touches off the unlimited cycle of infinite need growth with its inherent dilemmas. Liberal capitalism seems to have a remedy for this in the alleged harmony created by undisturbed market equilibrium, but in actual fact is does not have any such safe-guards. Infinite need growth creates disproportions (between states, regions, strata of population, branches of industrial production), generates tensions (between the haves and the have-nots), calls forth the ecological dilemma, and endangers the whole industrial universe because of finite natural resources. The advocates of command economy make two equally false promises in this respect: they advertise their alleged capacity to distinguish between 'true' and 'false' needs, thereby creating harmony in lieu of capitalist chaos, and they claim a near mystical ability to uncover new sources of production and universal affluence. One should add to the above dilemmas the traditional ones, always criticized by every socialist theory, all inherent in industrial development. These are the following: the price of the industrial development of one region is of necessity the industrially underdeveloped character of the other. Liberal capitalism cannot guarantee peaceful industrialization, rather it exists with the threat of wars. Wars have broken out twice in this century on a global level and constantly in between, in the form of armed local conflicts and clashes. Finally crisis (or recession) seems to be an inevitable collateral phenomenon of industrialization. All these factors, separately and collectively, in a sense call for another system of social and economic regulation, and command economy resurfaces again and again as the magic formula against liberal ills.

We have indicated those aspects of the original body of socialist theories which made the idea of a dictatorship over needs acceptable, even attractive. We circumscribed the social trends (meeting with the demands of underdeveloped areas, latent tendencies of every form of industrialization) which transformed the degenerated, originally socialist, impetus into the anti-capitalist but not socialist reality of dictatorship over needs. But we have not answered the question why precisely this type of ideology and movement were necessary for (or at least, adequate to) the task. First of all, even the most degenerate system bearing the name of socialism is still, at least nominally, a universalistic projection and both modernization and attempts at solving the dilemmas of global industrialization need universalistic projects. Apart from several other considerations, Fascism (or Nazism) proved inadequate to this task for the perfectly simple reason that it possessed, even in the short historical periods when it became a world power, too narrow a power basis: it was the ideology and power of one 'race' or nation. And, even if the concept of 'superior race' could be expanded elastically to include more and more nations, Fascism always had to have racial victims to persecute.

By contrast, the advocates of dictatorship over needs with a socialist origin have always had an urban, internationalist, 'this-worldly' (non-theocratic) and civilian character and power basis. The latter two factors have become tremendously important in the last decades. The non-theocratic character of these dictatorships is important because of the emergence of the contrasting fundamentalist regimes which, of necessity, have to undertake the task of industrial development but which will find themselves increasingly confronted by insoluble social problems in this respect, precisely because of their limitations as an originally religious body in regulating modern social relations. The civilian characteristic refers to the frequent emergence now of military juntas, not only in the original area (Latin America) from which the term comes but also in the Middle East, Asia and Africa. Their overdisciplined façade suggests more rationality than they actually possess. Whenever they really set out to modernize and industrialize, they are obliged at least to share their power with various branches of civilian bureaucracies. All the parties and movements advocating dictatorship over needs and their theories, have, for the reasons enumerated above, an enormous advantage over mere military juntas.

A further dimension of the success of the partisans of the dictatorship over needs is their perverted radicalism. It would be ridiculous to deny this radicalism precisely in the Marxian sense of the word: they grasp men at their roots, at their system of needs. An equally brief reference will suffice (after what has been analysed in detail in Parts I and II) to prove that they represent a radicalism that is perverted. Here perhaps one additional remark is necessary. We do not operate with any kind of mass psychological naturalism, we do not give credit to theories which suggest that it is a 'natural law' that masses choose the most extremist party, group or faction during any given social upheaval. We personally prefer the combination of anthropological radicalism with political realism (which includes the defence of all present achievements of democracy) and we also believe that it is a possibility that huge masses will have the same option. Without such a firm belief, our theoretical suggestion would be a rather private mental exercise. But two factors have to be taken into consideration. The first is that history, in contrast to Hegel's assumption, is a process of learning, for better or for worse. When certain movements — parts but never the majority of a population — chose the strategic suggestions of the advocates of dictatorship over needs, they had not yet had any personal experience of it, and later they had no opportunity to change their options. The second factor is that those choices had been made during vast social cataclysms (wars, concomitant famines and plagues, the collapse of centuries-old institutions and social prescriptions) or immediately subsequent to them. The hope at least cannot be abandoned that when people choose under somewhat more favourable conditions, they will pick a radicalism with a more humane physiognomy. But the fact that sometimes huge masses threw themselves in the arms of their 'liberators' in hours of a social apocalypse cannot be simply declared the result of 'childish immaturity'.

Finally, it should be mentioned that movements and theories of dictatorship over needs fulfilled a function Karl Mannheim attributed to Fascism alone: they implemented a change of elite in areas where such a change had for a long time been necessary but where it could not be implemented with the aid of the theories and movements then available. This aspect is closely related to the pervertedly radical character of the dictatorship over needs. Only a radical elite could replace the archaic, antiquated one, and only a pervertedly radical one would cling to its power with the unscrupulousness characteristic of the Bolshevik elite. Of course, this is a very complex sociological process and cannot be simply equated with the one observed and described by Mannheim after the pattern of Italian Fascism. Firstly, because in the case of the latter or of German Nazism it was the change of elite alone that this ideology and movement delivered: the basic socio-economic structure remained unaltered while this is obviously not so with Bolshevism. Secondly, and more importantly, the process during which the Bolshevik elite actually replaced the obsolete national Russian aristocratic elite was a long and extremely tortuous one. Originally Bolshevism consisted of internationalists of the most variegated extraction and conviction: Georgians, Ukrainians, Lithuanians. In particular, many leading functionaries were of Jewish origin. It was indeed a strange triumph of dialectic that it should have been Stalin-Dshugashvili who 'Russified' the elite during his repeated purges (notably by excluding all Jews but one, Kaganovich) in order to make that elite capable of performing its chauvinistic conservative functions. But all in all, the necessity for a change of elites in many areas where modernization failed, and the capability of the movements and ideologies of dictatorship over needs to implement the change, contributed to its worldwide success.

One may briefly summarize the above analysis as follows. Movements with an original socialist intent, largely transformed and degenerated theories with an initial socialist thrust, met real social demands and trends inherent in failed attempts at modernization and in ossified social structures, and in the underlying operative tendencies to industrialization. They produced regimes which are, in fact, anti-capitalist but which are not socialist but rather an abominable caricature of everything socialists have lived and fought for. Thus every militant with a will to genuine socialism is confronted with a situation which is far more complex than the first days of the outbreak of the First World War, when socialists whose moral integrity was still intact felt that the idea and the movement had already become hopelessly compromised.

CHAPTER 10

Hyperrationalist Preferences and Social Irrationality in a Planned Society

Rationality and irrationality

The general problem of rationality versus irrationality of dictatorship over needs has been repeatedly raised in the previous chapters and with good reason. Anyone entering these societies from the world of calculative rationality has, as a first impression, the feeling that he has arrived in Bedlam. Nothing functions, or at least nothing does in the way one would expect having been brought up in the spirit of rationalist standards; mysterious interdictions block the road from one point to the other in the shortest and most innocent peripatetics of everyday life, and usually the question 'why' receives no answer at all. But there is a general reluctance on the part of objective sociological observers who intend to produce scientific analyses and not political pamphlets, to declare of a society which has been existing (even expanding) for more than sixty years, which has created an enormous, technologically perfectionist army, etc. that this is a wholly irrational form of social organization. Behind this antinomy there lies a real social problem.

To resolve the antinomy, we have to distinguish two sets of categories. One of them contains the coherence, the internal logic, the capacity of continuous self-reproduction of any lasting social system, its existing channels which serve to integrate the majority of the population into the given system of domination. To take only one of these terms, internal logic means that the power centres attribute 'meaning' to men and things, thereby classifying them into their proper (and generally untranscendable) social place, assigning tasks to them which are vital in the social division of labour. This classification of men and things into pre-established places of social order can be rigid or loose (according to the more or less hierarchical, more or less traditional character of the society in question) but it is always necessary for any society to survive. In order to prove that this is not characteristic of every society many social formations, from certain nomadic empires to Hitler's Third Reich, can be mentioned which became for a historical moment seemingly irresistible world powers, yet disappeared just as rapidly as they had entered the *theatrum mundi*, and not always as the result of a military catastrophe. One universal, overall answer for their disappearance obviously exists only in the realm of the metaphysics of Stalinist diamat, the regime's popular philosophy. The real explanation is historically concrete in each case and we are not concerned with it here. The only general answer that can be given is that these social formations had not worked out precisely that internal logic, that coherence, those channels of domination, those capacities of self-reproduction mentioned above which would have attached meaning to things and men, and in this sense they remained inorganic.

But these mechanisms are neither 'rational' nor 'irrational' and it is ahistorical to raise the question of general social rationality at all in pre-enlightenment societies, in which the category of rationality had either not yet been theoretically formulated or else had been applied to individual behaviour alone. For it was early capitalist development, on the one hand, and the movement of enlightenment (as the theoretical elaboration of liberalism and democracy), on the other, which more or less simultaneously generalized the problem of rationality and rationalizability and projected it from individual action, behaviour and consideration to the whole of social development. Engels could not have coined his famous *aperçu* that the 'realm of reason' turned out to be in reality a 'realm of bourgeoisie' without sharing the intention of that same, historically existing, bourgeoisie to create a realm of reason, to transform the whole of society into a rationally functioning mechanism. For readers even a little versed in Marxism or in general sociological literature, the capitalist basis of this general rationality and rationalizability is too clear to require detailed analysis. Capitalism designed a society in which total harmony was based on a mathematically computable market predictability, and however often this 'scientific calculation' failed, the principle has never been abandoned up until the present-day upsurge of monetarism.

The representative theorists of enlightenment worked out a series of principles the fulfilment of which provided a society with the necessary criteria of rationality (and conversely, the lack of those criteria was sufficient ground to term the society in question irrational). The first of these criteria, destined to play a considerable role in the later, ominous career of substantive rationality was the postulate that a society should not come about in a spontaneous, organic evolution (in this sense, society was the exact counterpart to nature) but should be the result of a scientifically elaborated telos. The fabrication of constitutions, the favourite predilection of so many known and anonymous men of enlightenment in the eighteenth century served precisely this purpose. They tried to work out a blueprint for social change and the protagonists of the political turn, with apparent inevitability, had to realize its prescriptions with a doctrinaire zeal. Nor was this a total utopia. If we take the paradigmatic case, the creation of the United States of America, we are witness to the birth of perhaps the only theoretically preconceived society in world history which proved to be a lasting creation. And the obvious counterexample, the French Revolution, rather corroborates than refutes the thesis since it was the Jacobin (anti-capitalist) tendency inherent in it from the first moment and the concurrent demand of a 'substantive rationality' that upset the precedent calculations of a bourgeois enlightenment. But in all cases, both realized and unrealized, rational society is in principle the result in which a previous telos becomes reality. It is a negation of the organic character of social evolution.

The second component of general social rationality is achieving social harmony. In contrast to pre-romanticism and romanticism, enlightenment as an overwhelmingly liberal (or democratic) theory, acknowledged that in modern society there is no longer any homogeneity but rather heterogeneous forces at work (it regarded homogeneity as a characteristic of organicity to be overcome). It was the task of rationality (at the same time, it was evidence of rationality's existence) to be capable of creating social harmony between disparate and centripetal trends. Social harmony could come about in either an additive or a dialectical way. The concept of additional social harmony rested on a doctrinaire belief in market rationality. The (primarily economic) forces at play will somehow discard their negative effects and add up by themselves into a harmonious sum total and the end result will be acceptable in a mysterious way for everyone. The dialectical conception was much more outspoken. 'Private vices' will result in 'public benefits', stated the cynical Mandeville, and this was a maxim which would play a specifically ominous role, from Hegel's Evil that somehow fulfilled the role of moral Good to Marat's Jacobin-pre-Bolshevik principle of the 'tyranny of freedom'. But, one way or the other, social harmony remained the acme of all rationalist social theories while it was the lot of irrationalist prophecies to preach struggle and a cosmic will to create order, but not harmony, in social life.

Thirdly, certain substantive values had been elaborated in the enlightenment process whose fundamental character could not be denied by any theory claiming general social rationality, even if practically all of them gave a different interpretation of their content, their interrelationship, eventual conflicts, and the like. These values had already been set by the first prominent declarations of emancipated humankind, and most of all by the subsequent stages of the French Revolution: they were liberty, equality and fraternity, invariably with the leading role of freedom. When we emphasized that socialism cannot be defined in a value-free manner (and precisely for that reason the regimes of dictatorship over needs *cannot* and *must not* be regarded as socialist), we are only following in the footsteps of the best enlightenment traditions.

Fourthly, from all this followed the denial of the *raison d'être* of all discriminations up until then normal, perhaps even rational, between races, castes, estates. Equally, elitarian rule and social segregation guaranteed by legal prerogatives had to be eliminated. (This is one of the most remarkable features that makes any kind of reconciliation between genuine Marxism, or other socialist theories, as heirs to the enlightenment, on the one hand, and Fascist regimes or those of dictatorship over needs, on the other, impossible.) The idea that a human race as such should be exterminated for its alleged crimes or inferiority, or the equally attractive and humane idea (practised by Bolshevism) that social classes as wholes should be exterminated (or at least coercively segregated) from normal social life, are forthright denials of the legacy of enlightenment. These denials occur in an overt and clear-cut form in Nazism, and hypocritically in Bolshevism.

Finally, the postulate of overall social rationality included the idea and the requirement that certain forums should exist; there should be an at least formally free public sphere, which makes it possible 'to summon society in front of the jury of critical reason'. In more prosaic terms it meant (even in terms of a Hegelian conception of the supremacy of political state) that a political society, in which civil society is totally subjected to political state, was *a limine* unacceptable for enlightenment conceptions of general social rationality, since such an establishment excludes for reasons of principle any critical censorship of collective human reason over the results of human activity. In all societies in which these criteria of overall social rationality had not yet been formulated, it is ahistorical to raise the question of social rationality at all. But in all societies subsequent to their elaboration, it is a legitimate undertaking to inquire after general social rationality in the spirit of the above criteria and it is precisely because of their absence that we deem the societies of dictatorship over needs irrational, whereas we do not deny the existence of their internal logic, coherence of domination and oppression, nor do we call in question their capacity of self-reproduction.

Capitalism was the first society to claim overall social (calculative) rationality, and it was capitalism which at the same time degraded the hopes of enlightenment for the advent of a realm of reason, to replace the realm of the egoism of the bourgeoisie, with all the concomitant symptoms of social irrationality of which recurring crises is but one. There was no greater theorist of the resignation of reason's once high hopes than Max Weber with his famous distinction between *rationality* and *rationalization*. For him, rationality (in both forms, as value and as goal rationality) returns to the individual, to action. After Weber, and in keeping with his spirit, one can no longer state of a society as a whole that it is rational. The pertinent overall social category is rationalization which embraces the elaboration of the channels and social systems of rules in which, to an ever-increasing extent, optimization is always possible, the social roles are rationally distributed, the rules are worked out, in an equally rational manner. If there is progress at all (a dubious category with Weber) it appears in the sense of a perhaps more and more extended rationalization which is, however, no absolute refutation of the irrationally undermined character of modern life.

One of the main ambitions of socialist theories, but even of the movements working with a popularized understanding of social affairs, was to transcend this irrationality (or insufficient rationality) of capitalism. In this respect, an interesting dichotomy prevailed in socialism. Its great *fin de siècle* critics such as Pareto and Durkheim observed that for modern individuals there are basically two types of option for socialism. According to one, capitalism is an unjust society, according to the other, it is an irrational society. Even without statistical surveys, one can reasonably assume that in the actual individual options for socialism as a life-goal, the first played an incomparably greater role than the second for those joining this cause. Nevertheless the First World War decided in favour of the second. The Great War was an overwhelming refutation of the dogmatic belief in prevailing rationality. Every reproach made against insufficient market rationalism, every prediction summed up in theories of imperialism which forecast the advent of massive wars as a result of the irrational rationality of world market and capitalist transactions on it, now came totally true. In addition, this was an exclusively capitalist responsibility, it was the governments of capital, up until then regulating world politics in the haughty spirit of an alleged absolute expertise that failed without exception, that turned out to be playthings in the hand of 'history'. No wonder then that all the forces criticizing capitalism for its insufficient rationality set out to realize precisely a superior type of rationality. The first world-historical claim the new system of dictatorship over needs presented to an astonished world was this higher type of reason allegedly incarnate in its management of human affairs.

Part II analysed the fairly obscure concept of substantive rationality and came to the conclusion that it can only be distinguished from value rationality if goals (posited by individuals) are not in themselves regarded as values, and from goal-rationality (in its ordinary sense) in so far as substantive rationality embraces the objective of a well-defined change of social structure as a whole based on a preliminary knowledge of future realizability. Those positing this new telos make the practical efforts, cost what they may, to realize it. In principle, these preconditions were met in the ambitious initial claims (and as it seemed then, in the corresponding social premises) of the new system of substantive rationality. It regarded itself, first, as not subject to the arbitrariness of market actions. It was an enemy of market relations and it departed in lieu of the former from the collectively assessed needs of the toiling masses. Since at precisely that time market rationality failed spectacularly, this claim did not then seem to be totally lunatic. Further, it declared itself to be a scientifically predictive principle and, in addition, one which could formulate the ultimate goal of society. It was then perhaps Max Weber alone who (with his highly ambivalent relation to socialism) warned socialists that with this allegedly superior type of rationality they could only become bogged down in an unfathomable morass.

At the present time, when in Eastern Europe regular fights on barricades and popular uprising are needed to solve fairly pedestrian economic problems which are relatively easy to manage even with the undeniably deficient capitalist rationality, it no longer requires a prophet or a sociological wizard to state that there is something deeply and irreparably wrong with this superior type of rationality. It is more interesting to see what the causes of this new rationality crisis are. First and foremost, we have to refer back to what we have described as the central category of command economy: a 'goal of production' (*Zweck der Produktion*) instead of (profit-regulated) class- or group-interest. It has been formulated in such a way (in our firm conviction, adequately) that it necessarily entails an unresolvable contradiction specifically from the viewpoint of rationality. The objective 'goal of production' implies, on the one hand, a constant effort to increase the material wealth of society (dictatorship over needs is a dynamic and modernizing society), while on the other hand, this can only happen in ways which ensure the increasing power of disposition of the apparatus over this material wealth. Two frequently analysed results of this inner contradiction, the constant agricultural under-production (put more plainly, agricultural crisis) and the simultaneous production of waste and scarcity, together testify to a blatant lack of rationality in this society, at least as far as goal-rationality is concerned. (And there is no such present-day industrial society in which the daily violation of goal-rationality would not signify for the population a violation of rationality *in general*.) Let us emphasize again that this is not a by-product of a particular historical period which can be overcome by evolution but is rather inherent in the central category of the economic system of this society and inseparable from it.

Secondly, the very claim we mentioned amongst the ambitious objectives of this superior rationality, namely, that it is scientifically predictive, contains another unresolvable contradiction. The problematical element is, of course, the result not only of ambitious socialism, but to the same extent also of the ambitious evolutionism of the nineteenth century which believed itself to have scientific (and preferably quantifiable) answers to all dilemmas of social life. But the first attempts at realizing socialist doctrines had been committed to two self-contradictory trends, each of them irreconcilable with any type of scientificity. The first meant the abolition (or at least drastic reduction) of market relations which destroyed the only system of computing that would have made mathematical prediction, uncertain and capricious as it had always been, possible, at least in principle. The other was to gain true knowledge of the future which, as we have known since Aristotle, is in itself an impossible claim and undertaking, particularly if the only basis of a computable hypothesis of the present into the future is destroyed or drastically curtailed. No doubt, there is a legitimate way of planning the future: namely, to find public channels through which the social will to a particular type of future can be articulated. Socialism cannot renounce the objective of emancipation from the 'dead weight of the past' and of direction into the future. But the two simultaneous steps dictatorship over needs intended to realize were in themselves and in their contradictory entirety rather blocking the road to the rule of the future over the past.

Thirdly, these unresolvable contradictions have been further aggravated by the fact that substantive rationality had to be realized under the conditions of a dictatorship over needs. We do not want to enter here into a sterile discussion about the 'chicken-or-egg priority', namely, whether it was the idea of a dictatorship over the social and economic activities of man that meant the primary step towards the degradation of rationality in 'real socialism'; or the other way round, whether the previously analysed inherent antinomies demanded a dictatorial management of social affairs. For us, the results are overwhelming. The very fact that this society exists under the conditions of a constant dictatorship (which due to historical circumstances can be more or less brutal, more or less all-encompassing) suppressed all substantive values we mentioned as prerequisites for an overall social rationality, or turned them into a sheer hypocritical parody of rationality. Similarly, there no longer exist free channels through which individual needs in their social aggregate could be articulated in a free manner or through which 'society', this abstract entity, could be summoned to give account before the jury of critical human reason, of at least certain social groups. The result of this exaggerated enlightenment is, primarily, a total de-enlightenment. It creates a social condition in which the prevailing human experience is that there is one human faculty the individual does not need in its daily practice: the critical human mind. Furthermore, this makes the meeting of the system of needs and production possible only through constantly recurring cycles of economic and political catastrophes. Of course, this latter statement needs further qualification. We have mentioned in Part I that the gist of the post-Stalinist compromise between the apparatus and the population is precisely the former's intention to meet at least part of the population's elementary economic needs. But in a way, and together with this intention, they are still groping in the dark; they do not (because they cannot) have any clear picture about this need structure (apart from the truism that people always want something more of everything). The apparatus which itself established its rule as a dictatorship over needs and founded it on the goal of production of command economy, cannot eradicate the fundamental contradictions inherent in this objective goal.

Fourthly, the circumstance in itself that substantive rationality was meant as substantive precisely in the sense that it could not be simply reduced to economic rationality, was initially in harmony with Marx's most important emancipatory intentions. General social rationality as an arbiter over the merely economically profitable was and still is a central postulate of any socialist world order, and a key to a future worldwide redistribution unplagued by constant catastrophes. However, there were three accompanying factors necessarily bound up with dictatorship over needs which turned the emancipatory intent into its opposite, the hyperrationalistic aims into lunatic irrationalism. The first of them is that while command economy (like any other economy) was constantly computing costs of reproduction and distribution, after having destroyed or drastically curtailed its own basis of computation it never could find any objective basis of calculation. Secondly, while it has constantly costed the expenditure of its economic operations in terms of raw material, natural resources and their allocations, etc. (even if in a wholly arbitrary way), it never made calculations of the 'human price' of its grandiose planning mood, or at best did so only in cases where this *quantite negligeable* demanded some attention with arms in hand, on barricades. While the brutality of this practice has been eased in the post-Stalinist compromise, its guiding principles have never been altered. Finally, substantive rationality with its hyper-rationalist claims was highly critical towards the formal rationality of bourgeois society. As a result, it destroyed many of its channels of rationalization which were so important for Weber, primarily the formal legal system, which it replaced by the much more substantial caprices or arbitrary will of an individual or a collective tyrant. Needless to say, this was an unambiguous value degradation and in addition one which prompted the image of 'feudalism' or 'slavery' in many indignant observers of the untarnished state of affairs in 'real socialism'. Their comments might have been scientifically incorrect but what they were commenting upon was the crisis of arrogant hyperrationalist claims becoming an open and unprecedented crisis of rationality.

Guaranteed society

All those regarding substantive rationality not as a mystical notion serving the legitimation of the apparatus but as an actual principle of superior rationality believed that its realization was to be found in 'real socialism' which was for them *guaranteed society*. We have already mentioned that early proto-socialist trends demanded guaranteed society simply as a safeguard against a state of social affairs in which no social mechanisms protecting and granting physical self-reproduction of the wage-earners existed: areas of urban England, during the eighteenth and early nineteenth century, and during the famines of the French Revolution. This paternalistic streak of socialism seemed to have achieved a stunning historical justification in the late 1920s and early 1930s when the whole world with the apparent exception of the Soviet Union was living under the scourge of the Great Depression. Even sceptical socialists like the Webbs turned with admiration towards the proletarian miracle (although it is true that at the same time and for the same reason, the socialist Bernard Shaw turned for a moment with equal admiration towards Mussolini). We now know very clearly what the socio-economic background of this miracle was: command economy and its fundamentally irrational structure. In respect of economy, the guaranteed society (even if it had to admit certain limitations, as does any system of economy) possessed the following, fairly surrealistic, advantages. Firstly, it never functioned according to profitability, and so capitalist close-downs of factories working with deficit was a senseless category within it. But this meant no 'progress'. As we have repeatedly pointed out, it constantly and simultaneously produced waste and scarcity to a historically unparalleled extent. In objective social terms, that was a waste of human energy and usable raw materials which for a while remained an internal phenomenon of the Soviet systems. But the ongoing Soviet agricultural crisis, a classic example of this simultaneous production of waste and scarcity, now adds tremendously to the unsolved problems of a suffering humankind. While nineteenth-century Tsarist Russia was one of the main wheat exporters of the world, hyperrational Soviet agriculture (which can at least pay with gold for the cereals it cannot produce) is consuming the food of starving or pauper regions. Secondly, and linked with the above, command economy is also unfamiliar with the category of unemployment, for a variety of political and economic reasons, but the obverse of this situation is a nearly total disregard for the human cost of the growth of production restricted only by considerations for possible armed rebellion, and this only in the post-Stalinist period.

None the less, guaranteed society has a conceivable (and highly problematical) meaning, but Soviet societies worked out this meaning only during the post-Stalinist compromise. No doubt one can find an endless number of guarantees, which we analysed in Part II, in documents of earlier periods as well — guarantees of work, health care, free education, and the like. But most of them existed only on paper simply because the Soviet society was too poor to ensure them in fact, and, more importantly, they were meaningless as guarantees, even in their occasional realization. In a period of recurring waves of mass terrorization which annihilated millions it is small consolation if the population has free access to public parks. The post-Stalinist period brought one decisive change: the period of revolutions from above was at an end. This is a complex syndrome with many and variegated causes, the principal of which was apparently a consensual decision of the whole apparatus: its conviction that the concomitant bloodletting which does not stop at their door was too heavy a price to pay for too dynamic a social growth. But if one studies the constellation more closely, the limits of the power of the apparatus (as 'trustee' of command economy) so often emphasized in Part I, will once again be realized. The deeper underlying causes were twofold. Firstly, the urban population, no longer a simple raw material in the hands of the great planners, but a delicate machine producing and reproducing a complex technology simply would not have tolerated the total inhumanity of the revolutions from above and, for the first time in Soviet history, it had some clandestine weapons to strike back with: concealed sabotage, destroying the quality of important goods such as those of the armament industry, and the like. Secondly, since they simply proved incapable of solving the constant structural crisis in agriculture, there was a limit to the size of peasant work-force that could be forcibly transferred from the village into the big cities, or else the Soviet Union would have faced constant famines. All this means that guaranteed society has in fact set in and many of the guarantees on paper have been realized (in an imperfect way, of course, and so that they reproduce the structural inequalities of dictatorship over needs.)

If we intend to characterize the guaranteed society with its hyper-rationalist claims and inherent irrationality, the first thing to mention is that it is the exact opposite of welfare society. Whatever defects the welfare state may have (and monetarist reaction is now largely thriving on these defects), it is based on certain rights to certain benefits and in this sense, it is a formally free state. We have analysed that, in contrast, the guaranteed society of dictatorship over needs only recognizes requests and supplication on the part of the state subject. Further, in a way, the phase of guaranteed society setting in after the revolutions from above only completes the achievement of an earlier period: the perfect atomization of the individual. Despite the solemn promises that the past can never return, the subject in the Eastern European state still lives under Stalin's shadow and is aware of the possibility that the ghosts of Stalin, Yezhov, and Béria can be revitalized, therefore the individual generally respects the strictly circumscribed scope of social options which the state provides. But since for the first time in Soviet history, subjects are 'rewarded' for this obedience, even if in a very modest way, vast masses light-heartedly renounce the burdens of freedom. This phenomenon, combined with a general disappointment in Western democracies (which mainly has at its root the fact that the Western European countries have a clamorous propaganda, but no policy, in respect of Eastern Europe) is the key to many mysteries which are unresolvable as far as unprofessional Western observers are concerned. For example, this is the source of a newly and widely emerging fundamentalism whose main Russian prophet, but far from only advocate, is Solzhenitzyn. Similarly, this is the source of the unquenched hostility that not only Soviet Party functionaries felt towards the Chinese cultural revolution (which in itself would have been wholly natural). This hate was a feeling shared as well by those strata of the Eastern European population who had reason enough to watch with diffident eyes the bloody soap-opera taking place in the upper echelons of Chinese political life, but who also could have had at least some reasonable stimulus to show a minimum of sensitivity towards the militants who, later deceived, humiliated and suppressed, always gathering under false banners and themselves committing innumerable cruelties, still fought for social objectives which are in themselves popular in Eastern Europe. But what was happening in China was once again the ominous revolution from above, and the man in the street in Eastern Europe was happy to live in a guaranteed society. (Nothing can be more unpopular in this region than Trotsky's 'permanent revolution'.) Finally, guaranteed society means that, in exchange for the minimum amount of goods ensuring his physical and cultural self-reproduction at a low level, the individual renounces the possibility of social alternatives. The future becomes one and indivisible, predicted and fixed by the sovereign. But precisely these constitutive structural features of a guaranteed society testify to the new fiasco of hyperrationalist pretences. What has been, at least externally, designed as the proof of the triumph of superior rationality is nothing but the renunciation of basic components of rationality: individual freedom, the right to the critical use of human intellect, a release from general social tutelage.

The claim of the regime's propagandists, that 'real socialism' has already transcended the epoch of class rule in human history, belongs precisely to the catalogue of false pretences of hyperrationality. Before going any further, a certain ambiguity has to be noted here with regard to the regime's self-understanding. On the one hand, it admits the existence of classes in 'real socialism': there is a working class, a unified peasantry as one homogeneous class (after the physical liquidation of the kulaks). On the other hand, these are 'friendly classes', in a deeper sense: they are not collective entities akin in any way to those whose struggle allegedly propelled history forward up until now. This is not simply one of those masterpieces of *non sequitur* so characteristic of the official doctrine. It has a function: according to policy priorities, the interest conflicts between these friendly classes can be mobilized, one way or the other, to find an outlet for the regime's self-generated tensions. But basically this is one of the rare opportunities when we are in harmony with the regime's self-characterization. As has become clear from our analysis in Part I, we do not consider this society to be a class society either. The only question that remains to be answered is whether or not by transcending class structure, progress has been achieved.

If we look at history, we will find 'pure class system' (in the sense of socio-economic classes as Marx describes, for instance, the bourgeoisie) to be an exception rather than a universal state of affairs. Bourgeois rule as class domination with its at any rate theoretically free choice of social position not determined by birth and descent, but the result of realized capacities alone was the necessary social form of subordinating the politically emancipated individual to the rule of capital. This was the inevitable outcome of the parallel and interconnected processes of political emancipation and capitalist organization of economy, the deepest reason for the problematical but inevitable coexistence of capitalism and (at least) liberalism. Relative independence of the individual, the self-consciously professed class ethos as not only the rationalization but also the lucid manifestation of one's actual private and collective interests (in spite of, and together with all that has been said of ideology by Marx), abandonment of efforts to homogenize society as a whole in keeping with the patterns of one particular class, instead the sober acceptance of various social particularities as societary natural laws of societality — all this was constitutive of class existence proper both on its bourgeois and proletarian poles. One can, however, bear witness to quite opposite characteristics in the society of dictatorship over needs. The corporate character that we have described as the social mode of existence of the apparatus on the 'upper stratum' of this society, on the one hand, and myriads of totally atomized and only coercively organized individuals, on the other, are characteristic of 'classless' society.

In the corporate existence of dictatorship over needs, both at the top and the bottom, different as these two modes of existence are, there is no separate social existence of the individual: the individual possesses whatever he does possess, to a very different extent according to whether he belongs to the top or the bottom, by partaking in a 'collectivity'. The professed ethos serves to disguise real interests and real inner ambitions, no ethos or ideology is tolerated which tries to make the former manifest. The effort to homogenize society in token of the officially declared values is the real bathos and *raison d'être* of corporate existence. If our yardsticks are, then, individual freedom and the collective emancipation of labour, historical regression here can hardly be denied. We have indicated the only aspect in which the historical assets of the transition from estates to classes, the 'apparent' freedom of the chance of the individual could not be cancelled: social positions could not be created, even by this powerful trend of de-enlightenment, inheritable and inherited, nor could the only state subject be rendered into state property. But this double negativity can hardly be called progress.

In all other respects, the 'corporative existence' at the top, and the disjointed atoms at the bottom, are a regression from both a personal and a collective point of view. To begin with, the pyramidal structure of society often referred to here means that everyone has certain liberties 'downwards', but none 'upwards'. This amounts, however, to a general 'equality in inequality', to the state subjects' collective nullity before the leading bodies. This is characteristic of an old-style absolutism rather than of modern ways of (even oppressive) government; from here springs the scientifically untenable but quite significant theory of 'feudal socialism' (this is also the reason for using ante-diluvian categories in Part II). Further, such a situation is far more fetishistic than any class existence in capitalism for the simple reason that people have to speak (and, as a result, start to think) in terms of unity, general will and social homogeneity, whereas actually they lead a disjointed, heterogeneous and particularized life. In the language of the official ideology, this unity and homogeneity is the harmonious lot of the 'liberated toiling classes'. In the language of those not belonging to the apparatus it reads: we are all wage-earners of the state. But both languages perforce conceal the fact that behind this unity and homogeneity there are clearly describable, heterogeneous, particular interests and group aspirations which are not allowed to be formulated as such, and which accordingly are not always clear even for the members of the relevant group. The typical misunderstanding of one's objective group interest stemming constantly from this fetishistic constellation is frequently played upon by various factions of the apparatus when they oppose the alleged interests of the workers to those of the peasant, generating reciprocal conflicts from which both poles lose, and only a certain faction of the apparatus gains.

There are two particular aspects of the false homogenization of the dictatorship which are hated by the state subjects with a special passion, and against which whole social groups fight quite vehemently. The first is, obviously, the suppression (sometimes outlawing) of articulated particular group interests. All tolerable periods within the dictatorship, those of reforms and hopes, are characterized by direct efforts to give voice to specific interests of particular social groups which then become, usually for a short historical break, part and parcel of an existing but not overtly formulated ethos. Secondly, the quest for a separate group existence means at the same time struggle against the homogenization of society in token of a universal wage-earner relationship. It has become universalized (and distorted even in terms of the wage-earner's existence in capitalism) partly in so far as there are no alternative ways of life (one cannot live as a freelance or only in individual cases, there is no longer small 'artisan' private property except in very restricted areas of social life), partly in so far as the possibilities of labour exerting any pressure on the 'masters of production', even if increased in the post-Stalinist period, were very limited at least up until the recent events in Poland.

False homogenization of society, against which group interests lead a dogged guerilla fight, further increases the crisis of hyper-rationalist pretensions involving two important cases of 'false consciousness'. On the one hand, the categories of political economy in this society (not in the relevant departments of the academy where rubbish about them is taught, but in the consciousness of the 'man in the street') behave as if they were realizing the latent negative utopia of 'super-capitalism' never to come true under its normal liberal conditions. The total dependency of labour on the 'captains of production' always runs into obstacles there, while in dictatorship over needs this seems to come near its final and unalterable fulfilment, but — with a dialectical twist — not now as an increase in social and technological oppression but as the triumph of an allegedly 'superior predictive wisdom'. On the other hand, the whole production process seems to be circular, it appears as production for production's sake in its purest Ricardian form, which has never been the actually leading motive in profit-oriented capitalism. In Part I of this book we have argued against the conception that the command economy of dictatorship over needs was in fact oriented at production for production's sake. The whole definition of the 'goal of production' in it, as an objective social telos, speaks against such a cycle. But Marx was perfectly right when he attributed, as organic constituents of a particular society, certain necessarily emerging appearances in it. In this case, these false appearances are part and parcel of the crisis of rationality of the society, based on hyperrationalist pretensions and arrogance, in a double sense. First, guaranteed society is a false promise of the *enlightenment* which can only conclude, if taken seriously, in a paternalistic de-enlightenment, in a society which relieves the individual of the initiative, banishes critical thinking and does not tolerate the education of the educator who will become the general guarantor of public good. Second, there is one particular aspect in regard to which socialist movements have always sought for guarantees: maintaining political power if they were capable of seizing it. Of course, certain historical lessons demonstrate a relative justification of this behaviour. It will suffice to remember the bestial behaviour of the French bourgeoisie after the Paris Commune, to make comprehensible Lenin's exultation when he heard from Bukharin that the Soviet republic was one day older than the Paris Commune. But it is precisely in this respect that any quest for guarantees is prohibitive from the viewpoint of the vital interests of socialism. Namely, there can be only one guarantee for this: dictatorship, and history with the emphatic weight of instructive parable shows us that socialism simply cannot evolve under any regime of dictatorship.

Political society

As a further characteristic of dictatorship over needs as a social order with hyperrationalist claims, its organization as a political society should be mentioned. This has been repeatedly, even if cursorily, analysed from a directly political aspect. Here we must indicate at least its interconnection with the theoretical foundations of these arrogant pretensions and their full-fledged system. The obvious has been sufficiently belaboured: political society means the primacy of the political state over the whole of societal life; society is an annexe to the omnipotent political state rather than a relatively independent entity. We have also added to this, that it does not simply suppress the existing forms of civil society, but, to a varying extent in the various 'layers' of life, it uproots the whole system of civil society developed before the revolution (or the military take-over) and constructs a pseudo-version of it (therein lies the novelty of the modern Jacobin-Bolshevik-political state in contrast to its pre-enlightenment versions). This is at least its ambition, but we shall see that, similarly to its radical efforts in uprooting all market relations, there are limits to the omnipotence of political society in this respect as well.

Jacobin–Bolshevik efforts at establishing a political society have one serious advantage over all their weaker predecessors: they claim to embody, precisely through dictatorship over needs, an all-embracing economic justification (based on substantive rationality) as against the blind type of capitalist economy which causes catastrophes. Of course, in one way or the other, all their forerunners meddled with needs, totally or more often partially. It will suffice to refer to the institution of the French *police de robe* under the *ancien régime* which at least tried to enforce prescriptions and bans regarding the type of dress individuals were allowed to wear. In this respect, our use of ante-diluvian categories (such as absolutism) in the second part of this study simply underlined the historical continuity with *all* political states. But at the present stage of analysis it is rather the distinctive features that should be stressed. The Bolshevik outlawing of the whole of the empirically existing system of needs as dangerous because potentially leading back to capitalism is a totalizing act of the socio-economic establishment of a new society. One cannot emphasize enough that here and *not* in any emergency situation lies the root of the terroristic attitude of the regime. It is tyrannical even when and where the threat of restoration of capitalism by alien forces cannot be reasonably raised.

It stands to reason that political society is overwhelmingly suspicious of the individual, his need-dynamic, his independence. This feature follows from its tendency to be the supreme social arbiter (the adequate appendage to which in terms of economy is command, not planning), from its elitism. Corporate elitisms of that type always reject the individual person and his free associations, communities, his *Kommunikationsgemeinschaft* as the ultimate instance of need articulation because the latter are imperfect as compared to the perfection of hyperrational 'predictive wisdom'. Although the chicken-and-egg-priority is a sterile question here as well, in our opinion this is the primary act of establishing dictatorship over needs; the abolition of the market (to the extent that it can be implemented) is only derivative. The real political economy of the regime (as contrasted to the infantile propaganda about 'maximum satisfaction of all needs' as a 'law of socialist economy', which is a blatant lie, as well as theoretical nonsense) can be studied on the example of the Stalin–Bukharin debate, in three consecutive steps.

The first step is the tacit premise of all Bolshevik participants in the debate (and of every debate on economics among Bolsheviks): the declaring of unrestricted self-expression of individual needs to be illegitimate and dangerous (in critical times in a very harsh manner). As the second step, the priority between social groups is determined by a force which is neither part nor representative of any one of the particular groups but an arbiter over all of them. This process is partly an abstraction from, partly a mystification of, the empirically existing needs in which both those given and those losing priority find themselves in a disadvantageous position, and only the corporative elite wins in that it extends its power over social life. This is the practical victory of *general will* over the *will of all*. As the third step, a correct generalization of material and cultural needs, that is to say, an arbitrary assessment of the power elite takes place on this ground, already in complete separation from the only authentic fountainhead of the relevant information: the individual and his autonomous associations.

It is in this coercive need-imputation that one can find the real reason why dictatorship over needs based both economically and socially on commands, is despite all propaganda hostile to planning. In any reasonable sense of the word, 'plans' mean taking the natural resources into account and making, at least to some extent, a more or less free inventory of existing individual demands or their socially generalized aggregate. (We used the words, 'to some extent' and 'more or less free' because various social forces of domination manipulate and try to reduce or deflect from actual satisfaction the given sum total of needs in every society that has existed up until now.) Command, however, irredeemably comprises the elements of arbitrariness and the deliberate disregard of needs, and whereas after dramatic fiascos the ruling elite is ready to learn from the rigid resistance of natural resources, they never care to admit the *droit d'existence* of the actually given sum total of genuine needs. This is, of course, only true with provisos and historical relativization: we have mentioned the post-Stalinist compromise between government and populations aimed at increasing material goods available for the latter. But with a certain historical relativization it is a constant feature of the regime as a dictatorship over needs.

When analysing this political society, the general relation of state to civil society (or its artifically created substitutes) and the particular relation of state to proper legal authorities have to be scrutinized in some detail. The first and foremost feature to be mentioned here is the fact that contractual relations are minimal in the mutilated and fragmented, artificially created substitute for civil society in such a regime. Given that in the sphere of political power relations even the claim to a contractual relation between the citizen or subject and the state is a criminal intention in itself (because it is 'endangering socialist achievements'); that, further, up until the emergence of the first economically free Polish trade unions, labour relations had been contractual only formally, not actually, there remained only one social sphere in which contractual relations turned out to be irreplaceable: the family. In a strange way, general predictions regarding the areas which would resist the revolutionary hurricane and those which would be not capable of resistance disintegrated. Religion as a community and a way of life collapsed (except in Poland) whereas the nuclear family proved a bastion unassailable by even the most violent of social reformers. Of course, the above statement does not imply that religion as a *Weltanschauung* or an emotional attitude would wither away in these Eastern European countries. In many ways, and not only in the overt opposition, we can bear witness to precisely the contrary in the last decade. But observers of Russia in the early years of the Bolshevik Revolution believed that the institutional bulwarks of religious feelings would be strong enough to lend irresistible support to the Church as a competitor of the Bolshevik state, whereas in fact the former is now almost universally a servant of the latter. It has also been contended that 'communitarian' and 'amoral' Bolshevism, reinforced by the disintegrating tendencies of modern times, will totally dissolve the nuclear family, to replace it by collective forms of co-existence. However, despite the heavy pressure exercised on nuclear family relations during the heyday of Stalinist terrorism (when it was declared a virtue if children denounced parents, when there was not even a formal legal guarantee for wife and husband to abstain from damaging testimonies against each other — on the contrary, they were regularly set against each other during the 'trials' of the period), the nuclear family successfully resisted. General protest made a release of pressure necessary. A new phase now prevails: that of the idolization of the charms of parochial family life which also has a directly political character. Political society prefers the disjointed existence of political atoms within a nuclear family to any collectivistic way of life. Furthermore, dictatorship over needs is and must be a tyrannical-conservative authority over sexual behaviour. The sexual emancipation of women in particular is a non-controllable factor, even if non-political at the outset. Finally, the subtle argument that an authoritarian society likes to be bolstered up by authority in the family, holds true as well. But all in all, the defeat of the dictatorship before the walls of the nuclear family was the Stalingrad of its totalizing efforts.

State and law, the whole status and future of legal regulation within political society is so complex an issue that it can only be touched upon here. One of the widespread (and at least partly just) explanations of the shaky existence of law in this society is that already in theoretical Marxism prior to any attempts at realization, *Gesellschaftlichkeit* (social relations to be regulated by law) were largely substituted for *Gemeinschaftlichkeit* (communal relations which promote face-to-face relations, but do not tolerate 'formalistic' regulations). Without discussing the merits and demerits of this ingenious scheme, but at least admitting its partial truth tied up with the fact that Marx's perspective had always been the abolition of state (as a result, of the legal sphere), three other factors have to be pointed out here. Firstly, the source of law, the primary legal authority in every democratic (or at least liberal) system is a kind of consensus regarding the fundamental values on which the legal system should be based and the rights which originate from them, however complex it may be to define how this consensus comes about and what its character is. Needless to say, in a dictatorship over needs no such consensus can be freely articulated and no such consensus ever exists regarding the values which are declared from above to be the leading principles of society. Above all there is no such consensus regarding their validity. The maxim that the Soviet societies are ruled, not governed, holds true precisely in that sense. Secondly, in every society which is based on the above-mentioned consensus, the legal system is not a simple derivative of the state's will but presupposes the relative separation of legislative and judiciary powers from the executive. Of course the power centres exert a corrupting influence over the allegedly independent and impartial arms of justice everywhere. The well-known radical objection that 'formal justice' is abstract and lifeless is also true. But it is easily understandable that in dictatorship over needs, whose fundamental characteristic is that state and society are not separated from one another, the cure of the abstractness of law kills the patient, and the legal system has only a shadow existence.

Thirdly, even the formal recognition of certain individual human rights indispensable for the functioning of any legal system is lacking in most periods of political society, and when they are recognized as such, in a formal and very limited sense, they are very rarely practised. In a sense, the reason why a totalitarian dictatorship eliminates legal regulation is more comprehensible than the contrary, which really has to be accounted for: namely the reason why it returns to certain forms of legal regulation, even if in a very limited way, without abdicating from the prerogative of the sovereign (the Party) of overruling and violating its own laws. In our view, there are four main reasons for this. The first is the self-defence of the apparatus (coeval with closure of the period of 'revolutions from above') against the eventual and murderous caprices of any personal rule. In this sense, the Party resolutions restituting collective leadership including confidential and non-legal but legally binding decisions such as, for instance, that the secret police can only persecute members of the Central Committee with the prior consent of this body — that is to say, the decision of a non-legal body — and a certain (very fragmentary) legal formalization of law enforcement form a coherent unity. The second reason is the increased role of the 'fragmented' market (to which we will return later) which requires at least a minimum of formal patterns of economic transactions and behaviour. Thirdly, family relations, this bastion of resistance against the totalizing political society, is the nucleus of a legal system in Soviet societies. Fourthly, as from the moment when delinquency was no longer solved by Stalin's methods, for instance, with the mass extermination of the *besprisorni* (the homeless, wandering, partly delinquent, juvenile elements), the increasing formalization of the criminal penal code became inevitable.

The idea of a dictatorship of the proletariat has been inextricably bound up with the conception and the claims of political society. There are now endless and sterile debates on the Left about the 'necessary' or 'dispensable' character of such a rule, but very rarely is there any serious enquiry into its possible shades of meaning. All this happens despite the fact that the first thing that occurs to any observer is that dictatorship as a lasting form of government has never been the rule of a class where it has been invented, notably in the Roman republic, but rather a suspension of the class rule (if the term 'class' can be reasonably applied to Roman society at all). With Marx, when and if the concept returned, it was simply reminiscent of a 'Paris versus Vendée' situation, a doubtful idea politically, to say the least, but certainly not intended as a whole period in class rule. With Rosa Luxemburg, the notion was simply equivalent to a short-term emergency government between the revolution and the first general elections which Luxemburg logically considered the precondition of any democratic state of affairs. It was Lenin's dubious achievement to build up, with a highly questionable documentation and a sophist form of argumentation, a whole Marxist theory of dictatorship and declare it the lasting rule of a class, which was a symbiosis of incompatibles. But he and his successors had good reason to insist on the idea in spite of the tautological changes in the nomenclature. It is indeed an ingenious camouflage for political society. The latter is in fact a dictatorship which has its actual functions elsewhere, not in checking 'counter-revolutionary attempts against the new order' for this is only one of its functions in a very early period, but rather in a tyrannical regulation of needs, production and distribution. Further, in claiming a 'class against class' situation it is a successful façade. What is in actual fact a tyrannical administration of the whole society by an elite (the apparatus) is presented as the legitimate self-defence of a beleaguered social class. Finally, it is a term which covers the permanence of terroristic rule but which deceptively points to the allegedly transient character of its existence. In all these capacities it is the best disguise for dictatorship over needs.

Perverted radicalism

The final dimension of the characterization of dictatorship over needs is its *pervertedly radical* nature. But here we have to point out the measure of what for us is 'normal': it is the Marxian man rich in needs and the freedom to articulate them. It is precisely this man that is being oppressed in dictatorship over needs in a total way. This oppression is, therefore, a radical act and as such, a perverted radicalism for us.

Perverted radicalism can be discerned in the unceasing efforts of the power centres to turn society into a single community which only concludes in what can be called 'coerced togetherness'. (A feature of the unresolvable antinomies of this social system is that it is aimed at

once at homogenizing society into one community and at preserving
the duality of the corporate top and the social bottom constituted
by disjointed atoms.) Such a venture is doomed to failure at the very
outset unless it operates with the myth of race. A relatively successful
version (and the main logic of coercion in Nazism) was Hitler's
conception of the Nordic-Aryan society as a communal racial whole
which at least provided him with a firm home-front. Mussolini
already had failed spectacularly with a similar experiment: his neo-
Roman empire was a shabby façade for a nineteenth-century-type
colonizing nationalism rather than a genuine racist myth. Stalin's
totalitarian system could not even venture upon experiments of
such a kind because the historical and ideological genesis of a regime
was a stumbling block that could not be simply bypassed even by
powerful tyrants. But efforts in this direction never ceased to be
made and for good reason. The ruling elite with its perverted
radicalism only believed itself to have achieved its goal and 'cured'
the people of their 'bourgeois egoism' (in other words to have
subjected their homogenized needs to the will of the power centres)
if and when the relative privacy of *Gesellschaftlichkeit* has been
abolished and replaced by total *Gemeinschaftlichkeit*. The result was
neither the rule of the societal in any democratic sense of the word
because all elements of the voluntary unification of the economically
disjointed atoms, all elements of contract, legal regulations, and the
like were missing from it, nor was it genuinely communal, as the
overwhelming majority of the disjointed atoms never freely accepted
the values of cohesion. It was coerced togetherness which reached its
ultimate and lunatic height in the Pol Pot regime's interdiction to
keep doors closed overnight to enable people to prevent their most
private thoughts and acts from being spied on. But there was no
necessity to go to such an extreme: privacy was banned or drastically
reduced in more 'civilized' versions of perverted radicalism. And the
result was that coerced togetherness no longer remained entirely
external to one's innermost thoughts. Since people's lives, fate and
future still depend on 'public affairs' (in other words, the tyrannical
caprice of the central authorities), they live constantly 'turned
outward', whereas in fact they remain intimidated and consciously
isolated atoms.
    Another aspect of perverted radicalism is the terroristic claim of
'seizing' (re-educating and transforming) the whole human personality.
The word 'terroristic' should be emphasized here because the original
intention of abolishing the discrepancy between the private and
public spheres belonged to the principal original emancipatory thrust

of socialism, and it still does. But in a society whose act of establish-ment is the introduction of a system of dictatorship over needs, the free education of the whole human personality into a democratic communal life without rigid barriers between private and public (but admitting the existence of an undisturbed 'intimate sphere') is degraded into a nationalization of man which only has its limits where the dictatorship runs out of its power reserves (and since it does, it is not state slavery). A strange tension in this respect exists within Soviet societies. On the one hand, the sovereign — the Party leadership — has never renounced in principle what they call 'communist morality': the right of a self-elected power content totally to dispose of the lives, habits, ambitions, inclinations, future and even physical existence of individuals. The 'Party's right' to mobilize the whole man (and every man) in any given moment is constantly maintained, it is even acclaimed as a principle superior to 'bourgeois atomism' and is, again in principle, extended far beyond the confines of the vanguard. But then the Party has also to make concessions, and not only in the post-Stalinist compromise, to what Robespierre called 'the unvirtuous majority', to this mass of immoral egoists whom official propaganda declares to be the paragon of all virtues but who are regarded in the 'secret doctrine' as an incorrigible waste product unworthy of their status as subjects. The Party's constantly renewed attempts at the total transformation of man is a new act of de-enlightenment: in lieu of what Marx expected to be the education of even the educator, we now find the re-education camps of 'liberated' South Vietnam.

At this stage, a distinction between dictatorship over needs and manipulation and limitation of needs becomes all-important. The New Leftist denunciation of manipulation of needs as the restriction of human (individual and collective) freedom in the service of capitalist interests, as the subjection of human creativity, to profit-seeking enterprise, is still valid; there is no new historical evidence to refute it. But manipulation and limitation is not (cannot be) a totalitarian principle, whereas dictatorship indeed is. As we have already seen, a total subordination of the workers' needs to the interest of capital's valorization is an inherent negative utopia of (capitalist) industrialization, rather than the real state of affairs characteristic of its liberal edition or a fully realizable tendency in the least liberal variations. This is so for a variety of reasons. The achievements of the enlightenment process, certain individual and collective liberties of the workers (living barriers in themselves against excessive need limitation), could not be wholly revoked (and in the liberal version they have often even increased). Further, limitation of needs is only one of the options of capitalism and when the era of the so-called intensive period of capitalist development, mostly centred around the private household budget, set in, it was no longer the economically dominant one either. Manipulation of needs can be (and generally is) very powerful but – apart from the fact that it always leaves at least the *formal* freedom of choice open – it 'deforms' the structure of needs rather than impoverishing or delimiting it.

Of course, abstractly speaking, it is not in the interest of any government to keep its population artificially indigent: mass poverty is always fertile ground for rebellion. And in fact, even Stalin tried to raise the living standards of his subjects on pragmatic considerations when he did not set out to 'punish' them as he did in the Ukraine after the war imposing famine upon its population. But whereas for the ruling classes in capitalism, abundance for the wage-earners is in itself indifferent (just as indifferent as their indigence) and can even be, in the form of 'solvent demand', a source of profit, it is not so with dictatorship over needs. An anti-capitalist enterprise, the latter was designed and planned as a mere negation of its opponent; as a result, the expansion of the individual or group need system, its variability, a wider range of individual options and 'pluralism' within it, would mean the resurrection of precisely that individual on whose forced obedience, frugality and built-in servility alone the edifice of the anti-capitalist dictatorship can rest. The leaders of the regime must not necessarily be Stalins or Pol Pots. Sometimes they are normal petty bourgeois with an adequate system of needs (and an adequate indifference towards their fellow men); they may even be quite flexible towards similar inclinations in their subjects. But whoever they are, the free unfolding of the system of needs in the case of subjects with a wide variety of needs is incompatible with the survival of the regime.

The rationalization of dictatorship over needs

To what extent, particularly or generally, is the society of substantive rationalism really rationalizable? And, to approach the problem from the other end as well, what are the limits of its irrationality? It is easier to start with a reply to the second question. Despite the apparent omnipotence of 'hyperrationalist predictive wisdom', this basically irrational principle easily reaches its limits. When these systems violate *all* forms of rationality, when they do not respect the slightest degree of relative independence of the individual and tend towards a veritable system of state slavery, when not even the physical self-reproduction of the individual is ensured, or when it is regularly endangered, then they collapse. It was not by chance that after Stalin's death three regimes driven far beyond the 'rational limit of oppression' — the East German, the Polish and the Hungarian — exploded within three years. Therefore it is simple to point out the primary channel of rationalization of dictatorship over needs: it is the updating and 'streamlining' of the methods, principles and objectives of oppression. This has basically two aspects. The first is what we have otherwise repeatedly called 'post-Stalinist compromise' between governments and populations. The kernel of this compromise is the regular ensuring of the very slow but steady rise in real incomes and living standards of the state subject on a 'normal' level (which means very reduced standards), the change from non-paternalistic (non-rewarding) oppression to a paternalistic one which rewards the individual by a guaranteed physical existence in exchange for freedom, social initiative and critical thinking. The second aspect is the transition from a system of indiscriminate collective mass exterminations of social (national) groups to a regular but selective persecution of genuine enemies of the regime (by which of course should be understood every independently and critically minded person). These are still standards of an oppressed and unliberated society but such as can (and regularly would) be tolerated by huge groups of population, given the face of an overwhelming inner and outer apparatus of oppression and the general lack of democratic traditions.

There are also certain partial tasks whose implementation can be rationalized. A classic example is the development of the Soviet Army and the armament industry. It is now established as a fact beyond any doubt that the Soviet armed forces are undisputed competitors of their American counterparts, even from a techno-logical point of view, a statement which would have sounded totally ridiculous thirty years ago. For purposes of such a partial rationaliza-tion, the area has been deliberately relieved of the crippling presence of ideological dogmas. The opposite of this situation is clearly visible in the case of the army under Stalin where it suffered enormously and with consequences nearly fatal to the country, from the whims of the tyrant. Its best officers were executed, the data of its intelligence activity were neglected in the name of a 'superior wisdom', and so on. A particularly blatant instance of irrationality has been revealed by Marshal Zhukov. According to his testimony, one of the causes of the Soviet Army's backwardness in the 1940s and 1950s was that — for ideological reasons — the leadership prohibited the introduction of the results of the 'bourgeois' science of cybernetics into the various branches of the Army. When the Soviet leaders after Stalin's death set out to rationalize this field that was so important for world domination they immediately dismissed all ideological considerations from it and became dyed-in-the-wool pragmatists: cybernetics and every type of 'bourgeois' science was introduced in order to keep pace with the American competitors.

But there is an absolute limit to the rationalizability of the regime, and it is sufficient to cast a perfunctory glance at the series of mostly armed revolts (Berlin, 1953; Poznan and Warsaw, 1956; Budapest, 1956; Novocherkass, 1963; Czechoslovakia, 1968; Gdansk, 1970; Warsaw, 1975; Zilvalley, Rumania, 1977; Gdansk again, 1980) to understand its character. Dictatorship over needs is a system which boasts of the 'reign of the future over the past' but it is only able to recognize retrospectively even *prima facie* economic matters. The reason for this is simple enough: without a free social articulation of needs there can be no consistent social rationality. In less abstract (and more practically economic) terms this means that it is impossible for the regime to transcend the extensive period of economy and effect the transition to the intensive one.

CHAPTER 11

Market and Fragmented Market in Soviet Societies

In Chapter 1, dealing with the economic system of dictatorship over needs, we defined the basic terms of characterization of the market as follows. Firstly, we mentioned 'the subordinated existence of some elements of market regulation in Eastern European economies'. To this we added a division of the existing market relations into the 'administratively regulated pseudo-markets of consumption goods and labour power' which have in common, that neither of them has a pricing character in the strict sense of the term, but are both still separate entities in the sense that they are 'closed' in relation to each other. As a further restricting principle of the market character of these economic relations, we added that 'the liquidation of the equilibrating function of the market creates an economic basis *sui generis* for the social domination of the apparatus.' All these terms remain untouched in our further analysis and no forthcoming considerations will alter their validity. None the less, the social struggle unceasingly taking place over market and pseudo-market deserves further examination, since this has a direct bearing on the general situation of rationality in Soviet societies.

As far as intentions are concerned, the apparatus of dictatorship over needs, appealing to a superior wisdom, 'substantive rationality' has always unreservedly accepted Marx's idea of a marketless society. This is partly because of the theoretical orthodoxy of the elite, but there is no evidence whatsoever that they would have been interested in the great humanist mission Marx attached to the abolition of market. The whole syndrome revealed by Lukács in his *History and Class Consciousness*, the problem of reification, the dichotomy of man and world, man and culture, was for the apparatus abstract and meaningless. There were two other underlying considerations for the 'orthodoxy of marketless society' which appealed to them: the perfect homogenization of society and the (perhaps forcible) uniformization of needs. Once again, they were not so much concerned with Marx's humanistic utopia according to which the management of things should not turn into a 'government of men'. They were unconditionally prepared to manage and distribute things through a direct and very harsh management of human beings and their system of needs.

Both homogenization of society and uniformization of needs found an adequate training ground in the Russia of War Communism. This was perhaps with the exception of a few years during the Chinese proletarian Cultural Revolution (and, in particular, with the exception of Cambodia) the only period in which a Babuvian, and not Marxian, type of Communism came very close to realization. It was also a period of very strange contradictions which can only be accounted for historically. To mention just one of a long series of contradictions: on the one hand — as discussed in Chapter 4 — it was not yet a period of politically totalitarian rule, yet on the other, economic totalization, the total subordination of the system of needs of the whole population, had proceeded more resolutely than at any other time in Soviet history. There was a complete rationing system, money was practically abolished, and despite the fact that land was at that time legally and practically in the hands of the peasants, all transactions even resembling market activity were banned and replaced by a martial system of requisitions. Of course, Nove is quite right when he points out that things actually worked differently behind the military façade. In his estimation, 60 per cent of the provisioning of the cities took place through market relations between city and countryside which were never legalized but continued to function without interruption.

But the Tambov peasant revolt, a far more important event in a historical sense than is generally known, put an end to the only 'purist' attempt at radical social homogenization. Beyond any doubt, the New Economic Policy introduced under its impact was a compromise compared to War Communist orthodoxy, and this had been felt not only by moralizing Communists with qualms of conscience such as Lukács and Bukharin. Even the otherwise pragmatic Lenin (who had, however, as doctrinaire a character as his model in Maximilien Robespierre) felt ill at ease about it. The Tambov revolt simply meant that the Russian peasants were no longer prepared even formally to acquiesce in the above-mentioned system of natural taxation and requisitions, that they demanded certain elements of market relation in a recognized form and that the apparatus relying at least on the temporary and tacit consent of workers in the two capital cities (in whose dictatorship over the immense countryside the Bolshevik Revolution had originally consisted) had to yield in order to be able to provision the big cities. Even if for Russian peasants the worst still lay ahead under Stalin's — first requisitioning, later collectivizing — Party armies, the system of compulsory direct and natural taxation as an exclusive one could not be upheld as a 'law' of socialist construction. Certain elements of market relations had to be recognized by consecutive Soviet governments.

'Certain elements of market relations' are obviously not identical with genuine market, and this statement is simply a paraphrase of the results of our analyses in Part I. More importantly than making nominal distinctions, it is our task to describe exactly what fragmented market relations do and do not mean. First of all, we must make clear what we have in mind when speaking about limitations imposed on free need-articulation, and especially on free need-satisfaction. This policy moves between two extremes, neither of which is ever reached completely. One is a complete central prescription of the exact amount and nature of individual consumption which, as we have seen, was the latent (negative) utopia of War Communism: one which had never come to full realization. The other is a complete recognition of the individual's right as a consumer in an institutional form, in other words, in the form of 'open markets'. This has never been realized either. Between the two poles, there are constant social convulsions, struggles, etc. the character of which we will return to later. But these two very poles in themselves mark a situation which can be described as fragmented market. Secondly, what we have earlier described as administratively regulated and non-pricing markets (in the plural) that are closed to each other, reveal in reality an even more complex view. There are phases in the history of every Soviet society in which the central command authority exercised its power in such a brutal and direct way that nothing manufactured in Department I (the sector producing the 'productive forces' themselves) ever went near the 'socialist market' (in other words, the pseudo-market). Every article was directly distributed to, or revoked from, the collective unit in need of it. Now the constant aspiration of the factory managers (whose aggregate can perhaps be called technocracy) for the right to bargain between themselves, 'swap technology', sell machinery for each other, will most certainly not create a pricing and equilibrating market since the transactions, even if formally permitted, must still take place within the framework of the arbitrarily determined prices fixed by the central command authority. But these struggles are not without significance, either. They express certain 'needs' of the industrial units, they are indirect and certainly distorted, but none the less important, expressions of the approximate real costs of production, the gaps in technology and the like, and thus represent a revolt of rationality against the fundamental irrationality represented by the central command authority. In a sense, one can 'read' the degree of liberalization and the attempts at rationalization in the regime from the variety of articles which reach this 'inter-departmental' and closed market, rendering it at least fragmented. A separate type of closed fragmented market is created by the interactions between agriculture and industry, agriculture and consumer needs. It has no independence from the state either, of course, but it regains certain elements of a pricing market. What is popularly called the *kolkhoz*-market in the Soviet Union, an institution halfway between a gigantic, legally tolerated black market network and a normal agricultural market, quite doggedly determines its own prices. There is plenty of evidence to prove that the *kolkhoz*-market simply failed to recognize for many years the monetary reform of the 1960s in the Soviet Union which reduced the rouble to one-tenth of its value: peasants persisted in selling their goods for the same nominal price. This financial and economic absurdity growing out of an unnecessarily prolonged war economy shows, of course, that this is a caricature of a pricing market rather than a genuine one, but it also testifies to the fact that it has some pricing functions. Another component of the agricultural fragmented market is the constant fight of agricultural managers (resembling that of their colleagues in industry) for the right to buy machines directly from factories. This is a long story, endlessly complicated by the self-contradicting regulations of 'socialist law' which varies from country to country, from period to period. But there is one permanent factor in it. Despite the fact that even when this right is granted to them, cooperatives or individual peasants (where there are such) can feel themselves only conditional owners of their own equipment (that is to say, this equipment, even if 'legally' transferred to them for good, can be revoked from them at any moment), given the constant underproduction, even crisis, in Soviet agriculture and its direct political implications, the machinery (plus additional economic liberties) in their conditional possession provide the peasant productive unit with a certain amount of market liberty and a limited influence over the social strategy of the central command authorities.

Through these liberties they become a fragmented expression of the need for rationality, particularly in the period of post-Stalinist compromise.

Thirdly — this is a further argument for the fragmented character of any market relations tolerated or achieved in living socialism — demand is always larger than supply (because of the simultaneous production of waste and scarcity), and supply (production) remains partially, not wholly, unaffected by the growth and qualitative structure of demand. In the cynical Eastern European view, a good socialist customer is not a person who has something definite in mind when going shopping, but the one who buys whatever he can grab. Queuing, if not for bread (which also happens quite regularly, for instance, in the Soviet Union), then for more sophisticated commodities (such as East German brassières, modern novels or refrigerators), bribing the employees of department stores in order to have the commodities in question illegally reserved for you, the general atmosphere of war economy never ceases to be part and parcel of the daily life of Eastern European citizens.

The growth of demand is just as often reacted upon by centrally ordered price rises, in other words, by forcible need reduction, as by growth of production. Even more infrequently does the qualitative change in demand (the specific wish for a specific commodity) influence production, whereas it happens time and again that the 'supreme will' decides what preferences the state subject must have with regard even to minor details of everyday life. (Khrushchev, for instance, once ordered that production of 'tasteless traditional lampshades' should cease.)

In principle the ideal cycle (production increases needs, which in turn increases production) is disrupted. The best that can be said is that while production does not increase needs (being constantly below the level of given demand) needs may influence rises in production (through their express, and preferably violent, manifest political appearance), but they do not necessarily do so. It is the prevailing disruption of the normal relation between demand and supply that guarantees the non-pricing character of fragmented market relations but which, let us repeat emphatically, does not provide any superior principle of distribution, only the usual chaos of command economy.

Finally, we must briefly indicate the fragmented character of one particularly important closed market: that of the work-force. (A brief analysis will suffice since this question has been amply analysed in Part I and, to some extent, even in Part II). The pertinent facts are namely: 1. One's personal choice of work-place (the city, the factory or enterprise, the particular type of work one performs) has never been a right, but at best a concession on the part of the state. 2. Wages have never legitimately been an object of bargaining. 3. The famous 'right to work' carries with it the ominous obligation of being constantly employed or else one is liable to persecution. All three facts testify to the deeply fragmented character of the market of the work-force in dictatorship over needs. Events in Poland mark a new stage in the history of Eastern Europe in this respect as well.

What are the market relations *sui generis* enclosed in fragmented market? First of all, from the latter's very existence follows the practical, sometimes even legally formalized, recognition of the fact that diverse needs of individual persons and groups demand a satis-faction that is not directed (through rationing and the allocation of the necessary means) but one that functions by a certain kind of exchange. As has been repeatedly emphasized, this is a limit beyond which not even the apparently omnipotent system of dictatorship can proceed. These types of exchange take place between the individual purchaser—consumer and the state as the owner of consumer goods, between city and countryside, often between separate factories or branches of industry, between the state and particular social groups, and also between the individual vendor—individual purchaser on various kinds of semi-legalized black markets.

The question is no longer whether or not society can exist without all types of (fragmented) market relations, in other words, without certain types of exchange — this has been irreversibly decided in historical terms. The real purpose of the guerilla warfare waged by the population is to influence production by extra-economic methods. The first and foremost aim of such warfare is to 'emanci-pate' from central allocation, in other words, to 'marketize', as many types of commodities as possible. The fact that has relatively recently emerged in some (not all) Soviet societies, that there is an, albeit very limited, market in flats and houses, that the space in which one is living is no longer simply allocated by the state (at least not necessarily) is a real victory in this guerilla warfare. The general trend of such below the surface efforts is now to influence the increase in, and the diversification of, the production of consumer goods on the part of the people. Since, as we have seen, the applica-tion of this influence cannot take place through the normal cycle of need and production, it has always to make a political detour to reach its destination. When in a 'socialist' country one finds shops full of goods before a national, particularly a religious, holiday, one can be sure that the uproar leading up to this had taken on a menacing tone and the feed-back of the secret police was reliable.

A further important dimension of market relations *sui generis* can be grasped by understanding the exact obverse of what has been said about the lack of even a fragmented work-force market. The only 'progress' in dictatorship over needs (mostly fought out on the barricades which had been declared obsolete as early as the 1890s by Engels) is that even in this system there are now things which can no longer be done to human beings, and others which have to be done under pressure. Peasants, it seems, can as from 1980 no longer be tied to their village: they seem to have regained their right to inner migration and thereby the 'third serfdom' of the Russian peasants is nearing its end. (This much at least will be true if Brezhnev's solemn promise materializes, namely, that for the first time in fifty years, they receive their internal passports which up until now have been kept by the village soviet presidents.) Forcible population transfers, a habitual by-product (and precondition) of 'revolutions from above' seem to be suspended. In all probability the last of these was Khrushchev's ominous and ill-fated campaign of cultivating the Siberian 'virgin soil', which did much to increase the unpopularity of the de-Stalinizing First Secretary. Then there are other things which ought to happen and which increase (in a non-legitimized way) the scope and influence of fragmented market relations. To their utmost irritation, leaders of Soviet societies have to take several 'merely economic' factors into consideration in their 'social engineering'. On the one hand, and despite miserable living standards, the urban way of life exerts a certain influence on new generations of the peasant population which tend to migrate towards the cities. After thirty years of forced industrialization which obtained its manpower from the villages, the countryside is no longer an inexhaustible reservoir for all industrial projects, the apparatus no longer has an unlimited work-force at its disposal at any given moment. This, combined in a strange way with another, previously analysed, countervailing factor, 'unemployment within the factory', presses the governments to make use of non-legitimized and frag-mented market factors instead of extra-economic coercion. Various industrial managers simply adopt the technique of their bourgeois colleagues: resorting to 'illegal' means, they pay higher wages than in other sectors of industry or agriculture. (This is, of course, a very courageous and mostly a very unselfish act because this 'breach of legality' can be, and often is, turned against them; many such managers were persecuted and imprisoned in Hungary in the early 1970s.) A further possibility on the part of the authorities is to tolerate, even sometimes legalize, moonlighting activities by otherwise fully occupied workers, which adds to the enormous burdens and inhumanity of a worker's life in a 'workers' state' but which solves at least a part of the pressing problem of services and represents an indirect way of increasing wages.

If we say that, as a third element of market relations *sui generis* within the fragmented market, the regime introduces certain aspects of calculative rationality, this statement needs immediate qualifications – both negative and positive. A major negative qualification is the reconfirmation of what has been stated earlier: no attempts at introducing such elements can ever attain to a genuine system of rationality. The positive qualification is that no system of economy, including the often lunatic economic management of 'socialist primitive accumulation' can ever dispense with at least some elements of calculation: there is no such single moment in which unlimited reserves of manpower, raw materials, etc. would be at the managers' disposal. What does the introduction of 'certain aspects of calculative rationality' mean, then? Basically two things. The first is the necessary disappearance of certain habitual devices of extensive economy, both as regards manpower and raw materials. As mentioned, coercive population transfer has been suspended in the post-Stalinist period, so managers have to seek new methods for the 'construction of socialism' to replace mass deportations. The stock of peasant manpower that can be coercively fed into the channels of industrialization is highly limited, too, because of the ongoing agricultural crisis. Because of the dimension and consumption of Soviet industry there are unexpected raw material shortages which played simply no part in the economic strategy-making of the 1930s and 1940s.

The second decisive factor is that the period of Soviet autarchic economy is over. It was precisely this that Stalin felt and feared, for with the unerring instincts of a truly representative arch-reactionary, he perceived that the end of the autarchic period would, by the same token, mean an end to a hermetically closed world with 'secret' extermination and concentration camps, and would inescapably involve at least some respect for the general economic potential of the country, a most unfavourable atmosphere for his particular brand of political tyranny. This is why he proposed the infantile idea of 'two world markets' in his last work, *The Economic Problems of Socialism in the Soviet Union*. Nevertheless, that even he had to describe the 'socialist' economic interrelations in terms of market deserves some attention. But his political heirs are to a large extent living in an epoch in which no one can maintain even the principle, let alone the practice, of economic isolation. There are several reasons for this. Firstly, the Soviet leaders are dependent on other Western countries for wheat imports. Secondly, even the Soviet Union with its seemingly limitless resources can no longer find everything it needs within its national frontiers. Thirdly, there are certain consumer goods to which the population has become accustomed and which the apparatus must purchase (either in the form of ready-made goods or as licences) from their competitors. Fourthly, their own military technology compels them to be a regular customer on the world-market. It is the ensemble of these new types of attitude which the Soviet leaders have been obliged to adopt that we call 'introducing elements of calculative rationality' (as market relations *sui generis* within the fragmented market) into the system.

It is gradually becoming clear even to the non-theoretical observer that it is the system of needs that plays the crucial role in the battle waged for and against expanding (fragmented) market relations. Let us quote a very short passage from *Le Monde Diplomatique* (September 1979) which analyses the causes of failure of the so-called 1965 'reform' of the Soviet economy in the following way:

The failure of the material incentives had been explained by the insufficiency of the consumer goods available: for whom is it worth obtaining bonuses if one cannot spend them? The decree of 1979 takes this into consideration. It ensures that the plan of producing consumer goods should take demand into account and that their quality, just as their range of choice, should meet with this demand. *But who would define the needs of the consumer?* According to the text, it would be the planner in his own wisdom. . .

Whenever one breaks through the circularity of Eastern European economic thinking, one arrives at the key concept of dictatorship over needs.

Whoever abandons the regulative idea of social homogeneity abandons, by the same token, the programme of absolute equality as well. The only interpretation which is consistent and in which absolute equality makes sense is Babuvianism whose aim is reduction and uniformity of needs (forcibly if necessary). But a critique of absolute equality is not necessarily a critique of socialism, real or simulated. Marx himself, to speak of authentic socialism, as well as a considerable number of representative socialists considered absolute equality to be the abolition of individuality and as such indicative of despotic Communism and a negative abolition of private property. The pseudo-socialism of dictatorship over needs was partly a practical refutation rather than any realization of Babuvian-egalitarian Communism. They had only one thing in common: forcible need-reduction and uniformity. Stalin was a determined enemy of egalitarianism and in this respect more clear-sighted than Babeuf. His word for egalitarianism was *uravnilovka* (which gives equalizing tendencies a pejorative sense), labelled it petty bourgeois (in contrast with at least a part of the Trotskyist opposition which tried to mobilize 'public opinion', or what was left of it, against Stalin by allusions to equality) — and all this for just one political reason. He was perfectly aware that for dictatorship over needs, a stratum or elite is needed that exercises oppression, and this elite is by definition not equal with those it subjects to itself, and equally it will not remain satisfied with its merely politically distinguished situation. The ruling apparatus wants to obtain its bonuses in the form of material prerogatives which are organic constituents of the system of dictatorship.

Is the dictatorship over needs a universalistic system? As we shall see, the answer to this question is closely bound up with the status of market relations within the system, even if it encompasses other aspects as well. The universalistic claim in it is obvious. Eastern European Soviet systems advertise themselves as a general answer to all the problems of capitalism, as a universal panacea. The unceasing censorship suppressing all manifestations of what had been called during the Khrushchev period 'national Communism' (and which is really a contradiction in terms) is not a sign of the narrow-mindedness of an 'Asian' leadership but a shrewd perception of the vital demands of a system which simply cannot remain within national boundaries. The universalistic claim is not a total self-delusion either. In this regard the Second World War created a radically new situation. Three of the four regimes which called themselves (or were called by others) Fascist or Nazi disappeared and the fourth has been peace-fully transformed. In scientific analysis, and despite the utmost horrors committed by right-wing Japanese and Spanish dictatorships, only two of them deserved to be called Fascist, and three of them played a seemingly universalistic role. We emphasize the world 'seemingly'. Even if it is always a risky operation to ascribe necessity to an event that simply happened, there seem to have been intrinsic, and, if not strictly necessary, equally not merely accidental-external, reasons for the fact that in the competition of two types of dictatorship the Nazi Fascist type suffered an overwhelming defeat. The reason (apart from strategic logistic considerations) is that their basis was considerably limited in principle: it was race (in a pure culture in the case of Germany, somewhat dressed up and camouflaged by a theatrical nationalism in the case of Japan or Mussolini's Roman dream), with the concomitant, inevitable, 'racial enemy' mentioned earlier. Their adversaries, however, have a far better chance of universalization. They present themselves as mandatories of universals: of democracy or socialism or both, gaining thereby in certain periods several diverse supporters and relying eventually on a fairly general sympathy. To this, two important considerations should be added. Firstly, dictatorship over needs is a dynamic modernizing regime which, because of the specific character of the oppression it establishes externally, in contrast to old-time colonialism, does not need to keep dependent areas in industrial underdevelopment. Rather the contrary, it offers them (it even tries to impose upon them) its own system of industrial development, which from a distance is attractive for the population of underdeveloped areas. Secondly, the 'export of revolution' means largely the export of the oppressive technology of government perfected by the Soviet apparatus, which certain local power elites are only too eager to take over. It is a sterile undertaking to analyse to what extent the ruling groups of Ethiopia or Laos are Communist in a doctrinaire sense of the word. They are Bolshevik in the important sense that the Bolshevik technology of oppression (including its pertinent insignia) appeals to them for a variety of reasons, even though there is a strong likelihood that they are not acquainted with a single page of *The Communist Manifesto* (and they accept, to a greater or lesser extent, state ownership of 'forces of production', together with command economy as an annexe to this technology). But they do not need Marx in order to uphold their rule.

What are the intrinsic triggers of the Soviet thrust for world domination, in competition with liberal capitalism and its highly illiberal allies? What are the characteristic features of Soviet imperialism? It is no exaggeration to say that the Soviet empire's leap forward has been taken to escape from internally unresolvable problems. Soviet propagandists usually refer to 'American imperialist threats' when explaining their own aggressive acts. This reference is sincere, even though, contrary to the justified fear of the Bolsheviks after the seizure of power, and for decades afterwards, they no longer believe that the West would have the guts even to attempt to realize the 'roll-back' with arms. The examples of 1956 in Hungary, 1968 in Czechoslovakia, and even more recent events could satisfactorily convince the Soviet leaders that their Western competitors not only will not intervene but will not even put pressure on them. When they complain with conviction about Western threats they mean something different: the irresistible fascination of Western political pluralism, higher living standards, civil liberties for the average Western citizen, a fascination which is still valid despite the fact that capitalism has been undergoing the longest crisis it has ever experienced. The above syndrome seems to be an invincible threat to the leaders of dictatorship over needs, even if it is true that the population of Eastern European countries has far less trust (if any at all) in the political reliability of the Western countries, and even if the image of Western daily life is now being viewed more soberly than in the worst period of the Cold War. By this 'escape forward' the Soviet leaders' intention is to defeat a way of life rather than an army. They understand quite clearly that the former is more dangerous to them than the latter. The real motivating force of Soviet imperialism is the utopia of Soviet leaders, that by eliminating world capitalism they could eliminate 'dissenting wishes' from the minds of their subjects, and with them the danger of revolt as well.

The second aspect of Soviet imperialism can only be understood if we return to what has been called the 'goal of production' in the characterization of command economy, which was identical with the expansion of material wealth (the system is modernizing in character precisely in this sense) but only to the extent and in ways which increase the power of disposal of the apparatus over this accumulated social wealth. This principle accounts perfectly for both the reasons and the character of Soviet imperialism. A social system based on this 'goal of production', on this objective social telos and dynamic, simply cannot stop at national boundaries. At the same time, there will be no profit motivation in its policy of extending oppression and dependence, it is the political imperialism of a political society. Political imperialism implies exactly the trends inherent in 'the goal of production'. It contains an explicit tendency of industrialization which the nations and population of underdeveloped areas first perceive as an emancipatory mission as long as its total irrationality does not come to the surface. For instance, there can be very few doubts regarding the fact that at least one of the main motives of the revolt which was deceptively called the proletarian Cultural Revolution was protest against Soviet-style industrialization in China, which, had it been pursued to its ultimate conclusion by Stalin's methods, would of necessity have led to the collapse of Chinese agriculture and to the greatest famine yet known in world history. (Let us emphasize that we are speaking here of just one of the motives, not of the results of the whole undertaking or the means of implementation.) The really devastating impact of Soviet political imperialism is not what is usually summed up in a propagandist manner as 'exploitation' of the dependent countries. It is to Sartre's credit to have pointed out (in the special Hungarian issue of *Les Temps Modernes* in 1957) that, instead of 'exploitation', which is the central category of a profit-oriented capitalist imperialism with the necessary corollary of the industrial underdevelopment of the afflicted areas, the Soviet system is a complex of 'mutually disadvantageous economic relations'. Two qualifications are necessary here. The first is that the interrelations can only be economically, not politically, mutually disadvantageous. The 'goal of production' (and also of political imperialism) is the expansion of the political power of Soviet bureaucracy and in this regard they make no compromise. Secondly, the fact that it is not profit-oriented, that it does not imply industrial underdevelopment, does not imply that it is less disastrous than any other kind of imperialism, that it could mean any kind of liberation or emancipation. Apart from the political system whose newly created versions in the dependent regions differ from each other only in respect of the harshness or relative 'reasonability' of their terroristic rule (a factor which of course cannot be disregarded), Soviet expansions also export all the inner problems of the home crisis, the whole irrationality of the industrial cycle, and, above all, the agricultural crisis which is a life-and-death problem for the newly subjected countries, practically all of which are living on a bare subsistence level.

But it is precisely political imperialism, a field in which the Soviet apparatus, in particular its military arm, is likely to reap yet more successes, which shows the ultimate limits to the universalistic claims of dictatorship over needs. The case of Egypt will suffice here to emphasize the relevant points. Egypt is a society which has elaborated, through a caste of officers, a home-made technology of oppression not needing Soviet export, but which had a minimum of civil society and need-articulation on the part of the population, and a wide range of complex and variegated demands expressed through both. As a result, the only goods the Soviet masters could deliver, namely sophisticated weaponry (which the Egyptians could anyhow get from the West as well) was no compensation for the Soviet bureaucracy's domination of Egyptian society. Nor was it a response to any of the pressing problems the Egyptian ruling caste had to cope with. As a result, the leadership dropped their Soviet allies and made a radical *volte-face* (something similar happened, though on a different basis and for different reasons, in Somalia). And the same thing will recur in every case where the Soviet regime confronts a more complex social formula, when the overwhelming need is not weaponry, where at least a part of the population has some channels to express its will and needs, and where the Soviet presence is not direct and therefore overwhelming, as in the case of the Eastern European countries.

All this refers back to the phenomenon already analysed in Part I, namely, that in a particular sense, dictatorship over needs is a parasitic society. Not only does it borrow whole patterns of technological development from the capitalist West — a constant stumbling block of New Leftist criticism of Soviet societies, although this is only a surface symptom. Despite its now increasing threat to Western liberal capitalism, Soviet societies are dependent on their competitors in a deeper sense, not because they borrow their technology and purchase a substantial quantity of their wheat from them, but primarily because, strange as it may sound, they depend on them as their only basis for calculative rationality. A cynical but ingenious observation from one Hungarian economist will clarify this unique situation: after the worldwide victory of Communism, he said, we have to keep at least Switzerland under glass, in intact capitalist form, otherwise how could we make calculable prices? The real meaning of this *bon mot* is that fragmented market relations alone cannot provide a global rationality basis for any industrial society, and dictatorship over needs has not generated any new principle or basis of generating rationality, only the myth of the substantive one. It is not even likely to do so in the future. For that reason, the most likely forecast regarding its competition with the capitalist West is that neither will collapse or be totally dominated by the other, nor will they converge, but instead compete and collaborate at the same time. For despite their mutually hostility they are nevertheless mutually functional.

We are now, in the early 1980s, at a specific stage of this rationality crisis. From all statistics, even from those which work uncritically with Soviet data, if they do not further falsify them, it becomes clear that Soviet industry (whose fabulous impetus in the early days seemed to substantiate substantive reason) is nearing zero growth. In all probability, the channels which are socially open for command economy will not be sufficient to guarantee the transition from the extensive to the intensive period. This, however, has two consequences, both dangerous from the viewpoint of the regime. One threatens the basis of post-Stalinist compromise between governments and populations, and one can easily study the potential results of such a sudden halt on the example of the Polish August. The other is equally dangerous for the regime's own policy objectives: an increase in armament industry and army equipment adequate to the requirements of a global imperialism is impossible in a situation of near zero growth.

The question which often arises, especially on the part of the Leftist critics of Soviet societies is whether the (fragmented) market is an adequate battlefield on which the struggle for transforming this society into one really deserving the name of socialism, can and should be fought out. We have already responded to the theoretical background of this suspicion, a position which does indeed represent orthodox Marxism but which is unacceptable for us: the radical denial of the compatibility of market relations with socialism. Our answer to the problem will be three-pointed. Firstly, although correct in his critical phenomenology of the social ills created by the market, Marx was too radical when he denied all possibility of unification of a certain type of market with genuinely socialist social relations. The market as such did not emerge with capitalism; capitalism was only unique in that it totalized society under the sign of market relations and subjected the former to the latter. A democratic type of socialism is in principle capable of uniting a certain, critically supervised market as the basis of calculative rationality with emancipated human relations. Secondly, the social struggles in dictatorship over needs for a market, or more precisely, markets (a distinction we shall return to immediately), has a certain restricted enlightenment function. In a society where bargaining has only a negative connotation and under the disguise of an officially declared social harmony mostly brute force rules, where the chances of taking a careful inventory of individuals' and social groups' reserves and capacities, and testing their realism in decision-making are near zero, the struggle for markets can function to reconquer virtues which are not spectacular historical novelties but indispensable for a rational conduct of life. And here we have to account for the reference to markets in the plural. Various social groups which immediately appear as we have seen, as separate entities, look for various types of market as soon as the moment of 'thaw' sets in, and it is a historical exception if their efforts are synchronized. Technocrats (if industrial managers can concert their aspirations in such a way as to deserve this collective name) aim to open a market of industrial products, partly towards agriculture, partly between various branches of industry, partly towards the solvent markets of foreign countries without the state's interference. The state subject as wage-earner is rather interested in a free market of the labour commodity and the examples could be multiplied. Thirdly and finally, we have to express our reservations regarding the chances and the possible social extension of the struggles for a new type of market relations adequate to democratic socialism that are fought out primarily on fragmented market. Since fragmented market and all ensuing effects of social irrationality have come about as a result of the politicization of society, of subjecting society to an omnipotent political state, a real emancipation can only come through a radical political change.

CHAPTER 12

The Crisis of Dictatorship over Needs

Types of conflict

At the end of chapter 9 we stated the fact of an imminent or already
existing crisis whose essence has been summed up in the socio-
economic incapacity of the apparatus to implement the transition
from the extensive period of economy to the intensive one. It has
overt political symptoms as well, the most important of which is the
public existence of an (innerly variegated and structured) opposition,
almost for the first time since Lenin in Communist regimes. We shall
return to the cursory analysis and typology of this opposition later.
For the time being only two important consequences of this new
phenomenon should be pointed out. The first of them is that even
though Eastern Europeans still live under Stalin's shadow, fear is not
genetically inherited. This simply indicates, despite the fact that we
are so near 1984, that there is a limit to the scientific breeding of
obedient citizens, indoctrination, brainwashing or a brave new world.
This is an important argument for an optimistic anthropology and
demonstrates that what humanist Marxism called the indestructibility
of human substance and which with its old-fashioned pathos and
unscientific character provoked sneers both from its Althusserian
critics and disillusioned cynics, is a plain and important social fact.
Secondly, it is in itself a proof of the legitimation crisis of the regime
in that an influential minority within the society points out publicly
the untenable character of prevailing conditions and suggests several
other solutions abolishing the exemplary and binding character of
the existing order which we have, in the wake of Max Weber, called
a precondition of legitimation. This opposition is a factor to
anticipate everywhere, a phoenix resuscitated to new life by general
dissatisfaction, and nowhere is it clearer, come what may, than in
Poland.

But, against this, why not return to mass terrorization in the fashion of the 1930s? There are numerous reasons for the leading elite's inability to resort to such measures. To begin with, Khrushchev's historic action in exposing at least a small fragment of Stalin's murderous crimes, makes it impossible for the same or similar ones ever again to be committed in secrecy. A new Stalin could find minions, but not naive believers and certainly not an American ambassador prepared to report back to the President that his trials are 'legal'. He is equally unlikely to find general ignorance regarding the dimensions of his deeds which is all-important for a regime of mass-extermination (as could be seen from the confused doubletalk of the leaders of the Khmer Rouge and their supporters). Further, modern industrial relations are hardly compatible with mass terrorization: they are too vulnerable even to a reluctant, let alone an outrightly hostile, attitude on the part of the workers. Finally, as we have mentioned, the ruling stratum, the whole apparatus, learned from history that the rolling machine of mass terrorization once it has gathered momentum, never stops short at their doors, and they do not find this an attractive prospect.

To understand the present situation and its social alternatives, a promising point of departure seems to be the simultaneous considera- tion of the ultimate structural unity and the national specificity of the Soviet regimes in which the national problem plays the triggering role. But here a preliminary detour is necessary. This analysis suggests in itself that we expect the epicentre of the gathering storm to be located in the countries dependent on the Soviet Union, whereas in the Soviet Union itself the course of events will be more peaceful, even if not free of conflicts, and for a variety of reasons. Of course, this is a rough estimation, not a prophecy, and certainly not a realistic assessment of tendencies which simply cannot be accurately assessed in a country where no poll, either direct or indirect, of the popular view can be taken. No one can deny the theoretical possibility of a sudden Russian revolution, even with- out such spectacular warning events as preceded 1905. Only it is not very likely to occur in the near future. Therefore our forecast is that the constantly recurring series of tensions which cannot be reduced and defused will occur in the dependent countries and will affect indirectly the Soviet Union itself.

In order to understand these constant tensions, one has to com- prehend the forces of cohesion producing this ultimate structural unity in the Soviet sphere of influence. They are twofold. First of all, they are created by Soviet military presence. To put it simply, these countries are occupied territories of the Soviet empire and both population and governments have to be, and indeed are, well aware of that fact. If they forget it for a moment, as the Dubcek leadership did, catastrophe is inevitable. But it is necessary to point out the governments' national self-awareness as well. With the exception of Bulgaria, whose leaders rushed to be incorporated into the Soviet Union as the 17th Republic, all governments in this area showed themselves, at least at times, to be somewhat more than a pack of Quislings. Even the East German leadership blackmail their venerated Soviet masters from time to time into an economic policy advantageous to their own country. On the other hand, not only subjects but satraps too have to bear the limits of Soviet patience in mind. The second factor is economic dependence on the Soviet Union, whose character we have described as a system of mutually disadvantageous economic relations with the political prevalence of the Soviet apparatus.

Forcible cohesion, of course, provokes resistance of a nationalist kind. This is caused, first of all, by the inorganic character of Soviet domination. If one takes a look at the growing suspicion with which the activity of multi-nationals is being watched by the general public in the Western countries (an activity which at any rate can be somewhat controlled, even if not to a great extent), one will not be surprised by the hostility in the Eastern European states towards an economic and social power which is beyond the slightest, even formal, control and of which one thing is certain: it is not paying the slightest attention to the dependent countries' national interests. Communist reform governments, especially in moments of national crisis, try, as Gomulka did in 1956, to publish near-realistic figures of commercial exchange between their countries and the Soviet Union; they even emphasize the undeniable fact that whenever one of the dependent countries goes bankrupt, the Soviet government (that is to say, the peoples of the Soviet Union) have to carry a huge part of the burdens — all this is to no avail. Because of the fetishized character of the regime which simply makes it impossible for the man in the street to grasp the genuine character of the socio-economic interrelations (which are not better than people imagine, only different), the concept of direct Soviet exploitation is ineradicable from the average consciousness. Of course, it would be deluding oneself to believe that command economy plus a kind of independence of economic strategy would be a winning combination resulting necessarily in general affluence: one has only to look at Rumania to see the refutation. But whereas, as we have pointed out earlier, the presence of the apparatus in this particular type of economy is organic in the sense that the economic regime, due to its inherent construction, cannot exist without that particular type of commanding stratum, the presence, or rather aggressive omnipresence, of the Soviet apparatus in the economic life of the Eastern European countries is far from being an organic necessity. People rightly feel that all this is not happening in their interest and that they could manage without this daily, fairly brutal meddling in their affairs.

A further cause of the nationalist-centripetal trends and their unbroken vigour is the weakness of the integrating centre, Soviet Russia itself, in an economic, political and ideological—cultural sense. (The only aspect in which it can be described as indisputably strong is, of course, that of its military power.) Economic weakness needs no further comment. By political weakness is meant partly the complex of circumstances in which the dominating centre, the Soviet Union itself, is a multi-national empire and an intricate network of national domination and dependence, of mutual hatred of nationalities. We also include the result of the doctrinaire, ideological character of political society, which accounts for the slow and reluctant adaptability of its leading stratum.

But perhaps the weakest point of Soviet domination can be expressed in terms of the Gramscian theory of domination: it does not have a cultural hegemony at all. As is well-known, Gramsci's position was roughly that the measure of the capacity to rule of a class, social stratum, and the like, is its productivity of ideas, values and accepted attitudes in every field of social activity (that is, its cultural productivity in a wider sense) which are innerly binding and effectively steer human actions without the necessity of constantly deploying sheer coercion. Against this one could put forward as an argument our earlier observation about the export value of Soviet governmental methods as highly attractive for local power elites in many underdeveloped areas with weak (or non-existent) civil societies. However, the export of Soviet Marxism—Leninism as governmental technology may appeal to Asian, African or Latin American power elites (in the process of a change of elites), but it does not at all guarantee their loyalty to the Soviet empire. Sometimes just the contrary is the case and nothing proves it more emphatically than the example of China. It was beyond any doubt the Soviet-type Communist ideology in the 1920s which was the vehicle that brought the failing and dispersed revolutionary forces of the old China (whose crisis could clearly not be solved by the republican turn) to victory. Granted this, and even if one conceives of the attitudes of all consecutive Chinese leaderships in the last twenty years as treason (which would be an infantile way of thinking), it is still a corroboration of the fact that Soviet ideology has never had a binding force when additional coercion was not used or perhaps that it has lost its binding and steering capacity in its period of crisis (which we shall discuss later). A second pertinent observation would be that in the Gramscian theory hegemony was the capacity of the ruling class, group or stratum to promulgate new ways of life for the whole of a structure or society, to invent such, or at least to assimilate the existing ones to its ends. It is not enough for the fulfilment of cultural hegemony to devise a new way of governing and living only for those in the position of power. But the Soviet apparatus is specifically incapable of creating socially generalizable norms or rosters of values both at home, and even more so on foreign soil.

When it comes to the somewhat academic but necessary clarification of the types of conflict within Eastern European Soviet societies, it is appropriate to remark that they very rarely appear on the political scene simultaneously. This asynchronic character of the factors of the retarded and manifold social crisis in Eastern Europe is partly due to a certain amount of manipulative capacity on behalf of the Soviet power elite, which has drawn at least some conclusions from their own historical blunders and fiascos and acquired a portion of the manipulatory (not only coercive) technique of earlier ruling strata. This much was very clear, for instance, in Poland in 1968 when the Polish leadership immediately mobilized working-class prejudices against rebellious intellectuals (university professors and demonstrating students), and invoked traditional Polish anti-Semitism — against mostly non-Jewish dissidents — in order to acquire popular aid, and establish certain safety valves.

If the types of conflict are classified according to the needs which become manifest in them, the most primitive but most general one is focussed on the inadequate rationality (mostly as against the need for expanded, better structured and free consumption). The most elementary version of the demand for economic rationalization is the outcry against regular short supplies in most daily commodities, against the general unpredictability of economic perspectives in a system which incessantly boasts about being 'planned'. Striving for economic rationality is in a sense the most peaceful of social conflicts in Eastern Europe, for at this point, at least in principle, there is a certain amount of agreement between various social groups including the ruling elite itself. The elite would not concur for a moment in any trend aiming at political pluralism (and, as events in Poland show, is mobilizing divisions even against economic pluralism) but it is sometimes ready to go to some lengths in exposing the real weaknesses of its own regime. (For good reasons: the other option would be, and in fact is, the permanence of revolts.) The moments of relative consensus are the moments of economic reforms which already have a tradition of a cyclic character. About every five to eight years, subjects and masters alike realize that economic affairs cannot continue to follow the established patterns, that some change must be made. Consequent upon this usually come discussions (primarily officially supported ones), which are gradually toned down to a forced compromise. The upshot is, once again with the only exception of Yugoslavia where the story is more complex, a slow withering away of all half-hearted measures reluctantly taken (which does not necessarily mean that nothing at all happens). The leaders draw certain conclusions on the most pragmatic level imaginable: for instance they turn to the United States for more wheat or import more cars, or the like.

The second type of conflict is centred around the need for free cultural activity and cultural consumption. This is a widespread form of dissent, not limited to any particular social group, although it cannot include members of the ruling elite. There are good reasons for this. Whereas in the post-Stalin era it is compatible both to belong to the ruling stratum and to demand more rationality within the system (of course, in an appropriate, subject-like manner, and at appropriately chosen moments), it is wholly incompatible to demand more freedom in any respect. The concessions to the state subjects that are actually granted always have to appear to the members of the ruling stratum as the maximum possible realization of human freedom. There is, however, a politically and morally wrong corporative expression of this need. In an earlier period this frequently emerged in certain tendencies of intellectual groups which demanded unlimited freedom for the intelligentsia as a corporation but were wholly indifferent towards the liberties of other corporations. History is, however, instructive in this regard as well, and the most encouraging counter-example is the close alliance between Polish intellectuals and workers that has existed from 1975.

A wider and more universal conflict evolves in the campaigns for the free unfolding of civil society. This need is voiced energetically by many movements and actions which cannot be localized exclusively in one or the other social group but are 'trans-social'. Some of them are only *ad hoc* gestures to expose this or that *apparatchik* abusing his power, whereas, of course, the precise distinction between the abuse and legitimate use of power depends in large measure on the arbitrary decisions of the power centres. A more interesting symptom of the same type is action against certain prerogatives of the ruling elite (sometimes improvised by factory workers, sometimes systematically led by professional intellectuals). One of its typical forms is the effort to expose the non-monetary social amenities of the apparatus, this inextricable jungle of personal services which make the income of the apparatus incomparably higher than that of any other stratum and at the same time renders it impossible to exercise any kind of public control over social inequalities. But more important are the movements expressing the universal need for an autonomous legal system. At first glance, this seems to be an exclusive concern of intellectuals, another type of wrongful corporativism. As a matter of fact, many members of the old and the New Left aroused general hatred in Eastern European countries when they made light of this question saying: these only belong to obsolete bourgeois rights. Human rights, which in a dialectical ensemble are qualified as 'bourgeois inventions' superfluous for socialism and are simultaneously declared to be perfectly realized by the humanism of 'socialist law', undoubtedly represent nothing that is historically new. They are the achievements of the enlightenment and societies born out of enlightenment projects. But for precisely that reason their practical absence and their frequent out-of-hand theoretical rejection denounce the societies of dictatorship over needs as societies of de-enlightenment.

The supreme type of all possible conflicts is rebellion as an expression of need for collective autonomy, as was perfectly visible during the Polish August and has been ever since. This is a struggle for the economic, social and political autonomy of social groups, for workers' control over factory affairs, a nuclear form of self-management movement, an explicit need for free trade unions, outbursts of the universal need for self-organization and coalition. Whereas the possibility is not totally excluded that the regime can integrate some of these demands (primarily the existence of trade unions with a greater amount of independence), should these rights be demanded in their entirety, this would mean a state of total social upheaval, of revolution.

The negative dialectics of Marxism

Both at the top and the bottom, the phenomenon usually described as the 'crisis of Marxism' belongs to the social crisis of dictatorship over needs in various, often contradictory ways. Both the essence and the consequences of this crisis can only be grasped in a more or less sketchy historical presentation, for it is incorrect to speak of 'Soviet Marxism' as a continuous whole, as Marcuse did, particularly if one understands ideology functionally, as he himself did, and declares its truth content to be an abstract matter.

If we accept (at least partially) this functionalist approach to Marxism as ideology, we shall immediately see that there are clearly distinguishable periods of its historical—social existence in post-revolutionary Russia. There can be no question but that in the so-called 'Leninist period' (that is to say, from the Bolshevik *coup d'état* roughly up until the end of the 1920s) Marxism at the bottom of the social scale did not mean a thing, either in a negative or in a positive sense. Millions of peasants and workers were much too preoccupied (in a favourable or hostile way) with the primary, and brutally political, exigencies of a civil war and mass terrorization on both sides, and eventually with a famine unprecedented in modern European history, to be concerned about ideological niceties. Nor, with the exception of one question, did the victorious Bolsheviks demand that they should be. The one exception was the question of the cult of religion. Even here, Bolsheviks were less doctrinaire, as one would expect. The Pravoslav church was for them less a kind of 'opium for the people', as Marx described it, than the centuries-old servant of a conservative central power, dating from the times of Peter the Great. The church was also an immense corporative land-owner, a natural ally of the White Armies, a natural enemy of the Bolshevik power. The eminently lucid Lenin and his terror apparatus persecuted a this-worldly enemy rather than a prejudice inherited from pre-enlightenment times.

But Marxism was definitely a cardinal question for the ruling elite, the Bolshevik apparatus that had seized old imperial Russia in its grip overnight. For the members of the apparatus (and a wide entourage around them) it was a matter not only of doctrine, but also of a new way of life. This had a dual aspect. In part, the so-called 'purity of the doctrine', a loyalty to the corpus of Marx's works (naturally, in accordance with the dominant interpretation in Russian Marxism for a quarter of a century) was a test of the individual Communist's personal authenticity. This is valid not only in the case of clearly moralizing characters such as Bukharin, or that of philosophers of a possible new Communist morality such as Lukács. Even Lenin, a pragmatist by nature, a utilitarian in his conception of morality, suffered a shock when he acknowledged the overwhelming political necessity of introducing the New Economic Policy which he correctly deemed an absolute necessity but which he regarded, equally correctly, as a deviation from Marx's tenets about the abolition of market as a precondition of socialism. But if we are not speaking only of the protagonists of history (and if we disregard the now so controversial question of whether it was the individual called Sholokhov who wrote the novels for which he was awarded the Nobel prize, both *And Quiet Flows the Don* and his second, abominable novel about Stalinist collectivization), we can become acquainted with a series of types of Communist in the 1920s who were deeply, and sometimes in an infantile but always in an authentic way, concerned with the 'correctness' of their personal conduct of life from a Marxist point of view. In part, this period was the only historical moment in which Marxism and Communism meant an alternative to the traditionally existing ways of life. The first, mostly clumsy attempts at feminism (connected with the name of Kollontai) had been launched, agrarian Communists experimented with communes, later to have such a distinguished role in the aspirations of the New Left in the 1960s and the institution of monogamous marriage was definitely not in vogue among communists for equally doctrinaire reasons. It is a rarely discussed interconnection, but in our view a fact, that the simultaneous upsurge of a Communist quest for new ways of life and the Russian revolutionary *avant-garde's* coming into full bloom was far from a mere coincidence. To this picture belongs the additional (and already mentioned) circumstance that in this period relatively open debates within the Communist ruling elite (but of course, nowhere else) were accepted and widely practised. All this created a unique situation characteristic of a truly elitarian rule in which the ruling and mostly militarized elite and the bulk of the population subjected to it by force and by virtue of an intellectual superiority possessed totally disparate cultures, habits and languages, because of *disparate systems* of needs.

This anti-authoritarian tendency was nipped in the bud by the Stalinization of the apparatus, and not by chance. Here negative dialectics, the first phase of which was the emphatic elaboration of at least certain genuinely Marxist values in the elite and its opposition as elite culture to the majority of society, reached its second phase. On the one hand, Stalin and his followers definitely did not need any kind of anti-authoritarian, libertarian Communism. It was not necessary for the total subjection of the population, the leaders were suspicious of the spirit of rebellion constantly lurking behind its 'orthodox Marxist' façade, and they could not use a disparate elitarian culture for their main objective: totalization and homogenization of society. This implied a double operation. On the other hand, everything that was lively, dynamic, critical and truly an heir to the enlightenment in Russian Marxism had to be eliminated from it, and its accepted body of doctrines had to be reduced to a level which Orwell correctly called 'two legs bad — four legs good Marxism'. But, to describe a full circle in negative dialectics, parallel to this Stalinist Marxism ceased to be elitarian and became 'democratic' in the simple sense that it had been coercively imposed on everyone. Marxism (or the form it had been reduced to in Stalin's period) became a general iconography and a compulsory language for all state subjects in which they had to express their most intimate feelings as well as all their public functions. This created unbelievable, irresistibly comic situations in the portrayal of which the worst and most pedestrian enemy of Communism could not exaggerate the unbearable reality, but it was a comedy which aroused laughter only in distant spectators, not in those who lived it. Universal fear made Stalin's particular brand of Marxism a dogma bereft of all cultural achievements, of all the enlightenment features which were the great achievement and main theoretical ambition of Marx, a universal language. This is a well-known fact. Less known is the additional development that, precisely at this time, all aspirations to lead a life different to the narrow-minded standards of the Russian lower middle-classes had been eradicated from the Bolshevik elite by the iron hand of Stalin. His new man, as far as taste, habits and rosters of values were concerned, was an obedient subject of the state, a model bureaucrat, a pedantic (and mostly tyrannical) head of a strictly monogamous family, and most of all, an isolated atom without even the will to free association.

Paradoxically, the new, third phase of the negative dialectics of Marxism first appeared as a positive development. On the one hand from the revelations of the 20th Congress, and in this respect particularly of the 22nd Congress of the Soviet Community Party it seemed that even the apparatus drew radical conclusions from the total impoverishment of the theoretical body of Marxism. Ilyichov, an average bureaucrat for whom Marx's writing on any subject was obviously a matter of complete indifference, declared in his capacity as the then ideological Secretary of the Central Committee that during the whole Stalinist period not a single book on historiography, philosophy or economics had been written that deserved any scholarly attention. On the other hand, oppositional 'reform' Marxism whose greatest personality was beyond any doubt Georg Lukács, formulated this constellation with an even more merciless diagnosis. It was Lukács again (and perhaps not by chance within the Petőfi circle, that forum of preparation of the Hungarian revolution of 1956) who formulated the programme: the renaissance of Marxism.

Both developments seemed then to be something very positive, refuting rather than confirming the concept of the negative dialectics of Marxism. And in one respect, this new change turned out in fact to be positive. At least for a short historical moment, namely during the preparation of the Hungarian revolution and the Polish October oppositional efforts to galvanize Marxism into a new life, critical of the Stalinist heritage, the dissidents (and all dissatisfied elements of the population) were provided with a language in terms of which social complaints could be articulated. At this very early stage of still existing and virulent Stalinism, it was physically impossible to formulate individual or collective complaints in any language other than that of Marxism. The *cahiers de doléances* had to testify to an at least nominal trust in the sovereign, otherwise all dissent would immediately have been outlawed and mercilessly crushed. As a bonus for the services oppositional Marxism rendered to the dissatisfied population of many countries under Soviet domination, there was a historical moment when politically committed Marxist dissidents, young or old, dared to hope that after the years of isolation and popular contempt against Marxism (deserved, as they then felt) their world-view would finally be universally accepted for its emancipatory potential. In the mid-1960s this feeling was even amplified by the totally unexpected phenomenon of the New Left in Western countries. The subjects of states calling themselves Marxist but on whom Marxism was simply imposed, were dumbfounded to see huge masses choosing Marxism (of course, in a new form) in countries where it was not compulsory state doctrine. This tendency obviously reached its climax in the May of 1968.

But during this period (which also marked the gradual end of Khrushchevism) two tendencies became clear which together put an end to hopes for the renaissance of Marxism. One of them was the abrupt end of the honeymoon between those dominating and those being dominated (basically with the gradual degeneration of Gomulka's reformist regime, and the corrosion of Khrushchevism itself). With the demise of *pax Dei*, the apparatus gradually abandoned as too risky an operation any sanguine ideas of reforming its inherited Stalinist Marxism and invented instead a new method which we came to characterize somewhat later but which could hold no attraction for the population. At the top of the social scale, Marxism turned out to be irreformable. At the bottom, the disillusionment did not fail to come either. It turned out that even in its reformistic—oppositional version Marxism remained a language of domination, for the perfectly simple reason that, despite many critical remarks, it wanted to return (just as Khrushchev did) to Lenin against Lenin's successors. Along with many other critical elements, oppositional Marxism, too, wanted to retain continuity with the history of dictatorship over needs. But if it proves true (as we believe it does) that Lenin's successors intended a fundamental degradation of many of his original objectives and ideals, such successors could nevertheless only rescue his Jacobin regime, and in that case any return to Lenin rather than Stalin meant only a theoretical and political dead-end from which no real understanding of the genuine character of the Soviet regime could be derived. Oppositional Marxism missed its great historical moment, despite the sometimes heroic resistance several of its representatives (suffice to mention the Medvedevs, the then Marxist Kuron and Modzelewski and, more recently, Bahro) displayed in the face of an unscrupulous state power. This only corroborated the diffidence of those who watched with eyes suspicious of 'those allegedly dissident Marxists'. Apart from the all-important and still relevant intention and gesture of separating the radical project from the oppressive society which claimed to be its progenitor and realization, its perhaps sole remaining achievement was the rediscovery of the 'revolution of the way of life' as a dimension that was just as important as the political one.

Historically speaking, the period of the 'renaissance of Marxism' came to its end in 1968, in the days of the Soviet intervention against Czechoslovakia. In this event and during its aftermath, two inherent tendencies of the earlier period have surfaced in an unmistakable way. The first was that there can be no consensus between the apparatus and the whole population, but only very pragmatic, even if long-lasting, situations of equilibrium between rulers and ruled, as in Kádárist Hungary. The apparatus discarded all experiments with a consensus based on ideological reform together with Khrushchev and found a solution matching the conservative needs of a period which put an end both to 'revolutions from above' and to any kind of reformistic experiments. This solution implies a Janus-faced situation. On the one hand, as we have already seen, the sovereign — the Party leadership — never resigns the absolute prerogative of interpreting and further developing the body of dogmas itself. Any attempt on anyone's part at establishing an overt independence in this regard involves censorship and administrative measures of various sorts. To an equal degree, the insignia of the state doctrine (or 'the constant elements of Marxism–Leninism' as it is called) must remain unaltered and sacrosanct. But on the other hand, to an extent varying from country to country and from period to period, two changes take place. Firstly, a conservative–conformist observance of rules of etiquette is substituted for religious zeal: the state subject's actual belief is not tested regularly and in devious ways (although, of course, the files are still conscientiously kept), only his external obedience and good behaviour is required and checked. Secondly, there are certain areas of everyday life which are increasingly 'de-ideologized': these include religious belief, certain areas of cultural and other types of consumption, hobbies, a small degree of tolerance towards 'Western contacts' — to the greatest extent in Kádárism and in Poland, to the smallest in the Soviet Union. The decreasing relative importance of the ideological apparatus (as against, for instance, the increased role of the military) testifies to this change in an accurate way. There is a mirror symmetry to this at the bottom of society. Among those who are not part of the apparatus there is an unmistakable and fairly general hostility against *any* kind of Marxism, official or reformistic. The negative dialectics of Marxism, whose proud ambition was once to homogenize the whole of society, seems to have completed a full circle.

If our assessment of this situation is expressed in overwhelmingly negative terms, this is not because of our preserved, even if critical, allegiance to Marxism. Only advocates of totalitarian world-views try to tell people what they should believe, and it is hard not to see the reasons for such a hostility after so many disillusionments. Also we have to be faithful to Marx's genuine traditions: socialist ideas (his own among others) exist to serve the world, not vice versa. But it is equally difficult not to see the deeply problematical results of this fully completed negative dialectics. First of all, in the ideological vacuum thus created, a series of newly evolved fundamentalist ideologies of religious or nationalist character emerge, being in their extremely conservative and intolerant character a new corroboration of Marx's observation: the reaction is adequate to the action. Let us make it very clear: apart from not sharing these positions, we have nothing against religious doctrines and beliefs, and we no longer maintain what Marx, child of a rationalist century, so firmly believed, that an abolition of religious alienation is a necessary precondition of socialism. Equally, one can hardly object to the national feelings of millions who, like us, do not see supernational alliances such as the COMECON and the Warsaw Pact as anything but the front organizations of a brutal and arrogant political imperialism. But the new ideologies occupying the vacuum created by the negative dialectics of Marxism are not traditional nationalisms (which have already perpetrated more than enough collective crimes in this region for decades on all fronts), nor are they traditionally conservative religions (a conventional safeguard against many liberal social reforms): they are advocates of the new poison, fundamentalism, this direct enemy of the only basis of a possible socialism, democracy. Solzhenytzin, with his outright Dostoevskyan propaganda for a theocratic (as opposed to democratic–decadent) order is a direct follower of Ivan Karamazov's arch-reactionary dream about the monastery as the 'cell' of the new Russian society, and he is far from being the only such voice. An equal danger is represented by the growing intolerance even against raising the perspective of a socialist recommencement. With the (temporary) death of Marxism in the non-official, semi-underground *bon ton*, it became prohibitive even to discuss the chances of a type of society that would transcend liberal capitalism, lest one should be declared the agent of the existing power. History visibly took its revenge on Marxism because of its marriage with dictatorship over needs (even if only one very impoverished version of Marxism can reasonably be declared responsible for it). But this is not the end of the story. Equally, and in spite of the overwhelmingly fundamentalist ideology professed by the participants, one can say of the Polish events, with their unmistakable echoes of nineteenth-century proletarian class struggles, that Marxism with its ineradicably critical spirit takes its revenge on those who perverted its emancipatory message.

The alternatives

We pointed earlier to the opposition as a social factor which by its very existence indicates the legitimation crisis of the regime, irrespective of its actual and short-term fate in the face of an overwhelming military and police power. Now we come to its very sketchy typology. The method we are going to follow is to classify the opposition according to the perspectives they are drawing up for the 'silent majority' in the Soviet societies.

There is one question the answer to which is declared sterile and academic by that excellent writer and practically and theoretically respectable dissident, George Konrád. We, however, deem this answer to be crucial. The question is the following: is society in Eastern Europe socialist or not? There are the following typical responses to this. Firstly, it is answered in the affirmative which, as far as its social consequences are concerned, results in an interesting theoretical bifurcation and a functional homogeneity. The bifurcation is constituted by the fact that there are only two types of oppositional element who would answer it in the affirmative: the dissident Leninist and the militant conservative. The functional homogeneity comes about by the strange fact that the common answer, despite the absolute theoretical–political divergence, results in both cases in an obviously involuntary apologetic function. In the case of the Leninists in opposition it is so because no matter what sacrifices they have to bear for their stance, they constantly explain to everyone, as long as they have any audience at all in the opposition, that one should not go too far, one should not endanger the leading position of the Party, etc., not because of the obvious actual danger implied in such an act but in principle because the leading role of the Party is a guarantee against 'social deformations'. In the case of the conservative, for whom only the existing social situation, worthy of hate as it is, can be socialism, the apologetic function comes about simply by the circumstance that he cannot articulate his standpoint publicly up until the moment of the collapse of the regime, and so, apart from certain clandestine organizations, the conservative militant simply ceases to be a militating force.

Secondly, another typical reaction is that there is no answer to the question, not (or not primarily) for reasons of camouflage, but because a certain type of opposition is pragmatic in principle. No doubt there is an element of wisdom in such a pragmatic attitude, partly because it does not offer a vulnerable surface for Soviet propaganda and the secret police which is only too eager to accumulate evidence concerning the 'counter-revolutionary' character of the opposition, partly because it shows a certain amount of tolerance. The dissident activist does not impose his view of the future on those whom he represents only by tacit consent. At the same time, one can be literally sure that any poll taken in confidence of the 'intimate convictions' in this group would show a diapason of programmes ranging from centrist social democracy to ordinary liberalism, a most legitimate type of opposition which will have considerable impact on future events once Soviet hegemony is eliminated.

A third reaction is a negative answer as to the socialist character of these societies. Paradoxically (but, we think, understandably) this is the only socialist answer which has a future. In it, socialist doctrines cease to be the 'language of domination'; even in spite of themselves they finally cut the umbilical cord which has tied all oppositional Marxist (and other type of socialist) ideas to the very regime they oppose, and this independence can (not necessarily will) establish a new type of confidence towards them. But its chances at the present time are very slight, and its increase depends in large measure on the oppositional socialists' success in stripping the regime of its 'socialist' façade. As long as the population accepts the term socialism as the correct self-description of the regime, their chances are near zero.

A highly important line of demarcation between the various types of opposition is constituted by the priority given to the national rather than social aspect of the oppositional programme. Nor is this an artificial dilemma: if one follows closely the drafts of action programmes drawn by many — mostly Ukrainian — groups in exile, one can see the real presence of this alternative. We should like to make it clear that for us the only acceptable programme that offers any chance of a democratic, and preferably socialist, future in Eastern Europe is one that gives priority to social questions, despite the fact that it is undeniably the presence of the Soviet Army that maintains all the social ills against which the peoples of this region rebel. We do not believe that we are continuing the socialist radicals' tradition of mistrust against national existence (to which even Rosa Luxemburg fell victim); we have several arguments to make. The first of them is that, even if we disregard the past of reciprocal national hatreds in this region — which is hard to do — their resuscitation not only makes it difficult to synchronize social efforts at emancipation but directly plays into the hand of Soviet imperialism using the millennial 'divide and rule' technique. This can already be seen by certain typical configurations of mutual hatred — those between Czechs and Poles, largely mobilized in 1968; between Ukrainians and Poles; between Rumanians and Hungarians (which is tacitly sanctified by the Hungarian authorities and kept ready for the occasion of an eventual Soviet invasion against Rumania as a popular feeling of legitimization). Secondly, any theory giving the national aspect priority over the social, has perforce to be fundamentalist in the sense analysed earlier.

Finally, a factor should be mentioned with regard to all nationalist programmes of opposition: they forget the global background to their actions and cannot offer the slightest counter-alternative for their nations in world-strategy. This is a repetition of the traditional provincialism of regional politics and witnesses a blatant lack of responsibility. The practically total silence with which Eastern dissident Leftists (to our certain knowledge) followed events in Cambodia, the subsequent Vietnamese and Chinese interventions and the invasion of Afghanistan, is a most dangerous sign. They tend to forget that their nations (in isolation and even conjointly) are no more than puppets in the game of superpowers (where the plural has an importance as against Eastern European illusions and one-sidedness), that national narrowmindedness has repeatedly been misused by world-powers in this area, and that there is no guarantee, not even a reassuring sign to the effect that it will happen otherwise, unless the opposition plays an enlightening role in this regard as well and does not allow itself to be totally blinded by nationalist hatred. At present, the opposition's duty and responsibility consist primarily in the effort it should have made in order to avoid an all-exclusive preoccupation with the national (or even particularist–social) grievances of these countries. With regard to all 'external occurrences' in a possible strategical holocaust in preparation, which is not likely but again not impossible, every oppositionist ought to make it clear in his own world, for his own people: *tu res agitur*, if not, perhaps, in the present, certainly in the future.

Another important line of demarcation between several types of opposition can be grasped in the self-definition they give of their character and social function. In short, we are speaking of the phenomenon of an 'anti-Bolshevik Bolshevism', a type of dissent which claims the same vanguard role the founding fathers of the regime, against which they are fighting, claimed decades ago. Together with the true heroes, we are nowadays also witnessing the reappearance of Pjotr Verkhovensky, a well-known type from Dostoevsky's *Devils*, for whom values and collective morality are but empty words. These Bolsheviks of anti-Bolshevism reproduce all the diseases of the official sphere in microcosm; they introduce an atmosphere of reciprocal slander, envy and hatred, an authoritative definition of the 'correct' opinion — and all this is often supported and legitimized by some of their undeniable public virtues. There is, luckily, at least one counter-example to this new 'substitutionism': the activity, as courageous as it is unselfish, of the militants of the Polish KOR group. They simply regarded their unceasing struggle on behalf of Polish workers and political prisoners as a service that any progressive intellectual should offer without claims to leadership.

What are the actual predictable alternatives of a change such as the opposition strives for? Will it be a reform or a revolution, a short-term or a long-term process? Of course, no one possesses prophetic capacities and the highly covert, fetishistic processes in life in Eastern European societies make even normally predictive assessments very difficult. The possibility of a revolution, as mentioned, can never be totally excluded, but precisely because of the mysterious character of gestation of any revolution, it is anybody's guess and not a matter of sociological consideration whether it will come or not. Another question which can be historically and objectively assessed is whether Communist reforms from above have a real chance of long-term and positive development. Our answer, based on the experiences of Dubcekism, is unambiguously negative. Communist reformers find themselves under crossfire. On the one hand, the population, even if covertly, demand structural reforms from them which they cannot deliver; on the other, the slightest sign of a sincere (not Machiavellian) co-existence with their own population puts them under immediate Soviet suspicion and exposes the country to the danger of intervention. The most probable alternative is the highly inorganic one now coming about in Poland. Here, on the one hand, self-created organs of a counter-power are emerging which, if the crisis is particularly charged with other problems, are temporarily tolerated and at the same time put under duress in order that their directly political character may be loosened and they may slowly degenerate into pseudo-independent organizations. Should they fail to do so, or should the Soviet leadership be overconfident, armed intervention can put a swift end to this development. Yet even without this, the danger of their gradual self-degeneration is very grave. Nevertheless, they will inevitably resurface again, at the most unexpected times. But all those who see a social model in this coexistence of incompatibles are deluding themselves. The only way these organs of a counterpower can exist is through violence (imposing their will forcibly on the centre powers of the dictatorship); the only answer the state can give to their existence is insincere gestures of understanding and reconciliation, together with clandestine attempts at undermining them and, finally, clamping down on them. In all probability, this will be the way of life of most Eastern European countries in the next decade, with the possible upshot that all this could contribute to the inner erosion of the Soviet centre of domination itself.

Is liberal capitalism versus genuine socialism a real alternative in Eastern Europe? Before answering this question, we have to state unequivocally our attitude on the alternative of dictatorship over needs (which calls itself 'real socialism') and liberal capitalism. Despite the fact that we are radical socialists, or perhaps because of it, if there were a real alternative, and if this were the only one, we would not hesitate to accept liberal capitalism as a relative progress. Since we do not regard the present regime as socialist, there would be no socialist achievements to lose, the work-force could only gain liberties. Pluralism, and together with it the freedom of political life, could only grow. But there is no such alternative, for various reasons.

The usual counter-argument against the possibility of a capitalist restoration is that in the meantime (in the Soviet Union over more than sixty, in the Eastern European countries over more than thirty years) social changes have taken place of a width and depth that make such a restoration physically impossible. Even if we disregard the Deutscher-argument according to which the inhabitants of the Soviet Union would perish of mass famine in the aftermath of the disbanding of the *kolkhozes*, an argument which we do not consider to be particularly convincing, the other argument — namely, that the subjects to whom the forces of production should be restored are either no longer alive or indeed never existed, since the Eastern European, particularly the Soviet, industry is a totally new creation — is a strong and valid one. Of course, it is not one of absolute validity, because one can argue that under the right political circumstances, possibly created by the violent collapse of the Soviet apparatus, the gigantic combined power of multi-nationals could incorporate and transform the Soviet economy. This is not an impossible option and one which would conclude in a situation which we specifically reject: a total, unchallenged world domination of American capitalism.

But there is one argument which we regard as crucial: strange as it may sound, in countries where the population hates even the word socialism, there is no substantial social will to restore capitalism either. The cardinal evidence for this was provided by the Hungarian anti-Stalinist revolution of 1956, in the midst of the Cold War period. The streets were noisily but superficially dominated by Rightist groups, bloodthirsty Cold War anti-socialism at its most vulgar. Not even the words Left or socialism were tolerated. But the unanimously shared decision of the workers that neither factories nor land should be restored, cut both ways: it was directed just as much against the Stalinist state as against the one-time capitalist proprietor. The anti-authoritarian state subject of dictatorship over needs does not fight for a radical change in his situation in order to acquire a new master. Therefore dictatorship over needs versus liberal capitalism is not a real alternative. As George Konrád put it correctly, capitalism cannot be restored in a democratic way in this part of the world. Therefore all those whose real aim is democracy have to aspire to a genuine socialism as well.

In conclusion, the only slogan we could unhesitatingly accept is this: Oppressed of all three worlds, unite! But the sceptical question is unavoidable after so many fiascos: how is such an alliance practicable, especially in a world in which the word socialism has so deservedly lost its reputation? In early 1919 Max Weber wrote a letter of doom to his younger colleague and friend Georg Lukács, who had by then become a Communist and whom he regarded as the great promise of German theoretical culture. In this letter Weber warned Lukács that the audacious Russian experiment would bereave socialism of its reputation and authority for a hundred years. Let us conclude with the most optimistic sentence in this book: of these hundred, sixty years have already elapsed.

Index

absolutism, 250, 253
  system of domination, 160–61,
    162
abstract labour, 31
Afghanistan, xi, 296
agriculture, 200; *see also* collectiviza-
    tion
  bondage of labourers in, 17, 87
  Chinese, 276
  exports, 26
  goal-function of economy, 66–8
  increase in production, 27, 151
  market relations and, 265–8
Albania, x–xi
Alternative, The (Bahro), 38
And Quiet Flows the Don (Sholokhov),
  288
Angola, ix
apparatus, *see* bureaucratic apparatus
Arato, A., 111
aristocratic rule, 167, 168–9, 170,
  192
Aristotle, 167, 243
armaments industry, 97–8, 103–4,
  174, 178, 247, 278
  rationalization and, 262–3
army, 278
  rationality and, 262–3
  structure of power, 174
Asiatic mode of production,
  model of, 37–44
atomization, social,
  and mass-neurosis, 215–17
autocratic rule, 167, 168

Babeuf, François, 227, 273
Babuvianism, 272
backwardness, theory of, 228–30
Bahro, R., 38, 82, 86, 291
Bence, G., 90
Beria, L.P., xi, 248
Berlin, 21, 263
Bettelheim, Anton, 22, 92
Bolshevik Party, 235, 240
  early phase of legitimation,
    140–41, 144, 145, 148
  language of domination, 197
  morality, 205, 207, 208, 210, 211,
    213, 214, 216
  Party aristocracy, 168
  religion, 287
  system of domination, 157, 158,
    164, 165
Brezhnev, L.I., xi, 174, 184, 189, 270
Brus, W., 19, 62
Budapest, viii, 263
Budapest School, viii, xii
budgetary funds,
  competition for, 110, 172
Bukharin, N.I., 140, 143, 145, 165,
    192, 209, 252, 265, 288
  Soviet constitution, 160
Bulgaria, 170, 282
bureaucrat,
  relationship with bureaucratic
    apparatus, 106, 110, 111–14
  cf. technocrat, 112
bureaucratic apparatus,
  administrative power, 16, 22, 53–4

collective interest, 61, 64
goal-function of economy, 69
indirect power over labour, 71
logic of planning, 12
Marxian concept of class, 114—25
modes of execution of power,
174—8
organization of, 106—14
partial bureaucratic hierarchies,
107, 109
privileged stratum, 9, 11
proprietor of means of production,
71
self-appointed, 45
social costs of, 62—3
state interest, 55—65
will of, 11
bureaucratic capitalism, see capitalism
bureaucratic planning,
as social process, 77—83
Cambodia, 265, 296
Capital (Marx), 90
capitalism, 200; see also neo-capitalism
bureaucratic, 22
centralization and, 231
crisis of, 275
democratic, 15
disjunction of socialism and, 18—19
new social order, 221, 223, 224
possible restoration of, 253, 298,
299
rationality and, 241
theories of state, 22—37
Castoriadis, Cornelius, 22, 24, 36, 198
'productionism', 227
censorship, vii, 111
centralization,
and decentralization, 12, 63, 97
socialism and, 230, 231
structure of power, 175
system of domination, 158
charisma,
legitimation and, 143, 146, 147,
149, 150
China, 149, 283—4
cultural revolution, 248, 265,
275—6

dissent within ruling elite, 138
civil society,
conflict and, 285
and political society, 253, 255
class, Marxian concept of, 114—25,
249
class-conflict, Marxian focus on,
114—15, 118, 132
class-consciousness, among bureaucrats,
113
class dichotomy, and division of
labour, 125—33
Claudin, F., 10
closed-shop system, 13
Cold War, 149
'collective leadership', 169, 257
collectivization, 142, 148, 165, 266
command economy, 252, 282
bureaucratic planning and, 13, 77ff
consumption goods, 98
guaranteed society, 246, 247
industrialization and, 232—3
market relations and, 268, 275,
278
second economy, 98—102
social irrationality, 243, 244, 245
social stabilization and, 89
third economy, 102—3
waste and, 96
command structure, economy and,
53, 54
communal property, see property
commune, 288
Communist Manifesto (Marx), 114,
274
concrete labour, 31
conflict, types of, 280—86
Conquest, R., 147, 148, 169
conscience, morality and, 208, 209
consciousness, 'false', 251
consent, 203—4
forced, 203—4
tacit, 203—4
Conservatism, Soviet Union, 152;
see also social conservatism
Constitution (Soviet Union),
1918, 159, 160, 163

1923–4, 159, 163
1936, 160, 161, 163
1977, 159, 163, 164, 176, 181
consumer goods, 151
  market relations and, 269, 272
  price regulation, 29
consumption,
  individuality, 92–3
  market relations and, 266
  relationship with production, 14,
    86–91, 96–7, 98
  second economy, 99
convergence, theories of, 23
'corporation', primacy over individual,
  117
cost-estimates, and bureaucratic
  planning, 80
crisis management, Eastern Europe,
  20–21, 95
Cuba, ix–x
'cult of personality', viii
cultural revolution, 92–3
  China, 248, 265, 275–6
culture,
  and conflict, 285
  doctrine and, 201–3
  fossilization of, 152
  ideology and, 187
currency, double system of, 101
cybernetics, 263
Czechoslovakia, 42, 263, 275, 291
  housing, 28
  legitimation, 137, 138, 153
  Warsaw Pact invasion, viii
Davidson, A., 146
death penalty, 179–80
decentralization, see centralization
decision-making,
  agricultural cooperative, 67
  and ruling elite, 59, 121
  communal, 91
  function of experts, 186
  management and, 49
de-enlightenment, 217, 250
  ideology and, 194–6, 203
  morality and, 206, 210, 211
  social irrationality and, 250, 252

demand,
  market relations and, 268
  production and, 25, 97
demand-constraints, cf. resource-
  restraints, 83
democracy, as alternative system,
  152, 153
  Eastern–Western dialogue, 4–5
democratic capitalism, see capitalism
denunciation, 176, 212
dependence, as social divide, 123; see
  also relations of dependence
  economic, 282
Deutscher, I., 193
development, rationality of, 12
  dependent on Party leadership, 56
dialectical materialism, 188, 198–200
direct producer,
  cf. corporate ruling group, 125–7,
    130–31, 132
  resistance of, 126–7
dissent, 285, 296
  teleology of, 191–3
dissidents,
  de-enlightenment and, 196
  Eastern Europe, 4, 5, 6
  legitimation and, 153
  political orientation of, 6–7
  Trotsky, 9
division of labour, class dichotomy
  and, 125–33
Djilas, M., 198
doctrine,
  and culture, 201–3
  and ideology, 193
dogma, and ideology, 193
dogmatism, and ideology, 189
domination, see also social domination
  class dichotomy, 125
  language of, 196–8
  political structure and, 11, 176
  relationship of sovereign and state,
    159–66
  and social crisis, 21
  sovereignty and, 156–8
  Soviet thrust for world, 274
  types of conflict, 282–3

Donath, Ferenc, 66
Dostoevsky, Fyodor, 228
Dubček, Alexander, 282
Durkheim, E., 241
Dutschke, Rudi, 4
dynamic social production, concept
    of, 37
economic decentralization, see
    centralization
economic dependence, see dependence
economic development, see develop-
    ment
economic environment, lack of state
    control over, 52
economic mechanisms, self-regulating,
    12
economic performance, and distribu-
    tion of surplus, 50
Economic Problems of Socialism in
    the Soviet Union, The (Stalin),
    146, 271
'economic rationality', principle of,
    25, 29, 32, 36–7
'economic relations of property',
    interest of state and, 55
    Marx, 46–7
economy, see also national economy,
    planned economy, command
    economy, second economy,
    third economy
    criminalization of, 102
    dominated by politics, 56–8, 70,
        115, 116
    goal-function of, 65–71
    shortage, 84–6
education,
    as avenue of power, 119–20
    conservatism in, 152
    privilege, 123
    and structure of power, 182
egalitarianism, Stalin and, 227, 273
Egypt, 276–7
elementary norms, morality and, 206,
    215
employment, see also labour force,
    job security, overmanning,
    unemployment

control over conditions of, 15
and private ownership, 35
structure of power, 181
Engels, Friedrich, 140, 188, 189, 192,
    200, 224, 231, 270
'realm of reason', 238
equality, socialism and, 5, 273
equilibrium,
    bureaucratic planning and, 77
    goal-function of economy, 70
Ethiopia, 274
Eurocommunist parties, see also
    Western Left
    criticism of Soviet society, 10
    view of Eastern Europe, 1–3
exploitation, Soviet, 282
extended reproduction, 24
family, political society and, 255, 256,
    257
Fascism, 147, 233, 235, 240, 273
    mass hysteria and, 216
feedback,
    of apparatus, 182, 183–4
    of experts, 182, 184–6
    popular, 182–3
'feudal socialism', see socialism
feudalism, 210
    cf. Asiatic mode of production, 37
First Secretary, and structure of
    power, 169, 170–71
forced labour, 38, 40, 52, 180
Fourth International, 10
'fragmented' market, in Soviet
    societies, 257, 264–79
'free discussion', ideology and,
    189–91
freedom, 'tyranny' of, 240
French Revolution, 239, 240, 246
Freud, Sigmund, 216
fundamentalism, 248, 293
Gdansk, 21, 263
Gemeinschaftlichkeit, Gesellschaft-
    lichkeit as substitute for, 256,
    259
Generalkartel, 26
German Democratic Republic, 101
German Ideology (Marx), 114

Germany, 42, 157, 164, 216, 231, 274;
　see also German Democratic
　　Republic
Gesellschaftlichkeit, substitute for
　Gemeinschaftlichkeit, 256, 259
Giddens, A., 116
goal-rationality, 143, 185, 227
　social irrationality and, 242, 243
'goals of production', 243, 252, 275,
　276
　Marx on, 65
Gomulka, W., 282, 291
Gouldner, A.W., 119
Gramsci, A., 283
gross national income, waste and, 58
gross national product, direct
　producers and, 45
group interest, see also social group
　within bureaucracy, 69
　suppression of, 251
growth rate, fall in, 104
Grundrisse (Marx), 19, 65
guilt, sense of,
　morality and, 211–13
Gulag, 38, 180, 232
Habermas, J., 89
Hegedüs, A., 87, 99, 128
Hegel, Georg, 1, 17, 202, 234, 239
hegemony, Gramscian theory, 284
heredity, and structure of power, 169
hierarchical organizations, logic of,
　109
Hilferding, R., 26
History and Class Consciousness
　(Lukács), 264
Hitler, Adolf, 145, 146, 147, 149, 238
　perverted radicalism, 259
　slave labour, 232
household plots,
　agricultural value of, 67
　second economy, 99
housing, 13, 62
　state distribution, 28–9, 30
human rights, 286
Hume, David, 203, 204
Hungary, 40, 82, 271, 291
　agriculture, 66, 165

constitution, 163
economic reform, 13
economic waste, 58
education, 123
housing, 28, 29
legitimation, 137, 138, 153, 154,
　155
morality, 213
tacit consent, 203
unemployment, 103
uprising, vii, 21, 275
'workers opposition', 184
hysteria, mass, 216
ideology, 187–9
　de-enlightenment, 194–6
　dialectical materialism, 198–200
　'free discussion', 189–91
　language of domination, 196–8
　pseudo-socialist character of
　　official, 43
　teleology of dissent, 191–3
　totalization and control, 193–4
Ilyichov, L.F., 289
imperialism, Soviet, 174, 274–5, 276,
　293, 295
income, see also gross national income
　inequality in, 11, 57, 62
income policy, 13
industrialization,
　and market, 270, 271, 275, 276,
　277
　poverty and, 20
　socialism and, 230–33, 236
　system of domination, 165
industry, 200
　disparity with agriculture, 87
'inherent irrationality', see also
　　rationality
　and goal-function of economy, 65
　and shortage economy, 85
　theories of state capitalism, 30, 32
intelligentsia,
　conflict and, 285
　de-enlightenment and, 196
　ideology and, 190
　ruling group, 119–21
　structure of power and, 185

interest, concept of, 65
intermediary strata, Soviet social
  system, 121–2
investment,
  cycles, 27
  in first sector, 26, 81
  geographical distribution, 81
  industrial, 67
Italy, 146, 157, 164
Ivan the Terrible, 151, 162
Jacobin dictatorship, 179, 225, 226
  cf. Soviet legitimation, 139, 142,
    144, 145, 147, 150, 162
Jagoda, H., 211
Japan, 229, 274
job security, 15, 73, 76, 113
judicial procedure, see legal system
Kádár, Janos, 154, 203, 204
Kaganovich, L.M., 235
Kalecki, M., 83
Kamenev, I. B., 142–3, 212
Kant, Immanuel, 195, 202, 225
Kautsky, K.J., 226
Kennedy, John, 184
Khmer Rouge, 281
Khrushchev, Nikita, viii, xi, 59, 78,
    102, 150, 268
  agriculture, 270
  de-Stalinization, 152, 281
  legitimation, 150, 155
  'national Communism', 273
  'oppositional Marxism', 291
  removal from power, 170
  structure of power, 174, 184
Khrushchevism, viii, 291
Kierkegaard, Sören, 191
Kis, J., 90
Kollontai, A., 288
Komosol, 195, 206, 208
Konrád, George, 29, 66, 119, 185,
    294, 299
Korea, 149; see also North Korea
Kornai, J., 83
Korsch, K., 22
Kricman, J.N., 83
Kuron, J., 291
labour, see concrete labour, division of

labour, forced labour, non-
  market trade of labour
labour contract, state capitalism and,
  34
labour force, see also employment,
  forced labour, job security
  economic situation of, 71–6
  market relations and, 268–9,
    270–71
  and means of production, 36
  political control, 17
  slavery, 232
labour market, state capitalism and, 34
labour power, state capitalism and, 34
Laos, 274
Lefort, C., 22
legal system, 286; see also penal code
  political society and, 256–7
  rationality and, 245
  structure of power, 178
legitimation, 193
  charismatic, 143, 146, 149, 150
  difference between Soviet and East
    European, 153–5
  early phases of, 139–51
  legitimation crisis, 137–9, 280, 293
  negative, 150, 154, 182
  by tradition, 151–3
Lenin, Vladimir Ilyich, 169, 192,
    200, 252, 287
  dictatorship over needs, 224, 226,
    228, 229
  language of domination, 197
  legitimation of social order, 140–1,
    142, 143, 145, 146, 147
  and Marxism, 187, 291
  Materialism and Empiriocriticism,
    199
  morality, 205–8, 214
  New Economic Policy, 265, 288
  Philosophical Notebooks, 199
  structure of power, 169, 175, 179
  theory of dictatorship, 258
Lindet, Robert, 145
living standards, 20, 275
  rise in, 62, 98, 104, 143, 151, 261,
    262

Locke, John, 203
Lodz, xiii
logic of the market, *see* market
'logic of planning', *see* planning
loyalty, and shame-culture, 208, 210, 211, 212, 215
Lukács, Georg, 193, 202, 265, 288, 299
  History and Class Consciousness, 264
  'reform' Marxism, 290
Luxemburg, Rosa, 169, 222, 225, 258, 295
  'democratic centralism', 158
Lysenko, T.D., 189
Majakowskij, W.W., 209
Malenkov, G.M., 150
management,
  function of, 47–50, 53, 54
  market relations and, 270–71
  relation of workforce to, 75, 76
Mandel, E., 9, 17, 61
Mandeville, Bernard de, 239
Mannheim, Karl, 235
Maoism, 22
Marat, Jean Paul, 239
Marcuse, H., 10, 287
marginalization, and economic situation of workers, 73
market, *see also* 'fragmented' market
  logic of, 14
  Marx and, 288
  opposition between planning and, 14, 19, 91ff
  rediscovery of, 12
  regulative role, 93, 95, 116
market exchange, social use-values and, 88
market incentives, introduction of, 12
market mechanisms,
  command economy, 89, 94, 97, 98
  negation of, 77, 89
  and second economy, 102
Márkus, G., 90
Márkus, M., 99
Marx, Karl, 8, 92, 93, 140, 198, 200, 221, 252, 289, 292, 293

abolition of state, 256
Capital, 90
communal property, 69
concept of interest, 65
economic relations of property, 46–7
ideology, 188, 189, 192
logic of planning, 12, 18, 19
and market, 264, 265, 273, 278, 288
Marxian concept of class, 114–25, 132, 249, 258
'Mongolism' of Russian history, 37
private property, 228
'production for the sake of production', 32–3
'productionism', 227
religion, 287
scarcity of labour, 91
social crisis, 21
substantive rationality, 145, 245
surplus, 30–31
value of labour, 181
Marxism, 240, 280
  backwardness and, 228–9
  conceptual framework of, 7, 8
  Eurocommunist parties and, 3, 5
  ideology and, 192, 193
  negative dialectics of, 287–93
  opposition between planning and market, 14
  revisionist, 6
  theories of state capitalism, 22
Marxism–Leninism, 187, 188, 189, 192, 200
  dialectical materialism, 198
  'free discussion' and, 189, 190
  philosophy and, 202
Materialism and Empiriocriticism (Lenin), 199
means of production, *see also* Asiatic mode of production, 'mode of production'
  in capitalist society, 30
  ownership of nationalized, 46
  power of bureaucracy and, 22
  theories of state capitalism, 30, 36

Medvedev, R.A., 291
Mensheviks, 141, 142
Michnik, Adam, 6
ministries, structure of power, 171–2
'mode of production', *see also* Asiatic
　　mode of production, means of
　　production
　　economic relations property, 46
　　Mandel, 9
'modernity', 93–5
'modernization', *see also* 'pseudo-
　　modernization'
　　ideology of, 145
　　socialism and, 229
Modzelewski, K., 291
Montesquieu, Charles de, 178
morality,
　　Lenin and, 205–8
　　mass-neurosis, 215–17
　　purges, 213–15
　　shame-culture, 208–13
Mussolini, Benito, 145, 147, 164, 246,
　　274
　　ideology and, 194
　　perverted radicalism, 259
Nagy, Imre, 150
national economy, primacy of, 54
nationalism, 39, 293
　　legitimation and, 154
nationalist-centripetal trends, 283
nationalization,
　　of economy, 19
　　of man, 260
　　Mussolini, 164
Nazism, 233, 235, 240
　　mass hysteria, 216
　　perverted radicalism, 259
Nechaev, S., 222
neo-capitalism, 22
neurosis, mass, social atomization and,
　　215–17
New Left, 22, 290
Nineteenth Party Congress, *see* Party
　　Congress
nomenclature, Soviet system of, 38,
　　108
'non-market trade of labour', 17

North Korea, x
Nove, Alec, 61, 113, 265
Novocherkass, xi, 263
obedience, and shame-culture, 208,
　　210, 211, 212, 215
O'Connor, J., 89
Offe, C., 89
oligarchic rule, 167, 168, 169, 170,
　　183, 184
'one-dimensional man', Marcuse's
　　notion of, 10
oppression, *see* domination
Orwell, George, 289
Ossowski, S., 128
overmanning, 58, 74, 84
ownership, management and, 47
Pannekoek, A., 22
Pareto, V., 241
Parkin, F., 86
Party,
　　aristocracy, 168–70
　　culture and, 202
　　dialectical materialism, 200
　　dissidents and, 7
　　'free discussion', 189–91
　　legitimation of social order, 139
　　morality and, 206, 207, 209, 210,
　　　　212
　　organization of bureaucratic
　　　　apparatus, 107, 108, 109, 111
　　purges, 213–14
　　structure of power, 172–86
　　system of domination, 157–66
　　teleology of dissent, 191–3
Party Congress,
　　19th, 150
　　20th, viii, 152, 178, 289
　　22nd, 152, 193, 289
Party leadership, and economic
　　development, 56, 58
Party-state bureaucracy, *see*
　　bureaucracy
paternalism, 228
　　language of domination, 197
　　state, 76
　　structure of power, 174,
　　　　180–82

peasantry,
	market relations, 265—6, 270, 271
	social structure and, 128
penal code, 257; *see also* legal system
	structure of power, 174, 178—9
'personality cult', 149
Peter the Great, 151
Petofi circle, 290
Petrine Table of Ranks, 38
Philosophical Notebooks (Lenin),
	199
philosophy, doctrine and, 202
Pipes, R., 162
planned economy, cf. command
	economy, 78
planning, *see also* bureaucratic
	planning
	dictatorship opposed to, 254
	logic of, 11, 12, 14
	and the market, 14, 19, 91—8
	Marx, 11
	paradox of, 91
	as social process, 77—83
Plekhanov, Georgy, 140
pluralism, 261, 298
	culture and, 201
	economic, 285
	fascination with Western political,
		275
	ideology and, 192, 193
	legitimation and, 152, 155
	system of domination, 162, 163,
		164
Pol Pot regime, 259
Poland, 6, 101, 104, 183, 198, 251,
	269
	counter-power, 297
	housing, 28
	KOR group, 296
	legitimation, 137, 138, 153
	opposition, 280, 284, 285
	religion, 255
	Solidarity, xii
	tolerance, 292
Polányi, K., 230
police, secret, 257
	harassment, vii, 73, 190

structure of power, 171, 173, 174,
	178, 183
political elite; *see also* political leader-
	ship
	decision-making and, 59
	privilege and, 57
political leadership,
	decision-making, 59
	relationship with central planning
		organ, 81, 82
politics, domination over economy,
	56—8, 70, 115, 116
population,
	antagonism between urban and
		rural, 128
	transfer, 270
'possessor',
	cf. notion of 'proprietor', 55
power, structure of, 57
	aristocratic rule, 167, 168—70
	autocratic rule, 167
	and bureaucratic planning, 81, 82
	forms of feed-back, 182—6
	ministries, 171—2
	modes of execution, 174—82
	oligarchic rule, 167, 170, 183
	Party leadership, 58
	political police, 171, 173—4
	and self-preservation, 214
	as social divide, 123
Poznan, 21, 263
pragmatism, legitimation and, 155
private enterprise, *see also* private
	ownership
	and command economy, 99
	and system of domination, 165
private ownership, *see also* private
	enterprise
	concomitants of, 35
	and system of domination, 165
privilege,
	bureaucracy and, 62, 64, 113
	consumption and, 93
	and social hierarchy, 13, 38, 123,
		125
	and structure of power, 170, 182
production, *see also* relations of

production, 'specific relations of production'
and consumption, 14, 25, 86–91, 96–7, 98
dynamic social production, 37
and needs, 268, 269
production for the sake of production, 32–3, 252
second economy, 99
social costs of, 91
socialization of, 18
and system of domination, 164
'productionism', 227
productivity,
low growth rate, 58
overmanning and, 74
profit maximization, principle of, 26, 29, 51, 65, 88
profit-motive, bureaucracy and, 62
profitability,
and goal-function of economy, 67
and socialist management, 50–51, 53
and theories of state capitalism, 26, 27
property, see also economic relations of property, relations of property
communal, 69
private, 13
and theories of state capitalism, 33
property relations,
interest of state, 56–7
and Marxian concept of 'class', 115
'proprietor', cf. notion of 'possessor', 55
'pseudo-modernization', 42
purges, 235, 281
and Party ethics, 213–15
Radek, K., 141, 142, 148, 207
radicalism,
and dictatorship over needs, 234
perverted, 258–61
Rákosi, Matyas, 155
Rakovski, M., 49, 117
rationality, see also economic rationality, inherent irrationality
and irrationality, 237–45, 261, 262
market and, 264, 267, 271, 272, 277
structure of power, 177, 186
theories of state capitalism, 30, 32, 36–7
rationalization, 284
of dictatorship over needs, 261–3
market relations and, 267
rationality and, 241
raw materials, shortages of, 271
relations of dependence,
Soviet bloc, 41
state capitalism and, 35
relations of distribution, cf. relations of property, 9
relations of production, and theories of state capitalism, 33; see also 'specific relations of production'
relations of property, see also property
and apparatus of power, 45–54
cf. relations of distribution, 9
religion, 211, 287
political society and, 255
reserves, and shortage economy, 85
resource-constraints, cf. demand-constraints, 83
Révai, József, 202
Revolution (Soviet Union)
1905, 153
1917, 153
'revolution', ideology of, 297
as auxiliary form of legitimation, 145
Ricardo, David, 32
Rigby, T.H., 107, 143
Robespierre, Maximilien, 260
Röhm, E., 149
Rousseau, Jean Jacques, 93
ruling elite,
and division of labour, 125–7, 130–31
emergence in Soviet societies, 112, 114
general interests of state, 60
legitimation and, 138, 140

Marxian concepts of 'class', 115, 116, 117, 119, 120–21
Rumania, 40, 154, 170, 263, 282, 295
Saint-Simon, Claude Henri, 227
Sartre, Jean-Paul, 276
second economy, 99–102, 103
self-alienation,
   de-enlightenment and, 195
   morality and, 208
self-criticism, ideology and, 194
self-management, decentralization and, 97
self-recruitment, and organization of bureaucratic apparatus, 107
semi-urbanization, 42
separatist tendencies, and organization of bureaucratic apparatus, 111
serfdom, behavioural patterns, 153; *see also* slavery
shame-culture, Soviet virtues and, 208–13
Shaw, George Bernard, 246
Sholokhov, M., 288
shortage economy, 84–6
Sismondi, Jean Charles, 32
slavery, *see also* serfdom
   socialism and, 231–2
Smith, Adam, 12
social conservatism, Eastern Europe, 40, 42
social domination, *see also* domination
   and central bureaucratic planning, 77
   and corporate ruling group, 126–7
   and economic situation of workers, 73
   and goal-function of economy, 70
   legitimation of social order, 142
   Marxian concept of 'class', 115, 119
   organization of bureaucratic apparatus, 111, 113
   resilience of, 104, 132
social group, 254
   autonomy and, 286
   members of bureaucratic apparatus as, 112–14, 118

social justice, housing and, 28–9
social order,
   early phases of legitimation, 141, 142
   legitimation crisis, 137–9
social rentability,
   and theories of state capitalism, 26
Social Revolution (SR) Party, 140, 141, 142
social structure,
   class dichotomy and, 129, 132
   legitimating principles, 122
   organization of bureaucratic apparatus, 106
   Soviet-type societies, 112ff
socialism, 200
   alternatives to, 298–9
   and dictatorship over needs, 221ff
   disjunction of capitalism and, 18–19
   feudal, 250
   market relations and, 278
   rationality and, 241
'socialism in one country', 142
'socialist technocratism', 227
socialization, cf. nationalization of economy, 19
society; *see also* totalization of society, transitional society
   false homogenization of, 130, 132, 251, 265
   mono-organizational, 107
society, guaranteed, and social irrationality, 245–52
society, political, and civil society, 252–8
Socrates, 202
Solidarity, xii, 16
Solzhenitzyn, A.I., 8, 248, 293
Somalia, 277
South Africa, 231
South Vietnam, 260
sovereignty,
   relationship of sovereign and state, 159–66
   and system of domination, 156–8
Soviet Union, 9, 40, 78, 105

access to scarce goods, 64
agricultural labourers in, 17
closed shops, 30
culture, 201, 202
dialectical materialism, 199, 200
early phases of legitimation, 139,
   146, 148, 149, 150, 151, 152
Eurocommunist parties and, 2–3
execution of power, 174–82
feed-back, 182–6
forced consent, 203–4
investment projects, 104
language of domination, 196
legitimation crisis, 138–9
cf. legitimation E. Europe, 153–5
market relations, 264ff
mass-neurosis, 215–17
ministries, 171–2
one-party system, 156
political continuity, 20
political police, 173–4
'real socialism', 222
social irrationality, 246, 247
system of domination, 156–66
types of conflict, 281–3
types of rule, 167–71
'specific relations of production',
   Mandel's notion of, 9
Stalin, Josef, viii, xi, 9, 103, 200,
   224, 228
death, 20, 154, 171, 178, 262, 263
distortion of economic data, 78
egalitarianism, 273
ideology and, 189, 190, 193
legitimation of social order, 143,
   145, 146, 147–52
living standards, 261
market relations under, 266
Marxism, 289, 291
purges, 214, 235, 281
'real socialism', 222, 227
shame-culture under, 210, 211
social atomization, 215
Soviet constitution, 160
structure of power, 169, 170, 173,
   174, 179, 180
totalitarianism, 259

'two world markets', 271
Stalinism, 59, 290
denunciation, 255
slave-labour, 232
Trotsky and, 9
state,
and interest of bureaucracy, 55–65
and organization of bureaucratic
   apparatus, 108
primacy of economic interests of, 54
state capitalism, theories of, 22–37
Strasser group, 157
stratification theory, replacing class
   analysis, 129
structural inequality, and Party-state
   bureaucracy, 11
substantive rationality,
dogma and, 194
legitimation and, 143, 144–6,
   150–51, 155, 182, 193
market and, 264
and social irrationality, 239, 242,
   244, 245, 253, 261
supply,
market relations and, 268
restriction of, 89
surplus, 42
capitalism and, 24
interest of state and, 55
management and appropriation of,
   47, 49, 50
Switzerland, 277
Szamuely, T., 162
Szelényi, I., 17, 29, 34, 66,
   119, 143, 185
Tambov peasant revolt, 265
taxation, regressive system of, 182
'technocracy', 185
technocrats, cf. political bureaucrats,
   112
technological development, Soviet
   borrowing, 277; see also
   industrialization
terroristic totalitarianism, 144–50,
   152, 162, 165, 183, 192
terrorization, mass, and crisis of
   dictatorship, 281

'third economy', 85, 102—3
Ticktin, Hillel, 31, 92
Tocqueville, Charles Alexis de, 162
totalitarianism, 146—7; see also
    terroristic totalitarianism
    ideology and, 194
    and system of domination, 162
totalization of society,
    culture and, 201
    and ideology, 194, 196
    and structure of power, 175
    and system of dominance, 162,
        164—5
trade unions, 16, 265, 286; see also
    Solidarity
transitional society, theory of, 8—22,
    34
    Trotskyism and, 9—10
Trotsky, L.D., 9, 45, 158, 214
    and dictatorship over needs, 225,
        226, 228, 229
    and legitimation of social order,
        142, 145
    'permanent revolution', 248
    and structure of power, 168, 169
    'Thermidor' solution, 224
Trotskyism, 10, 12
Ulbricht, Walter, 59
'uncritical positivism', Hegel and, 17
unemployment, 103; see also employ-
    ment, labour force,
    command economy and, 246
    within the factory, 74, 270
    liquidation of, 72—3, 75
United States, 78, 151, 174, 182, 231,
    285
    creation of, 239
use-value,
    and corporate property, 53
    theories of state capitalism, 31—2
utilitarianism,
    Lenin and, 205, 206, 207
Vaganjan, Ter, 209

value, and use-value, 32
value-rationality, 143
Verfügungsgewalt,
    and bureaucratic apparatus, 60, 69
    and economic relations of property,
        55
wages, 72, 269
Warsaw, 263
waste,
    command economy, 96
    shortage economy, 84, 85, 86
    state capitalism and, 32, 58
Webb, Beatrice, 246
Webb, Sidney, 246
Weber, Max, 47, 187, 280, 299
    on bureaucratic power, 107, 177
    on class, 116
    rationality/rationalization, 241,
        243, 245
    social order, 137
    value rationality, 143
welfare state, 247
Western Left, see also Eurocommunist
    parties
    topic of unemployment, 72
    view of Eastern Europe, 3—5, 8
Wittfogel, Karl, 37
work force, see labour force
working class,
    economic situation of, 71—6
    employment of surplus, 55
    relationship with bureaucratic
        apparatus, 14
    social disenfranchisement, 17
    social rule, 15
Yaroshenko, L.D., 146
Yevtushenko, Yevgeny, 152
Yezhov, N.I., xi, 248
Yugoslavia, x—xi, 285
Zhukov, G.K., 263
Zilvalley, 263
Zinoviev, G., 143
Zur Kritik (Marx), 46